# The
# Terror

D1392531

# *The* Terror

## THE SHADOW OF THE GUILLOTINE: FRANCE 1792–1794

## GRAEME FIFE

PORTRAIT

# Visit the Portrait website!

**PORTRAIT** Piatkus publishes a wide range of non-fiction, including biography, history, science, music, popular culture and sport.

*If you want to:*

- read descriptions of our popular titles
- buy our books over the internet
- take advantage of our special offers
- enter our monthly competition
- learn more about your favourite Piatkus authors

**VISIT OUR WEBSITE AT:** www.portraitbooks.com

Copyright © 2004 by Graeme Fife

First published in 2003 by **Portrait**
an imprint of Piatkus Books Ltd
5 Windmill Street
London W1T 2JA
e-mail: info@piatkus.co.uk

This edition published in 2004

**The moral right of the author has been asserted**

*Picture credits: All pictures by kind permission of Bridgeman Art Library*

*A catalogue record for this book is available from the British Library*

ISBN 0–7499–5022–6

This book has been printed on paper manufactured with
respect for the environment using wood from managed sustainable resources

Edited by Richard Dawes
Text design by Paul Saunders

Typeset by
Palimpsest Book Production Limited, Polmont, Stirlingshire
Printed and bound in Great Britain by
Mackays Ltd, Chatham, Kent

For my mother (obit. 1997) and father
for their incomparable gifts to me

This book is also dedicated to the radiant memory of
Mary Lynch 1947–2003

# Contents

# *Author's Note and Acknowledgements*

Any account of the French revolutionary Terror must rely heavily on questionable evidence: the exaggerations of hearsay, the bloated testimony of witnesses at trials of former 'terrorists' as anxious to exculpate themselves as to blacken the accused; lesser officials protesting that they had only followed orders and the contradictions between actions they took and the orders – often not recorded – which set those actions in train. Moreover, a mass of archive material was destroyed when the Commune sacked the Hotel de Ville in 1870. I have, of course, sought accuracy at all points, nor can any disclaimer be more than tentative. However, a certain folkloreish element creeps in to some episodes: if not pure fiction, then certainly inflated fact. A noted commentator said of Tacitus: 'He may have got his facts wrong, but he told the truth', I have tried to verify all along, but confess to cleaving to Tacitus' kind of truth more than to stolid statistic, useful, in its place, as that is. Even the vexed question of orthography can complicate the issue – French spelling of the era is erratic and often sows confusion; more than one innocent went to the scaffold because of a muddle over names on a list. I have sought to eliminate vagaries of spelling, as far as possible. The titular 'de' can also be vexatious: should, for instance, one call the baron de Batz de Batz or plain Batz? Generally, I have preferred the shorter form but have elsewhere retained the de because it sounds more natural, anyway believing rigid consistency to be rather at odds with the uncertainties of that age. I have left patrie untranslated. 'Native land' is too twee for so potent a French word and 'fatherland' or 'land of my fathers' evoke quite the wrong picture.

The revolutionary calendar is such an oddity that it features hardly at all in the text, although certain dates – 22 Prairial and 9 Thermidor, for example – are totemic, so much a part of the revolutionary dynamic, that they must be retained. To explain the few other references made to the calendar, I include a chart as an Appendix.

To avoid cumbersome repetition of Committee for Public Safety, (the war cabinet), and Committee for General Security (the state police bureau), I opt for acronyms: CPS and CGS which have the added potency of a certain sinister ring.

In the writing of this book I owe much to many people. Lisa-Jane Graham, a specialist historian, guided my first thoughts and was, as ever, unstintingly generous with her time, expertise and insight. Marguerite and Jehiel's hospitality in Paris made the visits to the Archives much less stressful than they might otherwise have been. Through them, I also met Jean Artarit and Alain Gérard, head of the centre for historic research in the Vendée. Over lunch in La Roche-sur-Yon, Alain encouraged me in a perhaps disregarded aspect of historical investigation: that of intuition. His good friend Jean Artarit, a psychiatrist and psychoanalyst and himself a man of the Vendée, has written a masterly portrait of Robespierre and in several long conversations with him I have learnt much – about France, about the psychology of the 'terrorists' and about the tortuous politicking of a revolution which, even today, the French academic establishment insists cannot be censured one jot because it was a revolution of the people. Both men welcomed me with great warmth and a friendliness and charm way beyond mere politeness. The bookseller Jean-Luc Remaud was most helpful in supplying me with a number of out-of-the-way French tomes. To my daughter Lucy, no mean scholar herself, I owe helpful soundboard conversations and good-humoured encouragement, including that e-mail: 'Hope the Terror is going well (for you, obviously not for them).' Also to Jane, a latterday tricoteuse with a markedly more refined design sense than that of citizeness Hèbert and her gallery claque of harridans. Richard Divers aided me in picture research with his fine aesthetic acumen and inquisitive intelligence.

Sevenoaks Bookshop is one of the best bookshops I know: the friendly, intelligent staff have given me invaluable help on a number of occasions.

The staff of Sevenoaks library, who found many obscure volumes through the magnificent library loan service, and thus saved me from the expense and drudgery of incessant traipsing into London. So, too, the staff of the Nantes Municipal Archives and the Bibliothéque Nationale and the Bibliothéque historique de la ville, in Paris. The people at the Bridgman Library were kind, efficient and understanding.

Thanks to Leo Cooper for warm-hearted help and encouragement over a number of years; to Alan Brooke, who commissioned the book for Piatkus and through whose astute prompting it took its first shape; and Richard Dawes for his meticulous editing.

# Prologue

> We owe respect to the living; to the dead we owe only the truth.
>
> *Voltaire*

A T 11 on the morning of Thursday, 11 July 1793 a coach rumbled over the cobblestones of the place des Victoires in Paris and drew to a halt in the courtyard of the booking agent's office. A voluptuous young woman stepped out: she had taken the coach from her home town, Caen, the previous day, stopped overnight in Lisieux and caught the dawn coach for the capital.

Marie-Charlotte de Corday, 25 years old, came from an impoverished noble family. She had fine bones, a clear complexion, ice-blue eyes, long chestnut hair. An admirer of Rousseau, her initial enthusiasm for the Revolution had been soured by the perversion of the revolutionary ideals he inspired in men who purported to admire him.

She walked round the corner to the Hôtel de la Providence, the lodging house at 19 rue Hérold – she brought with her an introduction to the proprietor, citizeness Grollier, who showed her to room 7 on the second floor. A waiter, François Feuillard, came in to make her bed and the new arrival from Normandy asked him what people in Paris thought of Jean-Paul Marat, the extreme revolutionary leader. Feuillard told her that those who were lukewarm about the Revolution loathed him but that he was very popular with the people. Corday smiled. Feuillard added that Marat, a deputy in the national Convention, had been ill since 2 June and had attended no meetings. He was confined to his house with a dreadful form of eczema or psoriasis. This news seemed to trouble Corday somewhat. She told Feuillard that she would not, after all, go to bed for a rest after her long journey, and asked him to go out and purchase paper, pen and ink for her.

That April the moderate Girondins, denounced by Marat, now the acknowledged leader of the ultra-revolutionary Jacobins, had gerrymandered a vote in the Convention calling for his arrest. It was a desperate move; the liberal cause was in disarray. Marat appeared before the Tribunal; the jury was packed with men of the Paris Commune, the municipal authority, among them the public prosecutor, Antoine-Quentin Fouquier-Tinville. Marat was acquitted and borne from the courtroom on the shoulders of his supporters, howling their triumph. On 2 June, leading a mob into the Tuileries gardens, Marat, self-proclaimed people's friend and champion, read out the names of 22 leading Girondins who were to be expelled by force from the Convention and placed under house arrest. No one had any illusions what that meant. The Girondins were finished; the Convention emasculated; all power should revert, for the public good and safety, to the hands of those who would best protect it: the people.

Referring to an earlier crisis, in 1791, one of the Girondins, Henri-Maximin Isnard, had said: 'The gangrened limb must be amputated if the body is to be saved.' Marat, who had his own idea which the gangrened limb was, had duly obliged him.

Several of the Girondins who escaped arrest made their way to Caen, where the moderates were already in open revolt to the government in Paris. It was in the conviction that these men were the true champions of the Revolution, not Marat and the Paris mob, that Charlotte Corday had come.

Later that day of her arrival she asked Grollier for directions to the rue Saint-Thomas du Louvre, behind the Tuileries Palace, where lived another deputy, Lauze Duperret, a member of the Girondin party who had, so far, been left alone if not ignored. Duperret was dining with friends. Corday begged to be allowed to see him, if only briefly. She was shown to his study, where she gave him news of the Girondins who had fled to Normandy. She had other business in Paris, pressing business of national importance, and asked him if he could arrange for her to see the minister of the Interior. He offered to take her himself and promised to call for her at noon the following day. She gave him a card from the hotel and wrote on the back 'Corday'.

The next day, Friday, Duperret arrived as promised and took her to the Ministry, to be told that the minister could not see deputies until after 8 in the evening.

A few hours later Duperret returned to the hotel in a state of extreme agitation to tell Corday that his papers and house had just been put under seal by the police of the Committee for General Security (CGS) – the normal preliminary to arrest and interrogation. He was no longer safe to know. When did she plan to return to Caen? She did not reply, but merely said, in an urgent tone: 'Citizen Duperret, take my advice – leave Paris now and go to Caen.' He replied that it was his duty to stay. She reiterated her warning. He promised to cogitate on the matter and left.

She went back up to her room and wrote what she called *An Address to the French People*. It began: 'For how much longer, oh unhappy people of France, are you to suffer this turmoil and division? For too long, scheming men and scoundrels have advanced their ambition ahead of the common good. Why, unhappy victims of this chaos, do you rend your heart and destroy yourselves to bolster up this tyranny on the ruins of a France laid waste? . . . Oh my country. Your miseries break my heart; I can but offer you my life and I thank heaven that I am free to dispose of it.' In conclusion, she declared that upon Marat had fallen the condemnation of the whole universe, that his bloody acts had placed him outside the protection of law and that her family and friends were entirely innocent of any knowledge of what she intended to do.

The following morning, Saturday, 13 July, she got up at 6 a.m., put on a brown striped dress of textured silk and, at 7, as the shop-keepers and market traders of the street bazaar and the arcades surrounding the large open courtyard of the Palais Egalité arrived to start the day's commerce, made her way to citizen Badin's cutlery shop at 177 rue de Valois, behind the galleries along the eastern side.

Here, for two livres, she bought a six-inch-long butcher's knife in a green cardboard sheath and put it into a pocket in her dress. It being too early to proceed with her mission, she bought a newspaper and sat on a bench to read. The lead story: that very afternoon, to be taken to the guillotine, clad in the shameful red shirts of parricides, nine men convicted of the foul, the dastardly, the hideous slaying of Léonard Bourdon, deputy to the national Convention, representative of the people. These pernicious counter-revolutionaries tried before the august revolutionary Tribunal in Paris at 11 a.m. on 11 July . . . at the very moment Corday climbed out of the coach from Normandy.

Bourdon himself, the latest martyr to the cause of liberty and true patriotism, would, at some crapulous late hour of the day, when he woke from his habitual brandy-laden stupor, no doubt read, bleary-eyed, a similar account in one of the myriad revolutionary journals published throughout France.

This man, whose revolutionary principles were less exacting of his time and appetites than his bullying lust for power, had for some time been playing the tinpot dictator in Orléans, terrorising the provincials with the brand of revolutionary witch-hunt typified by Marat's near-hysterical denunciations of uncivic citizens, indifferents, anyone, indeed, not imbued with the most ostentatious, extreme and unbending patriotism. To a megalomanic drunken ruffian like Bourdon, this involved persecuting anyone showing even mild opposition to the whims and caprices of his volatile temper. One evening, reeling home after curfew, he was challenged by a sentry in front of the city hall in Orléans. He drew a pistol and fired point-blank, the shot went wide and the sentry lunged with his bayonet, grazing Bourdon's shoulder. Thus the full measure of his assassination. Bourdon at once raised a hue and cry; 20 'suspects' were rounded up and sent to Paris. The unlucky nine were to be made a salutary example. Bourdon's own account of his 'assassination', couched in the routine rhetoric, larded with heroic flourish, insists that he was set upon by 30 men, armed with bayonets and pistols, and savagely beaten but 'happily for me, my great coat buttoned over my clothes and my hat pulled down on my head did not allow the bayonets to penetrate more than about four to seven millimetres'. The assault, he ends, was expected 'because there is counter-revolution afoot everywhere here'.

At 9 a.m. Corday walked to the place des Victoires and asked a hackney-cab driver to take her to citizen Marat's house. The man did not know where Marat lived, asked another driver and came back with the information: 'Faubourg Saint-Germain, near the end of the rue des Cordeliers.' Corday wrote this on a piece of the paper Feuillard had bought for her. The cab drove off.

4

Marat actually lived at 30 rue des Cordeliers in the higgledy-piggledy of narrow winding streets and vennels of the old Latin Quarter. At around 10 a.m. Corday asked the concierge of the building in which apartment Marat lived, then made her way across the courtyard and up the stairs to the door of his rooms, and rang the bell. Catherine Evrard, sister of Marat's common-law wife, Simonne, answered the door. Corday asked to see citizen deputy Marat: she had important information for his ears alone. Catherine told her that Marat was ill and was seeing no one. He might be better in three or four days, she added, and shut the door in Corday's face.

She returned to the Hôtel de la Providence and wrote a note to Marat: 'I have come from Caen. Your love of your country must make you curious to know what plots are being hatched there. I await your answer.' She appended her address – room 7, Hôtel de la Providence – and gave the note to the desk clerk. He told her the letter would be delivered within the hour.

No reply came. Late in the afternoon she asked citizeness Grollier if she could find her a hairdresser and changed her clothes, putting on a spotted Indian muslin with a fichu of fine rose-coloured cotton. She replaced black ribbons with green on her tall black cockaded hat adorned with four black tassels. The hairdresser bunched her fine hair at the nape of her neck so that the tresses spread and hung to her waist; in the fashion of the day, he powdered the auburn fringe to make it look ash blond.

She wrote another note asking for an interview, in the hope that Marat would not refuse her, as she had matters of great interest to impart and 'my great unhappiness gives me a right to your protection'. To her bodice under her chemise she pinned her birth certificate and the *Address to the French People*, slipped the note into her pocket, put on a pair of white gloves and, carrying a green fan matching the green of the ribbons on her hat, stepped out of the hotel into the stifling July heat of the city streets.

At 7.30 p.m. her carriage drew up outside 30 rue des Cordeliers. She asked the driver to wait, perhaps expecting another refusal, and then walked up the stone steps to Marat's door. Denied entrance yet again, she pleaded the urgency of the matter; voices were raised. Marat, preparing the next edition of his journal *The People's Friend*, heard the altercation and told Simonne to let the Norman woman in. He had read her notes; he was preparing a savage denunciation of events in Caen. Charlotte Corday entered the dingy, ill-lit room.

On one wall hung two crossed pistols above a large sheet of cardboard on which was written: 'LA MORT' (Death). Light filtered in from a single window. Marat sat in a small hip bath of soothing almond water, a bandage soaked in vinegar about his head, a bathrobe draped over his shoulders, quill in hand, a writing board – papers and inkwell – across the rim. Whatever the shock of the sight of his twisted, diseased flesh and features occasioned in her, Charlotte Corday lost none of her poise. Voluptuous, finely dressed, the sight of her must have made him gasp; but . . . to business.

'You have the names?' he said.

She read them out: the Girondins in Caen: Guadet, Barbaroux, Pétion, Buzot . . . He scribbled them all down. This was no betrayal, she thought, naïvely: the names would die with Marat. She had planned to kill him in the Convention hall on 14 July, a superb dramatic gesture of true love of country; news of his confinement to the house had unsettled her but the task was more important than the venue.

'Excellent,' said Marat. 'In a few days' time I'll see them all to the guillotine in Paris.'

Corday at once pulled the knife from her corsage, unsheathed it and, stepping towards the bath, drove the blade full into Marat's chest, through one lung and into the aorta, with uncanny precision and pure luck. She drew the knife out of the wound, dropped it on the writing board and turned towards the door. Marat, in dying paroxysm, screamed: 'Help me, my beloved, help me.'

A geyser of blood spurted out of the gaping wound.

Corday walked out of the room as if in a trance. Laurent Bas heard the screams, and, in his own self-glorifying melodramatic account to the Jacobin club: 'Seeing the assassin walking towards me, I seized hold of a chair to stop her. The monster had got as far as the outer room and with a great blow of the chair I stunned her to the floor. The creature struggled to get to her feet. I grasped both of her breasts, overpowered her, despite her prodigious strength, and just managed to knock her down a second time and hit her a full blow. As I held her down another citizen came into the room and I cried: "Citizen, help me, oh help me, help."'

Three senior officials of the CGS arrived to arrest Corday formally and interrogate her. She told them that she had been convinced that

France was about to be engulfed in civil war, that Marat was the author of the worst disasters which had afflicted the country and that she wished to sacrifice her own life on behalf of the people of France. One of the men, Chabot, 34 years old, a former Capuchin monk known for two obsessions – women and luxury – and, like many of Marat's persuasion, a foul-mouthed, dissolute, degenerate, sanguinary ultra-revolutionary, eyeing Corday's small gold pocket watch, confiscated it. She asked him if he had forgotten his Capuchin vow of poverty. Her dress and fichu in disarray from Bas' assault, the papers pinned to her bodice were showing. Chabot reached out, tore open the laces of the bodice and snatched off the papers. Her breasts exposed to the gaze of the men in the room, she modestly hung her head to cover herself with her long hair.

They did not finish interrogating her till dawn was breaking; she was sent to the Abbaye prison a couple of streets away, from where she wrote this letter:

15 July 1793, year II of the Republic.
To the citizen members of the Committee for General Security:

Since I still have a few moments left to live, may I hope, citizens, that you will permit me to have my portrait painted, I would like to leave this mark of a souvenir to those whom I love. Besides, just as we cherish the image of good citizens, curiosity sometimes draws us to look out those of great criminals so as to perpetuate the horror of their crimes. If you deign to attend to my request, I ask you to send me a miniaturist tomorrow. I ask you once again to allow me to sleep alone. Believe me, I beg, entirely grateful. Marie Corday.

Citizen Hauër painted the portrait. He made sketches during her trial and she posed for him in her cell 'with an unimaginable tranquillity and gaiety of spirit'; she pronounced the finished work to be 'well-made and a good likeness'.

The night before her trial, Corday wrote to her father, expressing the naïve belief that Marat's death could put a stop to the insanity:

Forgive me, dearest papa, for having disposed of my life without your permission. I have avenged many innocent victims and prevented many other disasters. One day, when the people have their eyes opened, they will rejoice at being delivered from a tyrant. If I tried to persuade you that I was going to England it was because I wished to preserve my incognito; but I realised that was impossible and I hope you will not suffer any anguish. In any case, I believe that people will stand by you in Caen. I have a lawyer, [the Girondin] Gustave Doulcet de Pontécoulant. Such a crime does not allow for any defence. It is for form.

Adieu, dearest papa, I ask you to forget me or at least to rejoice in my fate – its cause is fine. I kiss my sister, whom I love with all my heart, as, too, my parents. Remember the line in Corneille: "Shame comes from crime not from death on the scaffold." (*Le Comte d'Essex*, 1678.)

I face judgement tomorrow.

This 16 July.

There was no possibility of acquittal, as she well knew. Horrified by the execution of the King, the decimation and expulsion of the moderate Girondin deputies, the ugly, shameful descent of noble revolution into mob rule, she had set out to amputate what she knew to be the gangrened limb of the sickly body politic. Her defence was actually conducted by another lawyer and Corday accused Doulcet de Pontécoulant of cowardice for backing out, unaware that he was under arrest.

The packed courtroom of that implacable revolutionary tribunal was like a drying kiln in the July heat; scrutiny of the strikingly beautiful young woman who had committed this murder with the apparent self-control of a professional killer was intense. But her unruffled, quiet self-possession astonished everyone in the room. There were no interruptions. The usual baying and catcalls from the assembled spectators were hushed. Even the *sansculottes*, even Simonne Evrard, said nothing. The fact, appalling to them all as it was, had superseded protest. The shock of it had struck even their rage dumb.

Charlotte Corday openly admitted that she had come to Paris, a city she had never visited before, expressly to kill Marat for his crimes: the desolation of France; the civil strife he was kindling; for his guilt in the September Massacres; for his desire to be a dictator; for his violation of the sovereignty of the people.

The earnest nature of the revolutionary lawyers produced moments of farce:

'How did you kill him?'

'With a knife that I bought at the Palais Royal. I drove it through his chest.'

'Did you believe that in so doing you would kill him?'

'That was indeed my intention.'

Pressed to reveal the names of her accomplices, she denied there were any: she had acted alone, there was no conspiracy.

She showed such lack of emotion during the cross-examination that some doubted the balance of her reason. Indeed, her lawyer was importuned to enter a plea of insanity. There could be no escape from the death sentence, but if she were shown to be mad, her act would lose its political impact, its anti-revolutionary motive, its professed patriotism.

Bravely, her lawyer Chaveau-Lagarde demurred. He told the court: 'Such calm, such composure, such serenity in the face of death in a way sublime, are abnormal; they can only come from an exaltation of spirit born of political fanaticism. That is what put the knife in her hand.'

Corday defended her action by an argument Marat himself might have used: 'anything was justified for the security of the nation. I killed one man in order to save a thousand. I was a republican long before the Revolution and I have never lacked that resolution of people who can put aside personal interests and have the courage to sacrifice themselves for their country.'

Wearing the red shirt of a parricide, she rode in a cart alone to the scaffold in the place de la Révolution through streets lined with spectators. A thunderstorm broke; drenched in the rain, the thin material of the shift clung revealingly to the lines of her breasts. It is said that Robespierre watched from a window, in company with Danton and Desmoulins, and quite uncharacteristically appeared very agitated, talking frequently to his colleagues.

On the guillotine scaffold, the executioner, Henri Sanson, stood at the top of the steps to screen the grisly instrument from her view, but she asked him to step out of the way. She had never seen a guillotine, she was curious to know what it looked like. When her head fell into the basket, Sanson's assistant, Legros, hired for the day, picked it out, held it up and slapped the cheek. Some of the spectators swore it blushed. Legros was dressed down for this shameless barbarity.

After her execution, the Girondin Vergniaud, like all the others doomed, remarked: 'She is killing us, but she is teaching us how to die.'

Her head and body were thrown into the common pit in the Madeleine cemetery.

Marat's funeral, which had taken place the night before, was a grandiose overblown affair: the catafalque on which lay his blood-stained corpse drawn through the streets, surrounded by women in revolutionary costume bearing pikes and flaming torches; some 80 of 749 deputies of the national Convention following behind the funeral bier, Robespierre in his finest clothes, young girls dressed in white waving cypress branches; the municipal authorities of the Paris Commune, people representing all the sections of the city with banners. Republican symbols, urns of burning incense, revolutionary hymns and solemn music played as, towards midnight, the hideously disfigured corpse was taken to temporary rest in the garden of the Cordelier Club, across the street from his house.

In the Jacobin club on the evening of 14 July 1793, anniversary of the Fall of the Bastille and morrow of the death of one of the Revolution's prime movers, Robespierre faced a ticklish emotional problem: Marat, self-styled 'friend of the people', had been their hero, their idol; murdered, he had become their martyr, apotheosised. And Robespierre had detested him, reviled and envied the power he exerted on the popular masses, the mob which had driven the Revolution, the great power base of Paris. He spoke, unable to mask the desperate, petulant clamour in his heart for their attention on *him*, the man who truly stood at the centre of the Revolution: 'Everyone talks of daggers. Well, daggers wait for me too. I have merited those daggers as much as Marat did and it was sheer luck alone that they struck him down before they struck me.' For himself he advised them against 'excessive hyperbole'; he twitted the notion of placing Marat's sacred mortal remains in the glorious pantheon of revolutionary saints, he derided the vanity of 'giving the people the spectacle of a funeral procession' before doing what they ought to be doing, namely 'hunting down the killers of Marat for their atrocious crime'.

Whatever Charlotte Corday had told her interrogators, Robespierre had no disposition to listen or believe: there were plots, he knew there were plots, perhaps only he knew there were plots, but, no matter, he alone would have to pursue them at whatever cost, if the Revolution were to be saved and reach its great triumph, the triumph he had conceived for it in his own apotheosis: a Panglossian best of all possible worlds.

# ONE

# *Rebellion*

To prevent a Revolution, one must want a Revolution and
set about making it oneself.

*Le Comte de Rivarol*

GEORGES JACQUES DANTON was born in 1759 at Arcis-sur-Aube,
in the lush countryside of the Champagne region. He grew up
a boisterous farm boy and remained a countryman at heart: sucking
milk straight from the cow's udder, he was attacked, when he was
two, by an irate bull who gashed his face with a horn – it gave Danton
the pug face and lip carved into what looked like a permanent sneer.
He played truant from school, swam in the river, ran wild in the
fields, got a good education, came to love Latin and French literature. Of the great French tragedian whose lofty drama greatly
inspired Charlotte Corday, Danton said: 'Corneille was a thorough-
going republican.'

Danton, a man of bustling energy, high animal spirits and acute
intelligence, typifies the kind of men who made the Revolution: a
coalition of the educated and the ambitious, shunted into limited
and trivial careers, their considerable gifts cheated of wider recognition by the exclusive protocols of old-regime France, the France of
an absolute monarchy bolstered by intransigent belief in the divine
right of kings.

Voltaire had cautioned against the injudicious franchise of those
not equipped mentally or socially to cope with it. 'All is lost,' he
wrote, 'once the people entangles itself in reasoning', but the indignant frustrations of men like Danton were, one might almost say,

generic, a crucial spur to revolution. 'The old regime,' he said, 'made a crucial error. I was educated by it as an exhibitioner at the Collège du Plessis. I studied there with great nobles who . . . lived with me on equal terms. My studies over, I was left high and dry . . . my former schoolfellows turned their backs on me. The Revolution came: I and all those like me threw ourselves into it. The old regime drove us to it by giving us a good education without opening any opportunity for our talents.'

He studied law and was called to the Bar at Reims, where the necessary certificates were cheap to buy. After moving to Paris he drank and played dominoes at the Café du Parnasse, on the right bank by the Pont Neuf, and married Gabrielle Charpentier, the wealthy proprietor's daughter. With her dowry and loans, he bought the legal practice and entrée to the law courts of Maître ['Master', the honorific title of a lawyer] Huet and was launched.

He and Gabrielle lived in the Cour du Commerce, in the Latin Quarter, very near the old Franciscan convent, by then disused, in the rue des Cordeliers. In its large refectory took place the meetings and debates of one of the foremost political clubs in the city, the Society of the Friends of the Rights of Men and Citizens, attended by all the patriots of the district: the Cordeliers, after the nickname of the Franciscan friars. This district of Paris, just south of the river, part of the old medieval city, an ill-lit, poky labyrinth of narrow vennels and criss-cross streets no wider than alleys, was a known hotbed of anarchists, a nest of truculent revolutionaries, intransigently opposed to all authority.

The Cordeliers were predominantly publishers, journalists, writers, booksellers and people of the theatre, among their most outspoken partisans men who played a central role in the Revolution: Fabre d'Eglantine, playwright, author of the revolutionary calendar; Jean-Nicolas Billaud-Varenne and Jean-Marie Collot d'Herbois, men of the theatre, both future members of the Committee for Public Safety; Jacques-René Hébert and the radical popular leader of the Commune Pierre-Gaspard Chaumette (who called himself Anaxagoras after the Greek philosopher who fell foul of the aristocratic faction in Athens in the fifth century BC); Jean-Paul Marat, 'the people's friend', author of a fescennine journal of that name; Louis Fréron, author, in the same vein, of another newspaper, *Orator of the People*; the printer-publisher Momoro, churning out political pamphlets; Elysée Loustalot

his *Revolutions of Paris*; and Camille Desmoulins, the progressive journalist – he and his wife Lucile were particular friends of the Dantons.

The cafés, restaurants and taverns of the Cordeliers district,
centred on the club, were alive with radical thinking, heated talk,
revolutionary fervour, polemical writing, the doctrines of social and
political change, fermented by a potent mixed society of convinced
intellectuals and impatient artisans. Desmoulins, addressing his
readers as 'my dear subscribers', encouraged the notion that the area
was the true heart of the Revolution, the home of the honest men
who worked actively for its integrity, its universal good, its protection,
without fear or favour, of the rights of *all* men and women, in stark
contrast with the finaglers, the shifty, self-seeking, self-serving men of
both the royal government and the Commune, the municipal
authority of Paris. In the Cordeliers district, the republic of ideas and
ideals had been brought into being. Even when the city's 60 districts
were reorganised into 48 sections, the Cordeliers remained the centre
of political influence on the left bank.

Across the river, the Jacobin club, the Society of Friends of the
Revolution, met in the former friary of the Dominican order, named
Jacobins after the rue Saint Jacques, in which their parent house
stood. Closer to the heart of government, they had a more presti-
gious membership – though Marat and Danton belonged there, too
– and the rivalry between the two most powerful political clubs in
Paris came, in part, to identify the war of factions within the
Revolution.

One of the Jacobins was a lawyer from Arras, a small town near
the Belgian border. Maximilien Robespierre was born on 6 May 1758.
On 16 July 1764, when he was but six years old, his mother, who had
been pregnant most of his short life with his elder brother Augustin
and sisters Charlotte and Henriette, died having just given birth to
a fifth child who did not survive. She was 28. Was it she who taught
Maximilien how to make lace? His father did not attend her funeral
and a few months later left the family home for good. The two boys
were taken in by their maternal grandfather and Maximilien was soon
packed off to the local Oratorian school, where he was taught that
Man was made to adore God and that God, the central pivot of all
Creation, did not exist to oblige or serve Man.

In 1769 young Robespierre enrolled at the Louis-le-Grand College
in Paris, named after Louis XIV. Former students included Voltaire

and the Marquis de Sade and among those there with Robespierre were Fréron, Desmoulins and Lebrun, who became minister of War after 10 August 1792. The daily routine had remained unchanged since the school was run by the Jesuits:

| Morning | | Afternoon, evening | |
|---|---|---|---|
| 5.30 | Rise | 1.15 | Studies and class |
| 6 | Prayer | 4.30 | Snack and recreation |
| 6.15 | Study of holy scripture | 5 | Studies and class |
| 7.15 | Breakfast and recreation | 7.15 | Supper and recreation |
| 8.15 | Class and studies | 8.45 | Prayer |
| 10.30 | Mass | 9 | Bed |
| 11 | Studies | | |
| Noon | Dinner and recreation | | |

This was the pattern of his life for 11 years, until he left the college aged 23. He graduated in jurisprudence in 1780 and a year later was awarded a degree at the University of Paris. These qualifications permitted him to be enrolled on the register of lawyers attached to the Parlement of Paris. He returned to Arras and practised as a barrister, on one occasion delivering an impassioned panegyric on England in defence of an Englishwoman arrested on charges of debt; on another, denouncing arbitrary imprisonment by *lettre de cachet* (a sealed order guaranteed by the King's private stamp) in the case of one Dupond. Under the old regime, any noble could issue this arrest warrant for the confinement or exile of anyone he deemed to be a criminal or an inconvenience: families seeking to safeguard the honour of their name in preventing misalliance, a family member disgracing them with debauchery, inebriation, debts. Abuse was rife. Strong representation against them increased during the reign of Louis XVI. A report of 1770 castigated a penal caprice which made 'none so great as to be secure from the vindictiveness of a royal minister . . . none so small as not to incur that of a farm steward'. A lettre de cachet confined Voltaire in the Bastille for a short while.

In the peroration of his defence, Robespierre voiced the profound indignation which informed so much of his thinking: 'The infinite being, who has created man for sublime purposes and endowed him with faculties worthy of those purposes, has destined him for society only in that state most proper for the development of those precious faculties, whose perfection is at once the object of all his strivings and the pledge of the felicity to which his nature is susceptible.

'All forms of society, all types of government, under whatever name one designates them, are good, from the moment they can lead to this important principle, and are essentially vicious and worthless whenever they go contrary to it; thus this principle is the foundation of the social contract of which we speak, so much of which is not at all the work of a free and voluntary covenant on the part of men but a contract whose fundamental conditions, written in heaven, were for all time determined by the supreme legislator, the unique source of all order, of all happiness, of all justice.'

On the evening of 13 July 1789 a lawyer called Lavaux attended a meeting of the Cordeliers where a speaker harangued the audience from a table, telling them in a tone of high rage that the citizens must take up arms 'to repulse the 15,000 brigands mustered in Montmartre and an army of 30,000 which is preparing to pour into Paris, to loot and massacre'. His whole demeanour was fanatical and he ranted on and on until he was hoarse and spent. The man was an old friend of Lavaux – Danton, whom he had always taken to be a rather peaceable, jovial, carefree fellow, but the times were neither peaceable nor carefree.

In 1787 an Assembly of Notables, hand-picked to eliminate troublemakers, had brusquely dismissed plans for much-needed fiscal reform. This can be seen as the first salvo of the Revolution. Ever more insistent demands were made for a meeting of the Estates-General, a sort of parliament called at the king's bidding which had not met since 1614. This, said the marquis de Lafayette, was the only 'true national Assembly' and only such a body, representing the whole nation, could agree to wholesale changes in taxation.

The Estates-General comprised elected members of the Three Estates: the First, the clergy; the Second, the nobility; the Third, the commoners, who had always been denied partnership in the Parlements, the sovereign courts established to render justice in the last resort in the King's name. The Third Estate, which groaned under the heaviest weight of taxation yet ordinarily had no say, was demanding to be heard. Under Louis XIV, the saying went, no one dared speak. Under Louis XV, they whispered. Under Louis XVI, they talked aloud. A contemporary cartoon shows a female commoner carrying a nun and an elegantly dressed noblewoman on her back. The caption: 'Let's hope they play fair.' The Abbé Emmanuel Joseph Sieyès, one of the leading theorists of revolutionary principles, put the point succinctly in his famous pamphlet *What Is the Third Estate?*, January 1789: 'What is the Third Estate? Everything. What has it been until the present time? Nothing. What does it ask? To become something.'

Marat reiterated much the same sentiments in his own pamphlet *An Offering to the Nation.*

Acceding to the pressure of calls for reform, the King formally summoned a meeting of the Estates-General in January 1789; elected deputies of all three Estates convened on 5 May. The debates and arguments foundered in the shoals of vagary, the indecision of the government and abject failure to agree on the way forward.

On 17 June the Third Estate, exasperated with the glaring insincerity of their partners in this supposed democracy, robustly declared that they alone embodied the true national Assembly and on 20 June swore an oath on the Tennis Court at Versailles to remain in session until a constitution had been established. The King reverted to type; such defiance could not go unchecked; he gave orders summoning an army of 30,000 to Paris and by 4 July the troops were encamped in the city and the surrounding area. It was neither a remedy nor an answer.

On Saturday 12 July barracking crowds invaded the theatres and forced them to close; dragoons tried to restore order; a mob occupied the Tuileries Palace. Paris was like a powder keg; one spark would set it off.

That same day Danton's friend Desmoulins addressed an 'expectant crowd in open-necked shirts' gathered outside the Café Foy in the Palais Royal, the gardens of which Philippe, duc d'Orléans, the King's cousin, had opened to the people of Paris, further making himself popular by periodic doles of bread. These gardens, enjoying Orléans' extra-legal status by proxy, were a sort of free enclave within Paris, flanked with cafés, haunted by prostitutes, rabble-rousers and intellectual agitators, seething with seditious talk.

Drawing on the text of a tract he had just published, Desmoulins bade his audience: 'Listen, listen to the voices of Paris and Lyon, of

Rouen and Bordeaux, of Calais and Marseille. From end to end of the nation there is one united cry: we want to be *free*.'

Free from what, exactly?

Of France's total population of around 26 million in 1789, only about 4.3 million lived in towns and, of that figure, 700,000 in Paris. This lopsided aspect of the country's demography was reflected in an equally lopsided cast in society, where the divisions cut by privilege, wealth and power effectively made France two nations: the enfranchised minority of the First and Second Estates, and the rest. The fearsome burden of taxation lay most heavily on those least endowed to support it: the poor were required to pay royal tax, church tax and dues to their local lords, the nobles, the seigneurs. Since many individuals, nearly crushed by the onus of this composite expropriation, had grown adept at evasion, and most were suspected of it, tolls were often levied on communities as a whole rather than on their individual members, which meant that those who were solvent would, most often resentfully, have to stump up to cover the shortfall due to the failure – or stubborn reluctance – of the insolvent to contribute. Moreover, taxes were calculated on gross product not net profit. Thus a tithe might levy a twelfth – a small slice of the gross on the net profit but this could work out to as much as two-thirds of the gross.

The most flagrant inequality operated in the levy of the gabelle, the hated tax on salt, a royal monopoly, which was levied per capita on a pre-assessed and *obligatory* consumption: a poll tax, in other words. However, the kingdom was divided into six regions of the gabelle, five paying substantially different levels of taxation and one entirely exempt, relative to the availability of salt from salt mines and the ease of manufacture in salt pans. The royal salt-houses took a varying proportion of the regional production by way of sanction. Cross-border smugglers were active.

The collection of taxes was the responsibility of the royal tax farm, a syndicate of private shareholders who leased a monopoly on the levy of all indirect taxation, by contract with the King, renewable every six years. The tax farmers were among the richest men in France and hated for it. Like the Roman *publicani* (the 'publicans' of the Bible) they mulcted the population in the name of the King and reaped a fat profit. Indirect taxes took the form of *aides* – customs duties paid by rich and poor alike; *traits* – stamp duty; *octrois* – local tolls on all goods and produce brought into a town; excise on the state monopolies of tobacco and salt and numerous other imposts on trade and consumption. A contemporary joke has dinner-party guests telling stories about thieves and thievery. It comes to Voltaire's turn. He begins: 'There once was a tax farmer . . . oh dear, I've forgotten the rest.' In his polemic *The Wealth of Nations* (1776) the political economist Adam Smith wrote of the French excise system: 'Those who consider the blood of the people as nothing in comparison with the revenue of a prince may perhaps approve of this method of levying taxes.'

France was a conglomerate of regions, each with a strong sense of identity and many with a long history of independence from Paris, straitjacketed into an idea of oneness but in fact totally at odds with itself. One, the Franche-Comté, 'Free County', made the point starkly in its very name. The despotic rule of Louis XIV, called the Sun King because everything in the kingdom revolved round him, might compel obedience but his death let loose the forces of dissent. The entire structure, already teetering, began to collapse. His successor, Louis XV, saw it and said: 'After me, to hell with it.'

The inequalities of the tax structure merely underlined the creaking inadequacies of the entire fabric of administration, but these inequalities were most cuttingly felt – and resented – in the system of privileges by which successive monarchs had bought the loyalty of noble grandees who would otherwise have been disinclined to pay any degree of fealty to the king. In England, with a population of around eight million in 1790, there were 220 male peers of the realm. By contrast, in France, with more than three times as many people, there were about 25,000 noble families and altogether some 110,000–120,000 nobles, most very far from being as rich as Croesus, but not one who did not enjoy exemption, enshrined in ancient privilege, from a large swathe of taxes. In 1788, when government expenditure totalled 630 million livres, over half the total was gobbled up in payment of interest on debt. The country was bankrupt by gross over-expenditure at court, the grievous toll of four wars waged between 1733 and 1783, chronic financial maladministration, and yet still the entrenched exemption of nobles from taxes held.

Privilege, which included the much-loathed right to hunt at will over whatever land they owned, extended over every aspect of the lives of the tenants of their estates, all beholden to the seigneur by feudal dues – even when feudal dependence had lost its meaning and usefulness. Tenants had to pay, in cash or kind, a bewildering number of imposts, such as several bushels of oats annually from anyone producing fire and smoke from that fire; to perform stints of guard duty (unpaid) on the lord's chateau, latterly commuted to a cash fee in lieu; to grind their grain, bake their bread and press their fruit exclusively in the seigneurial mill, oven and wine press. The celebrated right of the seigneur to deflower a newly married wife had fallen into desuetude long since but those who enjoyed privilege were very sensitive to the widespread popular hostility to them. Louis XVI refused to give Beaumarchais a licence for the performance of his play *The Marriage of Figaro* (1778), which satirised the 'right of the first night' and seigneurial arrogance, until 1784: he saw the danger in it. When it was at last performed, to great acclaim, the court looked on complacently at what Napoleon called 'Revolution already in action'. (Mozart's opera based on the play was actually banned from Paris.)

Privilege alienated not only the underclass but all those beholden to royal appointees: lawyers to high magistrates of sovereign courts; the minor clergy to those elevated to princely ranks in the church by patronage; town and city officials to great nobles, prelates, military governors and the King's personal agents in the provinces, the *intendants*, who wielded the full power of the absolute monarchy and acted as the King's long arm in every corner of the realm. There was no central government as such. The King, remote and godlike in the court at Versailles, did nothing which, according to sophisticated thought on enlightened despotism, entirely befitted his being and presence. And if, someone might ask, the King did nothing, who would govern? Why, the laws. This was, however, a queer even sentimental fiction riddled with incongruity, for those who supervised the quality and enforcement of the laws were generally the very people whose interests the laws best served. Besides, which laws, exactly?

In 1789 France had some 300 differing legal codes; those in the south based on paternalistic Roman law with particularly restrictive inheritance and property rights; those of the north rooted in customary law derived from the Frankish legal system. Attempts to unify the legal codex would inevitably seem draconian, insensitive to long tradition. Should the unified system disregard existing traditions and prejudices to reflect an abstract natural law, the basis of a perceived justice, or develop from the system known best to the lawyers of the legislative Assembly, precursor of the Convention, inevitably biased towards the customary law which prevailed in the north? Another cause of tension ready to add further strain. It was, however, entirely to be expected that the main motive power of the Revolution should come from hitherto obscure lawyers who seized the chance to transfer their pleading for justice in small-town court-rooms to the bar of the national legislature.

All royal office-holders, whether in lucrative sinecures or appointments of significant power, held their place in the hierarchy of influence, at whose apex sat the King, by a system of purchase, the *paulette* after Paulet, the man who initiated the idea in 1604. It was this antiquated mode of open promotion by wealth – as in the purchase of rank in the English army – which obstructed men of talent from the corridors of court and therefore of power; moreover, the paulette institutionalised the rot at the core of the governance of France: venality, the direct exchange of money for place and power.

The King spent some 5 per cent of the exchequer's annual revenue on the royal household, around 10,000 courtiers and servants. Versailles itself was the tenth-largest town in France, with a population of 50,000. The elaborate ceremonial, the *étiquette*, which surrounded the King's every appearance and action, from spectacles of state to the procession of the King's meat, was a complex apparatus of pomp designed to elevate him to that untouchable eminence above the people over whom he reigned. Not without cause did the master cook Vatel suffer a gross conniption of dismay and commit suicide when the arrival of the fish was delayed.

Since the majority of the people was ingrained with tradition, the popularity of the King's person was never much challenged, except by the one section of the people less awed by his majesty – a large proportion of the population of Paris – but then only spasmodically. When the young Louis XVI and his queen, Marie-Antoinette, daughter of Francis I and Maria Theresa of Austria, emerged from the ancient cathedral in Reims having been crowned and anointed with oil from the phial of sacred unguent bequeathed by Clovis, first king of the Franks (481–511), the people wept for joy. It was a very emotional, perhaps unthinking but nevertheless highly charged popularity: he was a king of France and the French people entire and as such he must be accorded all that made him *their* king, supreme, greatest king of all kings. He was the father and the saviour of the nation, a nation which had really only been defined as such, and paradoxically, in the wake of the disastrous defeats sustained in the Seven Years War (1756–63), at the cessation of which France gave up national sovereignty over a large proportion of her colonial holdings. In an essay of 1763 on *National Education,* the prominent political writer La Chalotais used the word 'citizen' in a specific, a French national sense, for probably the first time. And, while the King's person might be deemed to be inviolable, political thinkers had already begun to expose the cracks in the idea of monarchy vis-à-vis the reality. As the Abbé de Véri said: 'Today hardly anyone dare say in Parisian society: "I serve the King" . . . he would be taken for one of the chief valets in Versailles. "I serve the state" is the norm.' Jean-Jacques Rousseau's *The Social Contract* (1762) offered a quite contrary depiction of a free and just society to that of the hopelessly constrained and unequal society that obtained, inequalities which descended from and were most typified by the most sclerotic privilege of all: the royal privilege, whose tentacles had the whole country in a frequently brutal grip.

France boasted some 40,000 kilometres of the best highways in Europe; but they had been built and maintained by the annual *corvée,* a forced labour of between six and 30 or even 40 days exacted exclusively from the inhabitants of peasant villages sited within eight or 12 kilometres of the stoneyards or the areas of reconstruction. As if the poor landworkers did not work hard enough already at their own fraught subsistence.

When, in 1685, Louis XIV revoked the Edict of Nantes, which had guaranteed religious freedom to the Protestants, troops of royal dragoons were sent into recalcitrant regions and communities to compel adherence to Catholic worship and live high at local expense. The dragoonings continued long after the religious unrest had been crushed and became symbolic of the King's indifference to local sensitivities. More poignantly, if less reasonably, he was also blamed for food shortages, of which there was never a lack.

Turgot, one of Louis XVI's finance ministers, said that one should look for a famine every two years in France, chronic famines which were often trumped in devastation by epidemics of smallpox and typhoid. Shallow ploughing, a poorly sown crop, a pestilence in sheep and pigs, the calamities of inclement weather, might throw peasants who had nothing with which to pay taxes into vagabondage and mendicancy. From mendicancy it was a short descent to outright brigandage and, when smallholders were liable to be evicted at short notice by middlemen farmers to whom their rents were leased, the droves of landless agricultural labourers let loose on the countryside were a constant reminder of the age-old threat of rural violence: the so-called Jacqueries, or peasant uprisings, from Jacques (James), a sobriquet for 'peasant'.

Turgot equated the landless rural poor with the day-workers who scratched a living in workshops and factories and lived on top of one another in the crowded, insanitary tenements of the towns. Naturally, famine hit the poor hardest and so frequent were the famines that the poor suspected a conspiracy of king and nobles to starve them: a famine pact. When grain flowed freely, the King and his aristocratic lackeys were clearly in cahoots with the conniving, avaricious profiteers who manipulated prices ruthlessly to worst those who had little enough to pay with anyway. When there was no grain at all, it was clear that the fatties with plenty to eat were, as ever, indulging in the odious machinations of self-interest, hoarding grain and depriving the poor, who moaned in their distress: 'The King is starving us.'

Arthur Young, an English writer who travelled through France in 1788, made his own summation of the inequities of the nation: 'the magic of property turns sand into gold'. For the rest, it was dirt and thin air. Young met an old peasant woman in Champagne who told him that her husband had only a small parcel of land, one cow and a crank horse, but they had still to pay a quit-rent of 42 pounds of wheat and three chickens to one seigneur and 168 pounds of oats, one chicken and one sou to another, besides all the other taxes. She had seven children and used cow's milk to help pad out the soup. She told him: 'It was said that something ought to be done by some great folks for such poor ones but I do not know who nor how but God send us better because taxes, tolls and noble privileges are crushing us.' Of the region round Montauban in the south-west he wrote: 'One third of what I have seen in this province seems uncultivated and nearly all of it in misery.'

Young reported that bread prices in Abbeville and Amiens were 'five sous a pound for white bread and three and a half to four sous for the common sort eaten by the poor [about a third of a daily subsistence wage]; these rates are beyond their faculties and occasion great misery. At Meudon [just south-west of Paris], the police, that is to say the intendant, ordered that no wheat should be sold on the market without the person taking at the same time an equal quantity of barley. What a stupid and ridiculous regulation, to lay obstacles on the supply, in order to be better supplied; and to show the people the fears and apprehensions of Government, creating thereby an alarm, and raising the price at the very moment they wish to sink it.' In Nangis, south-east of the city, he saw a party of dragoons drawn up across the market to prevent any outbreaks of violence. 'The people quarrel with the bakers, asserting the prices they demand for bread are beyond the proportion of wheat, and proceeding from words to scuffling, raise riot and then run away with bread and wheat for nothing.'

The author of a pamphlet entitled *A Letter to the King* wrote: 'Sire, it is the high cost of bread to which we must attribute our recent calamities.'

Two things had, traditionally, propelled rebellion in France: empty stomachs and religion. In 1789 a third, more explosive ingredient was added: articulate political agitation within a consensus, albeit limited, of hungry and well-fed. The forms of oppression against which this consensus had long railed and now acted were many and various but, as the majority of petitions of grievance which poured into the Assembly of Three Estates in the autumn of 1789 show, the commonest complaint was against privilege and the indigence which privilege perpetuated.

The great 16th-century French thinker Michel de Montaigne wrote that 'poverty of goods is easily cured; poverty of soul, impossible'. Poverty and the effects of poverty drove the Revolution to its first violence, impelled it to its most unpitying extremes, distorted the noblest of its aims and forced the radical policies developed to secure those aims. It seemed, at first, to be only poverty of goods: it soon became evident that, despite the rhetoric of humanity, the sermons on virtue, the claims of mercy and the trumpeted declarations of rights, this wretched poverty of goods was underscored by a bitter and entrenched poverty of soul.

'Poverty is wretched,' wrote Juvenal, 'but it has no harsher pang than that it makes men ridiculous.'

Following a catastrophic harvest in 1788, bread prices rocketed, gangs raided granaries and attacked farmers, bakers and corn dealers. Mobs rioted in protest against the game laws and royal taxes. People's committees fixed bread prices and refused to pay more. Spring 1789 came wet and cold; whatever harvest there was it would be late; imports of grain could not peg bread prices. The average daily wage of unskilled workers hovered around 15 sous, and the cost of a loaf rose to 14 ½ sous in February. The eminent chemist and social reformer Antoine-Laurent Lavoisier wrote, somewhat optimistically: 'Today the nation is too enlightened not to recognise its duty to act in the interests of the majority and to see that if exceptions are to be allowed in favour of any class of citizens, particularly with regard to taxes, they can be made only in favour of the poor. Inequality of taxation cannot be tolerated except at the expense of the rich.'

Lavoisier was also a tax farmer and oversaw the building of a tariff wall round Paris to protect the city traders against competition from outside. However, the tolls imposed at the gateways punctuating the circumvallation were bitterly resented by shopkeepers, wine merchants and small consumers.

Opponents chanted slogans: 'The wall enwalling Paris/Sets Paris caterwauling' and 'Driven by pure greed/The farm has seen the need/To chop off* our horizon/And put us all in prison.' (*The French word means 'to shorten'; in slang, 'to guillotine'.)

Of 54 customs barriers, the insurgents burnt down 40 in four days of rioting, between 10 and 13 July. Sections of the wall itself were demolished. In an orgy of violence and street terror, documents, registers and customs receipts were incinerated, iron railings torn down, offices and furniture torched, terrified customs officers beaten up and driven out. In an earlier confrontation with the mob, a sergeant commanding a detachment of the royal guard had told his men to open fire: 'Shove some lead up the arse of this trash.' The remark encapsulates the continuing mood. Now 'this trash' were answering back.

On the nights of 12 and 13 July 1789, as the high-pitched alarm bell, the tocsin, rang repeatedly from every church belfry, gangs roamed the streets in search of caches of arms. On the morning of 14 July a crowd of 8,000 people marched into the Invalides military hospital and stripped its armouries of 30,000 muskets and four cannon. Later an armed mob, 900 strong, most of them artisans, masters or journeymen – joiners, locksmiths, cobblers, shopkeepers, clockmakers – soon to be reinforced by 100 of the Bastille guards who defected to them, marched on the Bastille, the huge royal fortress in the Faubourg Saint-Antoine used as a prison, its walls nearly 25 metres high and 1.5 metres thick, studded with eight demilune towers. Rumours had been flying that the court was bringing extra troops into Versailles and that several other regiments were on the march to quell any disturbances in the capital. It was known, too, that gunpowder from the Arsenal had been shifted in huge quantities into the Bastille, not far distant, through underground tunnels, and that the fortress guns were readily trained on the *faubourgs* (suburbs). The mob marching into their mouths had not much in the way of ordnance to match them.

The governor of the Bastille, Bernard-René de Launay, 59, offered to surrender on condition of safe conduct for the troops of his garrison. The mob refused. De Launay sent out a note to them: 'We have 20,000 pounds of gunpowder. Unless you accept our surrender we will blow up the entire quarter and the garrison. From the Bastille at 5 in the evening 14 July 1789. Launay.'

His note was waved through a newly cut firing slit next to the gate in the Great Courtyard. A group of men led by a clerk fetched planks from a carpenter's shop in the rue des Tournelles and pushed one out from the edge of the parapet wall as a bridge over the moat. Some men counterbalanced the weight of a cobbler inching his way gingerly along but the plank dipped and he fell off and crashed down, breaking an elbow. Another man (Marie Julien Stanislas Maillard claimed it was he) stepped up and inched along as the plank bowed under him and grabbed the note.

When the assailants heard the message they shouted: 'Lower the drawbridges . . . no capitulation.' Pierre-Auguste Hulin, 31, formerly a non-commissioned officer in the French Guard, which had mutinied, gave the order to prepare to open fire, but suddenly the gates swung open. De Launay had surrendered and the crowd poured in. Panicked, the garrison troops opened fire and killed nearly 100 before laying down their arms.

Hulin and Lieutenant Jacob Elie, who, after 20 years in the ranks, was now standard-bearer in the Queen's Regiment of Infantry, tried to get de Launay, wounded in the shoulder from a sword cut, away to safety. But the blood of the mob was up and there was no pushing through such a dense press of furious men with no grounding in, let alone taste for, military discipline. Some shouted for de Launay's head, others to hang him, still others to tie him to the tail of a horse and drag the hide off his back.

De Launay, in terror of his life, kicked out wildly when Desnot, an unemployed cook, sprang out of the mob at him; the kick caught Desnot in the groin. Desnot screamed: 'He's done me in, I'm hurt'; de Launay went down, stabbed by someone with a bayonet, and the mob were on him – firing pistols into him, sticking his corpse with bayonets and swords, all of them mad to have a piece of his slaughter. The brief frenzy over, a man bent down and hacked off the queue of de Launay's wig as a souvenir as one voice then another and another called for his head to be cut off. 'Here,' said a man to Desnot, handing him a sword, 'you do it, you're the one who got hurt.' Desnot took the sword, aimed and struck but he could not sever the neck. To fortify himself he drank some brandy mixed with gunpowder, knelt by the body and finished the job with a pocket knife. He boasted afterwards that he had done it because he thought it was a patriotic thing to do and deserved a medal.

The mob marched back to the Hôtel de Ville, the City Hall, to wreak their vengeance on Jacques de Flesselles, royal provost of merchants and head of the municipal administration, who, earlier in the day, had stalled when they demanded muskets and told them he had none left. They cornered, slew and decapitated him. In what became an emblem indelibly linked to the fury of the Paris mob, they mounted the two heads on pikes and held them aloft, like standards in the continuing rampage.

The English physician Edward Rigby, in Paris that day, wrote: 'We ran to the end of the rue Saint-Honoré. We here soon perceived an immense crowd proceeding towards the Palais Royal with acceleration of an extraordinary kind, but which sufficiently indicated a joyful event and, as it approached, we saw a flag, some large keys, and a paper elevated on a pole above the crowd, on which was inscribed "The Bastille is taken and the gates are open". The intelligence of this extraordinary event, thus communicated, produced an impression upon the crowd really indescribable. A sudden burst of the most frantic joy instantaneously took place; every possible mode in which the most rapturous feeling of joy could be expressed, was everywhere exhibited. Shouts and shrieks, leaping and embracing, laughter and

tears, every sound and every gesture, including even what approached
to nervous and hysterical affection, manifested, among the promis-
cuous crowd, such an instantaneous and unanimous emotion of
extreme gladness as I should suppose was never experienced by
human beings.'

The full complement of prisoners in the Bastille had been set free
and paraded as the first beneficiaries of true liberty: four forgers, the
Comte de Solages, incarcerated by his family for unnatural vice, and
two lunatics, one an Irishman according to the English, an
Englishman according to the French.

The Fall of the Bastille made 14 July the first of the 'historic days'
– red-letter days, red-blood-letting days in the calendar marking the
course of the popular revolution.

After the Fall of the Bastille, Joseph François Foullon, 74, an inveterate schemer, the 'Demon of the Parliament', who, when someone,
objecting to a finance scheme of his, asked: 'What will the people
do?' snorted: 'The people can eat grass', fled in secret to Vitry, near
Fontainebleau, and circulated news of his own sumptuous funeral.
On 22 July the mob rooted him out and hauled him back to Paris
on the end of a rope. They tied a symbolic bundle of grass to his
back, a garland of nettles and thistles round his neck, and brought
him past the Hôtel de Ville, across the place de Grève, the site used
for criminal executions, to the lantern on the corner of the rue de
la Vannerie, named after its many shops of rushworkers and basket
weavers. They threw a rope over the lantern – a projecting lamp standard – and strung him up. The rope broke, pitching him to the
ground. A second broke. The third held, his head was cut off and
stuck on a pike, his mouth stuffed with grass, and paraded through
the streets, his body behind, dragged over the cobbles till it was a
bloody wrack.

The procession set off to join others bringing Foullon's son-in-law,
Louis-Jean Bertier de Sauvigny, a royal intendant, back to the city
from his refuge in Compiègne. When the open carriage arrived at
the barrier, the mob brandished Foullon's head so that he should
have no doubt what fate awaited him. At the Hôtel de Ville, Bertier
broke away, grabbed a musket and, clubbing them off, fought like a
madman. But he was overpowered, borne to the ground and hanged.
His head and heart were skewered on pikes and taken with a deputation to Lafayette, appointed colonel-general of the new national

Guard of Paris on 15 July. He told them he had no time to deal with any more petitions.

The authorities made no attempt to control, even to oppose, these acts of brutality.

Chateaubriand saw the two heads pass along the street below as they were paraded through Paris. Other people in the room recoiled; he stayed at the window, fascinated but 'horrified by these cannibalistic orgies'. In his *Memoirs from Beyond the Tomb*: 'The murderers stopped and looked at me; singing and skipping and jigging about, they brandished their pikes so that the bloodless faces came level with mine. One eye from one of the heads had sprung out of its socket and dangled over the dark blood on the cheek. The head of the pike had been forced out of the mouth, clenched in the teeth . . .'

The murders caused sufficient wider public revulsion. Desmoulins, in *A Discourse on the Lanterne to Parisians*, censured the outbreak of popular, anarchic, justice as overhasty and alien to the intentions of 'enlightened' revolutionaries.

But, in Grenoble, Antoine-Joseph-Marie-Pierre Barnave, later to fall foul of the Revolution he so ardently supported and served, commenting on these horrors, said: 'This blood that flows, is it then so pure?'

In the sanguinary prose of his *Révolutions de Paris* published from near the Cordeliers, Elysée Loustalot made it clear that it was not only in Paris that the people had served notice on their oppressors – the city's authorities had received a chest packed with six heads from Provence, Flanders and other places. And he wrote of Bertier's death: 'Frenchmen you are exterminating tyrants. Your hatred is revolting, fearsome . . . but you will, finally, be free. My fellow citizens, I know how these disgusting sights torment your souls . . . but consider how ignominious it is to live as slaves. Consider what punishment should be meted out for the crime of injury to humanity.'

He was, by clear inference, substituting a newly defined dastardly crime of *lèse-humanité* for the ancient grievous crime of *lèse-majesté*, the crime of 'harming the king's majesty' – whether by an attack on the king himself or the state – the punishment for which had been gruesome.

On 5 January 1757 Robert François Damiens, a dim-witted 42-year-old jobbing servant, attacked Louis XV with a knife as he stepped out of his coach and inflicted a slight wound. Taken for public execution in the place de Grève, he was first put to the judicial torture.

The justice system of the old-regime criminal required a full confession before a criminal was sent to the scaffold and it was customary, in capital cases, to torture the victim one last time before execution, to extract a final confession. Similarly, in ancient Rome, the testimony of slaves could not be admitted in law except when coerced by torture. Criminality, like so many aspects of society in the old regime, was understood in terms of hierarchy. Therefore the police worked on the fixed assumption that only sophisticated people were capable of conceiving and executing sophisticated crimes.

Damiens' right hand, which had held the dagger, was burnt; his arms, thighs and breast torn with pincers; the wounds anointed with a mixture of hot oil, molten lead and pitch before each of his four limbs was tied to a horse. The horses were young, his executioners unpractised, and his sinews stretched but did not snap. The attempted dismemberment continued for an hour until doctors suggested that the sinews be severed. Damiens did not die until the last limb, the second arm, came away from his body. His sufferings expiated a crime against the sacrosanct person of the King, who represented, for his whole people, their lawgiver, their champion warrior, their father and their pardoner. This image of kingship had accrued over the centuries and 'the association of clemency with royal majesty, which stretched back to St Louis, possessed enormous persuasive power'.

Beheading on the block was reserved to men of noble blood whom dignity of spirit and gentility of birth set apart from the riff-raff who were dispatched at the end of a rope. These first lynchings and decapitations made it quite plain that the men, and women, of the Paris mob knew exactly what they were doing in terms of symbolism. More sinister, though, a terrible spate of energy had been unblocked: the Paris mob had acted and by their action initiated what they would always see as the true Revolution and their refusal to surrender that claim translated the shambles of street lynchings into the systematised havoc of state terror . . . *Liberty or Death.*

News of events in Paris reverberated across France.

Armed peasants gathered to defend themselves against the landowners' bailiffs and bully-boys. Gangs of brigands profited from the panic to go on more open rampage. The peasants were easily mistaken for more nefarious marauders. Everywhere tenants refused to pay tithes and rents by virtue of the new laws sweeping away the old privations, laws promised but not yet passed. In western Normandy, Burgundy, Hainault, Alsace, Franche-Comté, manor houses and chateaux were attacked. Dovecotes, wine presses, weathervanes, ovens for the roasting of the lord's meat, all symbols of feudal privilege were damaged. The document rooms containing records of landholding and feudal dues were ransacked and the papers burnt to erase all vestiges of written proof of divisions of property and status of master and serf.

On 19 July a manor house at Quincey, near Vesoul, was invaded and blew up, killing the intruders and destroying the building utterly. The owner, who was loathed, had obviously taken his revenge. There could be no question of the blame falling elsewhere. The myth of the holy innocence of *the people* had been born.

On 21 July, in Strasbourg, Arthur Young watched a mob hurling stones at the windows of the Hôtel de Ville, even though a detachment of troops commanded by an officer was drawn up in the square: 'The troops did nothing, the crowd grew bolder and, after some fifteen minutes of shouting and stone-throwing – which allowed the municipal officers to leave the building by a back door, the mob heaved the doors off their hinges with crowbars and poured into the building. From that moment, a shower of casements, sashes, shutters, chairs, tables, sofas, books, pictures, papers etc rained incessantly from all the windows of the house which is 70 to 80 feet long, and which was then succeeded by tiles, skirting boards and every part of the building that force could detach. The troops, both foot and horse, were quiet spectators . . . I remarked several common soldiers, with their white [royalist] cockades among the plunderers, and instigating the mob even insight of the officers . . . There were among them people so decently dressed that I regarded them with no small surprise; they destroyed all the public archives; the streets for some way round strewn with papers . . . This has become a wanton mischief, for it will be the ruin of many families unconnected with the magistrates.'

On 20 August the national Assembly received a letter of complaint and protest from the comte de Germiny, in the department of Orne: 'A group of brigands not of this neighbourhood, together with my own vassals and others from the parish of Vrigny adjacent to mine, 200 of them, invaded my chateau at Sassy, near Argentan, broke the locks on cupboards in which were stored my title deeds, purloined the registers which are invaluable to me and burnt them in the woods. My bailiff could offer no resistance, being the only warden in the area, where I myself do not reside. These villains rang the tocsin in neighbouring parishes to rally support. This saddens me the more because I have never imposed the hateful onus of feudalism on my people and I am sure that weight can be eased, now. But how can I ever prove the damage to my property, how can I ever testify to what I have lost and what has been destroyed? I appeal to you to pass a law whereby the national Assembly can redeem my losses, in particular bearing on the use of common land, which is of such benefit to my parishioners as well as to me, the title deeds for which have gone up in flames. I will take no steps against those people I know to have sided with the brigands who, not content with burning my documents, killed my pigeons. However, I wait for full justice in the spirit of equity which directs you and in which I have the utmost confidence.'

The seemingly pathetic appeal for the loss of pigeons may sound odd, but Germiny was no bird-fancier. The keeping of pigeons was another privilege of rank and wealth. Any man who could afford to build a *pigeonnerie*, one of those stubby, round, conical-roofed extensions to the manorial house familiar all over France, was making a very visible public show of feudal distinction.

The Assembly swept away feudal distinction and privilege on 11 August and, two weeks later, produced the Declaration of the Rights of Man, a political charter which proclaimed the liberty of each individual and equality of rights and, at a stroke, took France out of the Middle Ages. It began: 'The representatives of the French people, sitting in the national Assembly, considering that ignorance of, neglect of and contempt for the rights of man are the sole causes of public misfortune and the corruption of governments, have resolved to set out in a solemn declaration that the natural, inalienable and sacred rights of man, in order that this declaration . . . will always tend towards the maintenance of the constitution and the happiness of all.'

Before now, *rights* had been limited to those privileges accorded by birth to nobles alone; their birthright, God-given. In the very opening sentence of *The Social Contract*, the apostle of the Revolution, Jean-Jacques Rousseau, declared: 'Man is born free but everywhere he is in chains.' Such a statement went beyond controversy; it was, to the letter of its implications, positively blasphemous, but here it was repeated and codified in Article 1: 'Men are born and remain free and equal in rights. Social distinctions can only be founded on communal utility.'

From this, all else followed: the universal right to liberty, property, security and resistance to oppression. Resistance to oppression was the principle in which is grounded the right to defy and even over-turn a corrupt government. Since opinions vary as to what consti-tutes a corrupt government and since, in a revolution, opinions tend to be extreme and diametrically opposed, this offer of public demon-stration might easily be interpreted as an invitation to lawlessness, anarchy. So it was. In a climate of oppression, the determining factor in all human behaviour – of oppressor and oppressed – is mutual suspicion, fear. The more steadfastly fear is contained below the surface, the more potent its controlling effect, the more it distorts clear thought, the more it overloads reason with paranoia. The course of the Revolution was directed by a gradual narrowing of focus until the broad guarantees of its initial promise had been pared away to the sole propulsion of a psychotic version of human motive and desire: fear. It was the basis of the Terror, the engine of it, the justification of it in a shocking perversion of Article 3 of the Declaration of Rights: 'The principle of all sovereignty emanates essentially from the nation. No group of men, no individual, can exercise any authority which does not specifically emanate from it.'

Although all three guarantees of the revolutionary motto were to become horribly debased as the ideals of the Revolution grew more and more remote from its reality, there was, at least in the beginning, a fraternity of welcome for its brave hopes. The dashing of those hopes, though it took time to gain momentum, was, in the end, brutal, swift and inhumanly reductive.

'A man is guilty for opposing the Terror because he reveals a lack of desire for Virtue. There is something terrible in the sacred love of one's country: a love so all-embracing that it sacrifices everything ruthlessly, fearlessly, favouring none, to the public good.'

So said Saint-Just, the man they called the Angel of Death.

The Fall of the Bastille, climactic as it had been, of course did nothing to fill the bread bins. In the gap which, for the next five years, sundered promise from delivery, was spawned the desperation which formulated the doctrine of Terror.

On 5 October a large group of the notoriously irascible and vocal market women of Les Halles and the fishwives of the place Maubert decided to act.

A large company of them, with some token men, among them Maillard, now secretary of the association calling itself Conquerors of the Bastille, marched into the Hôtel de Ville to search for arms and powder. They tore up documents and ledgers. A wad of hundred 1,000-livre notes from the accounts office which disappeared from a cabinet reappeared some weeks later, and the City Treasurer told the police that more than three and a half million livres in cash had been left untouched.

From the start, there was very little theft of money and rarely did shops, other than bakeries, suffer any depredation.

Led by Maillard, the women, as many as 7,000 strong, hauling cannons and brandishing whatever weapons they had managed to get hold of, marched through driving rain to Versailles, to demand bread. They were confronted by the royal bodyguard at the entrance to the vast palace. In the confusion, some broke through the cordon, through the state rooms and as far as the doors leading into the Queen's apartments. The more boisterous screamed for the Queen's head and 'Down with the Queen. King Louis out, the duke of Orleans in – he'll give us bread.'

As the mob burst into the courtyard of the palace, a jittery royal bodyguard opened fire from a window and shot dead one Jérôme Lhéritier, a 17-year-old volunteer and journeyman cabinetmaker of the Faubourg Saint-Antoine. The crowd surged in a fury on the ranks of the guard and slaughtered two soldiers and cut off their heads. Order was restored by the arrival of 20,000 troops of Parisian national Guard and Lhéritier's body was borne away and later buried with full military honours.

The general in command of the national Guard, Lafayette, ushered the King and Queen onto the balcony to show themselves and mollify the crowd, who greeted them with roars of 'To Paris. Give us bread.'

Later the following afternoon a legion of 60,000 people set off for Paris, women, troops, the royal coach, cartloads of flour sacks from the royal granaries, the women chanting: 'The baker, the baker's wife and the baker's boy', this last referring to the young dauphin travelling with his parents. It took them nine hours.

The royal family was installed in the Tuileries Palace; the national

Assembly took over the former riding school across the way and began work on the first constitution for the new regime, to establish a constitutional monarchy and to reduce the overweening power of the central executive.

An article in *The National Lash* heralded the return of the King as a new dawn for France: 'May this happy day begin the most brilliant epoch of our history and show that the French people, so well known for revering their kings, have not degenerated and even in the throes of revolution maintain the same love and fidelity.'

The confinement of the royal family in Paris prompted the first émigrés, mainly from the military, to quit France with the intention of mounting an attempt to overthrow the Revolution. Alexandrine des Echerolles wrote: 'Every noble who was loyal to the King felt that he was performing a duty by going into exile. One saw old army officers, peaceable men, family heads, respond to this high-minded appeal and leave the comforts of the family hearth without hesitation . . . One must leave or be dishonoured.' Officers who stayed with their regiments or in the provinces, even old men in their country residences, received small parcels containing a white feather, the badge of a coward, or insulting caricatures.

# TWO

# *Division*

> What a peculiar mania in this incessant accusation of
> intrigue and ambition against men who have employed their
> soul and their talents only ever with the greatest devotion
> to the common good, serving it alone.
>
> *Madame Roland*

DEVOUT CATHOLICS across France perceived the Revolution not
merely as irreligious and impious, but as a direct threat to their
personal safety, their beliefs, their place in the nation. Alexis de
Tocqueville reflected that England was fortunate to have had its religious revolution before its political stasis, for 'the French Revolution
was a political revolution which functioned as and to a degree took
on the complexion of a religious revolution'.

Vicious feuds between the oppressed Protestant minority and
Catholics which had riven France for over 200 years flared up once
more. The prevailing mood of liberty hall had declared open season
on unsettled scores; old antagonisms, never but shallowly sunk, resur-
faced. In Montauban and Nîmes, large towns originally part of the
vast southern princedom ruled by the comte de Toulouse, the local
militia, the revolutionary national Guard, was recruited largely from
Protestants, the natural opponents of the established order. Sectarian
violence broke out on 10 May 1790 in Montauban, when a huge crowd
led by a file of Catholic women bore down on government officials
taking inventories of monastic property. A riot developed. The militia
moved in and the crowd turned on them, and killed five. The
Protestants fled in a panic. Order was eventually restored by the arrival
of the Bordeaux militia.

A month later, in Nîmes, the Protestant militia opened fire on Catholics who had raised their own militia. The murderous rioting went on for four days; some 300 Catholics were massacred, but only 20 Protestants.

On 30 May the Assembly debated whether the new penal code of the constitutional monarchy should include the death penalty. Russia had abolished it in 1754, Austria in 1787, Tuscany in 1786. One deputy, nobly born, Adrien Duport, a man whose thinking owed much to the teaching of the philosophers of the Enlightenment, posed the stinging rhetorical question which went to the nub: 'Does not a society which makes itself a legal murderer teach murder?'

Another deputy, a diminutive man whose quaint, outmoded, scriptural moralising, so well received by the unsophisticated audiences of the Arras Academy, had made him something of a laughing-stock in the urbane, sharp-witted, cynical forum of Paris, stepped up to the rostrum to plead for abolition. Better, he reasoned, that one innocent life should be saved than a hundred guilty die. The very thought of killing a fellow creature was abhorrent. Arguments from humanity far outweighed all political consideration. As to any argument for capital punishment, a deranged option, he learnt to reject it 'having seen so many scaffolds steaming with innocent blood' His voice was weak and reedy, even harsh, his northern accent grating, his manner far from assured, his demeanour pinched and introspective. As a 17-year-old student at the Louis-le-Grand College in Paris, he had been chosen to read a Latin oration as a loyal address when King Louis XVI (but four years his elder) and his queen stopped on their way back from their coronation in Reims. He stood with the rest of the scholars in the courtyard, in the rain, waiting for the royal coach to arrive. When it did so, the King and Queen kept to their coach, in the dry, to listen to the finely modulated classical lines and, no sooner was it ended than the coach moved off and the orator, Maximilien Robespierre, bowed his soaking wet head in due deference to his king.

The sincerity with which Robespierre held his opinions, the intense concentration on their detail, marked him out. He was a lawyer and legalistic scruples coloured his whole thought. He deferred only to his perception of justice and reason: inflexible and lacking in perspective, but irreducible by any other interest. Of him Mirabeau, the suave pragmatist, consummate politician, of easy cynicism, who had done so much to keep the Revolution on the rails in the early days, knowing that starting a revolution was comparatively easy but restraining it once begun near impossible, said: 'That man will go far: he believes what he says', the woeful implication being that few, if any, men in French politics set a high – if any – priority on believing what they said.

The death penalty was retained by a law of 25 September.

A few weeks later a decree made the wearing of the revolutionary cockade compulsory. Made of any cloth, though mostly of wool, the tricolour cockade – blue and red of the city of Paris added to the white of the Bourbons – was to be a regulation three inches in circumference and worn pinned to a hat or a coat as a badge of patriotism. Failure to wear one marked out the counter-revolutionary, although the sinister near-certainty that counter-revolutionaries would cynically sport the badge of revolution in order to fool honest patriots while they plotted and conspired in their hearts merely fuelled the pervading atmosphere of suspicion. A woman caught without a cockade was gaoled for six weeks in Coutances and women who wore their cockades other than in the hat – pinned to the bodice, for example – were denounced for unseemly coquetry; such diversity was condemned by one Jacobin in the provinces as 'unsuitable among equals'. The revolutionaries now distinguished themselves as partisans of equality by adopting a dress code which readily distinguished them from the cocks of the walk who had for so long ground the faces of the poor. Aristocrats were recognisable by their silk knee breeches, the *culotte*; true patriots wore calf-length loose trousers and were, therefore, *sans-culotte*, 'without breeches'.

The colours of the cockade tended to fade – the action of rain and sun – and there were cases when individuals were arrested on suspicion of royalist leanings, because their cockades looked white which, being the colour of monarchy, was taboo. This, presumably, encouraged the sansculotte predilection for dirty linen. Women and girls were asked not to tie their hair with white ribbons or bows.

The dress code of the sansculotte – the zealot – was red woollen cap (more generally worn as a winter-warmer), loose, knee-length trousers, stockings and shoes, and *carmagnole*, a short jacket as worn in the south, of a similar shape to the jackets of many Provençal folk costumes, the matador's bolero and so on. The sansculotte definition of an enemy of the people – a generic category whose separate phyla were diverse – was a 'man who had done nothing to ameliorate the life of the poor and who does not wear a cockade of three inches circumference; a man who has bought clothes other than national dress and who takes no pride in the title and clothing of a sansculotte. The true language of the Republic assures you that this definition is just and that the true patriot has done quite the opposite for the well-being of the Republic.'

Since the peacockery of the old regime – galloons of gold bullion and braid, lace and velvet, fur and silk – had been swept aside in the new spirit of sartorial uniformity, officials marked their status by wearing cross-shoulder sashes, carried in a pocket until the official function – making an arrest, for example – demanded that the man put on the panoply of revolutionary law. Under the old regime office was the thing and 'a dog's obeyed in office': the new regime made of its functionaries mere things, obedient to law, devoid of personal interest or influence. That, at least, was the theory which many of them bought and more exploited.

A year after the Fall of the Bastille, the proponents of this Revolution, bent on uniting the nation, oversaw a legal act which split it in two. On 12 July 1790 the national Assembly, presided over by the King (whose pious spirit recoiled at the nastiness of the measure) passed the Civil Constitution of the clergy, which, henceforward, would be an elected body subject to an oath of obedience to the civil power rather than that of the church, that is, Rome, and paid from the public purse – all ecclesiastical property and moneys to be sequestered by the state. The oath was to be administered on 27 November with a year's grace, on dire threat of loss of stipend, being declared in a state of conspiracy against the nation and deportation. A register of those priests who had sworn – constitutional priests – was to be made on 3 January 1791.

Hostility to corrupt churchmen and the overweening power of an ecclesiastical hierarchy with vast landholdings which operated largely outside the law and shored up its authority with what free-thinkers, not necessarily atheists, disparaged as superstition, was widespread but not wholesale. This anticlerical law affronted and alienated many for whom the consolations of the sacraments still carried weight and who regarded a church subordinated to the behest of the state as severing ties with heaven. Even Robespierre had grave doubts about the wisdom of it; in particular, the people of the Vendée took it most grievously and their dogged impassioned resistance to this godless edict helped spark the hysterical reaction which created the panoply of state terror.

When revolutionary France was divided into 83 new administrative departments, a large region on the Atlantic coast above La Rochelle, south of the River Loire, was named from an insignificant tributary river, the Vendée, cutting north past Fontenay-le-Comte through the salt marshes east of La Rochelle. And what the geographical fiction of the 'one and indivisible' Republic inaugurated by the Revolution failed to do, the divisive nature of its laws achieved: the unity of a region which had not, hitherto, existed. The landscape of the Vendée is varied: thickly wooded bocage enclosing pasture and meadow, interlaced with sunken roads and cart tracks closed in by tall hedges and trees; rolling heathland and open pasture; salt marshes some of which undergo periodic inundation; a generous sea littoral; a lacework of rivers. Touching Brittany to the north and Aquitaine to the south, the Vendée has characteristics of both terrains; save the absence of mountains, a sort of France in miniature. The climate is generally kind, the light luminous, the skies large.

The people of the Vendée, smallholders, peasant farmers, fishermen, reed-cutters, charcoal-burners, were of a deeply pious disposition, devoted to their priests, whose pastoral role played an essential part in the life of the community. Devotion to the ancient faith was central to the existence of peasants in this rustic backwater at a distant remove from cynical politics. Poverty keyed into and assuaged the simplicity of their life: basic demands were simply met. They were also profoundly loyal to the King and kingship. However closely wedded, heart and mind, to what they considered the inviolable institutions of the ancient kingdom, they greeted the Revolution eagerly, above all the abolition of feudal dues and punitive taxes. King on throne and God in his heaven did not make all right with the world and the Vendeans were at one with the general dissatisfaction – if not the stridency of Paris – which blighted the lives of the majority of the people of France. But they were of a loyal disposition and loyalty to France was a matter of honour, a deep vein of spirituality in the Vendée.

Dedicated to their king and, thence, to the nation he ruled over, they found this uncalled-for assault on their faith, the faith of their ancestors, the faith in which God had blessed France, insupportable. Though in violently anticlerical Paris few priests were brave enough to challenge the mobs clamouring for non-jurors to be lynched, of 333 priests in the Vendée, only 112 took the oath; of 150 minor clergy, only 38 swore. Rates of refusal were even steeper in the northern departments, where, of 1,057 clergy, only 190 swore and across Provence, where only one in five took the oath. Their reasons may be encapsulated in the apologia made by the abbé of the tiny village of Senez in the Maritime Alps in Provence: 'I can no more renounce the spiritual contract which binds me to my church than I can renounce the promises of my baptism . . . I belong to my flock in life as in death . . . If God wishes to test his faithful, the 18th century will find its martyrs as did the first century.'

This open reluctance to back what was plainly intended as a central tenet of revolutionary law – the disestablishment of a corrupt church which drew authority from a foreign power, Rome, rather than that of France – issued a stark warning which, when the central government came to address it, would force reluctance into defiance on the most dangerous grounds: those of conscience.

Two days after the decree imposing the Civil Constitution on the clergy, on the first anniversary of the Fall of the Bastille, the new nation celebrated a huge ceremonial Festival of the Federation on the Champ de Mars, to the west of Paris near the Invalides. Federation, fusion, unity, alliance, partnership – it was not a vision they all shared or could be forced to share. national Guards from all over the country paraded to renew their oath of allegiance to the King in front of a vast crowd of perhaps 350,000. The rain poured but spirits were high, the Revolution was progressing, king, people and nation all met to seal the first year of the changed world, and a new song went the rounds, a song that became the victory hymn of the sansculottes: *Ça ira* . . . it'll work out, we'll sort it out. Ominously, a new line was soon added, detailing exactly *how* they intended to sort matters out, as they had with Foullon, Flesselles, Bertier:

String the aristos from every lanterne . . .

from which would follow:

And a death to tyranny
Triumph then for liberty . . .
Send their whole infernal clique
Down into the depths of Hell.

Even the sansculottes, whose savage contempt for religion and the trappings of pietistic mummery was all but obligatory, could deploy the image of Hell in the imagery of their most virulent odium.

One of the extreme militants, the journalist Hébert, a trumpeting atheist and wholly despicable rabbler-rouser, was urging bloodthirsty methods in terms which had become the common currency of revolutionary sloganeering. In the pages of his scurrilous paper *Le Père Duchesne* this rabid hyperbolist exhorted his readers: 'To your pikes, good sansculottes, sharpen them for the extermination of aristocrats.'

The principal organ of revolutionary propaganda was Marat's *The People's Friend*, first published in the autumn of 1788. He took as its motto a line from Horace's *Ars Poetica*, a plea to the gods 'to restore prosperity to the deprived at the expense of the arrogant', made, however, by a man who is an 'admirer of benign justice and laws'. Benign Marat was emphatically not.

He was born near Neuchâtel, in Switzerland, in 1743. His father, a Sardinian, was a chemist and a teacher of languages. Marat himself became fluent in English, Italian and Dutch. Brought up in the strict Calvinist faith and precepts, he was an extraordinarily bright student seized with vaulting ambition. 'From boyhood,' he wrote in his autobiography, 'I have been consumed with lust for glory, a desire which has changed direction as my life entered different phases, but which I have never abandoned. When I was five I wanted to be a schoolmaster, at 15 a professor, at 18 an author, at 20 a scientific genius . . .'

Napoleon – another non-Frenchman – called glory *the* French passion.

Marat's mother died when he was 16 and he left home. He studied medicine in Bordeaux for two years, went on to Toulouse and then to Paris, teaching to finance his studies. He did not confine the rovings of his inquisitive brain to medicine. He pursued studies in physics, electricity, optics, political theory, philosophy, literature, ever more frantically obsessed with recognition. Recognition eluded him. He set up as a doctor in Paris, applying his studies in electricity and optics to diseases of the eye. Tireless, forever spurred by fame, quick to take umbrage, he quit unreceptive Paris for Holland – Utrecht, The Hague, Amsterdam, apparently making no friends, no acquaintances; all his time devoted to study.

In 1774 he published a book in English, *The Chains of Slavery*, the first salvo of many to issue from his battery of revolutionary propaganda. It contained 'an exposure of the intrigues among the princes of Europe against their peoples'. In 1775 he at last made something of a splash, an unlikely splash. *An Essay on Gleets* (a morbid discharge from the urethra) appeared, again published in London. It caused a stir in medical circles and, when he visited Edinburgh, home of a celebrated medical faculty, he was made MD of St Andrews University. Back in London, he published *An Enquiry into the Nature, Cause and Cure of a Singular Disease of the Eyes*, inscribed with a dedication to the Royal Society. He was gaining some attention, but still hankered for recognition in France, with all the desperation of a foreigner aspiring to acceptance by the established order of his adopted country. When the third volume of the French edition of his *Philosophical Essay on Man* came out, Voltaire launched a vitriolic attack on it. Perversely, that vilification by someone so famous launched Marat to notice at last and within two years, his fame as a doctor growing, he was appointed by Comte d'Artois, later King Charles X of France, brevet-physician to his royal guard, that is, physician with nominal army rank. Handsomely paid, he settled into the aristocratic lifestyle with relish and began to refer to himself as 'the Chevalier Marat'. 'Chevalier', equivalent of the English 'knight', therefore Sir, was one of those aristocratic titles he would later revile; far from shaking the chains off the oppressed poor, Marat had, for the moment at least, teamed up with the owners of the padlocks. He applied to the French counterpart of the Herald at Arms: 'You will not refuse my petition for a blazon of noble rank when you see how firmly established my family has been in the nobility of Spain as well as France . . .'

He opened a consulting room in the fashionable rue de Bourgogne. Here he cured a woman who was dying of pulmonary tuberculosis. His reputation soared; the upper classes flocked to see him and paid high fees. He had, for the first time in his life, leisure. He wrote a romance, *The Adventures of Count Potowski*, which remained unpublished till 1847. More neglect.

Turning more of his energies to work in his laboratory than the consulting room, he toiled ceaselessly, sleeping, he himself said, only two hours a night, wasting only an hour on meals and 'domestic necessities'. In three years he claimed to have had only 15 minutes' relaxation. Titanic ambition drove him headlong into relentless frustration. Refused admission to the Royal Academy, denied, therefore, any seal of official approbation of his genius, he made it his burning aim to humiliate the panjandrums of so-called science.

Courted by the aristocracy he despised, Marat was, to his worsening chagrin, still resolutely spurned by the intellectual establishment. The Royal Academy of Sciences rejected summarily his memoirs on heat, light and electricity, horrified by his audacity in challenging the theories of Newton. He was refused membership. In 1780 he published *Researches into the Physical Nature of Fire*, in which he claimed to have rendered the element of fire visible. He had seen it with his own eyes, and wasn't he an expert on optics? He had watched closely the flame of a candle in a closed container as the hot air round it pressed on it and squeezed the fire out. Fire, he said, was 'an igneous fluid. Contemporary theories about fire are like ideas on colour before Newton. Everyone takes it to be a material substance but it is, in fact, a fluid in a particular changed form.' The committee of chemists of the Royal Academy, including the chemist who eventually solved the riddle of fire, Lavoisier, evaluated the theory and dismissed it out of hand. Marat's work, they said, was utterly devoid of merit.

In 1784 he entered a thesis on Newton's theory of optics in a competition announced by the Academy. It was returned with acid comment on its negligible worth. He applied for a position in the Spanish Academy of Sciences in Madrid but the post was 'stolen by the insidious machinations of my enemies'. That seems to have been the final straw. He became a virtual recluse, thwarted ambition seething poisonously in his increasingly deranged mind and sensibilities. Apart from a translation of Newton's *Optics* (1787) and *Academic Memoirs or New Discoveries about Light* (1788), he published nothing. Neither book received any plaudits. However, his prodigious, and by now irrevocably warped, energies were about to find a conduit which would divert them from scientific research altogether.

Marat's inflamed sense of justice was decidedly idiosyncratic. He wrote with such venom because he took personally the hurts inflicted on the downtrodden in society; he transferred the slights and shafts of neglect which had so excoriated him, the undiscovered genius of the world, to the miseries of the unprivileged. For example, his attacks on Lavoisier, the man who had, he believed, vindictively thwarted his deserved ambition to high status in the academic world, were typical of his style: 'I denounce to you the coryphaeus, the chorus-master of charlatans, Sieur [English 'Sire'] Lavoisier, son of a land-grabber, apprentice chemist . . . who is intriguing in his devilish way to get himself elected administrator of Paris [a preposterous claim]. Why has he not been strung from a lamp-post?'

His own constantly repeated slogan was: 'We are betrayed.' The people had never been granted freedom of speech and the legal right of protest; now, at last, at this great turning of fortune's wheel, Marat unequivocally guaranteed them both. Into the pages of his war bulletin for the oppressed, the poor, the have-nots, the helpless, the powerless, he poured all the spleen of his own sense of rejection. In harangues shot through with a rabid fury, he vented all the outrage and resentment at the neglect which soured his own sense of worth. 'Rise up, you poor wretches of the city, workmen without work, homeless people compelled to sleep under the bridges or to prowl the streets, beggars with neither food nor shelter, tramps, cripples, aimless wanderers . . . you have a right to slice off the thumbs of the aristocrats in conspiracy against you, to split the thumbs of the priests who have preached the virtue of servitude to you.'

The people, whether the brigands who had ransacked comte de Germiny's estates or the Conquerors of the Bastille, lionised Marat; he spoke in a language only the truly poor could cleave to: words tempered in starvation, sentiments carved out of despair, anger forged by interminable subjection to injustice and tyranny. Marat's tone soon reached a hysterical pitch: 'The price of public tranquillity is 200,000 heads . . . '

This was the kind of arithmetic that even an unlettered have-not ignoramus could understand.

Unrest was not confined to the militant proletariat. Many of the new national Guard battalions, recruited across France from civilian ranks, did not bow submissively to the harsh regimental disciplines imposed by old-regime officers, most of them aristocrats who held their commission from the King. Their loyalty to the Revolution was, therefore, in question and the new men of the people's army refused to knuckle under. During the early summer months of 1790 Guard battalions in sensitive frontier garrisons – to the north in Lille, Hesdin, Metz, to the south in Perpignan, mutinied; so, too, in July and August, three regiments in Nancy, backed and encouraged by the local Jacobin club. General Bouillé, supreme commander of the departments of the east, marched on the town and stormed it. Twenty-three mutineers were hanged, one was spread-eagled upright and lashed to a large wagon wheel, his joints and bones smashed with an iron mallet, 41 deported for life. This savage reprisal by one of the King's high men and, therefore, in the King's name, caused wide revulsion.

During the night of 20 June the following year the King and the royal family left the Tuileries past a cordon of guards which had been doubled to prevent just such an eventuality and got to within a few kilometres of the Prussian border. The Queen had insisted that they should make their escape in a heavy berline coach which went at not much more than walking pace, instead of separate fast carriages. On the evening of 21 June, the longest day of the year, the postmaster at Sainte-Menehould, Drouet, saw an officer to whom the King had given an order salute. His curiosity alerted, Drouet, formerly a dragoon in the royal guard, looked closer at the occupants of the coaches and recognised the Queen and the man posing as her valet. He saddled a horse, galloped ahead to rouse the authorities in Varennes, and when the King's party arrived, Drouet made the identification. Revolutionary officials were summoned and the royal party was haled back to Paris.

Jacobin clubs clamoured for the King to be put on trial. Implicit was a call for a republic. The King had betrayed his people, denounced the Revolution and renounced France. A crowd of 30,000 marched on the Tuileries to deliver a petition calling for the King to be deposed. The Assembly, badly rattled, issued a proclamation urging calm. There was no need for precipitate action: the King had been kidnapped. This did not wash and the King was temporarily suspended from all functions. Executive and legislative power devolved temporarily to the constituent Assembly.

The radicals, led by Danton, Desmoulins and Marat, planned a massive demonstration after the second Feast of the Federation. On 17 July around 50,000 people gathered on the Champ de Mars and queued to sign a petition against the reinstatement of the King. Six thousand had already signed, when two men, discovered concealed under the altar dedicated to patriotism, were hauled out and lynched as government spies. Bailly, the mayor of Paris, evoking the Decree against Tumults of October 1789, declared martial law. The national Guard marched on to the field behind the red warning flag and the crowd retaliated with a hail of stones and scattered musket fire. The Guardsmen opened fire and the crowd broke and fled 'like chickens', one of the soldiers said. Fifty people died, more were wounded and in the weeks following what the revolutionaries remembered as the Massacre of the Champ de Mars, about 200 activists were arrested. Danton escaped to England, Desmoulins and Marat went underground. Radical newspapers folded, the clubs were marginalised, the Assembly prepared to deliver the Constitution it had been shaping for nearly two years. The Revolution had been wrested firmly away from the popular movement. But disaffection was general. The English Ambassador had already voiced a common belief earlier that spring: 'The present constitution has no friends and cannot last.'

The new Constitution, which made virtually all powers of the King subject to the legislature, was approved by him (what choice had he?) on 14 September, the constituent Assembly was dissolved two weeks later and the new legislative Assembly convened on 1 October. On 20 October one of its leaders, Jacques-Pierre Brissot, made his first call for war against the foreign despotism, the nations ruled by kings which threatened France.

Two decrees followed, one outlawing all those who had fled and gone into voluntary exile from France – the émigrés – and were now, many of them, fomenting counter-revolution, the second for the deportation of all priests who had not sworn the oath of allegiance to the state, with a year's grace to comply, which were vetoed by the King. His veto, allowed him in 1789 and enshrined in the Constitution of 1791, was a legal overruling which began in the Roman Republic, *veto* being the Latin for 'I forbid'. Since both measures were seen by even moderates as essential to the health of the Revolution, the King – deeply offended by both – was testing his already fragile position to the limit. To the extremists, his vetoes were plain evidence of his lack of sympathy for the founding principles of the Revolution, which required absolute loyalty to the nation before all else, before church, before previous status, especially before inherited privilege, which all the émigrés had enjoyed and refused to surrender for the common good and the common will.

The flight to Varennes polarised those who clung to a lingering hope of establishing a constitutional monarchy and those seeking to emulate the American revolutionaries who had so recently overthrown *their* tyranny and replaced it with a republic. When the Jacobin club voted a petition calling for the deposition of the King, several members, including Barère de Vieuzac and the Abbé Sieyès, refused to sign and on 16 July set up a rival club in the former Benedictine monastery on the north side of the Tuileries gardens, named after its parent house in the Haute-Garonne, Feuillants. Other moderates, including Lavoisier and the poet André Chénier, joined, and the Feuillants became identified with moderate pro-monarchic opinion.

The following February officials in the Vendée, as across France, began to impound and sell church property, the first protests erupted and continued sporadically until May: priests who *had* taken the oath were molested and hounded out of their parish. Priests who refused the oath were replaced by 'intruders'; their usurpation of the 'good priests' merely sharpened the rancour of the devout who now dreaded dying without the sacraments of holy communion and confession.

In the thickly wooded areas of the bocage, where a stranger to the district must quickly get lost in the maze of paths and tracks, the local people met for open-air Mass or gathered in the tiny chapels of the old pilgrimage routes. Revolutionary jargon referred to those who refused to accept the constitutional clergy as 'fanatics' and national Guardsmen were sent in to disperse them and destroy their chapels.

An apparition of the Virgin Mary, tutelary saint of one such chapel at Saint-Laurent-de-la-Plaine, was seen one night in an oak tree nearby. The Marquis de la Révellière-Lépeaux, one of the few Vendean nobles to side with the revolutionaries, gave orders for the tree to be cut down.

In early March 1792 the government, until now dominated by the Feuillants, who were bent on propping up a tottering throne and preserving a peace which was at best precarious, collapsed; it had lost a battle they could never win in the face of the growing force and expression of anti-monarchist opinion. Power passed to the republican Girondin party, named after the River Gironde which served as a broad sealane to and from the wharves in Bordeaux, led by Brissot.

On 10 March General Dumouriez, a career soldier in the royal army who, caught up in the disgrace of his aristocratic patron (privilege cut both ways), had spent part of 1773 in the Liberty Tower of the Bastille, was appointed Foreign minister. Dumouriez was much travelled, an urbane and intelligent man of wide reading, a professional soldier, dedicated to reform and at one with the Girondins on the need to defend the Revolution with vigour beyond its borders. Brissot, 37 years old, the son of a restaurateur, a vigorous popular pamphleteer, founder of a society for the protection of the black population of the Caribbean, Friends of the Blacks, had spent two months in the Bastille in 1784, on false charges of libel. He was the first to popularise the woollen red cap as worn in the winter by working men, later associated with liberty, and to disseminate the titles 'citizen', 'citizeness' and 'sansculotte'.

What had been a relatively broad description of the poor workers was, by now, narrowed to define specifically those who showed true patriotism by determined public acts of unimpeachable revolutionary spirit, the activists of the city sections, the men and women who could claim to have taken a leading part in the action of what were commemorated as 'historic days' – 14 July, 5 October 1789, 17 July 1791.

In these early months of 1792 the food shortages in Paris and disaffection in the provinces were imputed to the machinations of the émigrés, who, not without cause, were suspected of plotting to overthrow the Revolution. War fever ran high and Brissot saw in it a chance to seize power by harnessing the support of the popular movement. The Feuillant government was royalist and unpopular; the widespread conviction was that the King and his foreign – Austrian – queen, virtual prisoners, were plotting their liberation with the foreign coalition. War was a temporary inconvenience, but it would lead to political power. Brissot and his followers saw their chance. The émigrés, said Pierre-Victurnien Vergniaud, were gathering in Koblenz and along the banks of the Rhine; what must loyal citizens do: rush to defend the nation's frontiers or lay down their arms? The émigrés by their threats were controlling France. Because of French indecision they had become the arbiters of France's peace and her destiny. It was for France to decide whether such a humiliating role was worthy of a great people.

In a speech to the Jacobin club, Robespierre opposed the move towards war. It was being fostered for their own ends by court and other factions 'for the honour of France'. Such an idea was preposterous. 'Good heavens, the French nation dishonoured by this mob of fugitives, as ridiculous as they are impotent . . . The shame lies in being deceived by the unscrupulous artifices of the enemies of our liberty. Magnanimity, wisdom, liberty, fortune, virtue, therein lies *our* honour. The honour they speak of is support for despotism, the honour of aristocracy's heroes, of all tyrants; it is the honour of crime . . . and it is prescribed in the land of liberty. Leave this honour be or send it over the Rhine where it may seek refuge in the heart and head of the princes and gentlemen of Koblenz.'

France declared war on Austria on 20 April. Five days later Nicholas Jacques Pelletier, who, on 24 January, had been found guilty in fact and in law of armed robbery on 14 October 1791, in that he had waylaid a man and beaten him with a cudgel before robbing him of 800 livres in *assignats*, the promissory notes issued by the revolutionary government on security of state land from 1790 to 1796, was taken, dressed in the red shirt of a murderer, to a scaffold erected in the place de Grève and thereon beheaded by a machine invented some centuries before but recently modified and improved under the aegis of a Dr Guillotin.

# ✤ THREE ✤

# *The Sword of Justice*

> . . . a machine which humanity cannot contemplate without shuddering but which justice, and the welfare of society, make necessary.
>
> *Dr Cullerier*

D R JOSEPH-IGNACE GUILLOTIN was born in Saintes, north of Bordeaux, on 28 May 1738. Tradition has it that his heavily pregnant mother was out walking and, startled by the agonised screams of a man being broken on the wheel, gave premature birth to her son. The 'executioner was thus his midwife'.

He studied medicine, became an expert in the circulation of air and improved methods of ventilation and in 1770 set up as a doctor in Paris. Elected deputy to the first Assembly, he read a paper in December 1789 proposing:

*Article 1*
A uniform punishment for all categories of crime, regardless of rank or wealth of the accused. [Passed.]

*Article 2*
Offences and crimes are of the person – no stain ought to attach to the family in the case of execution or loss of civil rights.

*Article 3*
In no circumstances are the goods of an executed man to be confiscated.

*Article 4*

The corpse of a criminal to be returned to his family should they request so. The corpse to be given a normal burial and the public register not to specify circumstances of death. [Articles 2, 3 and 4 were adopted on 21 January 1790.]

*Article 5*

Any reproach offered to the family with regard either to the execution or to loss of civil rights to be reprimanded by judge.

*Article 6*

In the case of a death penalty, the mode of execution to be the same for any crime incurring the death sentence: decapitation by a simple mechanism. [Not debated until March 1792.]

The call for a humane method of execution keyed into the abolition of old privileges. Decapitation, traditionally reserved to men of blue blood in many societies, had its origin in Roman law which condemned a man convicted of treason to be beaten with rods and then beheaded. The *fasces*, the bundle of rods enclosing an axe, carried by the lectors who attended magistrates as a sign of their authority, became a symbol of republican law, the root of the word 'fascist'. Treason, first defined as the sacrilege of attacking the divinity of kingship or imperial majesty, becomes that of attacking the security of the state. The persuasion of privilege granted a swift death by the axe – always dependent on the competence of the man wielding the axe – as against lingering strangulation at the end of a rope, with the attendant indignity of evacuation of the bowels, ejaculation of semen and the prurient attendance of a crowd of spectators. 'In France, beheading has been the preserve of the high nobility and has thereby acquired a certain social distinction, a badge of respectability which makes it almost an honour. Rather than promote the masses to the dignity of the block, we should reduce the nobility to the common level of the gallows.' (Verninac de Saint-Maur in a debate, arguing for the adoption of the new machine.)

Experiments were conducted on commoners with beheading machines at various times in the 12th and 13th centuries in Naples, Holland and Germany and during the 15th and 16th centuries in Italy – the Mannaia – in Scotland – the Maiden – and in Yorkshire, England – the Halifax Gibbet; crude wooden frames with a descending blade. The Halifax Gibbett Law condemned anyone who stole goods above the value of thirteen and a half pence in the liberty of Halifax to be beheaded on the gibbet on a market day on a hill outside the town. Enacted to protect local manufacturers in the wool trade from theft of cloth, it ceased to operate after 1650.

> At Hallifax the law so sharpe doth deale,
> That whoso more than thirteen pence doth steale,
> They have a jyn [engine] that wondrous quick and well
> Sends thieves all headless into heaven or hell.
>
> *John Taylor, Works (1630)*

That 'wondrous quick and well' is what the French lawmakers were seeking.

In 1777 Marat entered a competition organised by the Society of Citizens of Neuchâtel; he advanced his *Plan for Criminal Legislation*, in which he called for penalties at once lenient and dependable. The beheading axe did not always cut first time and executioners needed skill for their work. 'Capital punishment should be a rarity . . .' he wrote. 'Life is a unique gift without equivalent; justice rightly requires that murder should be punished by death [as in the old law of a life for a life]. Execution should never be cruel; rather its aim should be shame. Even for the most serious crimes – liberticide, parricide, fratricide, the murder of a friend or benefactor – the machinery of death should instil fear but the death should be an easy one.'

He meant that it should cause as little pain as possible.

Six years later, in 1783, the University of Metz organised a similar competition offering prizes to the best and most persuasive arguments for the suppression of ignominious punishments. Robespierre took second prize; first prize went to Pierre Louis de Lacretelle, a lawyer of the Parlement, who was later one of 300 to be elected from the Paris municipality to the constituent Assembly. He argued that being broken on the wheel and being hanged on the gallows brought shame on the family of those executed whereas the blade that severs the criminal's head does not degrade his family in any way: it may even eventually be taken as a mark of nobility. Might it not be possible to take advantage of this consideration and extend this form of punishment to citizens of all ranks? 'We would thereby eliminate unjust discrimination of class . . . were we to replace a penalty which adds its own shame to the shame already attached to public execution with another penalty to which no sense of family dishonour attaches, one to which our imagination actually lends a certain lustre.'

After the law incorporating capital punishment had been passed, the public executioner, Charles Henri Sanson, latest scion of the family trade, was ordered to produce an expert report on the specifications of a killing machine by whose use no man's hands need be tainted with the blood of a fellow being. In March 1792 Sanson advised: 'The need for a good blade made of first-rate steel which would keep its edge. This would be expensive' and: 'Both executioner and victim would have to be equal to the task. What if the victim were to faint? to struggle? what if he could not be controlled?'

And, in such a case, what if the executioner were to give way to emotion? Nobles were accustomed to showing poise, dignity, composure; they had been schooled from youth in comportment, dancing, swordsmanship, they knew how to *hold* themselves, physically; but if the *lower classes* were placed in the same position?

An order to produce a design for a machine was delivered to the Permanent Secretary of the Academy of Surgery, Dr Louis, author of an article on Death for the great encyclopedia of the French Enlightenment philosophers, the *Encyclopédie*, long before there was any talk of such a machine. A good rationalist, he had dismissed without sentiment the familiar metaphor of the moment of death as the sweep of the Grim Reaper's scythe: ' . . . we do not see the sickle of Fate when it is about to cut off our life nor do we feel its stroke . . . the sickle is a figment of our imagination. Death does not come armed with a blade; no violence accompanies death. We die by imperceptible degrees.'

In his *Expert Opinion on Methods of Decapitation*, of 7 March 1792, Louis explores the chancy nature of beheading with an axe. When the executioner's axe fell on the neck of one Lally, kneeling and blindfold, the blade failed to sever his head; Lally toppled forward and had to be repositioned and his head was cut off only after four or five hacks from a sabre. He also referred to the machine used 'in England', namely the Halifax Gibbet. He stressed the need for a convex blade like an old-style battleaxe; a straight cutting edge delivering a perpendicular blow has little or no effect because the line of cut is far too small, being restricted to the point of impact. To work efficiently, the full sharp length of the blade must be deployed in a slicing motion. A convex blade is perpendicular only at the centre of the circle it has to cut – that is, the cusp of the neck – and as the instrument's edge penetrates it continues to cut obliquely – that is, in a slice. Louis also discusses basic mechanics; he stipulates a frame, a weighted blade whose force is increased by momentum proportional to the height or length of the drop; the mechanism to be operated by a trigger. Such a machine, he promised, would be ' . . . easy to construct and infallible'.

The prototype, built in less than a week by Tobias Schmidt, a fortepiano maker, was tried out on corpses in the Bicêtre prison on 17 April.

Helping Dr Louis in these experiments was that distinguished member of the Royal Academy of Sciences, Dr Guillotin. His name, to his lasting chagrin, was expropriated for the new device. Its feminine version, *guillotine*, rhymes with machine and, as Jacques-Claude Beugnot remarked: 'The poor man was a philanthropist, generous, erudite and intelligent but the misfortune of having that lethal machine named after him made his life bitter.' When the guillotine began its work in earnest, Guillotin made sure to give his friends lethal tablets – probably high-dosage opium – which he had made for them in case they were condemned to the scaffold.

A popular song wryly puffed his philanthropy:

> Guillotin's
> Medicines
> Social antibiotic:
> Imagine
> A fair new dawn
> When hanging's
> Inhuman
> And unpatriotic.

Guillotin carried out his own experimental work on the 'philanthropic beheading machine' in his house at 9 Cour du Commerce-Saint-André, opposite the house, number 8, where Marat's splenetic journal *The People's Friend* was printed.

The machine was also nicknamed 'Louison' and 'Louisette' but the monikers didn't stick, possibly because the innuendo of the King's name was too nasty. Dr Louis himself was, nonetheless, alarmed at the risk of notoriety he ran: 'I considered the guillotine to be humane and did no more than refine the shape of the blade, making it diagonal so that it cut cleanly and did what it was supposed to do. My enemies tried, they did everything they could via the press, to have the lethal machine called Petite-Louison although they couldn't replace the name guillotine. I was silly enough to be upset by these vile efforts and they were vile, even if they sought to pass it all off as a joke in perfectly good taste.'

The guillotine was designed to deliver judicial death mechanically, with virtually no involvement of any human agency. It would be efficient and the suffering attached to death momentary. As Guillotin put it: 'the head flies off . . . the victim is no more'. Its use would, most importantly, remove the stigma of cannibalism from a people which had already shown itself willing and able to take to itself the ritualistic expiatory wielding of the pike and sabre. There was, too, an inherent anomaly in the very rapidity of the death under the guillotine blade. The prolonged suffering inflicted by old forms of punishment were universally seen as a supplication to the Almighty, the torment endured part of the process of redemption of sin, the appeal to divine mercy. The automatic fall of the guillotine blade secularised punishment.

There was a certain amount of macabre speculation on the question of whether or not death was instantaneous. There was, of course, no way of knowing, although a man told his assistant to watch his eyes when the executioner held up his head: he would carry on blinking as long as he could. The young man counted 20 blinks. When the executioner's assistant slapped Charlotte Corday's face, the cheek blushed and the watching crowd was scandalised. That outburst of public anger at Corday's posthumous show of maidenly modesty did much to diminish public confidence in the humane efficiency of the machine.

To begin with, however, the public were not greatly impressed; indeed they were generally disappointed with the dispatch of the operation: it was too quick, there was no show, no spectacle, no long drawn-out procedural rite that fastened the solemn, the purgative nature of public execution. The rational, dehumanised machine lacked the complicity of feelings: horror at the crime, catharsis of the punishment, overt penitential suffering, the participation and collusion of the crowd, the mediating power of greater justice and the officer of the law, the *public* executioner. They preferred the old regime's methods: 'Give me back my wooden gibbet, give me back my gallows.'

Sanson, the chief executioner, once a master craftsman, had become a mere 'agent of public works . . . a simple representative of the executive', as Desmoulins put it.

Brissot's government did not last long. Its opportunist attempt to force a crisis and eliminate the King from any place in politics misfired. The King used his power of veto to block moves to set up a large garrison of troops brought in from the provinces, and reacted petulantly when he was reproved. He dismissed Brissot's government. The people felt affronted not from any great affection for Brissot but rather from outrage at the King's meddling in their affairs.

Paris had been divided into 48 sections, each with its own surveillance committee, national Guard post and police station. Some of the smaller sections could be traversed by patrols, street by street, in about half an hour and none was so large that the enforcement of a curfew posed any logistical difficulty. Surveillance was general, intrusive in every corner, constant. The city was a tight-knit community where gossip and rumour flew swiftly.

On 19 June it was common knowledge that mischief was afoot. The American Ambassador noted in his diary that 'There is to be a Sort of Riot tomorrow' and on 20 June a mob of between 10,000 and 20,000 armed demonstrators marched on the Tuileries along the direct road from the Faubourg Saint-Antoine, a serried column that tailed back 2.5 kilometres, led by Santerre, a brewer of the district who had appointed himself general-in-chief of the sansculottes. Their intention had been well bruited and they marched in a menacing silence, no tocsin, no drums, no voices raised, just the purposeful slow tread of the long phalanx.

The palace Guard made no attempt to stop them; they tramped up the grand staircase and swarmed into the King's apartments and there began to chant derogatory slogans – 'Down with the veto, to hell with the veto' – and the revolutionary hymn of the sansculottes:

> We'll sort it out, sort it out, sort it out,
> Off to the lamp with the a-ris-tos
> We'll sort it out, sort it out, sort it out
> A-ris-tos, we'll string 'em up.

The crowd filed past the King as he faced them with unexpected aplomb, whether from courage or stupidity is not clear. They waved sabres and pistols at him, but he did not flinch. It was the closest any of them had ever come to the royal personage. Part of Damiens' crime was to invade the regal presence. Here he stood before them, close enough to touch with impunity, tall, portly, awkward of gait, rather short-sighted, the rich finery of his garments apart, a mere man. A butcher called Legendre, friend of Danton, is said to have rebuked the King in his face: 'Sir, you are a villain, it's us you have to listen to, now. You have always cheated us and you are still cheating us. Enough. We are sick of your hypocrisy.'

'The King,' wrote the English Ambassador, Earl Gower, 'accepted a red cap of liberty with tricolour ribands and, upon their expressing a wish that he should drink to the health of the nation, His Majesty condescended to comply with their request and drank the remains of some wine in a cup, out of which a grenadier had previously drunk.' (The red cap or bonnet was often but mistakenly thought to be modelled on the cap worn by the ancient Phrygians and reckoned to be a badge of liberty.)

King Louis XVI had been reduced to a nobody, a mortal shell stripped of majesty, of his lofty distance from them, a figure of mockery as vulnerable to taunt – and physical wound – as a common criminal locked in the pillory. Far from bowing to the ignominy of having turned tail and deserted his people, the cowardice of betraying the nation, he had presumed, once more, to seek to impose his former sovereign will, to interfere with *their* elected government, to flout the popular will and their constitutional right to liberty.

A month later, as the forces of Austria and Prussia (which had declared war on 13 June) menaced the frontiers a decree proclaimed: 'The Nation in Danger.' On 25 July the Brunswick Manifesto, purporting to be the work of the Duke of Brunswick, the commander of the Prussian army advancing on Paris, but in fact written by an émigré friend of the Queen, warned that: 'The invading Prussians would treat any national Guardsman bearing arms as mercenaries beyond the pale of law and shoot them out of hand. Prussia and Austria did not seek war to enrich themselves, nor did they mean to meddle in the internal affairs of France but they would deliver the King and Queen to ensure their safety. The city of Paris and all its inhabitants were called upon to submit instantly to the King; responsibility for this rested squarely on the members of the national Assembly, on pain of losing their heads after judgement by military court without hope of pardon, and upon the authorities of department, municipality and districts, upon the national Guards of Paris, law officers and *others whom it may concern* [my italics] . . . rebels found guilty of illegal resistance shall suffer the punishments they have deserved.'

News of Brunswick's ultimatum reached the city on 28 July. The border against which the Prussians were advancing lay less than a fortnight's march from Paris.

The threat of invasion, backed by the machinations and intrigues of a large number of influential and wealthy émigrés, offered some hope of restitution to the King. The flagrant, ham-fisted attempt of the Manifesto to cow the national Guard into lame surrender and thus leave the city open and undefended infuriated the people of Paris: the campaign to remove the King gathered momentum rapidly.

The Assembly immediately ordered a distribution of weapons to all able-bodied citizens and two days later the first of the troops from the provinces –the *fédérés* – arrived in Paris: the men of Marseille.

There were some 500 hoodlums, led by a Pole called Lazowski and an unknown from the East Indies; the scourings of the Marseille docks, foreign vagabonds, Genoese, Corsicans and Greeks among them, marched into Paris, in sansculotte clothes, teamed up with the criminal dregs of the more unsavoury faubourgs, filled the taverns and danced their farandoles in the streets. The Paris Commune welcomed them; these were their people, brass-tacks sansculottes; national authorities were not to be trusted, all in cahoots with the placemen of the old regime. The people of Paris stood four-square for the Revolution. They signed a pact of unity with the Marseillais, a pact endorsed by Marat, whose influence over the sansculottes was now unparalleled. They worshipped him. He spoke the language of their heart; he voiced the reasoning of their grievances.

Marat, whose violent and sanguinary opinions underpinned that proletarian clamour for summary, bloody retaliation which led remorselessly to the doctrine of state terror, stood barely 1.5 metres tall, broad-shouldered, with a sturdy frame, no fat on him, short, bowed legs, strong arms which he flapped and wind-sailed jerkily when he talked. He had a broad forehead, pronounced cheekbones, a slightly squashed, aquiline nose, a small mouth with thin lips which frequently twitched in the corner like a sneer, pale eyebrows, yellowish-grey eyes, brown, dishevelled hair and a black jowl. He walked always as if in a tearing hurry, almost skipping along, head erect, hips rolling. His voice was deep, resonant, but marred by an impediment which nasalised his c's and l's.

In September 1789, when the new government issued orders for the arrest of this loud-mouthed agitator, he went into hiding; constantly on the move, living in cellars, sewers, basements, caves, attics; six weeks he spent in a room no bigger than a cupboard, crouched on one buttock. He rarely came out during daylight but eventually found a more permanent refuge in the Cordeliers district among uncompromising anarchists whose version of revolutionary law was unambiguous: big men (i.e. rich), bad; little people (i.e. poor), good. To someone accused of unpatriotic behaviour a Cordelier is reported to have said, with the kind of morgue affected by the feudal aristocracy, who admitted no slight to or diminution of their privilege: 'If you had 20,000 livres you would be guillotined. Since you are penniless, you are a brother.'

When the Marseillais arrived in town, Marat came into his own.

Following their invasion of the Tuileries, the sansculottes began to dominate both the political and the social forum. No doffing of hats, no deferential *vous* but familiar *tu* to everyone; *citoyen* ('citizen') replaced 'monsieur' ('my lord'); no wigs, silk waistcoats, scent or buckled shoes. 'Aristocrat' became a term of repugnance more or less promiscuously applied to anyone with property.

'Aristocrats are the rich, the wealthy merchants, monopolists, middlemen, bankers, trading clerks, petty-fogging lawyers, any citizen who owns anything.' Any citizen, indeed, whom the sansculottes decided was guilty of *incivisme* – uncitizenlike behaviour or attitude – guilty or even suspect. Since it was a fact that all sansculottes were hungry, theft and pilfering from those citizens who were not became legitimate, an egalitarian act, a revolutionary right. Thus revolutionary politics was reduced to the wants and demands of the sansculottes; their identity with the people an expression of the general will, the electoral consensus, a crucial narrowing of focus. 'I am,' said Marat repeatedly, 'the rage of the people.'

His nocturnal skulking while he was on the run, the long periods spent in fetid, disease-ridden, putrid locales, the lack of nourishment and the plague eating at his mind had reduced his health severely. His body erupted in blistering abscesses; he began to suffer chronic blinding headaches and excruciating pains in his limbs; he contracted the worst and most disgusting form of eczema; a purulent lesion extended the length of his perineum from the scrotum to the anus, causing maddening irritation. The scrofulous skin of his face had a sickly chlorine pallor. It was as if his body had taken on all the miseries and hurts of a diseased society and burst out in the corruption which ravaged the small people of France. The difference was that the cancer eating away at society had not been seen till he, Marat, the people's friend, exposed it. The disease and hurt of his torn body merely testified to the depth of such corruption: a Dorian Gray in reverse.

To compound the dismay of his flesh, he gave up any care of his appearance: his clothes stank, he rarely washed, he was a fright, a walking nightmare. It was a crude, a pugnacious and obnoxious self-advertisement of sansculotterie, a badge of his unadorned, unpampered, plebeian virtue.

The only relief he had from his appalling physical afflictions was to bathe in salts, a scarf soaked in vinegar tied about his head. He would sit, scribbling furiously on a writing board, in a hip bath the shape of an oversized gravy boat.

On 10 August 1792 Marat's people, the sansculottes of Paris, stiffened by the contingent from Marseille, marched once again on the Tuileries to remove the tyrant. Across the city the tocsin rang – in every church belfry the higher-pitched alarm bell, a horrifying din, each bell struck continuously with an iron rod or else the clapper grasped by hand and hammered against the inside of the bell casing.

And this time they came with the hollow slow roll of military side drums beating the general call to arms and cries of havoc to unleash the dogs of war.

The royal family were bundled off for safety into the Assembly meeting hall and took refuge in the box in the gallery set aside for the shorthand reporters. Most of the 2,000 men of the national Guard posted at the Tuileries immediately went over to the Commune. However, the Filles-Saint-Thomas battalion, drawn from the Place Louis XIV section, near the Palais Royal, which since 1791 had been heavily infiltrated by men of royalist sympathies, kept its post and, forever vilified for it, opened fire on the mob.

In the fighting, 600 soldiers of the royal Swiss Guard were cut down, including several who had been captured and promised safe conduct, their corpses desecrated – limbs lopped off, genitals cut out and stuffed in the dying mouth or fed to the scavenging dogs. From the Tuileries the mob rampaged through the city toppling statues, tearing down or defacing all symbols of royalty, even the word 'King' on street signs.

The royal family was first hustled into the Feuillants' building and then incarcerated in the Temple tower, a fortress dating from 1265, a few streets north of the Hôtel de Ville, the King separated, alone, in one room. The monarchy was finished. The Commune, the sansculottes, had taken power.

When the day was over, the bloodiest but most decisive historic day of the Revolution to date, the remnants of the King's bodyguards were loaded on to carts and dumped in common lime pits.

Two hundred and sixty men of the Commune fell in the mayhem; their corpses were laid out along the Pont au Change. Contemplating them, Robespierre nearly wept to think that any one of those corpses might have been of an innocent. Rising above his grief, he eulogised 'the most beautiful revolution that has ever honoured humanity'. He defended one Daubigny, who had been caught looting in the Tuileries the day the King and Queen were taken into custody. 'Whoever helped France on 10 August,' he said, 'is no thief.'

This kind of syllogism was common. Robespierre was taxed with engineering the election of one Desfieux, a man of very bad reputation, whom he subsequently had arrested and executed.

'This Desfieux of yours is a villain.'

'It doesn't matter,' he replied, 'he is a patriot.'

'But he's a convicted bankrupt.'

'He's a patriot.'

'He's a thief.'

'He's a patriot.'

And that was all he would answer: 'He's a patriot.'

All barriers were closed, the city sealed off. A few days after the attack, the papers of the Feuillants were seized and 841 members of the club declared suspects. The club was defunct but the appellation 'Feuillant' was retained, to be applied opprobriously to those who supported a policy of 'cowardly moderation'.

On 25 August the first political prisoner of the Revolution, Louis Collot d'Agremont, secretary of the administration of the national Guard, accused of complicity in the conspiracy to restore the monarchy, was tried and sentenced by a special court set up to try the crimes of 10 August. He went to the guillotine set up in the place du Carrousel, outside the Tuileries, where he was reckoned to have conspired. Being put to death at the scene of his crime most effectively expiated it.

The scaffold was not dismantled after his execution and on 23 August the Commune decreed that it would remain in place until further notice: its very looming presence to act as a stark deterrent.

For Paris was gripped with fear of the enemy within – refractory priests, skulking royalists, nobles professing loyalty to the Revolution but not to be trusted, hypocrites all. The arrests had begun, often on scant evidence and less proof; in two weeks nearly 1,000 people were imprisoned on charges of conspiracy in the foreign plot or disaffection from the Revolution. Most were priests but among the prisoners was the Queen's old friend, the Princesse de Lamballe. They were being flung in prison for plotting when they were at liberty; even when they were imprisoned, however, the abiding fear was that the plotters continued to cook up their dastardly schemes and that being all in one place made their conspiracy the more potentially dangerous.

On 27 August Paris solemnised the funeral of the 'martyrs of 10 August', their corpses on a sarcophagus drawn through the streets by oxen; widows and orphans wearing white robes with black girdles followed in procession.

Meanwhile General Dumouriez arrived at the vital strategic fort at Sedan, on the frontier with southern Belgium, in an effort to rally the troops. Morale was low; he had already failed to stir much enthusiasm north along the border in the camp at Maulde. The troops, most of them untrained recruits, had no stomach for war. The Prussians had already crossed from Luxemburg to the south into France and invested the fortress at Longwy. Their batteries opened fire but, before the day was out, Lavergne, the garrison commander, capitulated as the Prussian guns raked his defences, and his troops fled harum-scarum towards Paris.

Panic seized the city. There was chaos, a crisis in government: after the fall of the monarchy, the constituent Assembly, about to be dissolved, was leaderless and split by extreme divisions; by default, the government of Paris, *de facto* of all France, fell into the hands of the Commune. It reacted with ruthless energy.

The general Assembly of the Commune, under pressure from the popular assemblies of all the Paris sections, granted on 27 August that henceforth voting would be by roll-call, with deputies called to give opinion by public acclamation at the rostrum. This measure both protected that absolute sovereignty of the people demanded by patriots as well as avoiding secrecy and eliminating intrigue. Since the Hôtel du Châtelet, the archbishop's palace where the Assembly met, across the river in the rue de Grenelle, was too small for both the elected members and the public, sessions were relocated in the headquarters of the Jacobin club in the place du Marché Saint-Honoré, five minutes' walk from the Tuileries.

The Commune had set up a central communications bureau on 27 July, augmented on 11 August by two civic couriers nominated by the Théâtre-Français section in the Latin Quarter, locale of the Cordelier Club. These couriers were 'authorised to deliver messages wherever necessary . . . to gather and communicate all intelligence, liaison and instructions affecting the nation and report to the section'. Spymasters, in fact.

On 28 August Danton, recently appointed minister of Justice, authorised the first domiciliary visits to be carried out by patrols of ten or so men from the section committees armed with sabres, pikes and firearms. The justification of house searches for traitors or suspects was simple: 'When the *patrie* [homeland] is in danger, everything belongs to the *patrie*.' The lack of urgency in the matter of evidence reflects the willingness, already, to justify illegality by a supposed higher good. It was no less than an informer's charter, backed with arbitrary force, whose underlying principle was expressed by a statement from the Fontaine-de-Grenelle section, on the left bank opposite the Tuileries: 'The true patriot has no privacy; he relates everything in his life to the common good: the money he earns, his sufferings, he shares with his fellow citizens. This is the root of that publicity which is characteristic of fraternal, namely republican, government.'

The Commune rang the tocsin and proclaimed a state of siege: 'To arms, citizens, the enemy is at our gates.' Its central committee of surveillance, comprising 12 members from each of the city sections, had been established by decree of the Convention on 21 March 1792, to keep an eye on the activities of any foreigners in Paris. On 30 August their brief was extended to cover all suspects, monitoring and investigating sedition and counter-revolution within the city precincts, fielding denunciations, issuing certificates of civic rectitude to citizens whose patriotism had been tested and proved – by appearance at the historic days, regular attendance at section assemblies, activities conducive to the proper revolutionary spirit – and warrants for arrest. Their work reinforced the growing call for publicity, 'the people's protector', on which the rule of terror came to depend absolutely, namely that all words and actions must be deemed available and open to public scrutiny and judgement.

Several members of the commitee of surveillance became leading proponents of the Red Terror, that is, 'terrorists', the word applied to the Jacobins, their agents and partisans: Jean-Nicolas Billaud-Varenne, Jean-Marie Collot d'Herbois, Georges Jacques Danton, leader of the Cordeliers section, Jean Lambert Tallien, Etienne Panis and his close friend Marat. They now set about herding some 2,800 suspects, perhaps as many as 4,000, mostly aristocrats, political prisoners and priests, but also forgers, thieves, vagrants and prostitutes, into prisons, some of them housed in premises requisitioned from religious orders. In workshops hurriedly set up near the military hospital along both sides of the length of the avenue des Invalides and various other quarters of the city, muskets and some 30,000 pikes were hurriedly manufactured; weapons seized from suspects were handed out to the mob. An army of 20,000 volunteers flocked to recruiting tables to swear an oath not to return home until they had driven the nation's enemies out of France, an oath which not a few of them signed with their own blood. They marched out to join the army facing the Prussians. Defensive barriers were erected in Paris.

The commitee of surveillance next consulted the Assemblies of the 48 Paris sections as to what should be done with the inmates of the city's prisons if the invasion reached Paris. Marat, co-opted on to the commitee of surveillance on 2 September, said: 'Burn them to the ground, a purging fire.' Someone reflected that since there would be no satisfactory way of containing the flames, adjacent property would almost certainly be destroyed in the process of what was otherwise a commendable plan. A proposal to blow them sky high with mines was similarly rebutted.

Billaud-Varenne preferred butchering, a more poignant meed of justice, and when another committee member said that he would never find enough killers to do the job replied: 'Oh, I'll find them,' thinking, no doubt, of the men of Marseille who had already proved their ruthless worth at the Tuileries. Tallien later admitted that he opposed the scheme but did not, at the time, dare object. We may infer that the idea of terror was hatched in a very few minds, enshrined in emergency law and exploited by servants exculpated by the workings of a new definition of justice. The language used by obscure men and women to corroborate their own part in the administration of terror is couched in jargon, gutter cut-throat bravado, the vocabulary of the judicial abattoir. Bunou, from the Champs-Elysées section, demanded that a guillotine be erected in the section 'and that he would act as executioner if no one else could be found'; Lesur from the Luxembourg section, complained that 'the guillotine is not working fast enough and there should be more bloodletting in the prisons and if the executioner was tired he would climb the scaffold with a quartern loaf to mop up the blood'; Jayet, of the Gardes-Françaises section, declared that he would like to see rivers of blood, ankle-deep; Baudray, a woman lemonade seller from the Lepeletier section, said 'she would like to eat the heart of anyone opposing the sansculottes' and was going to bring up her children on the same principle. 'There's a lot of talk about chopping off heads,' she said, 'but not enough blood is flowing.'

To what extent Danton himself colluded in the details of the grisly business of the September Massacres is less clear, although he later said, or bragged – he was inordinately vain – to the future king, Louis-Philippe, the duc de Chartres, son of the duc d'Orléans, a prominent republican: 'You prattle endlessly and incautiously about the September Massacres without a clue as to who organised them. I did. I wanted to send the young men of Paris out into Champagne drabbled with the blood that would guarantee their loyalty. I wanted a river of blood coursing between them and the émigrés.'

Despite the state of emergency, many Parisians behaved with that indifference against which the more ardent revolutionaries struggled and upon which their extremism at last faltered and failed, when indifference turned to disgust. The Scottish physician and writer John Moore, living in Paris, having studied medicine there, records how: 'The Champs-Elysées were crowded with strollers of one sort or another. A great number of small booths were erected where refreshments were sold and which resounded with music and singing. Pantomimes and puppet shows of various kinds were exhibited and in some parts people were dancing. "Are these people as happy as they seem?" I asked a Frenchman who was with me. "They are as happy as that," he answered. "Do you think that the Duke of Brunswick never enters their thoughts?" asked I. "You can be sure that the Duke of Brunswick is the last person in the world they are thinking about," was his answer.'

If more prosperous, better-educated Parisians in the verdant pastoral of the western quarter affected such insouciance, in the over-crowded, rat- and refuse-infested, stinking factory and workshop ghettos of the east, the poor felt otherwise and ratified the strident rhetoric of their leaders. A 13-year-old apprentice sempstress, Marie-Victoire Monnard: 'Like everyone else, I shook with terror in case the royalists were allowed to get out of the prisons and come and murder me because I didn't have any holy pictures to prove I was on their side. That's why they did the September Massacres. It was horrible and we shuddered but we thought what they did was justified. We went about what we would be doing any normal day while it was going on.'

Speakers and stump orators at street corners harangued the crowds, weaving fury into fear; to the men who were about to march off to the war front, what dangers were they leaving behind them? Were they not afraid to leave family and children to the mercy of the aristocrats both in and out of prison? Was not a concerted breakout from their confinement altogether possible, likely? Even though nothing remotely like it had happened yet in Paris, when so many marched away, what better opportunity for the conspirators to burst free and work their revenge? And the crowds rising to the fury called back: 'No mercy. We must go on.'

Talk on these streets was brisk, overheated. Rumour fed rumour. Gossip fuelled paranoia.

Blood-curdling pamphlets were offered for sale at every street crossing and eagerly snapped up. One such went on sale on 1 September, entitled:

Louis Capet's great treason. Plot uncovered to assassinate all good citizens of the capital during the night of 2 on this month, to be carried out by the aristocrats and refractory priests, assisted by the thieves and criminals held in the prisons of Paris Signed 'Charles Boussemart, unwhiskered patriot'.

Boussemart used Capet contemptuously of Louis, referring to the post-Carolingian royal line, which began with Hugues Capet (987–96), who established his central authority in the capital and thus symbolised the Paris-based regal tyranny. The King always protested vehemently that he was no Capetian.

The side whiskers were later affected by the republican soldiers, in imitation of the infamously ferocious continental hussar regiments, but to begin with they were associated with royalist soldiers, including those of the national Guard whose loyalty was not yet dependable.

Marat kept up the pressure: 'Dissidents must be rooted out and hewn down. Rise up, you unfortunate poor of the city: workmen without work, homeless sleeping under bridges, beggars without food or shelter, cripples, outcasts . . . cut off the thumbs of the wealthy who conspire against you; split the tongues of the priests who preach servitude. A starving man has the right to slit the throat of a man who is well-fed and eat his palpitating flesh . . . This Terror is the measured price of public tranquillity, to drive out the legions of reactionaries lurking within our walls, poised for the moment when the patriots march off to face our enemies. They are all identified. Every single one by name. We are betrayed and we will flush out the traitors by fear.'

The traitors of whom he spoke were confined in a number of prisons.

The Bicêtre, perhaps one of the most terrible, had been built in the 13th century as a Carthusian monastery on the plateau of Gentilly, outside the city to the south, some 4.5 kilometres from the centre. Later converted into a feudal dungeon, it fell into disuse and dilapidation. The ruins were rebuilt and used as a hospital in the 17th century but eventually became a prison for madmen, syphilitics, swindlers, murderers, vagabonds and delinquents, sinners who were regularly and brutally chastised in expiation of their moral turpitude. In September 1792 most of the inmates were common-law prisoners and convicts awaiting transfer to the prison galleys off Brittany.

The Salpêtrière hospital was founded in 1656 as a home for aged or insane women on the site of a gunpowder factory close by the left bank of the Seine, in the Faubourg Saint-Marcel. In 1684 a wing was added to house criminals and, later, to accommodate elderly couples who could not fend for themselves. In 1792 there were said to be 8,000 people living there.

The Hôtel du Châtelet was used as a temporary lock-up by the Commune.

Sunday 2 September, 2 p.m.: open tumbrels (tip-up carts, originally an instrument of torture, perhaps a ducking stool) conveying
25 priests and members of religious orders rumbled through the
narrow streets of the left bank towards the Abbaye de Saint-Germain-
des-Près, now requisitioned as a gaol. Approaching the gates, they
were confronted by a large crowd shouting abuse, brandishing sabres,
pikes, axes, cudgels, shovels. In the jostling and shoving a man clambered on to the first cart and dragged one of the prisoners, a novice
monk in a loose white habit, to the ground. There was a sudden awful
silence, a moment of indecision on the one side, ghastly apprehension on the other. Shaking with fear, the young man sank to his knees,
raised his arms in supplication and begged for mercy in a barely
audible whisper. The soft grace of his voice jolted the mob into the
violence they had come to do. The men guarding the prisoners joined
the mob. A flurry of sabre cuts – an eyewitness calculated ten – hewed
the young man down. The horses drawing the carts jerked forward
in panic but the crowd was galvanised: they rough-handled the rest
of the prisoners out of the carts and hacked all but one to death.
The survivor, the Abbé Sicard, was saved by the intervention of a
national Guardsman, though one of his inquisitors said to him: 'There
is nothing more delightful to a patriot than the blood of his enemies.'

Sicard, rarely for a priest in the capital, was much loved and
esteemed, even by the poorer workers, because of his work in the
school he ran for deaf-mute children. When he was imprisoned, a
deputation from the school petitioned the Assembly for his release.
He was, the children said, like a father to them, he taught them, he
took care of them and he is shut up like a common criminal. 'He is
a good man, fair and pure-hearted . . . without him we would be just
animals.'

A deputy boldly offered to take Sicard's place but another,
Lequinio, objected that revolutionary justice allowed for no exceptions, no preferential treatment and the children were dismissed.

The man who intervened to save Sicard was later called a citizen
hero for saving a life which was so useful to the patrie.

The butchery in the Abbaye petered out for want of victims. Stanislas
Maillard said: 'We're finished here, let's move on to the Carmes.' The
mob, in full cry, surged south along the rue de Rennes to the Discalced
Carmelite convent, the Carmes, in the rue de Vaugirard, which they

knew held some 150 priests, and burst in through the gates. Maillard and his fellow 'officials' arrived and set up a table in the corridor at the head of a stairwell leading down to the garden. Elected president of this makeshift tribunal to 'try' prisoners by acclaim of his fellows, Maillard, tricked out in a tricolour sash of revolutionary office, promised to 'work like a good citizen'. It was agreed that the code word for 'condemned' would be 'To La Force', the prison close by the Bastille.

A number of Swiss Guards had been in detention since 10 August. Maillard proposed that examining them would waste time; they must be guilty *de facto*. The tribunal agreed with one voice: 'To La Force.'

Proceedings at the tribunal were brief.

Prisoners were stripped of wallets, jewellery, watches, and brought in one by one for judgement.

Once condemned, in a travesty of mock-execution with the words: 'Let him go', the prisoner was shoved down the steps to where his executioners waited at the bottom. One hundred and nineteen victims were dispatched in under two hours.

A few of the inmates had managed to escape over a three-metre wall into the rue de Cassette; the rest were systematically hunted down in every corner of the gardens and buildings; several, the Archbishop of Arles among them, were found kneeling at prayer in the oratory.

When the mob broke into the chapel, calling for him, the priests clustered round in an attempt to shield him but he pushed through and pleaded with the mob: let them be happy to kill him and spare the rest.

'I am the one you are looking for,' he said.

'So you're the one, you old bastard.'

'I am the Archbishop.'

'You criminal – you shed the blood of so many patriots in Arles.'

'I have never done anybody any harm.'

'Well, I'm going to do you some harm.' The man slashed him across the face with his sabre. Another struck from behind and split open his skull. The old priest put up his right hand to cover his eyes. A third blow and a fourth. He sank to the ground. A fifth sabre cut laid him supine, his dying eyes staring blankly up at their hatred. And one of them drove a pike into his chest with such ferocity that it couldn't be extricated. In a taking of fury, they kicked and trampled him underfoot before turning on the priests.

So runs the account of the Abbé Berthelet de Barbot, who, wounded in the thigh and hustled with some others into the Sanctuary, was somehow overlooked.

A commissioner sent by the committee of the Luxembourg section, Violette, saved several of the priests by concealing them under seats in a chapel, but he remarked to one of them: 'I am at a loss; I don't understand it at all. Anyone who'd seen what happened here would have been as amazed as I was. Those priests went to their death as cheerfully as if they were going to a wedding.'

One of the butchers, mopping blood from his wet hands with a handkerchief already steeped with blood, came in to ask Maillard and the tribunal for permission to keep a pair of shoes taken from an aristocrat. He explained: 'Our good brothers-in-arms killing these criminals will be marching off to the front tomorrow, but they're barefoot.' The committee consulted and unanimously granted the request and when he came back to complain of thirst and request some wine for the execution detail, this, too, was granted.

The funeral detail hired by the Commune – and most of the assassins were paid 24 livres for the job – finally tired of humping corpses on to the carts for dispatch to the common graves and simply heaved many of them into a well shaft. This hideous ossuary was excavated in the 19th century: most of the skulls had been dented or caved in with heavy bludgeons, jawbones smashed.

As night fell, the killers moved back from the Carmes to the Abbaye to deal with the 300 suspects incarcerated there.

At 9 p.m. a vinegar merchant, Pierre-François Damiens, entered a tavern kept by citizen Lévêque, accompanied by one Seguin, the hands of both men boltered with blood. They drank a bottle of wine and Damiens said to Seguin: 'Off to our work.' A witness saw Damiens disembowelling Delaleu, a sergeant major who'd been confined in the Abbaye, after which he split his side open and pulled out his lungs. Another man approached Damiens and asked him to hand over a young man in his custody. Damiens replied: 'You have never seen an aristo's heart – I'm going to show you one.' He killed the prisoner, cut open his chest, tore out the heart and made the man, who had been drenched in the spouting blood, kiss it.

Marie-Thérèse Louise de Savoie-Carignan, the Princesse de Lamballe, born in 1749, widowed at 19 when her husband died of syphilis, had, from 1785, been the Queen's closest companion. She went to London in 1791 to appeal for help for the royal family but returned to share their imprisonment in the Tuileries. The Queen's affection for her had cooled, but the Princesse's loyalty was unshaken. On 19 August the Commune authorities removed her, together with four other ladies-in waiting, Pauline de Tourzel, a governess, and her daughter, and took them to the Hôtel de Ville at 3 a.m. for interrogation. Three letters were found in the Princesse's hat, one from the Queen. Her interrogation lasted 15 minutes; others followed. From the Hôtel de Ville she was driven in a carriage through huge crowds under escort of gendarmes to La Force. During her incarceration she read devotional manuals and, with the steadfast calm which was the hallmark of her spirit, rallied the terrified ladies-in-waiting with whom she shared the grim cells.

Brought before a kangaroo court at around 11 a.m. on 3 September, she denied knowledge of any plots before or after 10 August and refused to take the loyal oath for Liberty and Equality and hatred of king, queen and monarchy. She accepted the first two but refused to forswear her former master and mistress. Her murder took place shortly after she was taken from the court, about noon; she was stripped of her fine clothes – perquisites of patriotic deeds – and one of her assailants ran her through and disembowelled her; the rest finished her off; her mangled body was delivered to the fishwives, who wound a belt of her entrails about the naked corpse; her heart, plucked out, was mounted on a pike, as, too, her head, and both were paraded past the Queen's window in the Temple tower.

The clotted remains of the Princesse de Lamballe were eventually tossed on to a pile of corpses near the Châtelet; *en route*, her head was grabbed by a wigmaker who, unwilling to let a quick profit slip past him, cut off the fine blonde tresses for reuse.

Madame de Tourzel was released after she had agreed to say: 'Long live the Nation.'

P.A.L. Maton de la Varenne, born in Paris in 1760, having been discharged from prison, walked over the Pont Notre Dame and saw a bunch of men smeared with blood sitting exhausted near a circle of corpses; even a drink of brandy into which one Manuel had put some gunpowder was not enough to revive them; a woman passed by with basket full of rolls, which they took and dipped into the gashes of the bloody torsos and limbs. Women rode by on carts loaded with corpses, singing the 'Carmagnole', a lively dance song adopted by the revolutionaries; pinned to their dresses, he says, were bits of flesh 'which modesty forbids me to describe'.

Who can doubt that such acts of wanton barbarity and cannibalism in the open streets bred exaggeration? Horror inflated sensibility. There was little truth to be had but it was distorted on both sides to the discredit of the opposing view. Perception is all and virulent hostility is a microscope outwards, a blinded lens inwards. Jean-Claude Hippolite Méhée (who signed himself 'Felhemesi') had been elected to the Revolutionary Commune for the Panthéon section on 10 August and appointed assistant secretary. He signed various warrants authorising the assassinations, though he protested that he had acted in a purely administrative role, that in fact he had done nothing more than 'hold the pen'. He said he saw Billaud-Varenne standing on corpses at the Abbaye and applauding the murder gang: 'Worthy citizens you have been killing criminals; you have done your duty; you will each receive 24 livres.'

Marat wrote a letter, countersigned by Danton as minister of Justice, which was distributed countrywide: 'The Commune of Paris hastens to inform its brothers in all the Departments that many of the ferocious conspirators detained in the prisons have been put to death by the people; the people considered this act of justice indispensable in order to subdue by terror the legions of traitors lying hidden within the walls, at the moment when it was about to march against the enemy; no doubt the entire nation, after the long succession of treasonous acts which have brought it to the edge of the abyss, will hurry to adopt a method so essential for the public safety.'

Fréron, in his *Orator of the People*, warned that 'the first battle we fight will be inside the walls of Paris when all the royal brigands crowded therein will die on the same day', and Fabre d'Eglantine, giving cheer to the 30,000 men of the Paris national Guard about to march for the frontier, assured them that the first holocaust sacrificed to Liberty would be exacted from the traitors in the towns 'so that, advancing to confront the common enemy, we leave no threat in our rear'.

The massacres lasted five days. On the last day, 6 September, in justification of this wholesale killing of suspects, the central Beaubourg section issued a 'proclamation of fraternity' in which it stated: 'The worse danger the nation is in, the more should the citizens unite.' It then changed its name by oath from the colourless

Beaubourg to Réunion in celebration of the fact that the entire section should be considered 'a single family whose members all coexist in perfect unity'. Having sworn the oath, the deputies exchanged the kiss of peace.

Mirabeau, who died before the massacres, said of earlier violence: 'There is nothing more appalling, nothing more revolting in such details as is a revolution, but there is nothing finer in its consequence for the regeneration of empires.' He voiced a central belief in the cleansing power of bloodshed, the redemptive sacrifice. Thus was Christ's body flayed, broken, pierced, exposed to public degradation; his very public torments offering a plea for divine justice and the cleansing of mortal ills in the passage through suffering to release from human taint.

Of the bestiality inflicted at the Salpêtrière, Madame Roland wrote: 'The women were violated brutally before being ripped apart by these tigers . . . You know well how enthusiastic I was about the Revolution; now I am ashamed of it. The Revolution has been disgraced by this scum and has become repugnant to me.'

But Marat's day had come. The massacres, he insisted, were a mild terror, a necessary surgical intervention to preserve the long-term health of the body politic; their purpose he expressed thus: 'He who could not bear to see an insect suffer wishes to prevent whole oceans of blood from being shed later.'

Pamphlets printed in the aftermath throughout September echo the howls of the righteous proclaiming the sanction of blood: *The People's Justice, Rage Justified, The Just Vengeance of the People*, the last of which reported the events of that terrible week in graphic detail: 'France has become a volcano more terrible than Vesuvius and we will conquer only by sacrificing our enemies. It is time for us to face our persecutors; they must learn to their cost what an outraged people is capable of. Many heads have been paraded, including that of the former Princesse de Lamballe, whose near- dismembered body was also dragged round. What terrors must these treacherous violators of the Rights of Man feel.'

Other tracts speak of the traitors as 'vampires, serving the tyrants to rob the people of holy freedom; or, in the prisons, wallowing in the idea of destroying the nation. A great strike was needed and the people of Paris delivered it.'

A new word entered the language and spawned other coinages: 'septembriser', 'septembrist', 'septembering', 'septembrisation'.

The Jacobins, controllers of the Great Terror, were taunted as drinkers of blood (playing on the popular slang for the rich, 'blood-suckers'), but most despicably as 'septembrisers'.

Robespierre stayed quiet during the massacres and was elected first of the Paris deputies to the Convention, which replaced the constituent Assembly on 7 September. Of the massacres, his own verdict was forthright and a chilling indication of that detachment, both moral and spiritual, routine in all servants of the Revolution, an impassivity through duty which rendered them *things*, mere *tools*, not *human beings*: 'The September Massacres were carried out in defence of the nation after the fall of Verdun. If they are to be lamented then so too must be lamented the death of patriots massacred by tyranny. I am always suspicious of delicate feelings offended by what happens to enemies of the state but not by the fate of its defenders.'

Those murdered enemies of the state included: in the Salpêtrière prison, women and girls, some of them under ten years old; in the Bicêtre, a large number of homeless beggars and vagrants, including 33 boys, 12 and 14 years of age.

The prison registers recorded the numbers of dead: at the Abbaye – 318; Bicêtre – 170; Châtelet – 223; La Force – 65; Carmes – 116. Unauthenticated – 692. A total of 1,614.

Maillard now rejoiced in the sobriquet 'Strike-hard' and 'The people's Chief Justice'.

Grace Elliott Dalrymple, former mistress of Philippe, duc d'Orléans, gave refuge to Champcenetz, the governor of the Tuileries, on the first day of the September Massacres. Driving through Paris in her carriage, she was taunted by the mob streaming past with the head of the Princesse de Lamballe stuck on a pike. She took Champcenetz in, his leg badly injured, although he was no friend of Egalité and therefore she held him in no great esteem. However, he was in danger, on the run, being hunted. She had come back to Paris from her house at Meudon, just south-west of the city, at the request of a friend who was sheltering the fugitive, armed with a passport for her and a manservant – she travelled alone but Champcenetz would pose as the manservant on the return trip. She was intending to return to Meudon by midnight, but, given the events of the day, the barriers were closed and she had no option but to stay in the city. A section night patrol searched her house, entered her bedroom – she sitting up in bed, Champcenetz concealed under the mattress. He had offered to leave, but she knew that if he did so he would have no chance of getting away. Danger was close, too: her cook was a staunch Jacobin.

'I felt doomed,' she said, 'but hearing him groan, God gave me more courage than I ever had before. When I accepted without much thought the task Madame asked of me I had no idea it would be so perilous. I naïvely hoped I would be helping – pardon me, sir – a closer friend than him. I confess that when the patrol arrived, I briefly regretted not having granted his wish and abandoned him to his fate. But under the threat of those wretches and the imminence of danger, I felt a sort of exaltation which was almost supernatural. Rather than escape the peril, I felt the urge to confront it together with all the innocent victims of today's barbarians. I suddenly felt ashamed of not sharing their fate. The horror of all the atrocities I've seen today is so strong that surely I would have been glad to climb the scaffold with him. If he had died I would have died with him. By losing the fear of death, I saved myself and him as well.'

An émigré marquis, speaking to a circle of English friends in the Canon restaurant in Jermyn Street, London, said: 'My word on it, gentlemen, I won't pretend that I haven't known for a long time that there would be a massacre, without knowing exactly when; and I promise you we must hope that more similar horrors happen in France. It may not be their intention, but the authors of these atrocities are playing into our hands. We must be straight with each other: if the French were to be amicably united, if they were to adhere strictly to their laws, respectful of their rights of Man, we could forget any notion of ever returning to our homeland. Opinion is against us; neighbouring peoples would, by and by, imitate them. But we need not fear that: the horrors that they are committing will draw opprobrium on the Revolution.'

Indeed there were those in Paris who firmly believed that the massacres had been instigated by English agents provocateurs. Jourdan, the president of the Committee of the Quatre-Nations section, home of the Abbaye prison, says he watched in the flare of torches a victim being dragged by his feet out of the church between two lines of onlookers as the murder squads hacked at him with sabres. In the crowd facing each other on either side, stood two Englishmen; one, a fleshy man in his mid-thirties, about 1.6 metres tall, wore an olive-green full-length frock coat; the other, thinner, had on a similar coat of deep slate grey. They were pouring out glasses of ardent spirits into glasses which they then pressed to the lips of the killers. One of the killers pushed the glass away: 'Fuck, leave us alone, we've had enough.' Jourdan claims to have known them to be English because he heard them in conversation and, though he did not speak the language, he could distinguish it from any other tongue by the accent. Sickened by what he had seen, he went home and drank several shots of brandy and spent the rest of the night in a state of mental torment which lasted for six weeks, when he suffered an apoplectic fit. The memory would stay with him for ever.

Questionable, perhaps, that strapping sansculottes, stalwarts of the Paris mob engaged in street thuggery, would so primly turn down free liquor.

Stanislas de Girardin, former head of the departmental administration of Seine-et-Oise, whose father, the marquis, had been a close friend of Rousseau, was unambiguous: the complicity of the English in these horrors was certain. Had not the English people been enthusiastic about the French Revolution to begin with and did that not spread alarm in their government, who feared they might imitate their French brothers? The fact is, that as soon as the events of 2 September were promulgated in England, the people clamoured for war on France. There was thus 'every reason to suspect that the Cabinet in London provoked this historic day of calamity'. Girardin later fled to England.

On 3 September Brissot reported Danton as saying that the massacres were necessary to appease the people of Paris, an indispensable sacrifice and that '*vox populi vox Dei* – the voice of the people is the voice of God – is the truest and most republican adage I know'.

And a new song entered the revolutionary hymn book:

> *Allons enfants de la patrie*
> *Le jour de gloire est arrivé*
> *Contre nous de la tyrannie*
> *L'étendard sanglant est levé*
> *Aux armes citoyens*

*Formez vos bataillons*
*Marchons, marchons*
*Qu'un sang impur*
*Abreuve nos sillons.*


(Come you children of the nation
The day of glory has arrived
For against us all the tyrant
Has raised his blood-drenched flag
To arms, citizens
Form battalions
March on, march on
An impure flood
Of blood soaks into France.)

The 'Marseillaise', the great anthem of the Revolution, was written in a single night, 24 April 1792, words and music, by a captain of engineers, Rouget de Lisle, stationed in Strasbourg. After a public banquet at which the city's mayor had called for a marching song to stir the garrison in the face of the Prussian threat, de Lisle sat up all night and produced his 'Battle Song for the Rhine Army'. It was an instant hit. The 'tyrant' was not, therefore, the French king but his foreign cousin and the émigrés – 'the horde of slaves, traitors and kings in league'. The song was polished by professionals and got its name when the regiment of Provençal volunteers from Marseille made it their own on the march from the south to Paris. It became the rallying cry for all patriots, and patriot the name of a loyal citizen.

The irony is that Rouget de Lisle was lukewarm about the direction the Revolution was taking; his loyalties had been formed in the royal army; as a result, he was cashiered and imprisoned, released only after the fall of the Jacobins.

## ✤ FOUR ✤

# A Republic, One and Indivisible

Here and today a new epoch in the history of the world began and you can boast that you were present at its birth.
*Johann Wolfgang von Goethe*, 20 September 1792

GOETHE'S WORDS can have brought little comfort to the men of the Prussian army who had reeled under the shock, first of the superbly handled French artillery along the Valmy ridge, east of Châlons, and then the charge of the volunteers, vastly superior in numbers but largely unblooded and untrained. With a mighty cry of 'Long live the Nation' they advanced on the Prussian ranks singing the 'Ça ira' and pitched into them with a ferocity that the cautious, manoeuvring continental armies had never witnessed and never deployed.

It was indeed an entirely new way of fighting. They came to the battlefield without baggage trains, carrying all their own equipment. There were no tents with which to set up camp – they bivouacked in the open under what shelter they could find, if any. Stripped of the encumbrances of the professional armies, they covered a vast distance at unsettling speed. And whereas old-style generals took great care not to waste the professionals of the royal armies – costly to train, costly to maintain – these amateur troops fought with a revolutionary fire in their belly, heedless of cost, indifferent to losses. Their tactic was attack, their strategy overwhelming fighting spirit fuelled by a highly politicised patriotic fervour: they fought for a new, liberated France against the viper's breed of European tyrants. The French commanders, Kellermann and particularly Dumouriez, whose prompt arrival with the northern army turned the battle, were lionised. In Paris, Dumouricz was grcctcd as a hero, invited to dinners and political meetings and widely applauded as the man who had sealed the birth of the Republic with its first, defining military victory. Save that Marat attacked him on a footling matter of military discipline, the taint of the old regime. Dumouriez looked him up and down with open disdain and said: 'So you are the person Marat? I have nothing to say to you' and turned his back.

In the 19 September edition of *The People's Friend*, Marat wrote: 'The gangrened members of the present legislature propose to install the national Convention in the manége (the school) riding school of the Tuileries, whose galleries hold no more than 300 spectators and will always be crammed with 300 informers for the senators and corrupt ministers. It is essential that the national Convention should be under constant observation by the people so that they may reproach and abuse it if it forgets its responsibilities. Thus, to keep it on the road to liberty, we must have a hall whose galleries will hold 4,000 spectators. This hall will have to be built; I demand that work on it continue without cease.'

More conservative opinion prevailed. Two days later the national Convention, to which Marat was elected as a deputy for Paris, took up residence in the riding school. Elections had taken place on 27 August and 2 September; fewer than one in five electors voted in the primary assemblies and of the 749 deputies, no fewer than 200 had sat in the Assembly, among them Brissot and others of the Girondin affiliation, such as the impassioned and eloquent Vergniaud and Guadet. Many of these men came from the big maritime and mercantile cities – Bordeaux, Brest, Le Havre, Lyon, Marseille – each claiming powerful status as a provincial metropolis and in no wise inclined to cede second place to what they considered the distinctly lower caste, and fiscally inferior, capital. The Girondin delegates from these wealthy, independent-minded provincial capitals – so they styled themselves – reflected the remove from the rather introverted world of the Parisians, who had little perspcctivc beyond their own self-importance.

The politics of these Girondins was shaped by very different influences from those of the urban lawyers, journalists and doctors who made up much of the Convention's numbers. The Girondins had a larger perspective: the France of their perception was more disparate than the singular, even absolutist, vision of the Parisians, more varied, its needs more complex than could be defined by the narrow vision of those deputies who saw the Revolution in simpler terms – as an uprising of the poor of the entire nation instigated by those of the capital. Their poverty defined the need for the Revolution. Their anger, resolve and energy had driven it. Their crushing of oppression defined liberty. Where, in this greatest hour of the Paris mob, had the rest of France been? so they argued. In the local Paris view, the provincials, largely of Girondin persuasion, lagged behind such acuity of understanding. Their ideas of liberty were in conflict: the Girondins, basing their vision on that of the ancient Roman republic, a gathering in of the nation, emphasised the *differences*; in Paris, the people was a single entity, the oppressed mass of Man born free but everywhere in chains. The cruel irony was that many of the Girondins' leaders were passionate and persuasive orators; carried away by their rhetoric, they delivered to the extremists, several resounding ultimata which became slogans for the Terror. Isnard in 1791: 'To save the rest of the body, the gangrened limb must be cut away.' Brissot: 'Why should we look for proof of conspiracy? Conspiracy never provides *proof*' and 'Any nation must be permitted to cast from its bosom anyone who seeks to do it harm.'

Of deputies in the Convention, the King's cousin, Philippe, duc d'Orléans, now Philippe-Egalité (Equality), the name conferred on him by the commune, was among the wealthiest. Jacques Chevalier, a mere peasant farmer. The deputies for Paris included some of the foremost radicals of the Jacobins: Robespierre, Santerre, Marat, Danton, Fabre d'Eglantine, Desmoulins, Collot d'Herbois and their adherents occupied the lofty bank of seats in the hall to the right of the president's chair, as lofty as their purist ideals. The steep rake of the benches set them high above the floor and gave them their nickname – the Mountain. Between them and the benches on the left opened those of the moderates, the Plain.

Collot d'Herbois, former actor-manager of dubious integrity and second-rate ability, made the most celebrated proposal of all early motions in the second session: he moved the abolition of the monarchy. Thus on 22 September, the autumn equinox, when the hours of daylight and night are the same, a perfect symbol of equality, balance, equipoise, the deputies of the Convention decreed that France was now and from henceforth would be a republic. Aristocratic titles – *monsieur*, sir, *le sieur*, sire, *le nommé*, appointed, etc. – were no more. The sovereignty which had resided in the person of the King was transferred to the people.

One deputy, seeking to affirm the Convention's absolute power, proposed that all existing authorities should be set aside forthwith and recreated as soon as possible. Chabot, ex-Capuchin monk, deputy for Loir-et-Cher, bristling with outrage, demanded that, on the contrary, it behoved the Convention to recognise an authority that could be neither abolished nor suspended: that power exercised by the sovereign people. 'I invite you,' he added, 'never to forget that you were sent here by the sansculottes.' Argument about precisely that was to cause intestinal differences which convulsed France and cast the long shadow of the guillotine over its people. Chabot was wildly applauded by the popular faction, listened to in pained, apprehensive silence by the rest.

Danton proclaimed himself devoted to the people whose minister he had been, whose mandatory he would be. He averred that the law should strike terror, just as the people had recently done. He also claimed for Paris the glory of the Revolution and appealed to the Convention never to confuse those people who had performed such brave deeds with the acrimonious Marat.

Robespierre launched into a cringe-worthy catalogue of the services he had performed for his country. Someone interrupted him and asked if he aspired to a dictatorship. He responded by resuming the history of his political career. It was out of place, niminy-piminy, loaded more with vanity than ambition.

Marat took the stand. 'It's a fact that I have many personal enemies in this assembly.'

Six hundred deputies rose and shouted: 'All of us. All of us.'

He was not fazed. 'Very well, I recall you to a sense of shame and of reflection. It was I who proposed a tribune of the people, or a dictator, or triumvirs – the name means nothing. Those are my opinions, I have published them; and if you are not up to snuff with me on that, tough: our troubles aren't over yet.' Seeing that he had cowed them somewhat, he pulled out a pistol, put it to his temple and said: 'If you have any accusation to make against me, I will blow my brains out here and now.'

There was to be much flourishing of pistols in this house, much vapid threatening to scatter brains on its floor.

Georges Couthon, deputy for the Puy-de-Dôme, intervened to calm things down. A mild-mannered, fair-minded lawyer from the Auvergne, he had, as a young man, lost the use of one leg after an amorous adventure: surprised by his lover's father, he took refuge on the parapet outside the girl's window and caught a severe chill. Already confined to a wheelchair, he had recently contracted meningitis.

The Convention, said Couthon, must concern itself with the public good, not individual persons.

Bertrand Barère de Vieuzac, a lawyer and son of a lawyer from a family estate near Tarbes, in the Hautes-Pyrénées, had an extraordinary memory, a sharp mind, great charm, a silver tongue and a slippery moral sense; vacillator, liberal, willing to manoeuvre and compromise, he leaned to the opinion of the most vocal and was known as the Anacreon of the guillotine after the ancient poet of graceful eulogy. Now he spoke against the general council of the Commune of Paris; even if the criminals of the administration were not to be prosecuted, at least the unacceptable organisation of the municipality should be reformed – they were cowardly and impotent.

Jean-Marie Roland, former minister of Justice and a leading member of the Girondins, indefatigably opposed to the anarchy which had erupted and triumphed on the historic days, delivered a swingeing attack on the 'unbridled breakers of all natural and decent laws who invoked without shame what they called their *principles*, flouting any measure aimed at repressing the most obvious of their excesses'.

The factions were beginning to stake their claims.

On 29 October a debate in the Convention opened with a report by Roland, the Girondin minister of the Interior, which blamed the Commune, and by extension the Jacobins, for the September Massacres. Robespierre demanded the right to reply and was soon vapouring about a subject close to his heart, on which he was a studied expert and of which he never tired: his virtue. The object of some mirth in the previous Assembly, Robespierre had sedulously honed his rhetoric and mastered his nerves and, more to the point, by tireless lobbying, parleying, ingratiation. Robespierre was too chilly, too self-contained ever to be liked by other than a few closer to him than most. However, he commanded, and retained, respect, often grudging, more often resentful, from convinced revolutionaries who nonetheless succumbed to the temptations of power. The moral norm was quite as malleable as among the unashamed tuft-hunters of the old regime and Robespierre's rejection of the profit motive was exceptional, matched, albeit, by a ruthless skill in the arts of political chicanery. Now that the first true revolution faced its first major ideological challenge, the removal of monarchy, he began to emerge as a real persuasive force. He represented himself as an honest broker, a man of the people's revolution, having extended his political power base wide in Paris: 'A system of calumny has been established,' he said, 'and against whom is it directed? Against a zealous patriot. Yet who is there among you who dares to stand and accuse me to my face?'

It was a challenge he did not expect to be met.

A voice at the end of the hall to the left rang out: 'I do' and a thin man with a bald pate and a pale, pale complexion strode like a spectre towards the tribune, where he fixed Robespierre with a level stare and repeated: 'Yes, Robespierre, it is I who accuse you.' Jean-Baptiste Louvet, a Girondin, editor of *The Sentinel*, a pink broadsheet posted twice weekly at street corners which did so much to rouse Paris against the court.

Robespierre was stunned, speechless. Danton stepped in to try to divert the debate to the subject of Marat's delinquencies – something on which they could all agree, but the Convention, no doubt consumed with prurient curiosity, voted to hear Louvet.

Robespierre regained his seat and Louvet began: 'The so-called friends of the people have tried to impute to the people of Paris all the horrors with which the first week of September were soiled; they have cast on them the most deadly outrage; they have slandered them shamefully. I know them, the people of Paris, for I was born and have lived among them: they are brave but, like all brave men, they are good; impatient but generous; they resent a wrong sharply but after the victory they are magnanimous. I do not mean to single out this section or that section but the vast majority, when one does not disturb their natural contentment. [Applause]

'The people of Paris know how to fight, they know nothing of murder. [Renewed applause] It is true that we saw them massed in front of the Tuileries on 10 August; it is not true that we saw them in front of the prisons on 2 September. [More applause] Inside the prison, how many executioners were there? Two hundred, fewer than two hundred perhaps; and outside, was it possible to count the spectators lured by a veritably incomprehensible curiosity? Double that, at the very most.'

He blamed the breakdown of the former legislative Assembly for the failure to address the problem. 'The weakness to which your predecessors were reduced is, in the face of so many crimes, the most serious of those for which the madmen whom I denounce to you should be punished. The legislative Assembly was every day tormented, slighted, degraded by an insolent demagogue who came to its bar to demand decrees of it; who did not go to the general council [of the Commune] save to denounce it . . .' There was, said Louvet, a Robespierrist plot against the lives of the Girondin leaders; Robespierre himself was guilty of a systematic slandering of his political adversaries, of setting himself up for idolatry, of tyrannising the Paris electoral assembly by intrigue and fear. (Brissot had been expelled from the Jacobin club on 10 October.) Billaud-Varenne cried out: 'It is false.' Several deputies seconded him, others pointed at Robespierre, one of them, Cambon, crying above the uproar: 'Wretch. There, there is the death sentence on dictators.'

Robespierre demanded the right to speak, but the vote was against him and Louvet continued the long, stark list of his accusations against him. He broadened his attack to include the much-reviled Marat, who never disguised his contempt for this assembly of milksop revisionists: 'Legislators, there is in your midst another man whose name will not foul my mouth, a man I have no need to accuse because he accuses himself. He himself has told you that it is his opinion that 268,000 heads must fall; he himself has sworn to you and he cannot deny it, that he pushed for the subversion of the government, the establishment of a tribunate, a dictatorship, a triumvirate . . . and this man is sitting here in your midst. France is indignant. Europe is astonished. They await your pronouncement.'

Louvet concluded by voicing the hope that the Convention would vote a decree 'against all those monsters who instigate murder and assassination and against a faction which from personal ambition was tearing the Republic in pieces'.

'The indignation,' wrote Dr John Moore, on his travels in France and an eyewitness of the debate, 'which Louvet's speech raised against

Robespierre was prodigious; at some particular parts I thought his person in danger . . . Although he drew the attack on himself by his impudent boasting, yet he was taken unprepared; the galleries in particular had been neglected on that day, for the audience showed no partiality . . .'

A week later, when Robespierre stood to defend himself, it was a different case. He had prepared his support. For what amounted to a vote of confidence the galleries were packed from an early hour and almost entirely by women, never shy of barracking. He disavowed his personal ambition. In law, of course, the Revolution had been illegal from its inception by its very nature, but different rules applied: it was the *natural*, the entirely legitimate right of the people to rise up in the face of tyranny and how, he asked, could there be a Revolution without revolution? He was roundly applauded; Louvet's demand to reply was turned down but he published it with a quirkily expressed English motto: 'In politiks there exists only two parties in France. The first is composed of philosophers, the second of thieves, robbers, and murderers.' The pamphlet, as was the common practice for disseminating opinion, was distributed through all the departments in France.

As a counterblast, Jacques Hébert wrote in his paper *Le Père Duchesne* of a dinner at the house of Roland and his formidable wife, the acknowledged leaders of the Girondin faction, at which 'at the top of the table, to the left of the virtuous Roland, sat the accuser of Robespierre, that dirty little tyke Louvet with his papier-mâché face and hollow eyes, throwing covetous glances on the wife of the virtuous Roland'. The word 'virtue' was, thanks to Robespierre, establishing itself fast in the revolutionary vocabulary and Hébert's use of 'virtuous' as pejorative and profane as he could make it.

Louvet was soon expelled from the Jacobins: he was a marked man.

Elsewhere in France, the impetus of the victory at Valmy began to spread. By early November Dumouriez, fêted in his home town of Cambrai, moved on to Valenciennes, a garrison town near the border with Belgium and declared that he had come to deliver the Belgians from the rule of the Austrian tyrants. This promise he made good on 6 November by victory at Jemappes, to the north-east of

Valenciennes, close to Mons. Wellington disparaged the battle, saying that Dumouriez had taken Belgium when there was nobody defending it but at least one poor little French mite born about the time was named Civilis Victoire Jemappes Dumouriez. Unquestionably, the victory owed much to his tactical expertise, energy and drive at every point of the fighting. It also exposed a rot at the heart of the administration, in the hands of the new minister of War, Pache, a Jacobin surrounded by Jacobins, animated by loathing and envy of the old-regime career general Dumouriez, whose former links with the royal army disqualified him politically from true patriotism; whatever actions he performed on the battlefield were vitiated by his entire lack of Jacobin credentials. Success did not matter: affiliation did. On the eve of the battle, Dumouriez's army was starved of money and provisions, the commissariat, filled with Jacobin placemen, was negligent, incompetent, inefficient. Dumouriez had had to borrow money privately to supply his troops; he had no doctors, no ambulances. By December his advance was stalled by lack of supplies. Pache was eventually replaced – at Dumouriez's insistence – in January, but by then relations between the military and their political masters had soured beyond repair.

To the south-east, Savoy, once part of the Frankish empire ruled by Charlemagne, had long been absorbed in the Italian territory of Piedmont. The day after Valmy, it sided with Austria and the coalition and on 29 September French troops commanded by General Montesquiou invaded and *liberated* two of the major Savoyard towns: Nice followed by Chambéry. In the Rhineland, three weeks later, General Custine took Mainz and then Frankfurt.

On 19 November a decree extended fraternity and offers of help from the Republic to all foreign peoples and on 27 November, pre-empting any request to convert the promise into action, Savoy was annexed. The new French Republic, brimful of confidence and vigour, was on the march and, in the Convention in Paris, a momentous decision was about to be made.

Louvet's *Sentinel* of 21 November showed the picture of a hand holding a quill pen writing on a wall the words in the book of Daniel directed at Belshazzar, the King of Babylon: 'God hath numbered thy kingdom, and finished it. Thou art weighed in the balance and found wanting.' To either side of the picture was a grossly overinflated assault on the character and reign of Louis XVI; as a result of his crimes and those of his ministers, the Revolution had come about. 'Since then, what has this man done? He has sworn fidelity to his nation and has done all he could to betray her; with the gold lavished upon him he has corrupted the members of the constituent Assembly, the ministers, the army generals; he has fawned on the enemies of France; he has cringed before the priests who have torn France apart; welcomed the nobles who burnt her, subsidised the foreigners who laid her waste. In short, greedy of assassinations, tortures and crimes of every kind, surpassing in horrors all that the imagination of man could lend to the tyrants of old, he meditates on the slaughter, in one day, of all patriots from the islands of America to the banks of the Rhine, from the Pyrenees to the shores of the Baltic. It is time to check his criminal career.'

The calls to bring Louis to account were already vociferous. A strongbox containing documents incriminating the King was found and on 13 November, making his maiden speech in the Convention, one of the deputies, a young man of 25, of striking features, haughty bearing and dandyish appearance, caused a sensation.

'The whole object of the committee investigating the conduct of the King,' he said, 'was to persuade you that he should be judged as a common citizen. I tell you that he ought to be judged as an enemy, that in fact we are not here to judge him at all but to oppose him and that the forms of this process are not to be found in civil law but in the law of nations . . . Judge a king as a citizen? The very idea. Judgement means to apply the law. Law requires a common ground of justice. And what common ground of justice lies between humanity and kings? What do the French people have in common with Louis that we should show him any consideration after his treachery? To reign is *per se* to be guilty. Tyranny is the crime and how can a king be innocent of that?' It is, accordingly, the right of the Convention as representing the people as a whole, to condemn the King to death and the sooner the better, for 'every citizen has the same right over him that Brutus had over Caesar'. Had not Louis committed murder – at the Bastille, in Nancy, on the Champ de Mars, at the Tuileries? He deserved no pity, no tears.

Antoine-Louis-Léon de Richebourg de Saint-Just's logic was ruthless; moderation he regarded as fudge. A month earlier, in the Jacobins, he had delivered a withering attack on the Girondins, the fathers of shilly-shally and political trimming, the party which repudiated the lead

that Paris had taken in the Revolution and continued to take. In Paris
the true virtue of the Revolution was alive; in the cosy, far-flung corners
of the nation, the Girondin nests, it was moribund. 'Give life to the
laws which destroy anarchy; bow down the factions under the yoke
of liberty; scotch all self-interest in politics . . . give the whole people
the call to republican virtue.'

Saint-Just had been something of a tearaway. His father died when
he was nine and he was brought up with two small sisters by his
mother in Blérancourt, some kilometres to the west of Laon, capital
of the Carolingian kings. In 1786, aged 19, he stole from her a silver
monogrammed bowl, a silver gilt cup, three silver cups, two pistols
inlaid with gold, several packets of gold braid from his father's
uniform and various knick-knacks; these he took with him to Paris,
where he sold them for 200 louis (1 louis equals 24 livres; very approximately, 15 years' subsistence wages).

He was arrested and confined in the asylum at 48 rue du Faubourg
Saint-Antoine, a sort of holding prison, where he whiled away his
time writing a long pornographic poem entitled *Organt*. This he at
first intended to dedicate to the Vatican – some indication of his reaction to the pious wish of his mother, a charming and charitably
disposed woman but 'of a sad and resigned disposition', that he should
enter the church. On reflection, he decided that *Organt* might better
stand as a testament to the mess he had so far made of his life and
he wrote, as preface: 'I am 20 years old; I have done badly; I will be
able to do better.' His mother wrote a letter pleading for his release;
he went home and started work in a legal office in Soissons.

The Revolution brought to flower in him a near-mystic conceit of
an ideal republic based, from his reading of the classics, a staple of
contemporary French education, on the ancient blue-blooded
Spartan model. The Lacedaemonian republic, an elitist polity ruled
by kings and aristocrats, all its energies and fit males canalised into
a professional army, served by slaves, made a harsh proving ground
of patriotic duty: weak infants exposed at birth; children schooled in
harsh military discipline in state training camps from the sage of
seven to manhood; the entire population subject to what amounted
to martial law and constant surveillance; dissent inconceivable;
informing on weak or slack behaviour in others encouraged and
rewarded; a formalist utopia of cheerless authoritarian rectitude.

In 1790 Saint-Just led a delegation of local peasant farmers to the home of a nobleman and, like the tyrant Pisistratos of Athens, who swished at the heads of poppies growing proud amid the barley, to show what happened to unruly subjects who got out of line, the fervent young rebel-turned-prig sliced off the head of a tall fern growing outside the chateau with a slash of his cane to leave the landowner in no doubt as to what might happen to him.

Saint-Just swore the civic oath of binding allegiance to the Revolution and, taking as his paradigm of republican virtue the Roman Mucius Scaevola, who thrust his right hand into the fire because it had failed in an attempt to assassinate the Etruscan king invading Rome, boasted solemnly that he would rather die than betray the nation, the law and the King. Around this time he wrote a letter to Robespierre: 'You who buttress the tottering nation against the torrent of despotism and intrigue, you whom I recognise as I recognise God, only by his miracles, it is to you that I address myself, to ask you for your help in saving my unhappy country . . . I do not know you but you are a great man. You are the deputy not merely of a province but of humanity and of the Republic.'

If this last allusion was premature and in marked conflict with oaths of loyalty to the monarch, it is apparent that there was no question in his mind that the Revolution must end in a republic or fail. He shared with Robespierre a faith in God and like him blamed priests, the church, for the baneful spread of superstition, fanaticism, perversion of morals. 'The early Romans, Greeks and Egyptians were Christians because they were good and kind, and such is Christianity . . . A people which has suppressed superstition [that is, the French] has made a great stride towards liberty, but it must take care not to stray from its moral principles because they are the basis of the law of *virtue*.'

Like master like pupil.

Elected deputy for the department of the Aisne, Saint-Just wasted little time in announcing himself and taking a firm stand at Robespierre's right hand.

Robespierre spoke at the Convention session of 3 December debating the trial of the King: 'Louis cannot be judged. He has already been judged. If he has not been condemned, the Republic is at fault. To suggest putting Louis on trial takes us back to royal and constitutional despotism; it is a counter-revolutionary notion because it puts the Revolution itself in the dock. For, if Louis can still be put on trial, he can be acquitted; rather, in law he is presumed to be innocent until he is proved guilty. And if Louis is acquitted, if he can be presumed innocent, what becomes of the Revolution?' He and his young acolyte were of one mind but the preponderance of opinion was that, as in England in 1648, to condemn the King without trial offended judicial practice too deeply. The lawyers of the Convention were sticklers for procedure. Robespierre, too, save that waiving a legal nicety counted, in revolutionary terms, with opposing unjust law.

The King was brought from his prison in the Temple tower to the Convention to hear the charges against him. The streets were lined with crowds; they stood in awed silence as he passed. Louis, not one jot inclined to submit lamely, rebutted every detail of the indictment and called for the right to a defence.

On 26 December the Girondin Raymond de Sèze pleaded his case but there could be only one outcome. The debate raged after he had left the chamber on the matter of punishment, sentence, reprieve, review. Louvet argued that the guilty verdict should not stand without first making an appeal to the people. He and the Girondins were, surely, expecting – hoping – that the provinces would never back a call for the King's death; that a public outcry from all corners of France would confirm the power of the moderates against the extremist Jacobins and their anarchic supporters, the Paris mob, the strident majority of the 700,000 occupants of the capital. The menace of civil war would compel this logic. Other Girondins, evading the issue of an appeal, voted for imprisonment or banishment. The party was fatally divided and in the eyes of their more stoutly republican opponents, openly compromised. Mercier, a deputy who later wrote a full account of events, remarked: 'The Girondins wanted to save the King but not at the expense of their popularity.' They lost both.

Marat had proposed voting by roll-call, each deputy to come to the bar of the Convention to deliver his verdict in public; this eliminated any possibility of conniving and evasion but it was immensely time-consuming. The voting, which proceeded without intermission, commenced on 15 January. Of 749 deputies, 20 were absent on government business, eight others through sickness; of the 721 present, 693 pronounced the King guilty; some abstained; there were no votes for acquittal. So without pause to the second vote, on an appeal to the people, and the split in the Convention became starkly evident: 283 for, 424 against.

The vote on the third matter – the sentence – began at 8 p.m. on 16 January and when the Girondin Lanjuinais, from Brittany, said that so grave a matter as the death of the King could not be passed with less than a two-thirds majority, Danton, just returned from a mission to the armies in Belgium, retorted fiercely that the size of the majority had not been an issue in abolishing the King nor should it be an issue in putting the King to death.

The galleries, says Mercier, were thronged; ushers working through the list barked the name and department of the deputies, who then approached the steps to the tribune slowly one by one through the spectral light of the candle lamps in an atmosphere charged with nervous tension. Riotous applause and cheering for those who pronounced the word 'Death'. Jeering, catcalls, vile abuse for the unpatriotic, lily-livered, self-serving hypocrites who wavered and said 'Banishment' or 'Imprisonment till the peace'. Vendors offering wine, brandy, ices and oranges supplied the spectators with sustenance; citizeness Hébert, a former nun, sat with her coterie of sansculotte viragos keeping count of the verdicts. In the neighbouring cafés and bars gamblers called the odds, bets were laid.

Mailhe, a lawyer from Toulouse who had been a member of the committee appointed to scrutinise the constitutional position with regard to the immunity of the King, gave his verdict, Death, but then mooted whether sentence should actually be carried out. Other Girondins, Vergniaud, president of the Convention, included, saw in this a possible route to a reprieve, but the tide was fast against them.

Robespierre worked tirelessly through these long sessions as a whipper-in for the Mountain, all ranged behind his wish to 'kill the King' and supported by their deputies, who fomented a climate of intimidation and menace throughout the debates. Mercier writes: 'If it needed a lot of courage in certain deputies not to vote for death, it needed still more in favour of a reprieve and that is what I did. As we spoke, we were greeted with threats and howls of anger. It is truly impossible to paint the frenzied agitation of this session as long as it was convulsed. The deputies who dared broadcast their desire to delay the death of the King were battered with invective.'

Robespierre was the first Paris deputy to vote. His speech was long, its message curt: massacring the people and pardoning despots were of a piece, inhuman acts. The last of the Paris deputies, Philippe-Egalité, had promised his former lover Grace Elliott that he would not vote for the death of his cousin. His republicanism had never been much more than a political convenience; he reneged because, he pleaded lamely, 'those who inflict harm on the sovereignty of the people' deserve to die.

The final count was 361 for death; 319 for imprisonment till the peace, followed by banishment; two for life imprisonment in irons; two for execution after the war; 23 for death conditional to a debate on a reprieve; eight for death and the expulsion of the entire Bourbon family, including Egalité.

The tally of votes was read out at 9 a.m. on the morning of 17 January. Malesherbes, the King's confidant, who had initially asked to be allowed to defend him before the Convention, took him the verdict and broke down in his grief. The King remained calm, tried to console his old friend.

Mailhe's proposal was debated and on 20 January defeated by 380 to 310.

That evening Philippe-Nicolas-Marie de Pâris, once of the royal bodyguard, entered one of the cafés within the precincts of the Palais Royal, now the Palais Egalité, and walked up to a table where sat a fervent Jacobin, the former marquis Louis-Michel Le Peletier de Saint-Fargean; he smiled, pulled out a large knife and stabbed the grandee of the old regime, who had just voted for the death of the King, again and again. Le Peletier's shirt, stained with the blood which poured from the gaping wound in his chest, was preserved and draped over his feet on the funerary catafalque.

In the Jacobins, the news of his murder just announced, Robespierre rose to deliver the first of the obsequies for Le Peletier, assassinated in the cause of liberty, 'the martyr of our sacred laws'. But, he cautioned, they must master their immediate grief and mourn him in due time to allow proper recognition of the glorious people's victim of so foul a crime. On the morrow, they had vital business for which to prepare themselves and 'It is round the scaffold on which the head of the tyrant will fall that we must rally ourselves and maintain a calm both imposing and terrible.'

The King asked for a delay of three days to prepare himself: denied. For a confessor of his choice: agreed. To be able to see his family from whom he had been forced to live separately: agreed.

He saw them that evening and agreed to see them again at 7 the next morning, but he had already decided that such a farewell would be too harrowing. He woke at 5 a.m., knelt on a cushion to hear Mass said by the Irish priest Edgeworth de Firmont, who had slept in the same room overnight and heard his confession. The King received the Eucharist and the priest withdrew to leave him to his devotions.

Between 7 and 8 a.m. there was a constant coming and going of warders and other officials, to mock and revile the King who was no king any more. Among them the extremist Jacques Roux, formerly a priest, who later boasted that he had said to the King: 'We aren't here to take your orders, we're here to bring you to the scaffold.' Finally, Santerre, commander of the Paris national Guard, arrived at the head of the armed escort to take him downstairs, through the first courtyard to the outer courtyard and into the waiting coach.

The drive to the place de la Révolution, formerly the place Louis XV, took a roundabout route along the wider boulevards to obviate any rescue attempts and lasted two hours. A heavy mist shrouded the streets, which were lined with soldiers. At the head of the procession, the cavalry of the national gendarmerie, followed by tight ranks of grenadiers of the national Guard, white equipment straps crossed over the blue uniform jackets, tricorne hats topped with horsehair plumes, muskets sloped, heavy ammunition pouches slung at their belt. Behind them the artillery pieces in twos, their metal-tyred wheels rasping on the paved roads, sinister bourdon to the heavy tramp of the infantry and the clop of the horses' hooves. Marching in front of the coach came a detachment of military drummers; the coach itself – windows blinded and speckled with mud – surrounded by a troop of mounted gendarmes. The vast crowd, some armed with pikes or muskets, the totems of their new authority, watched the procession pass in brooding silence.

As the long train proceeded along the boulevard Bonne Nouvelle, a man positioned on a section at the corner of the rue de la Lune which had not yet been levelled, suddenly pressed forward in the crowd and cried out: 'Frenchmen, let us save our king.' He was the Baron de Batz. In the mass of onlookers opposite stood a small knot of young men who had sworn to aid him in his bid to whisk the King to safety at this desperate last minute. It was madness. Even had they fought their way through the cordon of sentries and then held the armed escort at bay and got the King out of the coach; even had the people, against all expectation, rallied to their aid, where, in a Paris invested with 130,000 troops, would they have taken refuge, how escape the country? Unsurprisingly, Batz's small posse of adherents funked.

The police calculated that there were a large number of young men resident in Paris or recently arrived, all bent on saving the King, and that morning some 500 had been arrested and either held under house arrest or in their section police stations. None of Batz's fellow conspirators did anything to assist him. He was left shouting to the wind, then slipped away through the crowd and disappeared: but not yet from this story.

Edgeworth de Firmont travelled in the coach with the King. 'As soon as the King felt the coach coming to a stop he leaned over to me and said in a whisper: "We have arrived, if I'm not mistaken." One of the executioners came forward to open the door of the coach but the King stopped him and putting his hand on my knee said to the gendarmes: "Messieurs, I commend this gentleman to your care; be good enough to see that after my death he is not offered any insult. I charge you to see to this." They did not reply and the King began to repeat it, louder, but one of them interrupted: "Yes, yes, we'll take care of that" . . . in a tone of voice which would have frozen me, if at such a moment it had been possible for me to think of myself.'

The place de la Révolution was packed – Mercier reckons some 80,000 spectators. Opposite the scaffold stood the empty plinth on which had stood the statue of the King's father, toppled on 10 August.

The King stepped out of the coach and three executioners came forward and tried to remove his coat; he pushed them away and took it off himself, as, too, his shirt and collar. When they grasped his hands he recoiled, for he would not have them bound; they insisted; he refused. Edgeworth de Firmont came up to him: 'Sire, in this new outrage I see one last resemblance between your majesty and the God who is about to be your reward.' The King submitted and, because the steps of the scaffold were extremely steep, 'the King was obliged to lean on my arm and from the difficulty they caused him, I feared that his courage was beginning to wane: but what was my astonishment when, arrived at the top, he let go of me, crossed the scaffold with a firm step, silenced with a glance the 15 or 20 drummers who had been placed directly opposite, and in a voice so loud it could be heard as far away as the Pont Tournant [at the west end of the Tuileries gardens, leading to the Champs-Elysées] he pronounced these unforgettable words: "I die innocent of all the crimes with which I am charged. I forgive those who are guilty of my death and pray God that the blood which you are about to shed may never be required of France . . ."' but only Edgeworth de Firmont heard them all. As soon as the King began to speak, Santerre ordered the drummers to strike up to drown his voice.

The blade fell. The King, 38 years old, was dead. The executioner's assistant, 18 years old, plucked the head, spurting blood, by the hair from the basket and, holding it at arm's length, made a circuit of the scaffold. The abbé recoiled in horror from the bloody spray.

As the huge triangle of steel shot down to the foot of the frame, a huge cheer swelled up from the vast crowd. People nearest the scaffold struggled through the cordon of troops to soak their handkerchiefs in the deluging blood and, before long, according to Mercier, the executioners were selling off packets of hair, snippets of ribbon from the King's coat, some bloody remnant of the tyranny of which the French people had been finally rid.

Robespierre wrote a letter to his constituents: 'Monday, 21 January at 10h15 in the morning on the place de la Révolution, the man formerly known as Louis XVI, the Tyrant, fell under the sword of the Law. This great act of justice has consternated the Aristocracy, brought to naught the superstition of Royalty and created the Republic. It stamps greatness on the national Convention and renders it worthy of the confidence of the French people . . . It was in vain that an audacious faction and insidious orators exhausted their efforts in calumny, in charlatanism and chicanery; the courage of the republicans triumphed; the majority of the Convention remained unshakeable in its principles and the genius of intrigue ceded way to the genius of Liberty and to the Ascendancy of virtue.'

This extract was printed below an engraving of a hand holding the King's severed head: the superscription reads: 'Matter for Reflection for the Crowned Jongleurs' (medieval tumblers, clowns, entertainers) and the subscript, alluding to the 'Marseillaise': 'May an impure blood irrigate our furrows.'

\* \* \*

The unthinkable had happened. Within eight days the Convention declared war on England and the Dutch Republic, formerly under Spanish occupation and a constant irritant on France's north-eastern border. On 21 February the line regiments of the old regime were amalgamated with those of the new volunteers and on 24 February a decree called for conscription, a mass levy of 300,000 men: all unmarried men between the ages of 18 and 25 were immediately liable for military service; other males of the population were required for service in military transport, manufacture of weapons and gunpowder, and food production. Women were called for work in hospitals and clothing factories producing uniforms, linen, socks and shoes; children were set to make bandages from torn strips of linen. Even men long past the fighting age could rally patriotic spirit by parading in public places, exhorting the young men to courage and feats of arms, 'to a hatred of kings and a love of the Republic one and indivisible'.

Early in February Danton's beloved wife died. On 15 February Robespierre wrote to him with the army in Belgium: 'If, in the particular sorrow which must afflict such a spirit as yours, the certainty of having a sensitive, a devoted friend can offer you any consolation, I offer it to you. I love you more than ever and until death. At this moment, I am yours entirely. Never close your heart to the tones of friendship which feel all your pain. Let us weep together as friends and let us shortly feel the effects of our profound sorrow on the tyrants who are the authors of our public ills and our private woes. My friend, I have addressed you in this language of my heart when you are in Belgium; I would have been to see you before now had I not respected the first moments of your proper affliction.'

Two chronic material shortages imperilled this latest huge war effort, the mobilisation of an entire population: food and saltpetre. Despite prolonged efforts to woo the French to the idea of the potato – a staple in the Rhineland regions – a vegetable rich in carbohydrate, easy to grow, readily stored, the French persisted in their belief that only bread would serve as the basis of a solid diet and that the potato was good only for pigs and cattle. Between 25 and 27 February the capital was once more convulsed by riots. Since the beginning of the year the paper money issued by the revolutionary government, the assignats, had dropped to about 51 per cent of their face value; the price of sugar had nearly trebled and soap more than doubled since 1790. Popular petitions for a price cap, the maximum (first imposed by Henry III in 1577), flooded into the Convention and the Jacobin club. The outcry against hoarders grew shrill, but this was an inveterate bone of contention: the 'famine pact'. Marat led the clamour for all hoarders and speculators in commodities to be guillotined out of hand.

The petitions went unanswered; scrawled posters calling for action were pinned up in markets; women took to the streets, fixed prices at food shops, commandeered carts delivering foodstuffs. The shopkeepers could do nothing but accept the money these market enforcers handed over. For the most part the street transactions were conducted in an orderly fashion; there was pillage and pilfering, shops broken into, violence, threat and reprisal against recalcitrant bakers and grocers, but mayhem in the thoroughfares of Paris had become routine. The national Guard eventually quelled the violence; the Girondins predictably held Marat to account for the rioting; the Mountain accused Jacques Roux, leader of the extremist sansculotte faction known, for their intemperate radicalism, as 'the crazies' and a former priest who harangued the crowds which gathered outside the Convention. Mutual suspicions polarised the moderates of the government which promised reform and the increasingly frustrated popular elements which screamed at the failure to deliver.

The huge army of citizen soldiers even now mobilising posed massive demands on supplies of ordnance and ammunition; saltpetre, essential to the manufacture of gunpowder, was, therefore, of prime importance. Lime saltpetre is a mouldy efflorescence which forms on the damp whitewashed walls of stables, pigsties and cellars.

Gunpowder is made by first grinding together finely (in the contemporary proportion) 75.6 per cent saltpetre, 13.6 per cent charcoal and 10.8 per cent sulphur: sulphur to provide the combustion, saltpetre the latent oxygen, charcoal the fuel for the explosion. The ingredients are then moistened to prevent explosion, mixed into a paste which is first pressed between flat rollers, granulated through toothed rollers and dried. When the gunpowder is lit, the heated saltpetre, potassium nitrate, immediately gives off its oxygen and the resultant chemical result is to produce the gases nitrogen, carbon dioxide and carbon monoxide. It is the abrupt and violent thermal expansion of these gases which effectuates the explosive force.

The principal task of Antoine-Laurent Lavoisier, as commissioner of powder resident in the Arsenal, was to improve and expedite the production of saltpetre. Ordinary saltpetre is found everywhere, mingled with other nitrates on the surface of the soil and in the superficial layers of soil into which it leaches. Saltpetre is a by-product of simultaneous contact of decaying vegetable matter (which is rich in nitrogen), alkalis, the air and moisture. All excrement contains a fair amount of nitrogen.

Sodium salt, or sodium nitrate – the base ingredient of fertiliser – tends to pick up moisture from the atmosphere and becomes deliquescent, which renders it unserviceable for gunpowder. However, it can be converted into potassium nitrate by adding a calculated amount of potassium chloride (a by-product of salt manufacture) dissolved in hot water to a boiling saturated solution of sodium nitrate. When the hot solution cools, potassium nitrate crystallises out and can be separated and dried.

Lime saltpetre had always provided the main source of saltpetre for gunpowder, and its requisition enforced by royal privilege, but its recovery entailed a time-consuming hunt through dark, damp underground cellars and mephitic animal byres; the scraping of walls was laborious and, once they were scraped clean, the deposits of saltpetre took time to form again. Another source, animal dung from pastures where cattle grazed, was the subject of government levy – as a 'patriotic duty' – but landowners, wanting to keep the manure as a rich natural fertiliser, could, and did, buy off the salt diggers. A senior royal administrator complained, too, of the corruption attached to the task of collecting saltpetre: the collectors talked incessantly of the upheaval they caused in entering and working in properties: 'they exempt owners who give them money and degrade considerably the value of houses in which they conduct their searches'. By a decree of 1777, communities which constructed nitrate plants and transported to them the scrapings from house cellars, barns, stables, sheep-pens and byres at their own expense were exempt from official depredation.

The cull of saltpetre from farmland was meagre. Under the new system, instigated by Lavoisier, prices offered for the sale of saltpetre were more attractive. Another case of the old regime discovering too late that excessive greed at court engendered rapacity at the bottom. The price was adjusted only because the King's armies needed endless and vast supplies of gunpowder. Lavoisier devised a process to simulate the natural production of ordinary saltpetre: compost heaps in open fields. He mixed lime and wood ash with decaying organic matter in mounds piled with brushwood to promote air circulation. By the action of bacteria and the atmosphere, the combined nitrogen in the compost, or manure, is converted into ammonia, which later oxidises to nitrous and nitric acid and then potassium nitrate and calcium nitrate. These salts are extracted from the compost by mixing it with water, and the resulting solution is mixed with wood ash or potassium carbonate, which has the effect of converting the calcium nitrate to potassium nitrate. The liquid is then filtered to remove the insoluble calcium carbonate, and the residual potassium nitrate is crystallised.

Composting plants were set up all over France, regulated by a Saltpetre Commission, and by 1793, when the young Republic was at war with the armies of a hostile alliance, popular enthusiasm for the manufacture of this essential commodity was such that there were 6,000 saltpetre workshops across the country, churning out the precious stuff, ninefold more than ever before. One example of how the nation, relieved of its crass, absolutist governance, was pulling together against a common danger.

Having stepped up production of his vital saltpetre, Lavoisier now applied his skill as a chemist to refining the recipe to develop a gunpowder soon acknowledged to be the best in Europe, giving a longer range to French artillery, naval great guns and military small arms. He demonstrated, too, his fastidious efficiency as an administrator in organising the Saltpetre Commission.

In the works at Essonnes, a new recipe, proposed by Barthollet, replaced saltpetre with chlorate of potassium. This less stable mixture produced a violent explosion which killed two of Lavoisier's assistants instantly; Lavoisier himself and his wife Marie-Anne, present as ever to record the details of the experiment, escaped but narrowly. After the accident Lavoisier wrote to a royal minister: 'Monsieur, if you would oblige by acquainting the King with an account of this sad event and the dangers I have undergone, allow me to ask you to assure His Majesty that my life is His and at the disposal of the

State and that I am ready at all times to make any sacrifice which might result in some advantage in His service, whether it be in the resumption of work on a new gunpowder or any other work. This stems not only from the obligations I have as Commissioner for Powder, rather from my own heartfelt wish from which no sense of fear can divert me.'

Another chronic shortage soon threatened the war effort of all France: the obdurate refusal of all France to do what Paris told it. The Revolution sought to achieve not only a unity which not even the absolute monarchs enjoyed, but, more poignantly, a unanimity – of purpose, belief, commitment – which regional differences alone rendered a chimera. To begin with, there was the problem of language.

Regional dialects made France a small Tower of Babel: foreign influences spilled over the borders – German in Alsace, Italian in Savoy, Catalan in the eastern Pyrénées and, in the western Pyrénées, Basque, a language so difficult to learn it was said that even the Devil had never been able to master more than seven words of it, possibly the heptad of Deadly Sins, in which he has a vested interest. The provincials of Provence spoke Occitan, a tongue close to the old troubadour's mélange of Old French and the Spanish of Catalonia; the Bretons a version of the ancient Celtic language they originally shared with the Britons, residual in Cornish and Welsh; and, too, the dialects, the innumerable rustic variants of the language deeply rooted in its Romano-Gallic origins.

The educated could speak French with a varying degree of fluency; there were millions in the rural fastnesses who scarcely spoke it at all.

The dissemination of news, laws, revolutionary directives depended, therefore, on the work of local supporters and agitators: the message they delivered was attuned to their own level of dedication to the patriotic principles dictated from Paris, often quite at odds with local feelings and perceptions. Unanimity being vital to the cause but rarely delivered spontaneously, the tub-thumping radicals of the far-flung small towns passed quickly to coercion: they spoke with the voice of Paris in the terms of Paris to the uncomprehending, they dinned in the Paris version of events and duty, they spouted the familiar rhetoric of the central Jacobin club.

In the alarmingly extremists course it was taking, the Revolution was failing not only to speak *for* many of the people it claimed to set free, it was failing utterly to speak *to* them.

It took some time for this problem, which bedevilled France's long history, to be officially identified. Not until 27 January 1794 did Barère report to the Committee for Public Safety on multifarious dialects and foreign tongues and the teaching of French, 'the finest language of Europe, the first which frankly consecrated the rights of man and the citizen [and] assumed the obligation to transmit the most sublime thoughts of liberty and the loftiest speculations of politics to the world'.

Clearly, the foreign coalition ranged against the young Republic was targeting frontier regions with weaker ties to the French capital than affiliation to their own local interest. He singled out four danger spots: Brittany – Breton; Rhine – German; west Pyrenees – Basque; Corsica – Italian, as well as sundry other areas where argot and dialect were spoken. He stressed the urgent need to popularise the language, French for all France. To be a good citizen, one had to obey the laws and to obey them one had to know them. Government, laws, customs, manners and morals had been revolutionised, now language too must be revolutionised. His idea was to send out contingents of linguistic legionnaires, qualified by patriotism, to each rural commune of the departments named in his report to teach the French language and to inculcate the Declaration of the Rights of Man and the Citizen on alternate days to all young citizens of both sexes.

Language differences were treated with extreme prejudice at a time when the only acceptable test of what constituted a human being was physical characteristics. A young girl who emerged from the woods near Sogny in the Champagne district during the 1730s spoke a language no one recognised; she was painted black, her behaviour was savage. She might easily have been taken for a wild animal, save that she appeared to be physically the same as a normal human being. This, however, was not how many urban French thought of the queer creatures who inhabited the obscure geography beyond the towns. As La Bruyère put it: 'One sees certain savage animals in the countryside, blackened, livid and burnt by the sun; they seem to be able to articulate and when they stand on their feet they show human faces and, in effect they are indeed men. They retire at night into caves where they live on black bread, water and roots.'

This is no literary exaggeration – official reports concur. And the first of these queer creatures to declare themselves at odds with Paris were the men of the Vendée, whom the men of Paris described as being as dumb as and on a par with the animals they tended.

What the one and indivisible Republic inaugurated by the Revolution failed to do, the divisive nature of its laws achieved: the unity of the Vendée, a geographical fiction, a region which had not, hitherto, existed.

Rioting against the disestablishment and later the banning of the Catholic Church had sown deep disaffection in the Vendée, but the outrage the Vendeans felt when their king was taken to the scaffold was decisive. The levy, to force them into the army of a Republic whose ideals they detested and whose methods they scorned, brought them to action. When the recruiting officers marched in, the men of the Vendée reacted: sporting the white cockade of royalists, they rioted in Cholet on 4 March 1793. A week later a number of other parishes joined the protests and the administration of the department of the Loire-Atlantique reported the armed assembly of some 20,000 insurgents. The authorities in Deux-Sèvres wrote to Paris: 'We are under threat from the miseries which are laying waste the Vendée.' Another letter reported that Cholet was a pile of ashes but that republican forces were on the march: 600 men and two cannons from the interior, General Marcé from the coast with 1,200 infantry and 100 cavalry supported by artillery.

On 6 March the Convention sent out into the departments the first 80 of its members as representatives of the people to supervise and enforce the adoption of government measures. As under the old regime, the King's intendants acted as his bailiffs in the provinces, so the representatives were given full powers to speak and act for the government in Paris. They became an awesome part of the revolutionary machine. On 9 March a man who became one of the most notorious of them, Jean-Baptiste Carrier, 37 years old with but 18 months left to live, advanced to the bar in the narrow hall where the national Convention sat and proposed the creation of what became one of the most formidable weapons of state terror: the revolutionary tribunal. Born in the Cantal department, in the town of Aurillac, ancient capital of the High Auvergne, a remote, mountainous region in south-central France, he was an undistinguished man of sombre temperament, a lawyer of limited talent. Intended for the priesthood, he withdrew from the seminary at the age of 16, declaring that he had no vocation. He was not the only terrorist to have been or been close to becoming a priest. He entered the office of an attorney in Aurillac; from there went to Paris to study law, returned in 1785 and married the daughter of a local tradesman. 'A brooding, silent man, he often wore a brutal and sometimes a foolish expression; he had a violent temper and was slovenly, careless about his attire. His intemperance and the bitterness of his nature estranged him from his colleagues.'

At the beginning of the Revolution Carrier had joined the Jacobins and become an ardent clubbist. Surprisingly elected deputy for the Cantal in the national Convention, he had voted for the death of the King, but had done little else to bring himself to notice until this momentous day in early March. By the time of his death he had come to epitomise the ugliest excesses of the revolutionary Terror.

The decree he had proposed was passed, at the prompting of Georges Danton, the following day. 'An extraordinary criminal tribunal shall be established at Paris which shall have cognizance of all counter-revolutionary activities, of all attacks against the liberty, the equality, the unity, the indivisibility of the Republic, the internal and external security of the state and of all plots tending to re-establish the monarchy or to establish any other authority inimical to the liberty, equality or sovereignty of the people, regardless of whether the culprits should be employees of the government, military personnel or plain citizens.'

The Tribunal, comprising five judges, 12 jurors and a public prosecutor, would meet in the Palais de Justice on the Ile de la Cité in the centre of Paris, in a building adjacent to the Conciergerie prison. A Committee for General Security (CGS), formed on 21 March of elected members from the Convention, was to have responsibility as a central police administration for all activities coming within the definition of counter-revolutionary activities set forth in Article 1 of the decree, to investigate all matters pertaining to émigrés, foreign nationals and those already declared outside revolutionary law.

Vergniaud, speaking for many, not only those of his party, expressed his own dreadful anxiety about this sickening lurch to new extremes: 'Citizens, it is to be feared that the Revolution, like Saturn eating his own children, will, in the end, give birth only to a new despotism and all the calamities that must attend it.'

Carrier had no such apprehensions. Of pallid complexion, hollow-jawed, his eyes sunk in their orbits, his prominent cheekbones framed with the plaited sidelocks affected by the most fervent Jacobins, he had a spectral air about him. His role in the Terror was yet to be fastened upon him, but he typified many of those who served it so sedulously: humourless, unimaginative, a functionary and devotee of the extreme ideologues who conceived the Terror and propelled it to its murderous limits. Carrier idolised Robespierre: perhaps proposing the revolutionary Tribunal was his first major assignment.

# FIVE

# Revolt

> You can force the people to follow the principles of justice
> and of reason; you can't compel the people to understand
> them.
>
> *Confucius*

ON 18 MARCH 1793 the deputies of the Convention addressed
a measure proposed by the former noble Jean-Denis Lanjuinais,
a 60-year-old lawyer from Rennes, in Brittany. Lanjuinais' milder
Girondin sensibilities had been irked by the flare-up of opposition
in the Vendée – the theory of opposition being more manageable
than the act. He proposed that the decree outlawing émigrés should
be extended to the provincial counter-revolution – rebels taken in
possession of arms or *wearing the white cockade* should suffer the same
punishment. He did not need to spell out what that punishment
should be. It was death.

Opposition came from a surprising quarter: Marat, the most bloodthirsty of them all, denounced Lanjuinais' proposal as 'the stupidest
idea unworthy of a man of intelligence' precisely because it was
directed at murdering the people whereas those who needed their
throats cut were the rebels chiefs. (Many of them, perversely, were
aristocrats, whose relationship with their people was, more often than
not, one of affection.)

The stalemate was solved by a call for Barère to the rostrum. The
sansculotte claque in the galleries signalled their wild enthusiasm for
the suave-talking man who seemed always to be able to find exactly
the right phrase; echoing the thoughts of many of them concerning

this queer outpost of wilder France, he spoke of 'the inexplicable Vendée'.

He had, he said, but two propositions to lay before them. First, the necessity of establishing a mode of *revolutionary instruction* such that those guilty of counter-revolution might be apprehended and brought swiftly to the punishment due to their crime. The Convention agreed the notion in principle and the legislative committee was charged with drawing up the details of such a law. Barère insisted, further, that the assembly should deliver a short but vigorous address to the French people in summary of the current state of the Revolution and, finally, that the Convention should busy itself with a process of revolutionary instruction whose object would be to 'change our way of thinking, our former opinions, and to establish a moral code conducive to Liberty and the Republic'. The hint was brutal and plain: convert heads or chop them off.

On 19 March, towards 4.30 p.m., as the long session of the Convention debating Barère's measures neared its close, Cambacérès, the eminent jurist of the old regime and now the new, a foremost member of the legislation committee, mounted the rostrum and outlined the ten articles of the proposed decree which characterised the popular uprising in the Vendée as civil war, soon labelled by them all 'the Vendée war'. The law which changed the legal and social face of the Revolution punished with death not only the rebel chiefs but anyone who had taken part in any way whatsoever; all those who had worn the white cockade or 'shown any other sign of rebellion' – brandishing a pitchfork, concealing a red Sacred Heart badge – not excluding those who had laid down their arms. All were to be declared the enemy of the nation, outlawed (denied the protection of law) and delivered to criminal judgement, inside 24 hours, without appeal. One witness to the culpability of a suspect was sufficient to convict; all property was to be confiscated and made over to the Republic after redress of damages suffered as a result of the rebellion. In justification of the draconian nature of the law, Danton said that it was for the government to inspire terror so that the people did not have to take on that role themselves. He was thinking, obviously, of the September Massacres, which had been necessary at a time when the government, that is, the Girondins, had been guilty of a woeful dereliction. The people had stepped in to save the Revolution, to defend France when she was faced by an onslaught of foreign armies beyond her borders and arrant treachery within them. But such an onus of responsibility was too frightful, too complex, too large to lay to the charge of the people, whose devotion to plain justice was immediate and uncomplicated. It was for the elected members of a dutiful government to shoulder the obligation of taking a distasteful course of action for the general good. Wherever treachery, wherever opposition to the Revolution showed itself, it must be stamped out.

The Revolution had created the Vendée: now its leaders were hell-bent on annihilating it. Within a day every commune in the land had been required to establish surveillance committees to investigate signs of disaffection and counter-revolution, and every citizen was to accept as a civic duty the responsibility of informing on unpatriotic acts and opinions.

The brutal law which directed the full fury of the Revolution on the insurrection within the frontiers of France had come into being and, perversely, achieved what the airy promises of the revolutionary ideal had so far patently failed to do in its own favour: it united disparate peoples against it. Most of the deputies in Paris had no more than a vague clue as to where several key centres in this new department, the Vendée, were on the map. Suddenly, in righteous indignation, they were mouthing off about the atrocities committed in Cholet, Saint-Fulgent and, most poignantly, Machecoul.

Machecoul, a small market town some 13 kilometres from the Atlantic shore, was, until 11 March 1793, notable only for its proximity to the stronghold of Gilles de Rais, the French Bluebeard. Early that morning, according to one Boullemer, a former judge and crony of the local public prosecutor, Souchu, 3,000 peasants, armed to the teeth with pitchforks, broad-bladed billhooks, sickles, knives and long-barrelled duck guns, descended on Machecoul and confronted the detachment of the national Guard who had come to enforce the levy. The tocsin summoned others from the surrounding fields and within a very short time a furious threat had exploded in the wholesale massacre of the republican troops, the constitutional priest, known radical sympathisers and anyone involved with the municipal administration. Prisoners, their hands tied behind their back, were linked together with a rope passed under their armpit – the so-called 'rosary' – and dragged off into the fields, there to dig their own grave ditch before being gunned down into it. Patriots were hunted down, lashed to trees and emasculated. Patriot women were violated and cut down in the orchards. Souchu, eager to distance himself from his revolutionary sympathies, accepted the role of judge for makeshift tribunals, summarily condemning prisoners hauled in by the berserk peasants. Souchu, a Maillard for Machecoul. Boullemer reports the tally of the massacre at precisely 552.

The similarities with the September Massacres are crude, blatantly factitious and Boullemer's so-called eyewitness account a farrago of misrepresentation, a chilling example of revolutionary historiography, a propaganda coup which was used in justification of the viler excesses of the vengeance wreaked on the people of the Vendée. The truth is less dramatic. Even the 'rosary' is a conscious jibe at the counter-revolutionary pieties of the Catholic Vendeans.

On 11 March a large crowd of peasants did confront the national Guard, in protest against the levy. A nervous republican soldier opened fire and the enraged crowd retaliated. Between 22 and 26 soldiers were killed. On 23 March the insurgents, led by Francois-Athenase de Charette, minor nobleman, ex-naval officer, hauled out of his country gentleman's retirement in his chateau at Fonteclose, took the small harbour town of Pornic to the north-west and sacked it. A republican patrol surprised the Vendeans carousing in various cellars and killed between 200 and 500 peasants. In reprisal, the peasants killed a dozen prisoners on 27 March.

Boullemer wrote his account in Rennes, where he was taken after republican forces re-entered Machecoul on 22 April; he had, by his own admission, spent the entire intervening six weeks since the morning of 11 March hiding in a granary. His fanciful account of the 'massacre' was delivered to Paris in a slapdash, sensationalised recension by François-Toussaint Villers, constitutional priest and deputy to the Convention for the department of the Lower Loire, and played no small part in the hardening of official attitude to the Vendée.

Meanwhile, foreign revulsion at the news of Louis' execution led to the Spanish joining the British blockade of the French Mediterranean coast and very soon most of Europe had declared against the fledgling Republic. On 1 March General Miranda had been caught with 20,000 men outside Maastricht in a surrounding movement by 40,000 Austrians; he withdrew and was brought to battle at great disadvantage of position and numbers. The Austrian cavalry tore into his disorganised force repeatedly and left some 3,000 French dead on the field. Dumouriez was celebrating the capture of Breda after a week's siege. The vanquishing forces of the Republic were suddenly and calamitously on the back foot. On 12 March Dumouriez, exasperated by the incompetence, dilatoriness and sheer obstructive politicking of the War Office, openly rubbished French policy in Belgium: the victories of Valmy and Jemappes had been squandered, the army badly let down.

So recently the conquering hero, darling of the administration, he was now painted as a duplicitous self-seeker of meretricious patriotism. A week later his army fled the field at Neerwinden and the French invasion of Holland had collapsed. Dumouriez approached the Austrian commander, Coburg, the man demonised by the Jacobins along with the English Prime Minister, Pitt, and obtained a safe conduct for his army. It is clear that Coburg agreed only because he knew that Dumouriez intended to march on the Convention in Paris with the aim of restoring the Constitution of 1791 and placing the infant Louis XVII on the throne. Dumouriez marched out of Brussels; the minister of War, General Beurnonville, sent with commissioners to investigate the commander-in-chief's conduct, was arrested and given as a hostage to the Austrians; Dumouriez appealed to his men to march on Paris to restore the constitutional monarchy and, when they refused, on 5 April he and several high-ranking officers, including the son of Philippe-Egalité, the future king Louis-Philippe, defected to the Austrians. It was the ultimate betrayal, proof of the existence of a widespread conspiracy against the Republic *inside its very frontiers*, bitter confirmation that the old-regime military was not to be trusted, another symptom of the malaise of moderatism embodied by the Girondins, whose lapdog Dumouriez was. But, taxed with a betrayal of France, Dumouriez and others would retort: 'What *France*?'

'Citizens,' warned Robespierre, 'your enemies are more heavily armed than you, the conspiracy surrounds you, it is Paris they wish to destroy, it is in blood that they seek to drown the last hope of the triumph of the rights of Man.'

And, just as its vulnerable eastern frontier had been stripped of solid defence, the embattled Republic faced flagrant insurrection on its western marches. Rural Brittany had risen soon after the Vendée. Where the Vendean slogans were generally royalist – 'Give us back our king and our good priests' – the Bretons cut to the necessities:

no more taxes and, 'there being no king any more, how can there be any laws? Fuck the nation.' This bluntness had its match in Paris, where, incessantly, the actions of the defenders of the Republic spoke of 'firm and vigorous measures' always applied to the enemies within: 'We cannot possibly overpower our external enemies if our internal enemies can raise their head with impunity in the heart of France.'

The sansculotte Paris Commune had long been calling for the formation of a revolutionary army to march out to quell the uprisings within the borders and deter any new rebellion, in other words to impress on the rest of France the purity of their brand of patriotism. Danton and others supported the idea, believing that regiments of volunteers inspired by love of country would stiffen resolve in those inclined to buckle to the immediacy of threat from across the borders or else disinclined to take seriously the need for general unity as preached from Paris. The revolutionary army was, in fact, decreed in the wave of panic which ensued after Neerwinden but held in check by the caution of Robespierre and others, who, more animated by the threat within the borders than without, feared a loss of control over what might easily become anarchist forces ranged far and wide, distant from their guiding hand in the capital. Robespierre voiced his obsessive fears in the Jacobins on 13 March: 'No, I swear it, my *patrie* will never be enslaved by a Brissot, a Brunswick, and by several men whom I do not want to name. We will know how to die, we will all die . . .'

As to the Vendée, he could not admit that it was, from the very start, a *popular* uprising; such an admission would have entailed a complete revision of the basis on which he had constructed his power. Since the Revolution had been made by and for the people, that any sector of that holy (in his eyes) entity should oppose it was unthinkable. Yet, in the Vendée, a band of smallholders and peasants from Pin-en-Mauges marched up to the tiny house where lived the pedlar Cathelineau, a man noted for his piety and his resolute character, and asked him to lead them. And, on the very day Robespierre spoke in the Jacobins of dying, Cathelineau's men captured from the republicans a large cannon they nicknamed 'The Missionary', destined to become a symbol of the popular uprising.

That same day the peasants of the area round Beaupréau gathered in front of the Château de la Loge, where Maurice d'Elbée, 41 years old, a former army lieutenant and for a time a convinced revolutionary, warned them that they had little chance of success in their fight but finally agreed to lead them. Another of the Vendean leaders, the young Henri de Rochejaquelein, an ex-officer in the national Guard, who had narrowly escaped the slaughter of 10 August, told the peasants of his parish who had called on him to lead them: 'If I advance, follow me, if I retreat, kill me, if I die, avenge me.' It was the similar case with the other Vendean generals – Charles de Bonchamps, 34, ordered by the peasants who besought him to get off his horse and, like them, go on foot. And, near Clisson, the 37-year-old marquis Louis de Lescure. Leaders of the people who sang new words to the revolutionary hymn in their local dialect:

> Advance the Catholic armies,
> The day of glory is at hand.
> The Republic raises against us
> Her banner in a bloody hand . . .

The jostling for power, in the wake of Dumouriez's defection, showed the Girondins increasingly desperate. On 1 April, one of their spokesmen, Lasource, accused Danton of being the general's accomplice; certainly they had been friends, had mixed socially, perhaps even shared exasperation at the shilly-shallying of the Convention and the aggressive push of the Commune to usurp power. Danton retaliated with vigour and his central message was frank: 'No more coming to terms with *them*', meaning the Girondins, and 'all patriots', he said, 'must rally to the Mountain to initiate good decrees which can save the Republic and purge the Convention of *cowardly intriguers*'.

On 6 April a second committee of nine members of the Convention was elected: the CPS, effectively a war cabinet, to which Danton was elected, assuredly with the backing of Robespierre. (Across the country, many communes established their own committees of public safety in imitation, largely at the behest of local Jacobins.)

The Girondins had been fatally injured by their association with Dumouriez. Robespierre made no bones about the fact that the uprisings in Brittany and the Vendée, the fanaticism both royal and religious which had led the people of the countryside astray, were 'no more than the worthy fruits of the poisonous writings disseminated by the Girondin faction'. He demanded, with heavy irony, that they be brought before the revolutionary tribunal: 'I do not dare to say that you should strike with the same decree [of accusation] patriots as distinguished as *Messieurs* Vergniaud, Guadet and others; I do not dare to say that a man who corresponded day by day with Dumouriez should be at least suspect of complicity, for it is quite certain that this man is a model of patriotism and it would be a sort of sacrilege to demand the decree of accusation against *Monsieur* Gensonné.' The three men he named and to whom, with savage disdain, he gave the discredited, dishonoured old-regime title of 'Monsieur' were prominent figures in the Girondin faction. Vergniaud replied point by point but, to the charge of being 'moderate', as despicable a crime as any in these overheated times, he was indignant: 'Us? Moderates? I wasn't there on 10 August when you, Robespierre, were hiding in your cellar?' He continued: 'I know that in a time of revolution there will be as much folly in laying claim to calming popular violence as and when you choose as a fleet commander bidding the waves be still when they are tossed by the winds; but it is for the lawmaker to prevent, insofar as he can, the disasters of a storm by sage counsel; and if, under the pretext of revolution, it proves necessary to declare oneself the protector of murder and of outlawry so as to be a patriot, I am a moderate.'

But the game was up. Shortly afterwards, on 12 April, the Girondins made what was to be their final desperate throw at stifling the opposition: Guadet asked for and, somewhat surprisingly, obtained an order for the impeachment of Marat. Among other charges were those of inciting riot and unlawful assembly against hoarders and speculators in the pages of his *The People's Friend*, but this was seriously to misread the mood of a city populace who, having brought down the monarchy, were unlikely to see their hero pilloried. Marat, as sitting president of the Jacobins, had signed a defiant address calling the Convention to account and demanding a decree of accusation against 'the disloyal deputies' who constituted a 'sacrilegious cabal'. Robespierre, generally prompt to speak in such moments of crisis, remained silent; 220 voted for, 92 against. Stung by this assault on their heroic leader and, by that token, on their voice, 33 of the 48 Paris sections counter-demanded the expulsion of all 22 Girondin deputies from the Convention. Robespierre, protecting the interests of the nation's *elected* body, condemned the irregular, extra-parliamentary moves in support of a man whom, anyway, he detested.

Even as Paris was convulsed by this duel of the factions, the Vendeans crushed a republican force outside Chemillé, the great 'shock of Chemillé'. Two survivors of the republican army described the action: 'At about five o'clock in the afternoon of Wednesday 13 March a large number of men in a group, armed with guns, bill-hooks, scythes, forks and other farm implements, all wearing white cockades and decorated with small square cloth medallions, on which were embroidered different shapes such as crosses, tiny hearts pierced with pikes, and other religious emblems, appeared in the township of Saint-Pierre [the church in the centre of Chemillé.] All these fellows shouted: "Long live the King and our good priests. We want our king, our priests and the old regime." It was plain they wanted to kill off any patriots, including us, as we watched them. The whole band, which was terrifyingly large, hurled itself at the patriot soldiers standing against them, killed many, took many others prisoner and scattered the rest.'

Transported with the fury of battle, the victorious rebels were intent on slaughtering the republican prisoners but they were held in check by their general, Maurice-Louis Gigot d'Elbée, who ordered them to kneel, thank God for their victory and repeat the Lord's Prayer. When they came to 'Forgive us our trespasses as we forgive them who trespass against us' he bade them stop. 'You ask God to pardon you and you are unwilling to pardon? How, in all conscience, could you do such a thing? They may *preach* the brotherhood of man: we *live* it.'

They were shamed and this notable act of clemency set the seal on their treatment of prisoners for the remainder of the campaign.

In Paris, however, another justice ran its course. The revolutionary tribunal acquitted Marat on 24 April and, garlanded with flowers, he was carried off shoulder high in triumph by a horde of his devoted sansculottes.

A week later 8,000 of them trooped along the rue du Faubourg Saint-Antoine to the Convention building and demanded the maximum on the price of bread; they would not leave without it. On 2 May the Convention yielded, imposed a maximum and gave municipal authorities draconian powers of search and requisition of foodstuffs. The people had spoken; despite misgivings and attempted opposition, the Mountain fell into line behind them. A police spy told his masters that 'the Jacobins know only too well that they cannot stand against the people when they need them'.

Elsewhere the people were speaking, but in a very different language.

On 8 April a Conventional decree sent all surviving members of the Bourbon family, including Philippe-Egalité, to prison in Marseille on charges of complicity with the foreign plot. It was paramount to remove them from Paris and the proximity of the Girondins; the fear was that if they were sent to Bordeaux, the Girondins would proclaim Egalité king, but the Marseille sections, dominated by Jacobins, were nonetheless confused: the arrival of the Bourbons in their now strongly anti-royalist city delivered an apple of discord.

The Jacobins of Marseille, as in so many other towns and cities, were militant, seizing the opportunity to turn the tables on the bourgeois who had so long lorded it. In the big commercial centres, they were particularly fervent. Marseille's Jacobin club took as its motto: 'Death to the tyrant; no federalism.' They had grown impatient with the Convention and suspected Paris of not hastening on the death of the King fast enough; had not they provided troops for the attack on the Tuileries on 10 August and the purging of the prisons? Had not their 2nd Battalion of the national Guard brought pressure for the death penalty? All this talk of *Paris* . . . the patriots of Marseille had twice helped Paris to rise up against the oppressor and the foreign conspiracy.

When the Marseillais Charles Barbaroux was elected to the Convention, he proclaimed himself an ardent revolutionary, flourishing a dagger which, he swore, was to be plunged into his heart as a traitor to his townsmen's cause if he did not deliver France from the odious race of kings. 'Patriots of all countries,' he added, 'are Marseillais.' However, life in Paris had softened his politics. Away from the heat of his local club, he saw a more complex picture and, in the debate on the death of the King, he supported the motion requiring an appeal to the people – thus, to extreme opinion at least, manifestly betraying the melodramatics of the dagger gesture. He and other appellants were vilified by the Jacobins in Marseille and on 6 March the club called for the expulsion from the Convention of Brissot, Roland and their clique, who had penetrated the ministries and the armed forces, as well as recalling all deputies who had supported the appeal on the King's death sentence. This opposition to their deputies hardened when the men of the 2nd Battalion arrived back on 27 March with disgusted reports on events in Paris, particularly the intrigues and political shenanigans they had been subjected to.

They did not lack support. Paul-Francois-Nicholas Comte de Barras said: 'Paris needs the impetus of Marseille so that it can rise up a third time', that is, to defeat the Girondins, and Danton opined that the Marseillais' petition had showed them to be the Mountain of the Republic, but the official line was quite different.

Barère declared that the Jacobins of Marseille who demanded the recall of the appellants and thereby refused to acknowledge the laws of the Convention were 'federalists'. It was the new dirty word, the word attached to those provincial regions who had risen against Paris and thus seemed bent on secession.

Antagonism between Paris in the far north and the sun-blessed other world of the south was inveterate. The northerners of the Langue d'oïl said *oui* for 'yes', those of the Langue d'oc, in the south, *oc*, which marked them out as contaminated with foreign influence – of Catalan, of the old troubadour language, of looser manners and morals at odds with the polished etiquette of the sophisticated northern tranche of the realm. This was pure prejudice: the princely courts of Aquitaine and Provence had fostered a brilliant culture of poetry, literature, music and dance.

Differences in law also divided the north, where legal principle was rooted in ancient Teutonic custom, from the Midi, the south, which recognised written, Roman law, the Justinian Code. Under the old regime, Languedoc and Provence, like Brittany, the Franche-Comté, Lorraine and other pockets of the kingdom only recently absorbed into France, enjoyed a separate, so-called 'foreign' status, with unique rights of limited self-government and taxation systems. This independence of control bred a marked pertinacity of spirit. Moreover, the Mediterranean ports straddled lucrative maritime and overland trade routes. Envy spiked the suspicious disregard of the north. Marseille, ancient Massilia, a Greek foundation, could rightly claim to be France's first city and it acted like it. Granted the hugely important privilege by Louis XIV of a virtual monopoly of the Levant trade as a free port, exempt from the usual imposts, Marseille enjoyed a unique economic position and extraordinary political autonomy. Its citizens could only be invited, not forced, to pay tax.

These material differences were matched by a widely held belief that the Marseillais were a very odd, fractious, unseemly crowd. The royal intendant was based in Aix-en-Provence, a rather suaver, more genial centre, more conducive to polite and decorous spirits than the teeming port city of Marseille. The prefect Thibaudeau remarked on the propensity of Marseillais when abroad to disclaim all connection with France and Louis XIV told one of his agents unlucky enough to be sent south: 'You will have some odd characters to govern in Provence.' To most Parisians, the Marseillais were strange and unlikeable. Any man seen kicking a dog would be hissed: 'Look, a Marseillais' and there was an old saying: 'Aix-in-Provence, Marseille-in-Turkey, Toulon-in-Barbary.' An English visitor said of the population of Marseille and the Midi in general: 'The common people have a brutality and rudeness of manners more characteristic of a republican than a monarchical state.'

To Aix's fine architecture and grandiose style, Marseille opposed her commercial wealth; to Aix's Parlement and archbishop, Marseille flaunted her Chamber of Commerce. And it was this commercial strength which aggravated the hostility of the local Jacobins to the city burghers and determined the continuing resistance of those burghers to the radical shift of balance in the Revolution.

Barbaroux had, in fact, privately floated the idea of a republic of the Midi if the North should fall. This could not be kept secret and, inevitably, he was accused of promoting the idea as not only viable but desirable and of wanting to be dictator of this rival republic. But some enemies of all France were of more immediate danger, because much closer, to Provence: the Piedmontese, the émigrés who had taken up residence across the border in Turin, the Spaniards. Further to these overland threats, Marseille was vulnerable to attack by sea from the east and the west and its own defences were sorely depleted. It had sent a large number of volunteers to the army of the north.

The city was also gripped by fears that the Jacobins in Marseille were preparing massacres against the sections. A locksmith, Antoine Pillon, giving evidence before the Popular Tribunal of the Sections, said that he had been given orders to build an ambulant guillotine; and one prominent Jacobin, Maillet Cadet, the president of the Criminal Tribunal, was quoted as summing up the attitude of the Marseille Jacobins: 'Paris wants heads to be cut off and why not? Better hang than be hanged.'

The example of the Paris Jacobins had inspired highly politicised imitation throughout France early on in the Revolution, and by December 1789 the club was receiving a vast number of requests for associate membership and floods of correspondence from other clubs. By July 1791, 434 communes had affiliated clubs and another 500 were unaffiliated but modelling themselves assiduously on the one in Paris; by the end of the Terror, over 5,332 communes across France had clubs, some 3,000 of them founded after September 1793.

Full affiliation depended on recommendation by trusted patriots, proof of civism – good civic behaviour, notably participation in revolutionary activities, sworn references, the submission of each club's own by-laws for scrutiny by the Paris men. Although the Paris club never demanded uniformity of regulations, its lead was generally taken as the norm, particularly in the rhetoric. Thus the clubbists in Versailles wrote to the Paris Jacobins declaring that they would 'make a rampart of our bodies' if the city were threatened.

Affiliation was hard won, however: the Paris Jacobins could claim attendance at the great days of the Revolution – the Bastille, Versailles, the Tuileries; for those in the provinces, tests of revolutionary zeal were not always so convincing. Local jealousies came into play, feudal squabble and inter-town rivalry were ever a cause of social fissure; the clubs played on and exaggerated the divides.

Meetings took place in former churches and chapels for the most part, but also in private homes, college buildings, city and town halls, usually during the morning or the afternoon of holidays, otherwise between 5 and 7 p.m. on weekdays, three to five times per week.

The room was lit by oil lanterns, torches, chandeliers; at the front of the assembly, a podium on which stood the president's armchair, a table for inkwells, pens, secretarial paper; hung in some prominent place, the republican tricolour.

On the walls hung copies of the Declaration of the Rights of Man, lists of members, bulletins, plaques with the names of local volunteers killed or wounded at the front; newspapers for perusal, the texts of laws – on 25 July 1793 a law was passed which protected clubs from hindrance by any persons or authority, a clear indication of how crucial the government perceived the role of the clubs to be.

Placards and pennants exhorted the right spirit: 'WE HONOUR THE TITLE "CITIZEN" . . . THE REPUBLIC ONE AND INDIVISIBLE . . . LIBERTY, EQUALITY, FRATERNITY OR DEATH . . .', slogans which also adorned the flags borne by regiments of volunteers.

Paintings of revolutionary scenes: the Fall of the Bastille . . . the Historic Day of 10 August.

At the start of the meeting members entered to stirring music; a call for order and the communal singing of the 'Marseillaise', the fixed custom since 10 August 1792. Then cheers in unison – the by-laws of the club at Nîmes called for ten cheers with riders as follows: 'Long live the Republic.' 'Down with: moderates . . . those who show pity . . . aristocrats . . . federalists.' 'Death to all enemies of the Revolution.' 'Long live: the Mountain . . . constitution . . . defenders of the fatherland . . . the sansculottes.'

After official approval of the minutes came the highlight of the session – the reading aloud of correspondence and excerpts from revolutionary newspapers. With that slavish adherence to form which characterises the jobsworth men for whom civic duty is the paramount rule of all thought and action, the vast weight of mail which poured into the Paris Jacobins had to be read out, every single page, without précis or favour. Much of it was tediously inconsequential: parish-pump reports of civic fêtes, formulaic professions of undying loyalty and so on, swamping the important messages which were painstakingly extricated from the morass, copied and the duplicates forwarded to the government Committees.

The Committees, needing to respond, would first have to establish the names of 'sure, known' patriots in the provincial clubs to whom mail could safely be sent. Given that many patriots changed their names during the Revolution – dropping the old-style Christian names coupling saints – Jean-Baptiste, Marie-Joseph – in favour of Roman exemplars of republican virtue – Junius, Brutus, Scaevola – establishing who was or had been who was not always easy.

What characterised all the clubs was a united hatred of those whom the revolutionary leaders singled out and local patriots identified as the true enemies of the people and the Republic: the aristocrats, the rich, the haves, the bloodsuckers, the *egoists*. And a definition of 'egoist' framed by a Jacobin in Marseille may serve as general: the egoist 'loves only himself and does nothing except for himself . . . in a word . . . you will find that in him are combined all the qualities of marble: HARD, COLD and POLISHED.'

And in Marseille, the warehouse porters, sailors and workers, all of them dependent on the prosperity of the docks, were just as egoistic and aristocratic as the merchants and burgesses whose entrenched control of the city was so at odds with the emancipating aims of the Revolution. Indeed, so much a byword for opposition to the essential politics of unity and indivisibility was Marseille that it was bootless for Barbaroux to claim a wider vision, as he did in a letter to Marseille from Caen on 18 June 1793.

He spoke glowingly of a France whose economic supremacy over the rest of Europe was unchallengeable, and adamantly rejected accusations that such ideas were necessarily federalist: 'France thus parcelled out [in autonomous regions] would cease to carry any weight in Europe and our natural riches together with our commerce would pass into the hands of the English.' However, this liberal thinking, rooted in a broader perspective of how trade worked, how commerce functioned, on just how many diverse and disparate interests the economy of a nation depended, did not accord with the incessantly repeated mantra from Paris: the Republic, one and indivisible. The more worldly awareness of Barbaroux and the backsliders like him was no less than unpatriotic.

The local Jacobins stepped up their campaign against the city sections – the elected popular assemblies of citizens more concerned with the health of Marseille than with political correctness preached from nearly 800 kilometres north.

The sections, in their turn, saw their opponents as no better than that class of unemployed highway robbers who had terrorised the French countryside for generations – brigands – though now they had assumed an entirely spurious authority under the umbrella of radical politics as informers, intriguers, factious busybodies, Maratists. In sum: clubbists.

A similar antagonism was being played out equally across the southern portion of France but most significantly and, for Paris, most perilously, in three major centres: 80 kilometres along the coast from Marseille in Toulon, France's naval base on the Mediterranean; 700 kilometres to the north-east in Lyon; and at Bordeaux, which had come to epitomise the federalist poison, the gathering revulsion to dictates from the north. Worse than the ravages of political discord for the people of Marseille, and therefore the Midi, was the onset or real hardship due to the blockading of French sea ports by the English navy.

Toulon commanded a fine roadstead protected by the peninsula of Saint-Mandrier and, to the rear, by an amphitheatre of hills and town dominated by the fortified heights of Mont Faron. In its harbour was anchored the main force of the French southern fleet.

The prosperity of Lyon, called 'the second city [of France] in magnificence and size of population, its first city by virtue of its situation its industry its wealth', was founded on silk. Contemporaries envied it and sneered; the Lyonnais mentality was dominated by an obsession with trade: 'It is the spirit of commerce which dominates the city of Lyon; moreover, one sees here perhaps as nowhere else so much industry, so much pliability of character, nor so much focus on business matters.' There was a degree of social conscience: the Oeuvres de la Marmite and other systems of secular beneficence had produced substantial help for the poor and unemployed from 1787. But the prevailing belief was that Lyon had no time for revolutionary principles.

The Girondin minister Roland had lectured the merchants on their moral and social duties in the *Courrier de Lyon* on 6 February 1790, the day before a burst of food riots. A pseudonymous letter in reply took him to task: 'Count on the gratitude of all the Merchants and Businessmen . . . who . . . have learnt from you that someone who understands his own business better is not the right man to be expressing opinions about commerce . . . Learned Inspector, you are bold to be handing out lessons to merchants who are sufficiently empty-headed to believe themselves of some importance in the market place and whom you treat with the contempt that they deserve. You will inculcate in them that Agriculture improves mankind, as the manure of your writings betters our souls, whereas Commerce corrupts men . . .'

The relative autonomy of Lyon was long established, its administration firmly in the hands of wealthy guildsmen, elected *échevins* – consuls, city magistrates – and burghers. Madame Roland described Lyon as 'a sewer of everything most disgusting produced by the old regime' in a letter; and of the mayor, Palerne de Savy, one of the city notables, she wrote that he was 'an arrant traitor, filled with the prejudices of the old regime, the haughtiness of the gentlemen of the robe, the insolence of the King's men'. She found Lyon society crass and boring.

The Revolution had hit the city hard: foreign exports had all but dried up; internal trade was convulsed; above all, the market for luxury goods had plummeted. When vested interest was suffering so badly, the opinion of one silk merchant, Etienne Mayet, may summarise the Lyon attitude to the effect of political theory on fiscal health: 'To ensure and maintain the prosperity of our manufacturing industry, it is essential that the workers never get rich, that they should earn only so much as is necessary to feed and clothe themselves well.' Sporadic popular uprisings of malcontents, principally hatters and weavers, the 'small people', stirred fears among the bourgeoisie of a general rising that would 'make an omelette of the city'.

In 1792 the Conventional Louis Vitet, physician, wrote from bitter experience, after waiting in vain for a group of local merchants to produce a plan for alleviating unemployment: 'Don't expect to get anything from merchants; they'd rather die than lose their precious money . . . it is simply impossible to enlighten them.' This view is biased, but perception weighs heavy and from such opinion, whether just or not, stemmed Jacobin extremism in Lyon and elsewhere.

Madame Roland in a letter wrote of Lyon: 'My friend, the counter-revolution has begun here, it's a lost region, it is incurable.'

Geography helped. Lyon is remote; surrounded by mountains and narrow valleys, it stands near the frontier with Switzerland and Italy and therefore made a likely target for foreign invasion.

One of the Lyon Jacobins, Joseph Chalier, back from Paris and on fire with revolutionary zeal, had written in his *The Revolutions of Paris*, 1790: 'It came as little surprise to me to come home to my native Lyon and find it more anchored in aristocracy than ever . . . The cabal of those who occupy positions of influence and authority or who aspire to them, and their adherents, is, in truth, unthinkable . . . Oh, my God, what have we come to? What an infamous city this is. Ungrateful city, perfidious city, which, more than any other, houses in its breast the enemies of the most happy, the most astonishing of revolutions.'

And, addressing the national Assembly in 1792, he said: 'Lyon has always been divided between a large number of rich and privileged oppressors and a far larger body of poor, crushed by the weight of their burdens, demeaned by the weight of their humiliation. The former disdain . . . the Declaration of the Rights of Man and the Citizen; their hatred of equality lay at the root of the disorders in Lyon; these disorders began with the Revolution . . . they have continued, they still persist through the design and hope of re-establishing the old regime.' It was, he warned them, the incivism – the uncivic attitude and behaviour – of the rich which explained the deep-seated aristocratic tendencies of Lyon, not the seditious work of the émigrés in Koblenz, or the priests or the nobility.

This fiery demagogue dominated Marseille's Jacobin club, and he cranked up the struggle between moderates and extremists into violence. On 27 May, at the club, Chalier, well versed in the rhetoric of Marat and the others, allegedly said: 'We must seize the presidents and secretaries of each section, the whole bunch of them, and send them to the guillotine and wash our hands in their blood.' At the time, two representatives on mission, Nioche and Gauthier, were in the city. On 29 May fighting broke out between local partisans and Jacobins and gangs of section members took the two visiting Conventionals hostage. The city commune, in the hands of the extremists, was suddenly paralysed and surrendered next morning – 43 died and 115 were wounded during the affray. A general committee of the sections ordered the arrest of members of the commune and its committee for public safety, instituted on the Paris model. Chalier was seized, the Jacobin club closed and in early June all sectional clubs were abolished. That same day the moderates of Marseille finally took the members of the club into custody after three weeks of bitter factional unrest and the flight of the deputies on mission to Montélimar, whence they reported that Marseille was in a state of counter-revolution, which was, in truth, far from the case: uproar and confusion, more like.

Taking the lead, Lyon sent envoys to Bordeaux and Marseille to vow that the city would oppose with arms any attempt to restore the Jacobin tyranny.

Bordeaux, capital of Aquitaine, that vast ancient landholding of the English Plantagenets, had always been a thorn in the side of the French king. Wealthy, cosmopolitan, independent, Bordeaux thought well of itself. Its large port, replete with vested interests, looked out west into the vast other world of the Atlantic and beyond; trade with the French colonies in the Caribbean and America brought wealth and a wider perspective to the city and the bustling activity of the quaysides encouraged the Bordelais to be not so very concerned with what happened in the rest of France anyway. The central power lay very distant from their particular interests, both economic and political, which, at the end of the old regime, stood at their peak – trade was booming, profits were high, there was full employment, much immigration – all fostering an intense local pride and a building programme to reflect the gains of industry and opulence. Large sums were spent on embellishment of the city by its governors and royal intendants.

Arthur Young visited Bordeaux in 1787: 'Much as I had read and heard of the commerce, wealth and magnificence of this city, they greatly surpassed my expectations. Paris did not answer at all, for it is not to be compared to London; but we must not name Liverpool in competition with Bordeaux.'

Here was a rich, fashionable, cultured, modern city, its Grand Théâtre, finished in 1779, widely considered to be the best theatre in all France, Paris notwithstanding. The Abbé Expilly, in his *Dictionnaire* (1762), a sort of gazetteer, wrote of Bordeaux: 'Capital of Guyenne and the Bordelais, with an Archbishop whose archbishopric takes the title of Primate of the Aquitaines, a university [of acknowledged poor quality, suppressed by the Revolution], an Academy of Sciences and Arts, a Parlement [founded 1460], a court of taxation, a Treasury department, an Intendant [supervising a region the largest in France and largely independent of Paris, being so far distant; exercising control of a vast regional administrative machine], an admiralty, a Seneschal's court [royal appointee supervising finance and justice], a provincial governor, Présidial [judicial court of second instance], a Tribunal of municipal magistrates, a Stock Exchange, a Marble consortium, a superintendence of forests and waterways, a bureau of revenues, three forts, an elected body for determining financial admin, and one of the finest ports in the kingdom . . .'

What need had Bordeaux of a *revolution*?

In the Vendée, the royal and Catholic armies, now some 45,000 strong, were cruelly punishing the 15–16,000-strong Republican forces, 'the Blues' (from the colour of their uniform jackets). Melting into the thickets of the bocage, the Vendeans re-emerged to deliver short, furious attacks on the hapless Blues, floundering in the wild country of what was now being called 'the military Vendée'. Knowing their ground to the inch, often ill-armed Vendean ambushers waited doggedly for republican patrols straying into the labyrinths of heavily wooded tracks. Enemy morale faltered; patriotic zeal waned in the sapping round of what a Spaniard called a *guerrilla*, 'little war', conflict. At the approach of a republican column, news would fly to the waiting Vendeans; village mill sails were immobilised to signal danger. The rebels, armed with pitchforks, ancient duck guns and broad-bladed billhooks, knew their job: the best marksmen flitted along the dense hedgerows to pick off targets as the troops passed through; others fanned out in a screen, and hid – often in hollow trees – ready to swoop on the head of the column as it broke cover. A sudden shock attack and . . . gone. But they lacked strategy. Towns once taken were as quickly left ungarrisoned. Victories fed more victories, but never led to a sustained holding of towns or territory.

On 5 May the rebels took Thouars; on 25 May they captured Fontenay and were heading for the coast, where they might make contact with the blockading English fleet. By 7 June they had overrun Doué, advancing north towards the Loire, and on 9 June they captured the plum prize of Saumur, in the process trouncing the army of the Paris national Guard commanded by Santerre, who had arrived only three weeks earlier. General Turreau, who was to play a central role in the visitation of the Terror upon the Vendée, said of the sottish brewer-cum-imperator from Paris: 'He fights well, drinks better and has learnt to sign his name.'

The revolutionary government faced crisis and, in its handling of the crisis, took a direction which none of its key players had the courage or the nerve to alter, a direction which lead directly to the worst excesses of the Terror.

Towards the end of May, in Paris, sansculotte opposition to the Girondins had become more vociferous, more furious. Hébert, in *Le Père Duchesne*, called for the people to wipe out these 'traitors who plotted against the Republic'. The Commune sent a deputation to the Convention to further demands for the expulsion of the men who were now being openly labelled 'federalist'; one of their leaders, Isnard, who had not been shy of extremist talk in the past, now retrenched and hit back at the self-appointed champions of liberty: 'If the nation's representatives were to suffer injury as a result of these repeated insurrections, I tell you, in the name of all France, Paris would be razed to the ground.' Marat denounced him for exorbitant counter-revolutionary talk. Isnard ignored him. 'Soon,' he said, 'people would be searching the banks of the Seine to see if the city of Paris had ever existed.' Inflating the rhetoric, he was making a threat which chimed nastily with that of the duke of Brunswick in the late summer of the previous year, a threat which had little substance but which enraged the citizens of the capital, who took it as clear proof of Girondin disdain for their safety and well-being.

On 26 May, in the Jacobins, Robespierre called for the people to make another historic day and rise up against the corrupt deputies of the Convention.

The Commune had set up an insurrectionary committee; in the early hours of 31 May one of their members, Varlet, ordered the ringing of the tocsin; he urged the dissolution of the entire Convention on the grounds that the corruption was spread more deeply than among the few Girondins. Some focused on the 22 named; others thought that the Convention was probably by now sufficiently cowed to fall into line. Throughout the day the Commune mob thronged the Tuileries but the Girondins refused to bend; instead they referred the matter to the CPS, which, by the regulations of the bureaucracy, was obliged to instigate proper procedures for appeal. That same night Roland managed to escape and headed north for Caen; his wife was arrested.

The Commune had had enough. On 2 June, a Sunday, when the sansculottes were not at work, a deputation presented a new petition calling for the dismissal of the 22 deputies. Hanriot, commander of the Paris national Guard, had posted between 75,000 and 100,000 men round the Convention building and, when a group of deputies attempted to leave the building, he cried out: 'Cannoneers to your guns', sabres flashed from scabbards and the deputies retreated inside again. To a message from the Convention president, Hérault de Séchelles, ordering him to withdraw his troops, Hanriot replied bluntly: 'Tell your fucking president that he can fuck himself, him and the entire fucking Convention. If the 22 deputies aren't out here inside the hour, we'll blow the building to the ground.'

Barère, the voice of calm reasonableness, speaking for the CPS, refused to issue an order for the arrest of the deputies, but, as so often before, the presence of armed force outweighed the authority of nominal force. By the evening, gripped by fear and buckling to indecision, the members accepted they were beaten. Georges Couthon suggested that since there were only 22 deputies under order of impeachment, the rest of the assembly was in no danger and read the act of indictment. It would not be the last time that from his wheelchair he forced an issue which had reached an impasse.

The vote was taken. The Convention ordered the arrest of the 22 Girondin deputies and seven others who had been appointed to investigate insurrectionary activity in Paris. The voting was thin; most of the deputies present abstained. The Mountain, led by Robespierre, although they saw that yielding to this pressure would further incapacitate the Convention, were in no position to save those whom they had for so long vilified. Besides, once the Girondins had been crushed, the Mountain would be in clear control.

Assessing his last hours in the Convention before the Girondins were outlawed – despite the brave efforts of Lanjuinais to resist the crude tactics of coercion, being struck even as he spoke – Lacaze, deputy for the Gironde, said: 'I saw the tomb of liberty' and, in a letter of 2 June to his constituents, Gensonné said: 'We are close to a moment when I will fall victim to the conspiracies which are being woven against the liberty of the French Republic . . . I especially adjure the brave men of Bordeaux, my fellow citizens and the republicans of all France to examine with care the count of charges in my indictment (should there be one) laid on me. I commend to all my friends the cherishing of my memory; I charge them, in the name of the feelings they have expressed to me, to prevent its being besmirched: such a task will not be difficult . . . resigned to every eventuality, sure in my conscience, I embrace in my thoughts my dear fellow citizens, all friends of liberty and of the French Republic; and under the seal of my blood, the daggers of the conspirators, the hatchets of the factions at my throat, my last sigh will be for my patrie and my mouth will close expressing my most ardent desire: long live the Republic.'

At the close of the voting, Vergniaud stood and offered the deputies, assembled in what had become little more than an echo chamber of sansculotte will, a glass of blood to quench their thirst. His clarion call in the 5 May edition of his paper had gone into silence: 'Men of the Gironde, rise up. The Convention has been weak only because it has been abandoned. Support it against the mad furies who menace it . . . Men of the Gironde, there is not a moment to lose. If you build up a massive energy you will compel to peace men who provoke civil war. They will follow your generous example and virtue will triumph at last. If you continue to be apathetic, hold out your arms – the irons are ready and crime reigns.' The previous day he had penned another appeal 'with the knife at my throat'. Alas for them, it was another kind of virtue, the cold, calculating, patriotic virtue of ideological revolution which would supplant them.

Robespierre saw power and he took it. This latest coup effected by the people underlined their potency in the political bargaining; he elevated their readiness to take action on the enshrined revolutionary principle that it was their absolute, by now almost constitutional, right to overthrow corrupt government, into a philosophical abstraction which, so to speak, codified their reasons. The Paris sansculottes were the instrument of *the whole people*. He wrote:

What is necessary is one sole will.

The foreign war is a mortal sickness, so long as the body politic ails from revolution and the division of wills.

The interior dangers come from the bourgeois [he refers, largely, to the world of commerce – tradesmen, shopkeepers, merchants]; to vanquish the bourgeois, we must rally the people.

The present insurrection must continue.

The people must unite with the Convention and the Convention must avail itself of the people.

The sansculottes need to be paid and to stay in the towns.

Arms must be procured for them and they must be made angry and enlightened.

If imprecise and bombastic in its legalistic phrasing, the sort of flabby rhetoric which did duty as just cause, the programme behind the vagaries was eagerly seized on by the activists: here was a man who had secured them their rightful place in the power struggle. He had identified the enemies within, the traitors who, like the aristocrats before them, continued to make the life of the poor miserable. The famine pact had been usurped by the bourgeois. The people possessed the sole will which could save the Republic. The foreign war was a distraction fomented by the Girondin federalists. The civil war was the true danger, threatening the fragmentation of the patrie.

When 63 members of the Convention signed a protest against the popular violence of 2 June, Robespierre acted to consolidate his power. On 8 June he moved that the CPS should prosecute the excluded deputies and then proceed to the banishment of all foreigners from French soil. Four days later, in the Jacobins, he espoused the levying in Paris of 'an army capable of inspiring awe in all the despots [i.e. that ring-fence of tyranny inside which France existed as an enclave of freedom]. This army must consist of *all the people of Paris* [my italics].' It was just what all the people of Paris wanted to hear.

The expelled Girondins were immediately placed under house arrest; others of the party had already fled: their one hope was to coordinate the rebellion flaring up in the provinces.

In a brilliant stroke of psychological melodrama, Robespierre called upon the Convention to unite with the people, else 'you will be defeated, you will climb the scaffold and that will be the condign reward of your lack of foresight and of your cowardice'. In a clear, if inflated, allusion to Moses on Sinai, Legendre, Danton's friend, leapt to his feet: 'Robespierre, who has never misread political events, will come down from the mountain and electrify every heart by the soaring tone of his eloquence.' Robespierre turned on them one of the most potent weapons in his armoury: self-pity. He was at once the small vulnerable orphan, alone and battling to survive in the deprivation of all the comfort, all the support, all the protection he had never had from his absent father and his prematurely dead mother. Playing hard on their sentiments, attracting to his purity of soul and purpose all the self-doubt and nervousness with which their own consciences were clouded, he defied them not to respond to the luminous honesty of his own mind and spirit: 'I no longer have the vigour necessary to combat the intrigues of the aristocrats. Worn out by four years of punishing, barren travail, I feel that my physical and moral faculties are not on a par with a great revolution, and I announce that I will hand in my resignation.'

Several voices: 'No. No.'

He had engaged their desperate need of a man who could focus the Revolution, a man who could, while manoeuvring the factions to his will, at the same time appear somehow to stand outside the factions, to be of the sovereign people alone; he had engaged their need of *him*: 'If,' he told the Convention on 17 June, 'you decree that hardship exempts from the obligation of contributing to the needs of the patrie, you decree, thereby, the degradation of the purest party in the Nation, you decree the aristocracy of wealth and soon you will see these new aristocrats, dominant in the legislature, employing an odious Machiavellianism in concluding that those who pay no dues at all cannot share in the benefits of government; this will establish a class of proletarians, a class of helots, and equality and liberty will perish for ever.'

It was typical casuistry: if the poor have no money and cannot pay taxes they are effectively disqualified from the benefits of the Revolution for which they have made the hardest sacrifices. It called on all the old animosities which plagued the state and society of the old regime: aristocratic privilege and exemption, the oppression of the poor, the indifference of governments to the hierarchies of misery. He was telling the Convention that the new lodestone of power, the true inheritors of natural human right – because they were closest to it, unprotected by money and privilege – were the sansculottes, the have-nots. Consciously or not – and 12 years of Oratorian indoctrination had lodged deep in him – he was echoing the Sermon on the Mount: 'blessed are the poor in spirit, for theirs is the kingdom of heaven' (Matthew 5:3). In Coverdale's version verse 4 reads: 'Blessed are the meke: for they shall inheret the earth.' If 'meek' used of the Paris mob was to stretch the point wildly, Robespierre was pleased to paint the picture of the noble poor, the downtrodden, humble sansculotte rising up to take his just reward in the teeth of all despotic oppression and the machinations of the detestable bourgeois. Such religiosity fuelled his vision of the paradise which the Revolution promised. Meanwhile, the corruption of the world made by an amalgam of tyrannies must proceed apace, albeit the task was a lugubrious effort, 'done more in sorrow than in anger': 'I can assure you that I am one of the most defiant of patriots and one of the most melancholy to have appeared since the beginning of the Revolution.'

It was almost a commonplace of paradox: the man who had lacerated his own soul that day in Arras when, as a young lawyer, he came home from court, where, as judge, he had had to condemn a prisoner in the dock to death and lamented over and over again to his younger brother Augustin: 'I know very well he is guilty, that he is a criminal, but to send a man to his death?' The idea seemed insupportable, but, a few years later, he said of Foullon's lynching on 22 July 1789: 'Monsieur Foullon was hanged yesterday by order of the people.' That made it all right; so long as he didn't have anything to do with the practicalities, especially the lynch-law of the business. And didn't they say of the sanguinary Marat that he was the mildest man in private, wouldn't hurt a fly? The sentimentality of those who excuse violence is the more pernicious when it shelters behind law. And in

Robespierre's version of politics it was indeed the case that unity lends strength to even the most mediocre of men.

On 24 June, Midsummer Day, 1793, the Convention approved a new Constitution produced by the CPS: an extended form of the original Declaration of Rights; an enjoinder to citizens not to do unto others what they did not wish done to themselves; a proclamation of the one and indivisible Republic; paragraphs on what constituted the people and an affirmation of their sovereignty; universal suffrage; the political and administrative structure; a protracted definition of law and measures to be taken for general security; the system of elections to the one national Convention and a guarantee to all French people of rights of 'equality, liberty, security, property, public duty, the free exercise of religious worship, general education, social assistance, indefinite freedom of the press, the right to petition and to meet in popular societies, the enjoyment of all the rights of man'.

These declarations of the Constitutional act were to be engraved on posters and exhibited in the heart of the legislature and in all public places.

But revolutionary promise had not yet managed to overtake the harsher realities of existence. In many parts of France the high-sounding apophthegms of political ideology would have rivals claims to attention. As with this doggerel posted on the door of a baker's shop in the rue Judaïque, one of Bordeaux's main thoroughfares, and reported by section 10 in a minute of 5 August 1793:

> It's a fact there's naught to choose
> Between starvation and a king.
> Time runs out, brave Bordelais,
> So let's choose – Louis seventeen.

If the answer might not be widely upheld, the proposition could hardly be argued with.

When, on 10 June, Robespierre announced to the Jacobins the completion of 'a constitutional code, infinitely superior to all moral and political institutions, a work doubtless capable of improvement but which presents the essential basis of public happiness offering a sublime and majestic picture of French regeneration. Today calumny may launch its poisoned darts. The Constitution will be the reply of patriotic deputies . . .', the radical Chabot riposted angrily that the Constitution hadn't been read by everyone and that it 'fails to assure bread to those who have none. It fails to banish beggary from the Republic.'

There was loud applause.

Hunger allows no choice. Reductive sansculotte pragmatics or the imaginary state of Rousseau's Noble Savage. At one end of the extremist revolutionary programme the red-clawed tussle for food; at the other, the violet-hazed Robespierrist utopia. Each had to be accommodated somehow. And the Constitution, no sooner passed, was shelved: more pressing matters claimed the attention of the central power, namely the Committee for Public Safety.

# SIX

# *Destroy the Vendée*

Let us now consider the people of the Vendée . . . whose political existence, whose swift and astonishing success and whose unexampled ferocity were epoch-making features in the chronicles of the Revolution . . . who needed only an infusion of humanity and a better cause to possess all the characteristics of heroism . . .

*General Turreau*

T HE VENDEAN REBELS did not see themselves as federalist. They had backed the Revolution and the Revolution had failed them miserably. Fighting because of the affront to their liberty of conscience and fealty to God and the King, fighting because they refused to serve as soldiers in a cause they deemed a disgrace, fighting in defiance of what Marat called a 'dictatorship of liberty', they recaptured Machecoul from the Blues who had taken it in April. On 19 June they entered Angers, on the north bank of the Loire, vacated by the republicans, and began the advance downstream to Nantes, principal city of the region, which had declared for and stood by the Revolution.

The next day a Manifesto of the Marseillais sent out across the whole Midi was read out in Bordeaux, a clarion call to the middle classes of the city for a combined march from the regions in revolt on Paris, appealing to their sentiments of provincialism, legitimism and order: 'To arms. Save the Republic, save the Convention, save every good citizen, finally, save your age from all the exactions which might for ever pollute it in the memory of men.'

The Manifesto recalled the heroic, the defining part played by the fédérés from the Midi on 10 August and proudly promised Paris that it would see men from Marseille a second time saving the Revolution. [It prudently passed over their activities in the September Massacres.] 'Let us unite under the same banner; let us engrave on it these words: "UNITY OF THE REPUBLIC, RESPECT FOR PERSONS AND PROPERTY." May the Anarchists read the order for their destruction and may Europe, disarmed by admiration, demand of us peace . . . FRENCHMEN, TO ARMS.'

Recruitment and marshalling of ordnance and weaponry was set in train throughout the region but the push to rouse volunteers and furnish munitions was dogged by poor planning and low morale; there was no common purpose, no united sense of urgency, and there were few who did not baulk at the call to arms and the heavy financial burdens requisite to mount resistance to indeterminate forces so far from home. The reluctance ran deep: it was, after all, on Frenchmen that they were being asked to wage war.

Bordeaux had no arsenal of her own and whereas the men of the Vendée, ill-shod, ill-equipped, had been stirred to combat by a very particular vehemence, resolutely quitting hearth and home in order to preserve both, there was no such enthusiasm at large in Bordeaux.

On 29 June the combined forces of the Vendean armies launched their assault on Nantes, but the city beat off the attack. It was a setback but, six days later, at Châtillon, they confronted a softer target than their fellow regionals and inflicted another defeat on the Blues, who were led by General Westermann. His troops were inferior and had little stomach for the fight or any real idea what they were doing in this awful lost territory of tangled undergrowth and thick woodland populated by fanatics with sickles who materialised from nowhere and vanished as suddenly as will-o'-the-wisp.

Moreover, the high command was in disarray: sansculotte generals like Rossignol and Ronsin were at loggerheads with the former nobles of the royal army. Ronsin, a 41-year-old ex-actor, henchman of the minister of War, Bouchotte (who disbursed large sums of money from the public purse to distribute free copies of Hébert's *Le Père Duchesne* through the armies), had been sent to the Vendée on 9 May. In four days, 1–4 July, he was promoted captain, squadron commander, brigadier, general. Rossignol, 34 years old, a former goldsmith and a pure product of Parisian sansculotterie, was almost permanently inebriated. General Kléber remarked of him that 'nothing could compare with his stupidity and ineptitude, his brutality and his obduracy'. Gaoled for riotous affray, he was released on 10 July, went from brigadier to division general in five days and on 27 July was appointed commander of the army outside La Rochelle. These promotions encapsulate the catch-all political doctrine of the sansculotte: patriotism is enough; patriotism overrides all lack of experience; patriotism is a yeast of virtue which transforms volunteers into hardened veterans who will be a match for any flabby professional troops whose inner spirit has been cowed by subservience to tyrannical regimes.

Volunteers and politicians picked up quickly on the opening of the avenue to democratic protest. When the 5th Battalion had been forced to retreat outside Saumur in June, an officer wrote to the government, leading off with the formulaic statement turned into a catchphrase by Marat: '*We are betrayed.* Our general is in league with Santerre. We won't let this worthless knave desert us.' And on 11 September Robespierre, whose judgement of character was only ever based on a one-dimensional assessment of usefulness, said in the Jacobins: 'It is my firm belief that Rossignol has been the victim of a cabal in the Vendée. It is to that that I attribute the lack of success of the war in this region. Two types of men wanted such an outcome: those who had investments in the Vendée and wished to keep hold of their property and those who did not wish to see at the head of the Republican armies true republicans who could put an early end to this war.' The opinion was never more then merely serviceable. When Rossignol's turn came to attract Robespierre's revised opinion, contempt outweighed adulation.

A cannoneer of the Paris national Guard, Bon-Conseil section (today the Gare du Nord district), writes home from Caen, in the wake of Marat's murder, showing entirely the right spirit and well-tutored by the propaganda of *Le Père Duchesne*: 'I have no pity for the enemies of my country; they have spilled and continued to spill the blood of my brothers, who all demand vengeance, and those who have already played the part of counter-revolutionaries deserve death at angry hands . . . I have just been through the department of Calvados, which is far from being fully republicanised . . . there, in the commune of Caen, I fancy I saw all the knives of the partisans of Corday being sharpened, ready to assassinate the patriots.'

Mobilise that depth of paranoia and hardline vindictiveness and the battle was won. Such men as Rossignol and Ronsin certainly thought so; and they had no truck with the professionals of the old army: the old system of rigid discipline did not fit with the new doctrines of liberty and equality, never mind that battle recognises no liberty but superior conditioning. But the republican armies on the eastern front had shown the way to victory by sheer fervour and the sansculotte generals bragged that they could instil just that kind of brute force, forget tactics. Besides, Barère of the CPS mocked their ex-noble counterparts in the west, dragging huge baggage trains into the Vendée like the armies of the Great King of ancient Persia while the brigands fought on rations of black bread.

On 12 July a self-styled counter-revolutionary Popular Commission in Bordeaux decreed a parade of the whole national Guard of the city suitably equipped and armed, on the Champ de Mars, plus all volunteers to be ready for the march on Paris. Hardly anyone turned up. Even after repeated attempts to drum up numbers, fewer than half of the nominal roll made the parade. Conscription proved no more effective – besides, it smacked of the forced duty of the old regime – and eventually a mere 400 of the intended 1,200 marched out of city and got 50 kilometres up the Gironde valley to Langon, where this sorry apology for a strike force, already seriously depleted by desertion and discouraged by the long, gruelling trudge ahead, pitched camp among the vines. Jean Lafargue, a notary in Langon, sympathetic to the Girondins, scoffed at their 'armed rising' and dismissed this 'military pigmy' as a crude band of untrained soldiers recruited from among 'the thugs of the quaysides and the warehouses . . . a very caricature of the military, if it had not been drawn together by such distressing consequences'.

As soon as they heard that two representatives of the people from the Convention had arrived in Bordeaux – the big political guns from Paris – the liberating army decided that the real guns of Paris were no cheerful prospect, disbanded and straggled back home.

A rather larger body of combined Bretons and Normans quit Caen on 8 July, and four days later an estimated 2,000 arrived in Evreux, less than two days' march from Paris. But when republican troops opened fire on them near the Seine, they turned tail and fled without a fight.

The Marseillais responded no better to the manifesto issued in their name, justifying the revolt of the sections, arguing for a coherent and humanitarian view of the Revolution in contrast to that of Paris. Marseille declared itself 'in a lawful state of resistance to oppression' and called on 'upright men whom Paris still nurses in her bosom' to help the departmental coalition to defeat the 'factious'. Flags of the departmental army were to carry the blazon: 'Republic One and Indivisible: Respect for Persons and Property.'

The scheme was grandiose.

Plans had been afoot among disaffected deputies of the Convention to establish an alternative convention at Bourges and to organise a levy of regional armies which were to converge on Paris from seven secondary centres: Marseille, Lyon, Toulouse, Bordeaux, Rennes, Strasbourg and Rouen. A Central Commission was to be set up in the Midi to coordinate measures of self-defence – thus the Midi would be the unified centre of resistance to the radicals of northern France, the Montagnards as the supporters of the Mountain were known.

In every way, therefore, the success of the Marseillais' part of the bargain was crucial. Their armed force occupied Avignon – a papal enclave, foreign soil within France, governed until 1791 by the Pope's legate – by the second week of July under a non-commissioned officer promoted to general, Rousselet.

Behind him, in Marseille, the newly dominant sections were behaving as autocratically as the abhorred Jacobins. Anyone who spoke in favour of the Constitution or decrees voted after 31 May was declared a traitor. Marseille had become like the wider Republic, obsessed with the enemies within, directing domiciliary visits to suspected radicals and nocturnal patrols to break up clandestine Jacobin meetings in and around the city.

While the Vendeans were beating every republican force sent against them – notably at Vihiers, on 18 July and Les Ponts-de-Cé on 26 July, the Marseillais sansculottes showed rather more vim than the rebels who talked much of overthrowing the Paris Jacobins. Yielding to the advance of the republicans under General Carteaux, Rousselet's bedraggled volunteer army limped back to the city. The so-called federalist revolt of the Midi and north-west had all but collapsed, save in Lyon and Toulon.

The overthrow of the Jacobins in Lyon had been resisted with some ferocity, clear enough indication of the real divisions in the city between rich and poor – as sharp and militant as those in Paris, thanks to Chalier's vehemence, inspired by the chilly thrust of Jacobin logic. The 'small people' of Lyon hated the so-called *muscadins*, the 'pastille-eaters', the nattily dressed fops who despised the slovenly, ragged-trousered sansculottes, flaunting their stinking body odour and down-at-heel shoes, if they wore any shoes at all, as badges of honour. The section insurgents were pelted with stones as they marched along the Quai du Rhône, having taken the city Arsenal at 8.00 on the morning of 29 May; several were hacked to death in the darkness of the streets near the Hôtel de Dieu hospital, where they sought refuge from Jacobin cannon fire. Mother Jarrasson and her daughters dropped rubble out of their window on to the wounded insurgents below, convinced that it was their civic duty to kill muscadins. But the Jacobins enjoyed only localised support in the poorer districts; there was no great popular upsurge. The extremists had alienated diverse sections of the Lyon populace and the radical agitators were greatly disliked. Some 100 of them were arrested between 30 May and the end of June, 43 of them between 29 and 31 May; only nine were tried in civil courts and nearly half were detained until the rebellion was crushed in October.

On the evening of 26 June a Jacobin municipal officer, Sautemouche, was released from the Roanne prison, situated in the anti-Jacobin bastion of Porte-Froc. An angry crowd was waiting – he sought refuge in a section assembly, was thrown out, cornered by the crowd and hacked to death.

The departmental authority, anxious to promote the idea that, far from secession, it was moderate compromise they sought, appealed on 30 May to the minister of the Interior, Joseph Garat, defending their rebellion as a legitimate act of resistance while paying respect to the rule of law, calling on that central tenet of just revolution: 'the right to resist, within the frame of law, an oppression which is the most audacious violation of all Law'. It promised to await the decision of the government of France, though it made it implicit that it would not accept the restoration of the former Jacobin Municipality.

In the city, the language was more explicit. The Jacobins were 'vile criminals, impudent schismatics, [who] dare to menace free men . . .

we, too, know how to march on those who rebel against the national will'.

For the government in Paris, the revolt in the Midi was a powerful, if undefined, threat. Lyon, at the southern end of the Alpine chain guarding the eastern frontier, and Auxonne at the northern end, were of huge military importance. Lyon was the principal supplier for three armies – of the Alps, Italy and the eastern Pyrenees. Its massive arsenal contained 83 artillery pieces, 782 muskets, more than 10,000 sabres and large stockpiles of powder, cartridges, cannonballs and shot; its foundries produced four cannon per day. These armaments suggested the very real possibility of another Vendée centred on Lyon.

On the morning of 2 June Edmond-Loius-Alexis Dubois-Crancé, one of two representatives based in Grenoble, ordered General Kellermann, the commander of the eastern republican armies, to cancel the departure of 4,000 men for Toulon and instead to march on Lyon with ten infantry battalions, each with an established strength of 1,000 men plus auxiliary cavalry and siege artillery. The situation in Toulon was by no means quiet – dock workers were being pushed round the clock to fit and repair the fleet for action against Spanish and English ships; they were being paid in depreciating assignats and resented the flood of immigrant workers brought in to boost production. However, for the moment, Lyon was the powder keg with the fuse burning.

On 7 June a Conventional decree authorised Dubois-Crancé and his colleague Antoine-Louis Albitte in Grenoble 'to take any measure of general security proper to re-establish calm and public tranquillity in the city of Lyon'. But, to ensure that the two representatives would bear full responsibility for any precipitate action, the CPS wrote to them the same day 'to recommend them once again to use the authority invested in them by the decree only with extreme prudence'. It was the kind of vague, foggy order with which the CPS from the very start wreathed its orders to the men out in the field: 'destroy opposition but do not exaggerate'. Placing Lyon at Dubois-Crancé's mercy could only intensify the hostility of the Lyonnais; hampering his taking immediate decisive action gave Lyon time to consolidate.

Lyon was awash with rumour, alive with fears that the decree of 7 June which had ordered the Army of the Alps to attack them 'at a moment when our city appeared to be threatened by the worst misfortune, by the perfidy of men who had been empowered exclusively by the national representatives, ordering them to carry against our city all the forces which had been destined to push back our enemies and putting them at the disposal of men whom we rightly regard as our greatest enemies, it is necessary to ensure that all the artillery and munitions which are presently in the city . . .' should be retained.

Lyon was a fortress border town, they were saying; it needed to concentrate on the foreign enemy, not the inflated apprehensions of northern politicians. When one of them, Robert Lindet, arrived as representative of the people on 8 June, he brought with him in the same coach Chalier's close ally Gaillard. Although this dubious alliance compromised Lindet, a man of intelligence and integrity, in the eyes of the section rebels, he behaved sensibly and patiently to start with, yet got nowhere. The department authorities refused to accept his credentials: their overriding belief was that the Convention which had sent Lindet was far from being the voice of the whole people but was, rather, in the control of the same factions which had dispatched Dubois-Crancé against them. Was not the decree of 7 June proof of this far more sinister intention?

The sections called for his arrest; one section president demanded that 'we deploy the most careful surveillance to deprive citizen Robert Lindet of all means of harming us'. This was fighting talk yet tempered with what Lindet saw as a profound reluctance to break with the Convention. Even violent diatribes against the national Assembly were at pains to separate specific grievance – against the extremists – from the general truth that 'the people of Lyon want only liberty, equality, the unity and indivisibility of the Republic.' Placated, he left the city on 16 June.

Matters deteriorated fast. The fury of the Jacobins found an equal and opposite fury in those determined to expunge them, seeing in this a struggle to save the patrie from the Parisian anarchists. They also vilified the plenipotentiary representatives on mission, sent on the bidding of a small clique of the Convention – the CPS – in the name of the whole assembly, comparing them to the great tyrants of history: 'Nero, Tiberius, the Dukes of Alba, the Inquisitors of Spain, the Mikados of Japan.' They were no better than travelling dictators sent with illicit powers to oppress the departments at will; their activities were a condemnation of the arrogance of the Convention. 'Who are these cowardly despots who dare to come thus to establish this atrocious dictatorship in the departments, to dismantle their powers, to violate all laws of justice and humanity, to hire bestial agitators? And they call them *representatives of the people.*'

A Conventional decree of 17 July confirmed that 'orders given by representatives of the people being provisional laws, no other authority but the national Convention can obstruct their implementation'. The behaviour of these representatives afforded the most powerful rationale for resistance to oppression. It was time to act.

Chalier, still in prison, was brought to trial on 15 July and executed the next day as an instigator of murder and civil war. The evidence was thin, but he was widely hated, a class traitor, branded by the *Journal de Lyon* of 17 July as 'the prime author of all Lyon's troubles'. In fact, he embodied all that the anti-Jacobins hated and feared in the Jacobin domination. The same edition of the paper ran a report of the execution: the exultant crowd scrambled over the scaffold before the victim arrived, but when it took four drops of a misaligned blade to sever his head, 'several bursts of applause were quashed by the indignation roused by the ill success of the instrument. It was deplored.'

Sending Chalier to the guillotine cast the die. Robespierre himself admired him as the first man to unmask Roland and he treated all talk of conciliation with his murderers, namely the Lyon authorities, as an outrage. He declared himself implacably hostile to 'a patriotic municipality destroyed' wherein 'hundreds of patriots [are] entombed in prison cells . . . the national Representation repudiated'. In his harshest verdict of all, he dubbed it 'the Koblenz of the Midi' and preached the need of 'making a terrible example of all the criminals who [in Lyon, Marseille, Toulon, the Vendée, the Jura] have outraged liberty and spilt the blood of patriots'.

In line with this, the CPS identified anti-Jacobinism *per se* with counter-revolution and on 10 July, under pressure from the Mountain, the Committee was reconstituted, with the original 14 replaced by nine members of whom a majority were in favour of extremist measures to crush insurgency. Danton, unwilling to associate himself with what he saw as a rapidly insensate reaction to circumstances, and unable to uphold so crude a consensus as 'either for us or against us', was pushed aside, no matter that he insisted he had no wish to stand for re-election. Of the nine, three were Robespierrists – Saint-Just, Couthon and Jeanbon-Saint-André – re-elected together with Hérault de Séchelles, Lindet, Gasparin and Barère; newly admitted were Jacques-Alexis Thuriot and Prieur de la Marne. News of Chalier's execution reached Paris shortly after another momentous death – that of Marat. The darling of the sansculottes, detested by almost everyone else for his violent outbursts, the hyperbole of his popular rhetoric, the visceral hatred of his attacks on the all and sundry who disagreed with him, had, till now, acted as a distraction from the radicalism of the Montagnards. In truth, Robespierre's own programme of revolutionary ideals was quite as inflammatory, but, couched in the staider, more measured tones of the lawyer speaking under the aegis of justice and the heart-tug of liberty and human rights, it appeared, at least, so much more reasonable.

On 14 July 1793 *La Gazette Française* reported, straying somewhat from circumstantial fact: 'Today at eight o'clock in the evening Marat was assassinated by a woman who, for several days, had been trying to see him in order, it is said, to obtain a pardon for the citizens of Orléans. He was at the time in his bath and the murderess plunged a dagger into his breast, causing instant death. The woman made no attempt to escape. She waited calmly in her carriage till they came to take her. "I don't care," she cried, "the deed is done, the monster is dead." This incident has made a great sensation and untoward consequences are feared.'

That same day other consequences were launched. Dubois-Crancé and Albitte, chafing in Grenoble, at last received specific orders telling them to send forces to subdue Lyon, for some long time adjudged to be technically in a state of rebellion. Kellermann refused to go: his absence would compromise the frontier from Grenoble all the way south to Val de Barcelonnette, 15 kilometres from the Italian border. He said he would march on Lyon only if Dubois assumed responsibility for the frontiers. Dilemma or not, Dubois-Crancé had no option. Kellermann marched.

That very day a popular tribunal in Toulon, set up to purge the town of extremists, arrested two representatives on mission. As in Lyon, the mood was emphatically not one of counter-revolution as Paris would have it, but of a desire 'to enjoy in peace our goods, our property, the fruits of our labours and industry'. That cut little ice in Paris. Toulon was declared outlaw.

Less than two weeks later, on 27 July, the day after a Conventional decree imposed the death penalty on all hoarders of foodstuffs and essential supplies, Gasparin, almost certainly levered out by Couthon, resigned from the CPS on the grounds of ill health; he was replaced by Robespierre, known as 'The Incorruptible' from the title of a pastel study of the young politician published in the *Salon*, 1791. He dominated the Jacobins, he was the firm voice of the Convention and, though this was the first governmental post he had held since the start of the Revolution, with his arrival the CPS became the real seat of executive power. He accepted the mantle of responsibility with customary self-effacing unworthiness masking a stiff spiritual pride: 'Called, against my inclinations, to the CPS, I have seen things I would never have dared to suspect. On one side, I have seen patriotic members striving in vain for the good of their country, on the other, traitors who, in the bosom of the Committee, plotted against the interests of the people. Now that I have seen the government close up, I have been able to perceive crimes which are being committed daily.'

It was the first resounding utterance of his manifesto of *suspicion*. On to every other member of the Convention, Jacobins, even the CPS itself, he projected the formidable apparatus of his own paranoia, his own suspicious nature, his fragile psyche, the brittleness of his own temperament. Knowing that he was beyond reproach, the rest of them, who were very far from spotless, felt the constant dart of his eye, the incessant pulse of his suspicion, the readiness of his finger to point accusation. The solitary who never played with the other pupils at the Oratorian school, the prissy lawyer of Arras who lived with his sister, the revolutionary whose moral stand had from the beginning been untouchable as he himself shrank from human touch, human warmth, any intimacy, now glided into the wings of a theatre of violence whose terrible acts he directed but never joined; like a puppet-master he pulled strings and others jerked and danced at his silent behest when he chose, at the behest of his fulminations against their cowardice, their treachery, their diseased morals. In the French fairgrounds, the try-your-strength machines are called Turk's Heads. The name goes for butt, scapegoat, whipping boy. These were Robespierre's routine fodder, the flexible men, the venal, the impure men who had failed his own purist vision. At them he shied his barbs of contempt.

Spanish forces threatened Perpignan, which straddles a corridor extending from the Pyrenees into France; Coburg's Austrians had just overrun the frontier fortresses of Condé and Valenciennes and General Custine ordered his garrison to abandon Mainz to the advancing Prussians. Custine was the fourth commander appointed to the army in two months. His first task was to nerve the badly demoralised soldiers and his prestige as a career officer – he had been affectionately known as General Moustache – was so great that his mere threat of death for failure to obey orders brought the army to order. But, struggling with the ungrateful work of reorganising the entire military operation, he was undermined by diversion of generals and troops to the western Vendée front; his strategic withdrawal from the exposed position in Mainz to concentrate efforts on a more consolidated front was misinterpreted by politicians whose sole strategy for the armies was 'attack and attack in mass'.

The CPS had Custine arrested as a traitor and Robespierre gave the Convention a taste of his new confidence in the matter of rooting out corruption: 'Do you know what efforts our enemies are making to snatch [Custine] away from the just vengeance of the people awakening compassion for him so as to make them bothered whether he lives or dies? One does not resist the tears of a pregnant woman; a woman will throw herself at the feet of the first man she sees to beg his pity. And for the rest of us, sansculottes, we have no women to snatch us away from death when the conspirators of Lyon drive us in our hundreds under the knife of the assassin. This is the man [Custine] whom your revolutionary Tribunal would spare.'

'We sansculottes,' he said, standing before them in silk breeches and coat, and powdered wig, the very model of a muscadin of Lyon.

Custine went to the guillotine on 28 August 1793.

Within four days of Robespierre's joining the CPS, the full force of republican violence was unleashed on the provincial rebels, its focus trained ruthlessly on the Vendée.

On 1 August Barère walked on to the tribune of the Convention holding an agenda, a medal and a letter. 'Know that universal and incalculable danger hems us in. A letter [he flourished the pages] tells me of the very instant that Valenciennes would surrender.' Consternation. 'A horrible conspiracy covers the earth of the Republic and threatens to attack it and to scatter it in fragments.' Proof lay in this letter, dated 29 June and discovered in the portfolio of an

Englishman captured outside Lille. The author, in London, used it to send instructions to one of his cousins based in Saint-Omer, who, under cover as director of a commercial firm and a college in Flanders, commanded a comprehensive spy network throughout France, the work of its many agents subsidised by the highest authorities in England, including the Prime Minister, Pitt, in person. A major strike was planned for 10 August.

Of course, said Barère, the CPS doubted the authenticity of this letter to begin with, but all the intrigues contained in it had been validated by events. And the medal found with the letter was irrefutable proof that the entire conspiracy could be traced back to Pitt – it bore his image and was, therefore, 'the token for rallying all his emissaries in France'. There was, said Barère, but one recourse. 'You must, on the same day, strike England, Austria, the Vendée, the Temple [where the Queen and her family were held prisoner], the Bourbons.' On the Vendée in particular, on its 'parricidal guilty populace', must be doled out 'political medicine':

Destroy the Vendée and:
. . . Valenciennes will no longer be in Austrian power . . .
. . . the Rhine will be rescued from the Prussians . . .
. . . the English will no longer occupy Dunkirk . . .
. . . Spain will be carved up and conquered by the armies of the south . . .
. . . part of the army of the interior will go to reinforce the northern army . . .
. . . Toulon will rise against England and Spain . . .
. . . Lyon will no longer resist and Marseille will raise itself to the level of the Revolution.'

In fact he prefaced each affirmation with the deadening words 'Destroy the Vendée' and ended: 'The Vendée and again the Vendée is the cancer which is devouring the heart of the Republic. It is *there* we must strike.'

The letter was a forgery. Purporting to frame an agenda starting on 'Monday 24 January 1793' (actually a Thursday) it used pages of a diary for 1791, for a 'Memorandum *commenced*' on that date, a use of the word without precedent in English; the misspelling 'arranged' which follows has no citing in the *Oxford English Dictionary* and the handwriting is discernibly French secretarial, quite distinct from the calligraphy across the Channel.

Barère's call for the 'extermination of this rebel race' save for old people, women and children, who were to be deported, and the putting to the torch of all that could be burnt in the Vendée, was adopted by the Convention and, in the momentum of that decision, it also decided to transfer Marie-Antoinette from the Temple to the Conciergerie and ordered the destruction of the royal tombs in the crypt of Saint-Denis on 10 August.

Some 40 years earlier, Voltaire, former prisoner of the Bastille, apostle of liberty whose plangent views on the Church and vested interest contributed much to revolutionary thought, had denounced clerical corruption in the memorable words: 'Destroy that infamous thing *superstition*'. The twist that Barère and the CPS for which he spoke gave to Voltaire's cry was a terrible reverse of infamy.

In that same session of the Convention, responding to Jeanbon Saint-André's gloomy verdict that 'the evil which besets us is that we have no government', Danton proposed that the CPS should be formally recognised as the nation's provisional government. The Convention refused: the CPS disposed of powers quite adequate to its task. Ten days later two military experts joined its ranks. Lazare Carnot, a mathematician of some distinction and a highly qualified and capable captain of military engineers, was in character sober, austere, preoccupied and, by force of intellectual concentration, apparently rather chilly; he was, in fact, a man of generosity of spirit. Claude-Antoine Prieur-Duvernois, known as Prieur de la Côte-d'Or, to distinguish him from his colleague, Prieur de la Marne, was a military engineer. They were drafted into the Committee specifically to manage the war effort. In this, their contribution was a spectacular success, particularly that of Carnot, 'the Organiser of Victory', who is deservedly credited with shaping the streamlined republican army and making it the best in Europe.

The CPS was never actually called the government but it effectively governed without the title for a little short of a year. It met in the Tuileries, in what had been Louis XVI's private office, overlooking a long ornamental garden, used as a public park stretching west to the Pont Tournant. Beyond the bridge lay the place de la Révolution, originally named after Louis XV, a fine open square, and beyond this the new Champs-Elysées, an area drained and planted in 1670 after

Le Nôtre's plans, and rearranged in 1770 by the marquis de Marigny, brother of Louis XV's mistress, Madame de Pompadour.

The front door of the Tuileries was flanked by a pair of primed cannon, matches kept burning, and a file of soldiers of the national Guard in red-lined, blue tailcoat uniform jackets with white facings and red cuffs, crossed white shoulder belts holding ammunition pouch and sabre, white shirt and breeches, and red-plumed cocked hat.

From the entrance hall ran the Queen's Staircase to a long corridor of communicating chambers, offices for various ministerial functionaries. A constant mill-race of clerks, messengers, army officers, politicians waiting for meetings or interview, errand boys, porters, couriers waiting, booted and spurred, ready to leave, others bringing in dispatches from outside the city, a constant tide of bustle poured back and forth along this artery of government.

In the last chamber met the CPS. A clock bearing the inscription 'clockmaker to the King' surmounted the fireplace; a rich green carpet overspread the floor; polished mirrors lined part of the walls; heavy chandeliers lit the room at night; in the centre, a large oval table covered with a green cloth matching the green wallpaper; on the table inkwells and piles and piles of paper: letters from provincial authorities, reports from generals, dispatches from representatives on mission, requests for action in a sundry multiplicity of problems faced by the drones scurrying hither and thither on revolutionary business far from the central hive, who assured their masters, however, of their tenacious adherence to the 'inflexible principles' of the Jacobins; the locust swarm of official paperwork which consumed the hours and lives of the men who came from their individual offices to meet in the green room.

Prieur de la Côte-d'Or describes a day: 'At 7 a.m. or earlier, those with least time went to their own office to read the dispatches, above all those from the armies, or to prepare particular work. [Reports to the Convention, proposals for legislation, directives to representatives, the endless correspondence.] Towards 10 a.m., the members of the Committee who were in Paris [and several never were] began to deal with current business, framing resolutions and orders . . . At 1 p.m. some of the members went across to hear the Convention's principal daily agenda. So the day went until around 5 or 6 in the evening, at which point each of us went home to dinner, or, if pressed, to a local restaurant. At 8 p.m. the session recommenced and continued into the night, most frequently until 1 or 2 in the morning.'

Robespierre was 'always present in the morning, worrying over food supplies, the war, conspiracies, generals'. Carnot and Barère were the most assiduous in attendance. They often did not go home at night but slept on a camp bed in the green room where the Committee met. Green, the most expensive colour available for dyes or paints, had long been a mark of opulence, much favoured by royalty as a mark of exceptional wealth.

On 23 August the Republic effectively declared total war in a decree which stated that:

1. From this moment, until the enemies of France have been expelled *from the territory of the Republic*, all Frenchmen are in a state of permanent requisition for the army. The young men will go to fight; married men will forge arms and transport food and supplies; women will make tents and uniforms and work in hospitals; children will find old rags for bandages; old men will appear in public places to excite the courage of the fighting men, the hatred of kings and the unity of the Republic.

2. Public buildings will be converted into barracks, public squares into armament workshops, the soil of cellars will be scraped clean to extract saltpetre . . .

And so on. The CPS to be 'charged with taking all measures to establish, without delay, an extraordinary factory for arms of all kinds, to cater for the determination and energy of the French people . . .' A sum of 30 million livres was set aside for the Ministry of War to fund the war effort. But a war to remove all enemies 'from the territory of the Republic' was clearly targeted first and foremost at various pockets of resistance which the government had lumped into the *federalist revolt.*

Lyon was under siege. On 25 August Carteaux and his republican army entered Marseille. The leading sectionaries had fled to Toulon. The representatives travelling with the army set up a revolutionary government and a revolutionary tribunal, released patriots, restored the Jacobin club and those Jacobins expelled from the administration, purged the national Guard, conscripted men for the recapture of Toulon from the federalists and levied four million livres from the city's trading community to fund the operation.

Two days earlier the English admiral Samuel Hood, whose fleet had command of the main roads outside Toulon, deeming the outlawed port ready to negotiate, offered it military protection if it would declare for the uncrowned Louis XVII. After anguished deliberation the town's administration agreed, the only major urban centre to do so. It took three more days to persuade the sailors of the entire French Mediterranean fleet that resistance was futile and on 27 August the English fleet sailed in and occupied the harbour and town unopposed. News of Toulon's fall reached Paris on 2 September.

A Conventional decree of 6 August had repudiated all measures sanctioned by the counter-revolutionary Popular Commission in Bordeaux as threatening the freedom of the sovereign people; its members were stigmatised as traitors to the nation.

This decree was to be implemented by the representatives on mission, Claude-Alexandre Ysabeau, a former Oratory priest, and Marc-Antoine Baudot, elected to the legislative Assembly when he was only 25 and to the Convention two years later, a man known for a hard, unbending line. He was no fanatic, however. His hero was Danton, whom he called 'the only man who possessed the genius of the epoch' and in his *Historic Notes*, bequeathed to Edgar Quinet on his death in 1837, claimed proudly that supporters of Danton had played a large part in Robespierre's fall. Baudot and Ysabeau were transferred from Montauban and Toulouse, now quiescent after some agitation.

They arrived in Bordeaux on 19 August; there was no sentry on the gates. They signed in at a hotel, ignorant of a city by-law which required visitors to report to the municipal Council. That evening, walking along the Cours Chapeau Rouge, near the river in the old quarter, the men from Paris, easily identifiable by their northern city clothes, were, as Baudot claimed, 'assailed by more than 800 young men richly and elegantly clothed, in the style known in Paris as square-cut, all of them armed with daggers and swordsticks. They began to shout murder and assassination at us, quarrelling among themselves for the honour of delivering the first blows.' This in wretched contrast to the courtesy they had experienced elsewhere in the south.

Abraham Furtado, a magistrate and former member of the popular Commission, was appalled at this monstrous failure of courtesy, when the representatives came to the Council chamber to report the incident. But the reception was little better there: the galleries were packed with a hostile, jeering crowd, and the two Conventionals were eventually escorted out of the building to their hotel at 3 a.m. under a continued hail of 'whistling, mockery, abuse, insidious questions, bursts of insolent laughter, in a word everything characteristic of madness and fury'.

Ysabeau described the hecklers as 'all the salesmen, office clerks, clerks of various administrative departments, joined by informers, spies, men in the pay of foreign powers, royalists and aristocrats of every stripe'. The cost of supporting this 'immense mob of clerks' fell on the Bordelais; it was they who were subsidising these 'lazy, insolent and cowardly' young men seeking posts in the administration to avoid military service. To Baudot 'they were vampires on the people' and police files show that they were all in their twenties, in minor administrative posts or, more commonly, employees of the various commercial houses of the port. These were the men who, on 6 August, had formed a Society of Bordeaux Youth 'to oppose the moral influence exercised on the people by the Jacobins day after day'.

Ysabeau and Baudot left the next day, their carriage door slashed by a sabre cut, a crowd jeering. At the first staging post they learnt that the coachman had been bribed 25 louis d'or to kill them by tipping the carriage over the Pont de la Maye on the south-eastern outskirts of the city, towards La Réole, their destination, where they found an altogether more congenial atmosphere.

Baudot informed the Convention that the popular Commission of Bordeaux 'wanted to preach a different evangelism from that of the Republic with the aim of founding its own little empire' and thereby confirmed the resounding image of Bordeaux in Paris.

When the battalions of the Bordeaux national Guard back from duty in the Vendée were not replaced, Bordeaux's loyalty was brought further into question. Would it follow Toulon?

However, on the day that Toulon welcomed the English and elements of the Spanish fleet, Bordeaux's Jacobin club reopened, having been closed since March. The men of the club were later praised by General Brune, commander of the local revolutionary army, for 'saving, all by itself, the city of Bordeaux, which was within an ace of ruin and would have become a second Lyon'.

On 11 September Baudot and Ysabeau wrote to the club encouraging its members' work and assuring them that they were 'the rallying point for all those who love the Republic'. In pursuance of their task of bringing a proper revolutionary spirit back to Bordeaux, one of the Jacobin section assemblies ruled that applause should be banned at meetings as 'a sign of joy unworthy of true republicans'.

In Paris, the urgencies cut closer to the bone. On 4 September a mob invaded the Commune offices chanting: 'Bread. Bread. Bread.' That evening in the Jacobins, so one of the revolutionary journals reported, Robespierre queried: 'Brissot in prison and his accomplices at the head of the ringleaders? All suspects must be arrested and the national razor must pass over the necks of all the guilty. The CPS has taken vigorous measures; each day that passes it will expend even more energy.' And, when the demonstrators headed for the Convention the following day, Robespierre, as sitting president, addressed them as they poured into the chamber and filled the benches: 'I call upon good citizens to close ranks around the Convention; may they combine their forces; may they have but one and the same direction. The arm of the people is raised, justice will bring it down on the head of traitors, of conspirators, and there will remain of this impious race neither trace nor vestige; the earth of liberty, for too long befouled by the presence of these perverted men, must, then, at last be emancipated.'

It was a masterpiece of manipulation, flattering their vanity, binding them to the Convention as its one hope of integrity and security, assuring them of their essential role as exterminators of those plotting against them, and promising nothing, aloof from such squalid considerations as 'Bread. Bread. Bread.' And, with polished cunning, Robespierre now removed himself from the transaction of violent measures which followed hot on this session. He resigned from the Convention presidency and took no further lead until the vengeful popular demands for the trial of the Girondins and Marie-Antoinette.

In that same session, two leaders of the Hébertist sansculotte faction entered the CPS: Jean-Nicolas Billaud-Varenne, an extreme radical from the start, was particularly virulent in his execration of the church: 'However painful an amputation may be when a member is gangrened, it must be sacrificed if we wish to save the body'; this fatal metaphor of gangrened limb spread like contagion through French politics for five years – it became a commonplace in the clubs and a sort of motto of justification for the work of the guillotine. 'The only cry to be listened to,' said Billaud-Varenne, 'is that which takes for its devices Conscience and Truth.'

Jean-Marie Collot d'Herbois had been a professional actor and thus, under the old regime, a social outcast, discriminated against by law, custom and religion. Two sallies as a theatre manager in Geneva and Lyon had hit bad luck and both ventures failed. If bearing grudges was not characteristic of all revolutionaries it certainly marked out the splenetic, hard-mouthed, antagonistic men of the Hébert persuasion. The advent of Billaud-Varenne and Collot to the great Committee was not so much a sop to the populars as a neat way of exercising even a limited control over them, by jobbing in two of their principals to the heart of government.

It was left to Billaud-Varenne to propose the measure that addressed the current state of apprehension, aggravated by news of Toulon's treachery and cranked up by popular agitation into a paralysing fear of treachery everywhere: adopting Danton's coinage of the order, the Convention decreed that 'terror should be the order of the day'. Simply put, this meant that at the head of each day's agenda of business would be repeated the pressing and continuing need for the prosecution of all enemies of the people, in whatever guise, in whatever quarter, by a policy of terror designed to flush them out and eradicate them, at the same time dissuading any others so inclined to plot or oppose the one and indivisible Republic. To this end, levy of the long-called-for revolutionary armies – an ad hoc militia – was at last ordained.

Within a few days the army in the field registered its first victory of the year at Hondschoote, just outside Dunkirk, which was under heavy siege by the English commanded by the duke of York, whose dilatoriness in the campaign was derisively summarised as marching his men to the top of the hill and marching them down again.

Carnot's presence had infused some organisational and tactical expertise overall but the French very nearly dissipated their advantage. Attacking enemy outposts in overwhelming numbers on 8 September, they expended both energy and ammunition. Recruited and resupplied, they advanced the next day, but the general in command, Houchard, more concerned with relieving Dunkirk than with the defeat of the enemy – a result, surely, of inadequate detailing of priorities in the orders he received – had divided his forces and held off from all-out attack.

The representative on mission with the army, Delbrel, conspicuous in his tricolour sash and plumes, the badges of his office, emblematic of the revolutionary cause, riding up and down the lines on a white horse to encourage the troops, sensed that Houchard was not engaging the enemy as hotly as he ought to be. In the opinion of the civilian representatives sent to the war front to inspire the Republic's fledgling armies of volunteers with revolutionary fervour and courage, there was only one way to fight, just as the Revolution had only one way to advance: attack, the hellish tactic in which (in the words of a former royal French officer who fought against the republicans) 'fifty thousand savage beasts foaming at the mouth like cannibals hurl themselves flat out on soldiers whose courage has been inflamed by no such passion'.

Delbrel urged Houchard to order his centre forward; Houchard demurred. The English general, seizing the advantage, ordered the fearsome Hessian infantry to advance, firing their trademark rolling volleys as they marched in steady line, bearing down on the French volunteers. Such a measured thrust by well-disciplined veterans, the steady volume of fire they delivered along the full front of their line, was a formidable test of nerve. The inexperienced republicans broke and began to scatter; once the Hessians had forced the breach, the entire French army would almost certainly buckle and cave in.

In the crisis, Houchard gave the command which was to prove his death warrant; he ordered the retreat. Delbrel rounded on him in a fury, countermanded the order and galloped across to the right wing to stir resistance, leaving the front-line general, Jean Baptiste Jourdan, to rally the centre. Had they then moved forward, action might have stayed their panic; instead they began to crumple again. Delbrel galloped back and confronted Jourdan. 'You fear the responsibility [of attacking on his own initiative]. Well, I assume it. My authority overrides the general's and I give you the formal order to attack at once.' Then, softening the rebuke, he added: 'You have forced me to speak as a superior; now I will be your aide-de-camp.' At this he hurried off to bring up reserves and dispatch the cavalry to round up the deserters. Jourdan fell wounded; Delbrel raced back and led a wild bayonet charge and Houchard, arriving opportunely with 500 sabres, flung himself on the enemy, who reeled before the combined weight of the French impetus.

Arraigned for treason, Houchard delivered a calm and reasoned defence of his conduct but, when one of his judges said 'Coward', the old soldier broke down in tears, pointed to his scars and slumped into lethargic indifference. He went to the guillotine on 17 November. (After his arrest, Jourdan had, with many misgivings, accepted command.)

On 9 September Danton, who had refused to join the CPS again, proposed that the production of arms be increased so that every patriot could be provided with a musket, and that the revolutionary tribunal be split up into a number of courts so that it could get through more trials. He also moved an end to permanent section assemblies, packed as they were not with wage-earners and the genuine poor sansculottes, 'hard-working men who live by their sweat', as he put it, but with low-grade political agitators who thrived on the froth of club meetings and the heady talk of the revolutionary cafés into which they slouched after the formal meetings, there to continue the planning of their radical empire.

Instead, Danton proposed that there should be but two meetings per week, all those who attended to be paid 40 sous. This would give an immediate incentive to those of the sovereign people, on whose needs and demands the Revolution was (purportedly) endeavouring to meet, to contribute – though not too extensively – to the political debate. It would also bind the section assemblies more closely to the Convention, the one conduit of official law-making, and divorce them, if only subtly, from their allegiance to the Commune, whose interests had been largely in agitating opposition to the legislature. The general thrust of the Jacobin direction of government was thus declared: away from the anarchy of the mob, useful as it had been in the isolating of the moderates, the federalists, the back-sliders, and towards a solid grip of the central authority – the CPS, the CGS and the Jacobin leaders – on the whole state.

Baudot, in a dispatch from Fontenay-le-Peuple to the CPS on 13 September, wrote that from the citadel of Blaye, on the right bank of the Gironde, 30 kilometres north of Bordeaux, and now safe in republican hands, 'the counter-revolutionaries of the Gironde' could be held in check; 'their plan,' he said, 'is plainly to deliver their city to the English; an accomplice of their treason has forewarned us in the hope of receiving our pardon . . .'

On 17 September the Convention passed a law framed by the CPS which ushered in the formalities of the reign of Terror adumbrated in the earlier decree. The Law of Suspects gave untrammelled power to the surveillance committees set up in March in every section of the nation's cities and communes to arrest anyone who 'by their behaviour, their contacts, their words or their writings showed themselves to be supporters of tyranny [royalty], of federalism or else to be *enemies of liberty*'. Thus definition of 'enemy of the people' was left to the caprice or interpretation of those keeping watch on their fellow citizens. It was, in fact, an informer's charter, but, since the Bourbon kings had, through their network of police agents, paid spies and snoops, an obsession with disaffection expressed in 'ill opinion' and 'ill disposition' of citizens, of whatever status, the leaders of the Revolution were doing no more than replicate an old-regime scrutiny and surveillance. For example, the Master Weavers of Amiens wrote to the King in May 1765: 'In denouncing, as guards of their guild, a public utterance which offended the royal Majesty, they had done only what the law required, failing which they risked being considered accomplices to the crime . . . it had been a patriotic act worthy of loyal subjects.'

As Alphonse Karr, commenting on later French convulsions, put it: 'The more things change the more they stay the same.'

Specific targets were identified, as ever: 'former nobles who have not made clear their attachment to the Revolution' and anyone who hoarded goods or cash. The charge of counter-revolution had become so vague that almost any aberration might be reckoned inimical to the safety of the people. It was a legalised expression of Robespierre's own peculiarly febrile psychosis and the rigid polarities of Saint-Just's pronouncements.

His trenchant and lucid intelligence, as well as his fiery spirit, had contributed much to the tempering of Robespierre's political acumen. One observer said that 'Robespierre had no real eloquence until he had lived in familiarity with that of Saint-Just'. The younger man's frank admiration of the Incorruptible had inculcated a confidence, a self-esteem, which enabled Robespierre to harness his formidable moralising proclivities and apply them to his speech-making. Saint-Just's character was undoubtedly a paradigm of Robespierre's ideal revolutionary, this young man whose face has 'the stiffness and intolerant pride of a man who has reformed himself and is atoning for a youthful error by a life of virtue'. A man, indeed, who, born into the chains of corruption laid on him by an impure society, had shaken them off and been regenerated as a free man, albeit in a self-fitted straitjacket of moral rectitude.

Referring to the institution of terror as the order of the day, Saint-Just read the Convention an improving lesson: 'Your committee [the CPS] has weighed the causes of our public misfortunes and found in them the weakness with which your decrees are executed, in the wastefulness of the administration, in the lack of a consistent policy and in the party passions which compete for influence over the government. It has therefore resolved to explain the state of affairs to you and to submit the measures it thinks best fitted to establish the Revolution, to confound federalism, to support and to secure abundance for the people, to strengthen the armies and to cleanse the state of conspiracies which are the plague of its existence.'

Punishment was to be an essential part of the programme and it was Saint-Just who did not shy away from the hard talking. He wrote to Robespierre: 'We make too many laws and too few examples. You are punishing only obvious crimes: the crimes of hypocrisy go unpunished. The way to frighten ill-disposed people and to remind them that the government has its eye on everything, is to punish a small offence in each department of public life . . . Induce the Committee to give special publicity to the punishment of faults within the government.'

Punishment, purgative punishment, the doctrine of the self-flagellators. 'The revolutionary,' wrote Saint-Just, 'is the irreconcilable enemy of every lie, indulgence and affectation. Since his aim is to see the triumph of the Revolution, he never finds fault with it but condemns its enemies without involving it in their disgrace.'

They were obsessed with hypocrisy, 'the homage vice pays to virtue' (La Rochefoucauld), the besetting sin of dishonesty, lack of self-knowledge, individualism, egoism, the creeping for place which had characterised the snivelling manners of court; as to the 'faults within the government', flagrant examples of them were ready to hand: the Girondins were sent for trial on 3 October. And in the Conciergerie waited the woman whom such as the Hébertists blamed for all the evils brought upon France, 'the Austrian bitch' Marie-Antoinette.

# SEVEN

# Retribution

The Provisional Executive Council, ministers, generals and
constituted authorities are placed under the supervision of
the Committee for Public Safety which will report weekly
to the Convention.

*Article II decree*, 10 October 1793

WHEN THE QUEEN was transferred to the Conciergerie prison
on 2 August 1793, the desperado who had attempted to rescue
the King from the scaffold knew that time was running out.

The baron de Batz had dedicated himself to saving the royal family
and restoring the Bourbons to the throne of France. The botched,
even farcical attempt to wrest the King away from his executors had
not deterred him and his continued presence in or around Paris was
of extreme concern to the revolutionary authorities. Batz, this man
of the shadows, a confidant and trusted courtier of the King, an indefatigable traveller with contacts – and ready and ample sources of
royalist subsidy – comported himself with almost casual disdain for
his own safety and, more to the point, for the competence of his
hunters to track him down.

Fleeing Paris after the King's execution on 21 January, he had
taken a boat for England out of Boulogne, stayed a week, returned
on 9 February and was back in Paris by 12 February. Named on a list
of émigrés, he was denounced by several people. A law passed in
March restricted the movement of émigrés; Batz returned to
Boulogne in the week of 17–24 April and obtained false certificates
from the authorities attesting that he had never quit France after

January of that year. Taking this documentation back to Paris, he persuaded the public prosecutor of the Paris department, Le Sieur Lhuillier, to establish his credentials as a non-émigré. Batz's command of the black market of certification was masterly and, without doubt, expensive.

In late May Batz mounted an audacious attempt to rescue the Queen from the Temple prison known as the Eyelet affair, from the concealing of a secret note in the eyelet of a shoe.

He had close contact with a police commissaire of the Commune, Michonis, who had charge of the surveillance of the royal prisoners in the Temple. Michonis, a member of the General Council of the Commune, enjoyed the protection of Pache, elected administrator of police in April 1793. Influence was nothing without bribery and Batz spent lavishly. The Commune, in the hands of Hébertists, had official jurisdiction over and responsibility for all prisoners in the city, including surveillance of the Queen. Outspoken proponents of radical reform against the iniquity of wealth and the rich, they were, nonetheless, eminently bribable; indeed, their willingness to turn a blind eye in return for cash was almost laughable.

Batz's plan centred on Michonis sharing watch duties in the Queen's rooms on the same night as another of his stooges, Cortez, his exchange broker, to whom he was very close. The Queen, attended by Madame Elisabeth, the King's sister, lived in a single chamber of the four-turreted Temple tower under constant surveillance with no more than minimal regard for her privacy. Batz and a number of hired accomplices would form the patrol on curfew duty and the Queen and Madame Elisabeth, supplied with large uniform cloaks, broad-brimmed hats and a musket apiece, would be taken through the various inner doors, past sentinels who had been bought, down the main staircase while Cortez gave orders to the watch to make their night rounds, and on through the main door and outside. There they would be delivered into the care of the patrol, who could then pass to the outer courtyard and thence to temporary refuge in a safe house belonging to a banker, Laborde, and onwards in a covered coach to Metz and the border with Prussia.

Concealed round the stalk of a carnation, messages of instruction were brought into the prison by one Rougeville.

A few days before the date set for the attempt, Cortez arranged with his section's police commissaire, Chrétien, an agent of the CPS, the CGS and the revolutionary tribunal, to include him in the list of captains of the detachments of guards detailed for duty at the Temple.

Michonis was at his post in the Queen's apartments when another of the Commune's policemen on duty, Simon, was handed an anonymous note informing him of the escape attempt: 'Michonis will betray us this night. Keep watch.' Simon went straight to the Commune to inform the authorities, returned to the Temple and confronted Cortez: 'I would not rest easy if it were not for you being here.' It was a gauche warning, but warning enough.

Cortez, on the pretext of hearing a suspicious noise in the street below, sent out a sentry to signal the alarm to Batz, who was waiting with the guard detachment in the street. Batz's immediate impulse was to kill Simon, but the game was up and he disappeared into the night.

Taxed with his complicity in this affair, Michonis dismissed the note as mischief. He was innocent. Besides, what had happened? Nothing. In the way of things, at least in the way of things which involved the elusive Baron de Batz, the Commune let the matter drop. There were other factors at play.

The Austrian diplomatist Metternich wrote to count Trauttmansdorf on 2 May 1793: 'I have this minute heard that the national Convention has proposed to marshal de Cobourg [Coburg] to give freedom to the royal family on condition that freedom will also be accorded to the members of the Convention, including M. Beurnonville, arrested by Dumouriez.' Metternich later confirmed this report about an abortive exchange of prisoners. It may be that the Queen's natural reluctance to be separated, for however long, from her children imperilled Batz's plan from the start and that the Jacobins refused any negotiation with the Austrians.

In the autumn of 1793, whatever plan Batz hatched to remove the Queen from the Conciergerie, the holding prison for the revolutionary tribunal in the Palais de Justice on the Ile de la Cité, this also failed, and on 3 October she was sent for trial, the same day as the Girondins.

Danton was unequivocal: 'The men leading Marie-Antoinette to the scaffold are destroying all hope of our ever coming to terms with Europe.' It is a stark measure of the widening rift between his view of the Revolution and that of the hard line, now dominated by the Jacobins but the Jacobins still paying lip service to the extravagant demands of the sansculotte agitators. Hébert, in *Le Père Duchesne*, had waged a vicious campaign of incrimination against 'the Austrian she-wolf . . . the arch tigress . . . the monster thirsting for the blood of the French'; as a queen she had condemned herself, echoing the *ne plus ultra* of Saint-Just's judgement on the King. Royalty was a crime and she had heaped upon that innate crime the orgiastic abominations of unnatural lust, treachery, the purchase of foreign conspiracy, the subversive design of making her guards drunk with the wine she kept hidden under her bed.

As an adjunct to this torrent of abuse directed at the Queen, the so-called 'madmen' of the extreme faction were demanding the full implementation of the Constitution, enjoining wide democratic changes, including a newly elected legislature. In the circumstances of the federalist revolt this was absurdly impractical but the CPS moved to counter the demand with the declaration of an official state of emergency. On 10 October, speaking on their behalf, Saint-Just announced in the Convention: 'It is impossible for revolutionary laws to be implemented if the government itself is not constituted in a revolutionary way.' The CPS therefore proposed that it should take upon itself the central control of all the machinery of state law and function; that, in fact, the government of France should be and remain 'revolutionary until the peace' and in the hands of the great Committee in the green room. This unconstituted law gave carte blanche for the worst excesses of the Terror; the men who framed it and then acted by it had too great a respect for law per se to attribute the course of action they took other than to law.

Two days later, when the news that the siege of Lyon had ended, the Convention passed the vindictive decree bringing down the full wrath of the Terror upon recalcitrant citizens:

*Article 3*
The city of Lyon will be destroyed. All buildings inhabited by the rich will be demolished; there will remain only the house [*sic*] of the poor, the dwellings of patriots who have gone astray or been proscribed, edifices employed specifically for industry and monuments consecrated to humanity and public instruction.

*Article 4*

The name of Lyon will be effaced from the table of cities of the Republic. The collection of houses preserved will, from henceforth, bear the name Ville-Affranchie [Emancipated Town, as of a manumitted slave; soon changed to Commune-Affranchie].

*Article 5*

There will be erected on the ruins of Lyon a column attesting to posterity the crimes of the royalists of this city and their punishment bearing this inscription: "Lyon made war on liberty; Lyon exists no more."

Of those areas which had risen against the central power, only the Vendée and Toulon still held out.

On 13 October Danton, sickened by the news that the Girondins were to be taken to trial and exhausted by the ravages of emotional ferment and, no doubt, horror at what the inflated rhetoric – not least his own – was leading to, this regime of punishment without consideration, wrote a letter to the Convention: 'Following my recovery from a serious illness, my doctors have informed me that to shorten my period of convalescence I must retire to the country and breathe my native air. Accordingly, I request permission from the Convention to proceed to Arcis-sur-l'Aube. I need hardly assure you that I shall hasten to return to my post as soon as my strength permits me to share the Convention's labours'. Recently remarried, to a 16-year-old girl, Louise, he had recently clashed savagely with Robespierre. When Danton called to account the activities of the CPS in the Convention, Robespierre, in his wonted style, deflected the pointed attack with a general assertion: 'Those who denounce us today will be denounced in their turn . . . those who accuse us now will one day be accused.' He capped this hanging threat with a challenge to the entire body of the deputies. Scanning the benches he declared: 'If you do not have confidence in the Committee's fixity of purpose, then dissolve it. I propose that a new CPS be elected.'

That was a poisoned chalice from which none of them dared propose a toast. 'No,' they shouted, as required. 'No. No.'

About this time Danton and Desmoulins had been walking back to the left bank from the Convention, and as they crossed the Pont Neuf the Seine was ablaze with scarlet reflected from the dying sun.

Seeing how the river seemed to run with blood, torrents of blood, Danton told Desmoulins: 'You must start writing again, demand clemency. I will support you.' *Clemency* . . . it would sound their death knell.

The Queen's trial was a showcase for vile opinion. In the course of the inexorable demolition of any defence she might offer, the vilipending Hébert accused her of compelling her son to commit incest with her after having already enfeebled his morale by teaching him to masturbate. Lambasted first by this foul-mouthed, disgusting calumny and then by demands from the jury to answer it, the Queen, who had held her revulsion in check, finally broke silence: 'If I did not answer it is because it is unnatural for a mother to reply to such a charge. I appeal to all mothers here present.'

It was the only way, and the best way, to trounce the sacrilegious Hébert, but Robespierre was outraged that the despicable man had given the Queen opportunity for this last great throw of imperishable dignity. The following night he dined at Barère's house with Saint-Just, and another guest, Vilate, a juryman of the revolutionary tribunal who had been at the trial, spoke of Hébert's intervention. At that moment Robespierre, 'struck as if by an electric charge smote his plate with his fork and broke it' and said with a fury that shocked everyone present: 'That imbecile Hébert. It's not enough that she should be a second Messalina [emperor Claudius's nymphomaniac wife], he has to turn her into another Agrippina [emperor Nero's incestuous mother] and give her a public triumph of sympathy at her last moment.' Sympathy, a dangerous thing.

Pronounced 'the declared enemy of the French people' by Fouquier-Tinville, the Queen was taken to pass her last night in her cell in the Conciergerie. A prison trusty, Barrassin, originally condemned to 14 years in chains on the prison hulks, rejoiced in her woe. 'La Capet? She was really down in the mouth; she used to mend her shoes so as not to walk on Christendom. Slept on a bed of blood, like you, dressed in a black dress all torn; she looked like a magpie, a trull, trollop. A Blue stood guard on her door day and night, outside, but he could see what she was doing through a screen with holes in it.'

He may have been peering in that last night as she wrote on a devotional book: '4 – in the morning – my God have pity on me. My eyes

have no more tears to weep for my poor children; farewell, farewell.
Marie-Antoinette.' Somehow gathering herself, she wrote a last letter
to Madame Elisabeth, whom Hébert had implicated in the lubricious
charges against her. It was now 4.30 a.m. on 16 October 1793.

> I have been condemned not to a shameful death which is only for
> those who have committed a crime but to go to join your brother.
> Innocent as he was, I hope to show the same firmness in these my
> last hours. I have nothing in my conscience to reproach me; I am
> calm. I regret deeply that I must abandon my children. You know
> that I live for them only and you, who have by your friendship sacri-
> ficed everything for us, what a plight I leave you in . . . Farewell,
> may this letter reach you safely. Think of me always. I embrace you
> with all my heart as, too, my dear children. My God, how terrible
> it is to leave them for ever. Farewell. Farewell . . .

Her husband had ridden to the scaffold in a closed coach, shut off
from the prying eyes of the crowd. She rode in the indiscriminate
open tumbrel exposed to their stares, their jibes, their mocking, their
anger and, somehow, preserved her calm until the last minute, when,
on the scaffold, she faltered, stepped on Sanson's foot and apolo-
gised. Hébert shrieked with obscene delight in the pages of his report
the next day: 'The bitch was insolent and shameless to the very end
but her legs went when they tipped her over to shake the hot hand
of the knife.' It was, he said 'the joy of all joys of the Père Duchesne
to see with his own eyes the female veto's head part company with
the fucking tart's neck'.

The chitty of expenses incurred by the municipality for the disposal
of her remains details: 'The widow Capet. Coffin: 6 livres. Grave and
grave-diggers: 15 livres 35 sous.'

Just over a week after her execution, the 21 Girondins, chief of
them Brissot and Vergniaud, who had not fled Paris, 'whose death
had been demanded so often', were brought to trial. One of them,
Jean Duprat, deputy for the Bouches-du-Rhône, had been condemned
by his own brother for liaisons with Barbaroux the Girondin from
Marseille. He wrote, and had printed for general distribution, a long
letter to him which begins: 'I have not the glory of being denounced
by Marat and Robespierre; it is my own brother who assassinates me
. . . I suppress within my soul the profound indignation at your scarcely

brotherly conduct which has penetrated me; to this unbearable feeling is added another feeling of pain which has filled me through with the opprobrium with which you are heaped in the eyes of all just and sensitive human beings.'

Fouquier-Tinville and Nicolas-François Herman, in charge of the trial, quickly found themselves under enormous pressure from not very far behind the scenes to cut short the proceedings in order to cut out the accused. The government needed to get rid of them without having to run the not inconsiderable gauntlet of Girondin eloquence. Jacobins packed the chamber of the Convention, clamouring for a speedy end to this farce of a trial of men whom everyone knew to be steeped in guilt.

After three days of evidence, the pages of the report blotted and marred with erasure, the jurors were asked if their conscience had been enlightened – that is, 'hurry up' – and the sentence was pronounced. Standing up in the dock, Valazé drew a knife from inside the lining of his coat and plunged it into his heart. Lasource cried out to the court: 'I die on the day the People has lost its reason – you will die when they recover it.'

They were taken back to the Conciergerie and, that night, held a fraternal banquet, a last supper in a large communal cell. Vergniaud had a phial of poison by him, but the dose was sufficient only enough for himself; he threw it aside.

That same night Camille Desmoulins, further and further distanced from his 'dear Robespierre', suffered agonies of remorse. In Vilate's presence he cried out: 'Oh my God, my God, it's I who am killing them; my *Brissot, unmasked*. Ah, my God, that is what is killing them.'

Five tumbrels took them to the scaffold; in one of them, Valazé's corpse. They sang the 'Marseillaise' at the foot of the scaffold, the full-throated chorus depleted voice by voice to a pitiable diminuendo as the plank swung flat and the blade dropped 21 times, parodying the lines:

> Against us now is raised
> Tyranny's bloody *knife*.

It was the first time so many were executed in one batch. It took 36 minutes to execute them all.

At Arcis, hearing what an excited neighbour called 'the good news', Danton was shocked: 'You call that good news?'

'But they were factious, they—'

'Factious? We're all factious. If they deserve to be guillotined we all deserve so. Those men in Paris will guillotine the entire Republic.'

Four days later Olympe de Gouges, a champion of women's rights, followed them to the guillotine. Author in 1791 of a *Declaration of the Rights of Women and Citizenesses*, which she dedicated to the Queen, and of a play condemning slavery at the Comédie Française; she offered to defend the King at his trial – and thereby caused a scandal. She abhorred violence: 'The blood of the guilty stains the Revolution for all eternity.' She also demanded radical interpretation of the much-bandied 'equality'. Where, she asked, was the woman's voice in politics, in government? For 'if a woman has the right to mount the scaffold she also has the right to mount the tribune'.

She supported the cause of the Girondins even after their arrest and was imprudent enough to write a pamphlet, *The Three Urns*, putting forward the idea that France should choose its form of government by referendum of the Three Estates. Before it could be published, she was arrested, on 20 July; taken to the Abbaye, she continued to write, including *Response to Maximilien Robespierre*. 'Robespierre, you have just enlightened me: you inform us that you have renounced the just vengeance of right that you have against those who make accusation. You demand only the return of peace, the forgiving of private hatreds and the maintenance of liberty. What an abrupt metamorphosis. *You*, disinterested? *You*, the philosopher? *You*, the friend of your fellow citizens, of peace and of order? I could cite this great maxim: when a wicked man does a good deed, he is preparing great evils . . .'

She ends: 'I propose you take a bath with me in the Seine; but, so as to wash you clean from the stains with which you are covered since 10 August, we will tie leaden billets of one pound or a pound and a half to our feet and we'll jump into the waters together. Your death will quiet the ghosts and the sacrifice of one pure life (yours, without doubt) will disarm heaven.'

As she went to the scaffold on 5 November, she harangued the crowd, among whom stood someone who later remarked that on this day 'they were killing intelligence'.

Three days later Madame Roland, 39 years old, a woman of striking beauty followed her. In the last pages of the memoirs she had been writing secretly, she wrote: 'I no longer wish to leave this prison save to die' and, on the scaffold, turning towards the statue of Liberty which had replaced that of the King, she is reputed to have said: 'Ah, Liberty, what crimes are being committed in your name.' Even if she did not say it, the sorry example of her death and countless others gave the bitter anecdote a poignancy of such weight as to hang heavy on every severed neck that fell after hers.

Hearing the news, her husband walked out of Rouen, fell on his swordstick and was found, slumped against a tree, with a note which ended: 'I no longer wish to live in a world overlaid with crime.' It was a sentiment that so many in France shared, of great estate or no estate at all, joined only by the common thread of supposed guilt.

Of the others who had escaped, Guadet, who had called Marat 'a croaking toad' and, when he visited the Queen after the invasion of the Tuileries in 1792, told her that if the dauphin was to survive 'you must bring him up to love liberty', went to the guillotine in Caen, the drums beating to drown out his voice. Hearing of his arrest, Buzot, Pétion and Barbaroux left their refuge with a local hairdresser, Troquart, and were crossing the fields when they were spotted and hunted down; Buzot and Pétion committed suicide and Barbaroux tried but succeeded only in inflicting a terrible wound. He was, even so, taken to the guillotine, for 'it is nevertheless of purpose that the law be executed'.

The bodies of Buzot and Pétion were later found in the cornfield, half-eaten by dogs.

Shortly afterwards Danton, at home in the country tranquillity of the Champagne, received a letter urging him to return to Paris. 'Robespierre and his party are preparing to destroy you.'

He left for the city on 17 November.

On the day Marie-Antoinette went to the scaffold, the northern French armies under their new commander-in-chief, Jourdan, veteran of the American war, delivered a timely, and resounding, vindication of the new government order. Jourdan and the CPS military expert Carnot, together with the citizen representatives, stood in the front line as the republicans drove through the siege lines of Coburg's Austrians to lift the siege on their eastern-frontier fortress at Wattignies. It was, above all, a triumph of the new warfare, vast numbers of troops directed with uncompromising determination; if such methods were prone to calamity in the hands, of, say, a general of the old school, whose will faltered at the prospect of an exorbitant butcher's bill after battle, the combination of unflinching political decision (taken by those who had little or no experience of battle) and the do-or-die fanaticism of patriotic troops primed to fight for patrie, for liberty, equality, fraternity and for the one and indivisible Republic – or death – was, or could be, unstoppable. If the CPS needed any proof that the new revolutionary order would work and was, therefore, justified *whatever action it took* then Wattignies provided it.

Before the battle, a letter from the CPS was read out to the army:

Paris 11 October 93
Republicans,
The army of the Republic has entered in triumph into Lyon. Traitors and rebels have been cut to pieces. The standard of liberty floats upon and purifies the city's walls. See in it a presage of your victory.

Victory belongs to courage. It is yours. Strike, exterminate the satellites of tyrants. Cowards. They have never known how to conquer by valour, but only by the treasons that they have bought. They are covered with your blood and still more with those of your wives and children. Strike. Let none escape from your just vengeance. Your country watches you, the Convention supports your generous devotion. In a few days, tyrants will be no more and the Republic will owe to you its happiness and its glory. Long live the Republic.
[Signed] Hérault de Séchelles, Collot, Billaud, Barère, Saint-Just, Robespierre.

Some men plucked from the benches of the Convention to assume a military role as representative of the people jibbed at the task.

René Levasseur, deputy for the Sarthe department, had the following exchange with Carnot:

Carnot: The army of the North is in open revolt. We need a firm
    hand to put down the rebellion. You are the man we've chosen.
Levasseur: I am honoured but firmness is not enough. Experience
    and military ability are needed and I lack these essentials.
Carnot: We know you and how to value you. The sight of a man

who is esteemed a friend of liberty will be enough to bring back those who have gone astray.

Levasseur: But the truth is I lack the physical powers. Look at my short stature and tell me how can I inspire the respect of grenadiers with such an appearance.

Carnot [in Latin]: Alexander the Great was small in stature.

Levasseur: Yes, but he had spent his life in camps, he had been apprenticed to arms. He knew how to manage the minds of soldiers.

Carnot: Circumstances make men. Your strength of character and devotion to the Republic are our guarantee.

Levasseur, having little choice, it must be said, accepted his commission and the next day he received his decree of authority from the Convention and the tricolour sash which was his badge of office. Within a short time he found himself in action at the battle of Hondschoote, in the front line, cheering the soldiers on. When the Hanoverians broke and withdrew with heavy losses across the frontier to Veurne, Levasseur urged pursuit, to be rebuffed by General Houchard, who replied, with that aristocratic superciliousness so hateful to the impatient revolutionary: 'You are not an army man' and stayed put. Levasseur set about restoring order to the disorganised French battalions and it was another representative, Hentz, who on 20 September denounced Houchard in Paris. Removed for his 'failure to throw the English into the sea', Houchard went to the guillotine two months later.

However, the fledgling Republic was still gravely embattled: against Sardinians of Piedmont, former masters of Savoy, in the Alps, Spaniards in the Pyrenees, Prussian-Hessian forces advancing on the Rhine, Austrians loitering close to Alsace. There was, too, the federalist revolt, yet assessment and analysis of the situation on all fronts was carried out by politicians with virtually no reference to military experts, who, in the eyes of those same politicians, were for the most part already discredited or yet to be proved, if not habitually untrustworthy.

And if the situation on the frontiers was dictated by imperatives that were not susceptible to political solution – foreign armies had to be fought – the solution they arrived at in the provinces, where the federalist forces, whatever threat they had posed, real or imagined, had spent themselves, was unreservedly political. The desk men of the green room dictated a continuation of the war inside the nation because it suited their political construct, not because it made any practical sense. Never mind that, as Danton accurately put it, they were all factions of one sort or another. Robespierre's policy was shaped round the extirpation of faction: faction was the hydra of division, its heads must be cut off with ruthless obstinacy one by one even as from the severed necks sprouted a new head: Lyon, Bordeaux, Toulon, Marseille, the Vendée.

In this he was backed to the hilt by Couthon and Saint-Just; Carnot, concentrating on the army, was rarely in Paris and Saint-André, with the navy, never. That, in itself, was significant. As early as June, Robespierre had voiced the essential of his approach to government, albeit he had yet to join the CPS: 'The people is sublime but individuals are weak. Nevertheless, in a political turmoil, a revolutionary tempest, a rallying point is needed. The people in mass cannot govern itself. This rallying point must be Paris . . .' He was in Paris: his world enclosed within the small compass of the three distances he had to walk each day: from home to CPS, to Convention, to Jacobins. A stroll to all three would take no longer than ten minutes. From here he made stipulation about all France and Europe, too.

The republican army advanced in four columns converging on the Vendée: from Sables d'Olonne, to the south-west on the coast, Luçon to the south, Thouars and Doué to the east, burning houses and granaries as they went. Like beaters flushing game from the coverts with fire, they scorched the earth and drove the native Vendeans north. Fleeing their land, their country, because they did not want to abandon the nation to which they had always been among the first, loyal, the Vendeans, armed men and non-combatants, the old, the women, the children whom the Blues hunted as spies, quit their homes and took to the familiar bocage, the wooded coombs, the tangled undergrowth, the deep-sunk lanes canopied over with trees, the dense copses and thickets, ideal terrain for their hit-and-run tactics, the ambushes which picked off segments of the advancing Blues without committing to full-scale battle for which they were ill prepared and quite untrained. The Blues, moving into the bocage concealing the elusive enemy, were jittery, terrorised by the fear of sudden attacks which melted away after one bloody rush.

On 8 October the Convention in Paris ordered the amalgamation of the two main armies, those of La Rochelle and Brest, into one single army group of the West. On 11 October General Westermann's army sacked Châtillon, and the Vendeans, some 40,000 in all, together with around 5,000 republican prisoners, drifted further north towards the River Loire, beyond whose banks lay what might pass for temporary refuge in Brittany. The presence of women, children and elderly hampered their flight to no better than a slow walk. The Blues, in pursuit, came on fast; the enfeebled rebels were herded to a stop outside the town of Cholet, some 40 kilometres south of the river and, on 17 October, forced to battle.

Denied their usual sharpshooting tactics, the Vendeans advanced in a single column like a regular army. It was a counsel of despair, a mode of fighting for which they had neither the training nor the discipline. They had never lacked courage or spirit, but their shambling retreat now turned into a suicidal onslaught. Fighting to defend their religion and their homeland, the ancient traditions and culture of faith and hearth, they launched their attack on a ruthless enemy, so-called fellow citizens of the one and indivisible Republic, directed to annihilate both.

They moved up towards the waiting Blues. It was no time to be blooded in the dreadful shocks of open warfare. Staggering under the first massed salvo of the republican muskets, their nerve failed, the line faltered and broke. As they ran, their leaders trying valiantly to rally them, to steady them into some order, one of the republican generals, Marceau, gave the command to uncover batteries of cannon placed ready to do their dreadful work. They opened fire with grapeshot, canisters packed with loose fragments of metal, which launched a devastating hail of jagged splinters into the insurgent ranks and cut them to pieces. The battle was over, and the bloody slaughter of any survivors trapped in the streets or house, or stumbling away from the ruined town, began.

Afterwards the republican commander, Kléber, said: 'They fought back like tigers and our men like lions.'

The rebel leaders, Bonchamps and Elbée, fell grievously wounded, Bonchamps mortally; what remained of their army, a terrified rout, fled with the rest of their people north to Saint-Florent-le-Vieil, where the fourth-century abbey overlooks the river.

During their retreat they had been compelled to leave some 400 of their wounded behind in the hospital at Beaupréau. These the pursuing Blues had massacred out of hand, on government orders to hunt down and destroy all outlaws. There were calls among the defeated Vendeans to serve the 5,000 republican prisoners equally, but Bonchamps, in his dying hour, intervened. 'Set the prisoners free, Bonchamps wills it, Bonchamps orders it.'

The men of the Vendée had treated their enemy prisoners with decency, to their cost. As the German military theorist Clausewitz observed, when one of the two sides fighting a war denies itself at the outset even the possibility of going to extremes in matching whatever injury its opponent inflicts without quarter, it is generally already beaten.

The broken force and all their people, some 60,000, fled north to the Loire. Leaving her dead husband behind, Bonchamps' widow wrote: 'We were obliged to follow the army, and the republicans, knowing that we could follow only one route, caused an enormous heap of wood to be transported on to the road we had to take. They then set fire to it. The whole road presented the aspect of a long avenue lined with trees felled and in flames which formed throughout its length a blazing unbroken river. We had no choice but to traverse this inferno with all our artillery at the risk of our ammunition wagons blowing up. The soldiers preceding the guns tried, as best they could, to extinguish or throw aside the burning brands to clear a space . . . but we looked with anguish at piles of gunpowder being dragged across smoking ground, blackened and starred with sparks as red-hot pieces of timber broke on to it. The passage through this hellish stretch was so terrifying that a deep and mournful silence fell on us all.'

A long string of victories had ended. The Vendeans' last great triumph was in the defeat of the feared veterans of the siege of Mainz, in French Mayence, under the formidable General Kléber. The Mayençais, marching behind their reputation as the fiercest troops in Europe, advanced as one of four columns penetrating the Vendée, burning and destroying houses, farms, habitations, as they went. The Vendeans had shrunk from engaging this vanguard of the professionals sent to fight them in the wake of the unschooled volunteers, but it was their women who taunted them with a failure of nerve. 'Soldiers of Mayence?' they jeered. 'Soldiers of faience', and, outside Torfou, the crack regiment which had endured such a scarring in the siege of the fortress town, tasted a further withering at the hands of the Vendean amateurs. But Cholet finished them.

From Vannes, far to the north in Brittany, the representative on mission, Julien, 18 years old, son of a deputy, protégé of Robespierre, wrote to the CPS: 'The Vendée is destroyed, the rebels dispersed and the leaders either killed in battle or dead by suicide. There are a few priests left in the countryside but we have the republicans on their heels and fanaticism will repent of federalism.'

If the report was accurate – and, at such a distance, how could it be? – the CPS signally chose to ignore it, as they ignored so much delivered in sackfuls to the Tuileries.

The same day as Cholet, 17 October, Ysabeau and Baudot made a solemn triumphal entry into Bordeaux with an escort of 1,650 men under General Charles de Frégeville to put an end to the city's federalist plans and herald the institution of the Terror in the Gironde. The Jacobins had already been active. On 1 October their committee of surveillance, endowed by the March decree with powers of interrogation and arrest, had sent a number of men who had taken part in the revolt to the revolutionary tribunal in Paris for trial. The day after the representatives arrived, an official announcement declared that it was time to execute those who 'wished to make a new Lyon of Bordeaux' and decreed military government in the city. The use of military tribunals, empowered to dispose of summary punishments such as were appropriate in the field, was sanctioned by the CPS as dictated by necessity and circumstance. In all operations of the Terror, the instruction from the CPS in Paris to the representatives on mission was an unspecific: do whatever you have to. There would be no redress of written evidence to cover *what* was done, only a general pressure to do *something*. As in Bordeaux, the Committee's aim was to purge the departments of all elements deemed by the Mountain to threaten the internal security of the Republic, by enforcing the Law of Suspects and the decree of 6 August against the federalist leadership of the city. Beyond that, what needed to be said? Let the law, they insisted, take its course.

The CPS had now established itself as a compact body possessed of a powerful unified will, the first time such a focused authority had existed in France since Louis XIV. For too long the Revolution had been misdirected by a gallimaufry of inexperienced legislators trying to revolutionise politics, society *and* the administration simultaneously.

The lack of experience could not easily be overcome; the lack of homogeneity could and, now, was.

At the beginning of September the CPS had sent two new representatives to Marseille: Barras and Fréron, who reported that if Marseille were left to itself, it would admit the English fleet. Albitte, who had been in the city for rather longer, was more cautious: republican laws were beginning to command respect and patriotism was reviving. He counselled more moderation. If all those who had been even nominally guilty were condemned, some three-quarters of the population would disappear, for almost all citizens had participated in the federalist revolt, whether by conviction or fear. This was a humane, even politic, assessment, and the Committee agreed that, in principle, the man who had merely gone astray at the time was not to be confused with a criminal who must still harbour anti-republican sentiments.

However, Fréron and Barras were bent on bringing the full panoply of revolutionary government home to these recalcitrant southerners: in their decree of 12 October they emphasised before everything that terror was the order of the day, 'to save Marseille and raze Toulon'. There was to be a vigorous enforcement of revolutionary laws: arsenals and workshops organised for war production, workers requisitioned, some to tear down buildings where the rebellious sections had met; iron, lead and copper to be stripped from churches and chateaux; the ashes of the comtes de Provence to be thrown into a common cemetery; dungeons and castles demolished; shirts requisitioned from the rich and stocks and goods from merchants for the immediate needs of representatives, their wives and retinues. Naval construction was to be reorganised.

On the matter of social reform, theatrical representations of a sturdily patriotic hue were to be patronised, gambling suppressed; decrees passed against prostitution, although even the Jacobin municipality softened the abrasive attitude of Fréron and Barras by distinguishing between persevering offenders and any women who, swayed by extenuating circumstances (hunger? desperation?), had been 'perhaps more weak-willed than culpable'. A census was taken to regulate the distribution of food; a tax on wealth for redistribution to patriots who had lost money under the rule of the sections; a festival to mark the overthrow of feudalism, accompanied by the burning of any remaining feudal titles.

In what became a common ploy – to convince the CPS that the slackness of the former representation had been replaced with an unyielding grip, Fréron and Barras attacked Albitte for his 'obdurate repugnance for grand measures'. In particular, Albitte had disgracefully allowed merchants to get off the hook, forever saying that 'it was essential not to render the Revolution hateful'.

Fréron went further, implying that their predecessor had lost – or surrendered – his chance for a full programme of repression after General Carteaux had entered the city. To his political master and former fellow collegian Robespierre, he vowed not to let this happen when Toulon fell. In Marseille, he said, 'Federalism is but dormant.'

The CPS was united in its aim to make a horrific example of Lyon and thereby to deter further revolt at a time of continuing military crisis. Paris stressed the need to plant 'dependable men' as the nucleus of a revolutionary colonisation to eradicate counter-revolution and to regenerate the waverers. Dubois-Crancé was relieved of his powers by the Committee on 1 October for failing to win a quick victory over the contumacious city.

Georges Couthon was convinced of the innate disposition of the Lyonnais to revolt: 'I believe these people are stupid by temperament and made more so due to the fogs of the Rhône and the Saône which fill the atmosphere with vapours which also dull thought processes.'

Couthon was sent south to begin implementation of the 12 October decree of the Convention for the destruction of the city. His reaction, faced with the reality of *doing* what they had *imagined*, sums up the wide, the irreconcilable, gulf between the theory of punishment and the practice. Couthon had no stomach for this annihilation of Lyon. He set up special courts which, by their nature as stillbirths of bureaucracy, proved very slow to operate, as he might have predicted from the slow grinding of the justice mills in Paris.

At 7.30 one morning towards the end of October, accompanied by a few soldiers and city officials, Couthon drove into the Place Bellecour, a rich district of Lyon, and, in his wheelchair, read the decree of the Convention which condemned Lyon to be razed to the ground. Making a round of the finest buildings, he solemnly struck the walls with three strokes of a hammer and declared: 'In the name of the law I condemn you to be demolished.'

The inhabitants had been given time to move but the wreckers, local demolition gangs, did not hurry. Even some Jacobins protested that this war on sticks and stones was absurd.

On 21 October the military commission, set up during the siege to identify and condemn rebels bearing arms, was now supplemented by a Commission of Popular Justice for those taken unarmed and for non-combatants.

The tangle of red legal tape grew ever more bedevilling, the bickering between legal officials as to the partition of responsibility more pained, the inefficiency of the bureaucratic machinery installed to deal with an imponderable process of justice – suspicion, testimony, evidence, trial, sentence of an amorphous mass of people tinged with a plain guilt, no guilt, some guilt, putative guilt – steadily irrecoverable.

The fact is that Couthon was unwilling to continue with the harsh manner of the decree, to abide by the simple edict of the Law of Suspects. Robespierre wrote to him on 12 October: 'You seem to have given yourself up to a people which flatters its conquerors . . . you must unmask traitors and smite them without pity . . . execute, with inexorable severity, the salutary decrees with which we entrust you.' It was all true and Couthon asked to be replaced.

Robespierre was undoubtedly prompted by the rhetoric of one Gaillard, who won rapturous applause at the Jacobins in Paris, when, on 19 October, he addressed the brothers as 'an oppressed patriot' and again on 29 October, when he persuaded them to allow him and eight other patriots to accompany Couthon's replacements to the Emancipated Commune the next day.

The replacements were Collot d'Herbois and Joseph Fouché. Fouché was cold, calculating, canny, a close associate of Gaillard, a former physics teacher, most recently at the Oratorian college in Arras, where Fouché had, briefly, wooed Charlotte Robespierre; the slur of jilting her hung about him still. Having moved to the college in Nantes, Fouché was elected to the Convention from there and had voted for the death of the King. He had already announced his credentials as representative in Nevers, not far north of Lyon, where his fulminations against the rich won the praise of Chaumette, the *procureur* (public prosecutor) of the Paris Commune, who was visiting his sick mother: 'Rich men, egoists, it is you who have caused all our ills: it is in your houses, it is in your shadowy secret assemblies that treason and crime have been hatched; it is with your gold that corruption produces disorder and the bloody reverses in our armies. You ask what reproaches we can have against you: the misery of your fellow citizens, the long, the incessant sufferings of the honourable families of those who pour out their blood for the defence of their properties, do not they lay evidence against you? Their tears, their despair which have dried up at their source . . .'

It was all sound, copybook Jacobin stuff, the sort of model answer an ex-college priest might have been able to dictate in his sleep.

Fouché and his colleague, Collot d'Herbois of the CPS, as chief agents of the Terror in Lyon, reported to the Convention on 17 November 1793: 'There is nothing innocent in this vile city other than those who were oppressed or loaded with chains by the assassins of the people.' A while later Collot expressed the view to Robespierre that the majority of former Lyonnais could be regenerated only if they were scattered throughout the Republic: 'By disseminating them among free men they will take on their feelings. This will never happen if they are left together.'

Meanwhile, Fouché and Collot established a temporary Commission of Republican Surveillance to supervise and energise local patriots, arrest priests and despoil the rich and the church and to redistribute the wealth to 'the politically virtuous poor', namely those imbued with ultra-Jacobin and sansculotte principles. This kind of action backed with violence was later called 'the infernal machine' of the Terror.

They also reconstituted the municipal authority of the Emancipated Commune with the cream of the Lyonnais Jacobins and informed them, with allusion to the theology of shared guilt, sins of fathers visited upon son, and so on, the stock-in-trade of the comminatory priest: 'You have great crimes to expiate, the crimes of the Lyonnais rebels are yours.' Whatever Couthon's reluctance to incur the wrath of posterity, Collot and Fouché had no such qualms. Collot expostulated with the reedy voice of moderation: 'Some wish to moderate the revolutionary movement. Can a tempest be steered? The Revolution is one. We cannot and we must not check its motion. Citizens, patriotism must always be at the same height. If it drops for an instant it is no longer patriotism . . .'

Robespierre had said of the Lyonnais: 'These monsters must be unmasked and exterminated or I must perish.' That he should have been instrumental in sending Collot, a womaniser, devotee of Hébert, inclined to rant, bellow and gesticulate, a man he loathed and did not trust, to wreak the CPS's notion of vengeance on Lyon, gives some measure of the cynicism which lay at the heart of the so-called purificatory programme to be carried through with the aid of what Collot called the 'national tool, otherwise known as the holy guillo- tine'.

In the last two weeks of September, following the Law of Suspects, the prison population in Paris rose from 1,607 to 2,365. The scraps of paper on which were scribbled denunciation multiplied like autumn leaves, often no better than a scrawl, the spelling haphazard, addressed to the CGS in Paris:

> I denounce civically [name illegible] for royalist tendencies.
> [Signed] Gonace (?) Molin, Jacobin for ever
> . . . It is very important that this man be arrested and his papers seized. He is a notorious counter-revolutionary, very cunning and bold.

Or, to the surveillance committee in Nantes:

> It is entirely at odds with my principles to make a denunciation, but when it is a matter of revenging outraged humanity and the viola- tion of natural rights, I believed that it was my duty to bring to your notice what I witnessed.

All this information, whether from obscure citizens doing what they perceived as their civic duty or fingering a neighbour against whom they bore a grudge, from malice, ignorance or sheer stupidity, or else the work of police-paid spies and snoops, every lead was there to be followed. Evidence – often thin, circumstantial, vindictive, prepos- terous – accumulated and was assessed, acted upon, even laid aside, forgotten. When the grounds for accusation were, in law, so vague, where were the grounds of innocence? As the poet Juvenal wrote, under an earlier regime of terror: 'Who will spy on the spies them- selves?'

The entire apparatus of criminal justice depended on this termite hill of informers; information translated from spoken or written dela- tion to formal charge; suspects arrested, very often at home in the early hours of the morning when the police might be sure that everyone was in the house – walking abroad after curfew was as good as an admission of guilt – and taken to the section police headquarters, often no more than a room in a large building. From there, the bureaucracy extended to the CGS's offices, from which was issued authorisation for transfer of the suspect to prison and, from the chief gaoler at the prison, issue of a receipt for the new detainee.

In addition to those few edifices built as prisons, some 45 premises had been taken over as gaols, excluding the temporary lock-ups at the police stations in each of the 48 city sections. These new prisons included former mansions and chateaux like the Luxembourg palace and the Grande- and Petite-Force (together, La Force); army barracks; a large number of former religious houses – seminaries and convents whose austere architecture and a large number of small austere living cells were easily adapted; a number of colleges and hospitals; and a dozen convalescent homes which acted as holding prisons for wealthy detainees who could afford to pay for a laxer regimen and better food and conditions until such time as their money ran out and they were transferred to the very much thinner commons of the main prisons. Even there, cash bought a distinction between those who had the pistoles (gold coins worth ten livres) to afford separate room, bed, table, chair and decent food and drink brought in from outside, and the unfortunates who had to make do with communal living on straw mattress and communal latrine bucket set up in the long corridors of the overcrowded, unheated, airless, insanitary detention houses.

Baron Honoré Riouffe, known as All Saints, born in Rouen, was on his way thence to Bordeaux on business, when, during the hue and cry for the Girondins, he was arrested at La Réole on 5 October 1793. Interrogated by the revolutionary committee of the Francklin section in Bordeaux, he was taken back to La Réole to appear before Ysabeau and Baudot, the representatives, who sent him with three other prisoners to Paris in three six-horsed berlines with cavalry outriders.

At meal stops, the chief of the escort – crinkly black Jacobin hair, bilious complexion, heavy moustache, huge belly, spouting Jacobin, Mountain, sansculotte jargon like a Lutheran parish beadle mouthing off about the pope – swaggered about the place brandishing a sabre, pistols stuck in his belt and his pockets stuffed full of civic certificates, no doubt. Riouffe teased him: 'Monsieur Jacobin, you, crowned with a red bonnet, by virtue of which article in the Declaration of the Rights of Man do you load a citizen of France with shackles?'

He was delighted to see Riouffe was an anti-Jacobin – it relieved him of every shred of remorse and it was the only gain to be got in any exchange with him.

One of the escorting gendarmes took the party 40 leagues out of their way to pass through Agen so that he could show off what a powerful man he was, having originally been a cook in the town. He lorded it at supper in the inn where he had been employed and, next morning, in front of a large admiring crowd, he called up two farriers to put irons on Riouffe and the Spaniard with whom he had been arrested – who had fled Spain and its religious inquisition only to fall foul of the political inquisition in France.

Riouffe spent the next 149 hours in the carriage without changing position, shackled to the Spaniard.

They arrived on 16 October in Paris, where, there being no authorisation for any of the gaolers to receive them, it took a further three hours to go from the Luxembourg to La Force and thence to the Abbaye, even the sight of which gave Riouffe the shivers, until finally they were admitted to the Conciergerie, 'this abyss of the living'.

The turnkeys sat Riouffe on a chair so as to remove his chains but the blacksmith couldn't get at them, so he was made to lie down on the floor. When the work was done, he tried to get up, but his legs were so weak that he tottered around like a drunkard.

He was confined in a dank, windowless cell deep inside the building already housing several thieves and a murderer condemned to death. Three turnkeys making a routine round later that night, with enormous dogs, revealed the size of the cell by the light of their flares: it measured 1.1 square metres.

Listening to the talk when they thought he was asleep, he learnt one of the stratagems used by thieves: to enrol pretty young men to tart on an old satyr and then open the house doors for the robbers at night.

As his confinement went on, other ploys came to light: prisoners forged assignats using a nail or the prong of a belt buckle, squeezing oil out of their salad to saturate the wick of a candle for ink and, since so much paper was of inferior quality, made from pulped rag, using strips of shirt for the paper.

In the permanent dark, the mephitic air, the filth, the worst scourge was having to sit in their own shit and piss. He wrote a poem to the harvest as a distraction:

> Harvest, whose zephyrs over these smiling leas
> Races and stirs in aimless wave and eddy;
> Ceres in her grain-stores summons your argosy,
> And solitary Pomona loads the trees . . .

He stopped eating, not because he wanted to die but emulating the Stoic fortitude of Seneca or Epictetus: by not eating he found he could rest on one side motionless for 48 hours with need neither to urinate nor defecate; food made his blood race again, anger surged back and he was, once more, in hell.

One morning, at about 11, the bolts shot on the four or five doors which separated the outside world and their cell; the heavy, iron-shod doors groaned on rusty hinges and crashed shut again; then, the rattle of the key in their door lock, the door opened and it was the gaoler, the concierge, Lebeau, to take him to interrogation. One of Lebeau's children, who had come with his father, recoiled as the pestilential air of the cell gusted from the interior of the cell. Lebeau, an old hand, prudently kept his distance.

Riouffe did not return to this dreadful oubliette and a few months later, as the pressure of numbers of political prisoners grew, Fouquier 'exiled all thieves from the Conciergerie, their former domicile, wanting to suffer only probity, talent and enlightenment; my cell was abandoned as unhealthy'.

He joined the Girondins two days before they were condemned.

They were all unaffectedly calm, hope could not touch them. Their souls had risen to such lofty remove, they were beyond the reach of ordinary consolation. Brissot, sombre, reflective, had the demeanour of a sage battling with misfortune; and if any disquiet was etched on his face, one could see that it was only for the patrie. Gensonné, withdrawn in himself, seemed scared of soiling his tongue by naming his murderers. He let slip not a word about his situation, only general reflections on the happiness of the people for which he so wished. Vergniaud, by turns grave and less serious, quoted reams of pleasant verses with which his memory was adorned, and sometimes delighted us with the last ringing tones of that eloquence already lost to the world, since the barbarians had stopped his voice. As for Valazé, his eyes had something godly about them. A soft, a serene smile ever on his lips, he took pleasure in the foretaste of his death. It was obvious that he was already free and that he had found a great resolution in the guarantee of his liberty. I said to him once or twice: 'Valazé, how fond you are of so beautiful a death and what a punishment it would be for them not to condemn you.'

The final day, before mounting the tribunal, Valazé turned back to give Riouffe a pair of scissors he had with him, saying: 'It's a dangerous weapon, they're afraid we'll do ourselves mischief.' Riouffe called it an irony worthy of Socrates; but hearing that 'this Cato of our age had stabbed himself with a dagger that he'd kept hidden under his coat I was not at all surprised, indeed, might have suspected it. They hadn't found it when they searched him as they did, frisking them like cheap criminals before they went up. Vergniaud threw away the poison he'd kept, preferring to die with his friends.'

The brothers Ducos and Fonfrède kept aloof from this stoic tableau to indulge more tender, more vibrant feelings springing from their youth, their friendship. Ducos' gaiety, unaltered to the last, their gracious spirit, said Riouffe, made the rage of their enemies the more odious. 'Once only Fonfrède took me aside where his brother could not see him, and let go a torrent of tears for his wife and his children; his brother saw this.

'"Now, what's wrong?" Fonfrède, ashamed, held back his tears. "It's nothing, something he said" . . . and the two of them became stoical, true Romans. This happened 24 hours before their execution.'

Etienne Clavière, ex-minister of Contributions, born in Geneva, accused at the same time as the Girondin deputies, took Riouffe aside in a corridor of the prison. He had just read the list of witnesses summoned against him, among them one Arthur, a foreigner who had become a member of the Paris Commune and was more extreme and sanguinary than even Hébert and Chaumette. He told Riouffe: 'These are assassins, I cannot face their fury.' He went off to his room and 'a quarter of an hour later, he was no more'.

Two others from Bordeaux, Girey-Dupré and Boisguyon, were brought in horribly bruised from their shackles, but Girey was not a jot downcast. Interrogated he replied: 'I knew Brissot, I declare he lived as honest as man as Aristides and that he died like Sir Philip

Sidney, a martyr for liberty.' Riouffe called this 'a courageous reply which disarms great souls and vexes the mediocre'.

Riouffe gathered his material from the executioner, who regaled the gaolers with stories of the scaffold. He relates the death of Sylvain Bailly, the distinguished astronomer who calculated the orbit for Halley's comet when it appeared in 1759, and who, as mayor of Paris, had precipitately declared martial law on the Champ de Mars, on 17 July 1791, when the national Guard opened fire on a huge crowd of demonstrators. Bailly retired to Nantes; he moved from there to Melun, where he was recognised, denounced and brought before the revolutionary tribunal in Paris on 10 November. When he was taken to execution from the Conciergerie on 12 November 1793, he was spat at and pelted with mud by the crowd, who burnt a red flag, the signal of martial law. The scaffold had been specially set up on the Champ de Mars, but, the mob howling protest that so sacred a site should not be desecrated, the scaffold was dismantled and removed to the riverside. The whole business, carried out in a freezing torrential downpour, took three hours, the while Bailly waited, his hands tied behind his back; intermittently showered with rubbish.

When the platform and the guillotine were finally ready for him, one of the executioner's assistants sneered and asked: 'You trembling, Bailly?' He replied: 'My friend, it is with cold.'

# EIGHT

# *The National Swimming Baths*

> The sole pardon one can extend to rebels is to kill them
> promptly.
>
> *Jean-Baptiste Carrier*

A FEW HOURS after hearing of Bonchamps' act of clemency,
Merlin de Thionville, a representative, wrote to the CPS: 'These
cowardly enemies of the nation have spared more than 4,000 of our
men whom they were holding prisoner. The fact is true for I have it
from the very lips of several of them. Some of them allowed themselves
to be moved by this incredible hypocrisy. I harangued them and they
soon came to see that they should show these brigands no recognition.
But, as the nation has still not attained the heights of our patriotic
sentiments, you act wisely in not whispering a word about such an indignity. Free men accepting life at the hands of slaves. This is not revolutionary. We must bury this unhappy event in oblivion. Do not speak
of it even in the Convention. The brigands do not have time to produce
journals. This will be forgotten along with many other things.'

Another representative, Jean-Baptiste Carrier, filed his own report.
Each of the prisoners released, he told the men in the green room
in Paris, had, expecting to be dispatched, tattooed 'liberty' on his
right arm, to show his fellow citizens that he had died a free man.

The men of the Vendée had treated their enemy prisoners with
decency, to their cost.

On 19 October the representatives reported that 'the Vendée no
longer exists'.

\* \* \*

Cholet marked the end of any possibility of victory for the Vendeans; whereas in the past they could leave the field triumphant and go home to tend their crops and their animals, now their home no longer existed: they were, and would remain, on the run. The survivors crossed the river below the abbey at Saint-Florent and so began what they called the 'veering of the north-west wind' through Brittany to the coast and back.

That terrible day when the Blues took Cholet, the people's representative on mission, Carrier, sent from Paris to stiffen the revolutionary resolve of the republican armies, had spent several hours running through the town berating battle-crazed soldiers intent on looting, tongue-lashing them back to some modicum of discipline. The following day he arrived, with his colleague Francastel, in Nantes.

The English writer Arthur Young, travelling through France in the late 1780s, reached Nantes and was astonished at the opulence of the city: 'Mon Dieu, I cried to myself, do all the wastes, the deserts, the heath, ling, furze, broom and bog that I have passed for 500 kilometres lead to this spectacle? What a miracle, that all this splendour and wealth of the cities of France should be so unconnected with the country.'

Nantes' wealth was built on maritime commerce and the slave trade which flowed into and from the city along the wide course of the Loire out into the Atlantic. Cargoes of cotton and sugar, brandy, wine, manufactured cloth, and spices were unloaded into the vast warehouses on the wharves along the banks of the Loire west of the Ile Feydeau, mid-river, on which stood the grand mansions owned by and built for the great merchant families, the shipowners, the corsairs. These grandees of the municipality in their silk suits, red-heeled shoes, tall canes topped with gold knob, the sword at their side – a privilege accorded shipowners by the King – had, for the most part, declared for the Revolution; now that the Revolution had stiffened with the ideology of the mob, the have-nots, the radicals who preached that wealth was, *per se*, a sink of depravity, the Nantais merchants would become one of its prime targets, they and the priests.

Nantes was home to a large number of religious houses, seminaries, convents, churches: in revolutionary parlance, nests of fanatics, dens of 'black animals', corrupters of morals, impenitent enemies of the one and indivisible Republic to which all civic obedience, duty and loyalty were due. All kingdoms, including that of God, were anathema, the hearth of tyranny, the despotism which had so long oppressed the people.

Through Nantes, on the night of 28 October 1793, drove a closed carriage; in it, Carrier and Marie-Pierre-Adrien-Francastel, plenipotentiary proconsuls of the central government. Their power as agents of the national Convention backed by its decrees was absolute. They served the revolutionary law without question or favour. Where others wavered, they were inflexible, entertaining no consideration apart from the dictate of the laws which governed the actions, ideas and opinions of every French man and woman. As Francastel himself put it: 'I am no more than an atom, public matters take precedence before everything.'

Curiously, this complete abnegation of personal interest, favour or opinion might also be taken to define the perfect servant, the minion at the instant beck and call of the old-regime master, a member of that underclass whom it was the Revolution's intent to rescue from the iniquities of *service*.

The representatives saw themselves, were required to see themselves, as embodying the people's will, the people's voice, the whole people, the voice of the Revolution itself. The people was, by definition, the combined mass of true patriots, the good citizens who constituted the essential spirit of the Revolution. Their representatives were, in their name, commanded and required to advance the cause of revolutionary politics in whatever city, town or district to which they had been dispatched. The charisma of their power was awesome; their authority, vested with the authority of the people's elected assembly, overrode any local authority.

Carrier added his own take on the isolation of the representative – both in virtue and in circumstance. It is as good a summation of their role as any: 'The character of the national representation deploys itself with greater force and sovereign authority when the representatives do not stay in one place, when they have no time for multiplying their relationships or their acquaintance; and when they strike heavy blows en passant, except for making sure their orders are carried out, they leave the responsibility to those charged with their execution.'

The carriage turned into a large gateway surmounted with a crucifix. A seminary for priests. Carrier, who might have become a priest himself and was now, like all extreme revolutionaries, vehemently anti-fanatic, reputedly swore at the coach driver. 'Fuck, you're taking us into a house of liars.' Self-conscious blasphemy was very much part of the vulgar revolutionary rhetoric.

In the courtyard stood some 50 men wearing sansculotte revolutionary uniform, with blue and red sashes round the waist of their breeches, dog-ear side-locks and bristling full moustaches.

These men formed the Brutus company, named after Lucius Junius Brutus, first consul and traditional founder of the Roman Republic, who, epitomising dispassionate republican virtue, country before sentiment, inflicted capital punishment on his sons for the crime of treason. Self-glorifying echoes, too, of the tyrannicide Marcus Brutus.

As the doors of the carriage opened, and the two representatives, swathed in their tricolour sashes of office, bicorn hats with voluminous tricolour plumes, stepped out, the men of the Brutus hammered the butts of their pikes into the stone paving and shouted: 'The Republic or death . . . long live the people.' Three of them, Goullin, the man who had agitated for a revolutionary committee in Nantes, Bachelier, its president, and Chaux, stepped forward to greet the men from Paris. Apologising for this somewhat insalubrious venue, Goullin explained that the day before the superior of this seminary had been served with a requisition order to put his refectory at the disposal of the Brutus company; however, the Brutus men would soon be setting up quarters in premises more worthy of sansculottes, the large town house of an American, now deputy Cottin de Melville. They moved inside.

Long tables ran the length of the white-walled refectory; a jetsam of empty bottles and glasses. The men of the Brutus had already drunk much and sat to drink more. Goullin handed Carrier and Francastel each a glass of the white wine and proposed a toast 'to the Republic and the national Convention'. One of the men mounted the superior's big carver chair at the head of the table and, to jeers and cheers, launched into a foul-mouthed tirade on priests and fanatics, the revolutionary mantra for the anti-patriots who put religion before republic. The wine was exceptional, liberated from the college cellar, fine burgundy, shipped down the Loire. Goullin remarked: 'These black animals don't stint themselves.'

Goullin and the members of the revolutionary committee had voted on 14 October to inform the citizen representatives that, reliant solely on the police for making arrests of one sort and another and for setting up a full and efficient surveillance network, it lacked muscle. What it needed was a revolutionary company of good sans-culottes – vigilantes – attached to the committee, to enforce its authority, and principally on the rich, who, in the language of the Revolution, were, variously and interchangeably, reviled as criminals, malevolents, indifferents, hypocrites, egoists, plutocrats, extortionists, from the nabobs of the Ile Feydeau to the grubby grocers guilty of flouting cynically the law of the maximum by selling merchandise at extortionate prices. These merchants were also partly, and against all the evidence, blamed for sustaining the Vendeans of the royal and Catholic army, the 'brigands'. For good measure of their morbid malignancy they were also guilty, it went without saying, of 'honing the daggers of fanaticism'.

There was, naturally, no need to search for *proof.* The culprits were well known.

Carrier addressed the company: 'We, representatives of the people on mission, approve and confirm the formation of your revolutionary company. There is not a moment to lose. The hoarders of food, the egoists, the moderates, the indifferent, are each and every one suspect. Energetic measures must be taken against these miscreants helping their comrades in the Vendée, supporting the brigands, selling them provisions at cost. Arrest the conspirators. Make a terrifying example of them. Strike every hoarder with terror.'

It was just what the men of the Brutus wanted to hear – they whooped and brandished clenched fists.

Goullin gestured for quiet and asked Carrier: 'Do you give the revolutionary company police powers?'

'The police?' chipped in one Durassier, 50 years old, a ship's broker. 'What are the police good for, except going round taverns after hours and arresting a barman serving liquor? Or arresting *the people* – domestics, workers, sailors – for so-called disturbing the peace? And if you need a policeman where do you find one? Patrolling the streets of merchants' and aristocrats' houses. The police are worthless. We're in control, now.'

Goullin then introduced the members of the Brutus company to the representatives, singling out individuals for mention such as 'the good patriot who had changed the names of his sons from André and Antoine to Pick and Iron out of the new revolutionary calendar'.

The rational calendar, invented by Fabre d'Eglantine and recently adopted by decree of the national Convention but dating from the official declaration of the Republic, had jettisoned all reference to religion. The months, named after seasons: Foggy, Frosty, Snowy, Rainy, Windy . . . were composed of ten-day decades, each day named after an item of fruit, a vegetable, an agricultural implement, an edible live creature, to reinforce the idea of revolutionary humankind in perfect accord with the works of that Nature whose perfect nurture had been so poisoned and corrupted by the chronic inequalities of despotic society. (English contemporaries poked fun at this pastoral confection, nicknaming the new months Slippy, Nippy, Drippy, Freezy, Wheezy, Sneezy, Showery, Flowery, Bowery, Heaty, Wheaty, Sweety.)

Carrier and Francastel handed each man a separate warrant, instructing him, in the name of the representatives of the people, to keep under observation all citizens of Nantes suspected of enmity, ill will or an unfavourable attitude towards the French Republic; any strangers entering and taking up residence there or seeking refuge; all hoarders scheming to withhold or fraudulently conceal merchandise and essential foodstuffs. Further, to denounce any individual implicated in conspiracy against national liberty or the general security of the Republic, to the surveillance committee established in Nantes, to any constituted authority which might have a concern in the matter and to the representatives of the people. The warrant also bestowed powers within Nantes and the whole department of the Lower Loire, to arrest or cause to have arrested any suspect individual and to make any such house visits as were judged fit; to search any cupboards, storerooms, outhouses and apartments deemed necessary and, in the case of obstruction or refusal, to employ skilled workmen to open the doors, if necessary to break them down; in case of further resistance, the national Guard would be required to afford due support and aid: those offering resistance to be seized forthwith and, as rebels to the legitimate authority, punished.

Given at Nantes, 7th day of the 1st decade of the 2nd month of the year II, of the one and indivisible Republic. [Signed] Francastel and Carrier.

To loud applause, Carrier then informed the assembly that 'as earnest of our desire to hunt down all suspects, the ex-deputy Coustard has just been arrested'.

The aristocrat Coustard de Massy, of the King's household, a plantation owner with 1,500 slaves, had served in the musketeers. Elected deputy to the Convention and, from there, representative of the people on mission, he had, whether from prudence or conviction, declared against the nobility and the clergy. However, he had voted against the death of the King and thus marked himself out in extremist circles as a detestable moderate, no matter that he, like many others of his class, had helped man the defences of Nantes when the Vendeans invested the city at the end of June.

'He was declared an outlaw,' said Carrier, 'on 18 July for ignoring Robespierre's order recalling him to Paris to answer the accusation that he had conspired with the rebels. He went into hiding and was planning to escape on an American ship with his young blonde mistress who sells tobacco in a shop on the waterside. He leaves tomorrow to face judgement by the revolutionary Tribunal in Paris.'

Voices from the floor:

'Ah, he'll get away with it – no one will testify against him.'

'He didn't get far when he flew off with his girlfriend in the balloon.'

(On 19 January 1784 Flesselles' hot-air balloon rose to a height of 915 metres above Lyon with seven persons in the car but descended after only 15 minutes, owing to a large split in the upper skin.)

Coustard, condemned by the revolutionary Tribunal, without formal charges, was guillotined on 6 November, five days after his arrival in Paris.

On 30 October Carrier and Francastel organised a revolutionary Tribunal under the presidency of Phelippes in Nantes to judge *without appeal* all persons with counter-revolutionary leanings, all persons sympathetic to or supportive of the Vendeans, all persons guilty of hoarding.

Two days later Goullin and Chaux brought the men they reckoned to be the nucleus of the revolutionary company, the ultra-reliables, to visit Carrier. They climbed the stairs to his apartments in the large Maison la Villetreux in (La Petite Hollander) Little Holland on the waterfront of the Ile de Feydeau, requisitioned by the representative for his stay in the city.

Carrier told them: 'Be sure, my boys, the Republic will pay you well. Nantes, this new Capua, is gangrened with the corruption of the aristocracy. The rich, the hoarders, the federalists have to be bled to render them incapable of harming the patrie. This we must do to consolidate the Revolution and I believe you are good fellows. I hope you will execute the powers I have given you to accomplish this.' (Ancient Capua, possibly the wealthiest and most prosperous city in Italy, produced spelt, wine, roses, spices, unguents, perfumes, bronzes; its luxury – and pride – became proverbial.)

This elite corps swaggering behind the man of power, Carrier set off to the former church of Saint-Pierre, now a Temple of Reason, through the streets of the city in which they were now his paid myrmidons, men at the heart of the revolutionary Terror. In front of the main door stood the rest of the Brutus company, smoking their pipes as a mark of their pure sansculotterie, many of them with their breeches slashed in good patriotic style, several sporting newly acquired sabres. Good men. None meaner. Such men as were needed to bring the aristocrats to book.

They greeted Carrier and the others with the customary cries of 'Long live the Republic' and 'Down with all suspects'.

The interior was littered with all manner of debris – confessional boxes seized from other churches, ready to be chopped up for firewood, heaps of liturgical vestments. Here and there workmen had set up workshops for the repair of wagons and carriages. A fire was ready for the fitting of metal tyres to wheels. The men sat in the choir stalls.

Francastel informed them that, following the defeat of the Vendean brigands at Cholet, he and Carrier had, the day before, established a military commission in Nantes, presided over by Lenoir, to deal with prisoners brought in by the army. Moreover, the CPS had sent a solemn undertaking to all revolutionary and criminal tribunals, military commissions and public prosecutors. He read out the text, signed by Robespierre, Billaud-Varenne, Carnot, Barère, Prieur [de la Marne], Lindet and Couthon.

Social regeneration has begun and is under way in all parts of France. Laws appropriate to the crisis, strengthening the health of the body politic, are setting it on its feet; no matter where they go, the guilty, fleeing in terror, meet the Republic; they cannot escape it; it pursues them, catches them and sends them sprawling in crowds under the sword of vengeance which, by these powers, you hold in your hands.

Such is the situation of a regenerated people who are shaking off the trammels of slavery: they must accept the destruction either of their enemies or of themselves. There here can be no negotiation between virtue and crime. As soon as the need to punish arises one must punish promptly. Thus the penalty which, in its principle, has been established only for example, attains its end more effectively and strikes with a salutary terror.

So, too, come on more swiftly the days of the people's happiness when the axe will rust with disuse because all men will have been made virtuous.

One final consideration must hasten on the punishment and it is a consideration drawn from revolutionary principles: the hope of a change of luck or circumstances makes a large number of people flock round criminals; often the guilty themselves admit their guilt because they count on being able to escape punishment or on the soft heart of those who have to administer it.

Purge your soul of all weakness: it is not just a matter of rising above common temptations, of resisting the demeaning snares with which the statue of justice was formerly hemmed round. Finer victories await you. May the adamant of the law wrap round your souls, unmoved by the tribunal. Have no family but the patrie; sacrifice to it, as did Brutus, your brothers, your friends, your children, if they are guilty, such is the high calling of your duty. Know, too, the limit placed on the law: here lies another reef on which ardent patriotism can founder. To aggravate the weight of the law, to corrupt its spirit by misconstruing its sense, by misinterpretation, by misusing its provisions, is a crime which calls down punishment even upon the head of the judge. The law is precise in all particulars: you are charged to apply them and them alone. If the literal sense of the laws presents a difficulty, you must ask the Assembly of the people's representatives for clarification.

In the interpretation of the law, which was far from precise in all its particulars, the final resort and ultimate responsibility was, therefore, laid on the representatives. The CPS, by implication, took no blame, present or future, upon itself.

The revolutionary company was then sworn in.

Liberty. Equality. The revolutionary committee, following the outline of powers delegated by the representatives of the people to the new revolutionary company as a body and to each individual member, in consideration that such authority could become dangerous if separated from the principles which conduce to the formation of this company, in consideration that it might be infiltrated by certain royalist lozenge-suckers or federalists who, having the right to requisition armed force might then use such force for the furtherance of anti-popular and liberticide schemes, orders as follows: No citizen will enter the new revolutionary company without first passing the purifying scrutiny of this Company and then of the surveillance committee; no citizen, besides, will be admitted without the preliminary taking and signing of this oath: I swear that Marat, so calumniated, so reviled by the moderates, by the toads of the Marais [a rich quarter of Paris] in a word by the counter-revolutionaries, lived only for the people and that he died a victim of his devotion to this same people. I swear that the revolutionary principles which he dared to profess, both in his writings and at the tribune of the national Convention, were, are and ever shall be mine. I swear that the popular societies are the true pillars of liberty and equality and that I will for ever regard them as such. I swear to denounce and to pursue to the utmost of my ability the calumniators of these beneficent societies. I swear death to royalists, fanatics, lozenge-suckers, indulgents, moderates of whatever stripe, of whatever mask, in whatever disguise they may adopt. I swear never to compromise with regard either to my family, my personal interests, even my friendships, and to acknowledge as parents, as brothers, as friends, only zealous defenders of the Republic. I swear, finally, to defend to my last breath the good order of the indivisible Republic and to submit in strict obedience to the military regulations of my company. All these conditions being met, the new member will be admitted and inscribed in the roll of the revolutionary company.

The reading out of the oath completed, amid cries of 'Glory to Marat', 'Marat tore off the traitors' false mask of patriotism', one of them marched up to the table and waved a sheet of paper, asking for quiet.

'I am going to read you,' he said, 'what Jacques Roux, the people's friend, has written in the Publicist of the French Republic: "Marat, oh thou who prophesied the triumph of liberty, Marat, whose name alone evokes courage and virtue, intrepid defender of the people's rights, surely you are still among us." We will march in your footsteps. May the revolutionary company of which we were members be called from henceforth the Marat company.'

Uproar. Jubilation. Shortly after the death, the martyrdom, of the people's saint, Marat, Roux, a former priest turned inflammatory sansculotte leader of the *enragés*, the revolutionary 'rabids', had called for a proper, a virtuous severity: 'It is only by instilling terror in the soul of traitors that you assure the independence of the patrie.'

Carrier called for silence and spoke: 'Marat is not dead. His shade keeps watch on intriguers, on royalists, on criminals and he denounces them to the people. Let us unmask all hypocrites, all conspirators, all hoarders. Let us make them pale before our pikes and sabres. May they pay with their money and with their life. Yes, at them. The time is upon us. People, be as courageous as you have shown yourself to be generous and great. The sacred fire which quickens a republican heart can never be extinguished.'

The company was sworn in.

The next day, Sunday 2 November, a party of Marats marched from the place du Port-au-Vin, on the right bank of the Loire, over the three-arched stone bridge leading to the place de la Petite Hollande on the Ile de Feydeau. Their target: the grand town house belonging to the Grou family, wealthy shipowners, who had made their fortune in sugar, coffee, indigo and cotton from the Caribbean islands. Guillaume Grou, administrator of the main hospital in Nantes, had donated a sum of 200,000 livres in 1774 to build and administer a house for orphans and abandoned children.

A chambermaid opened the main door, the Marats barged in and mounted the long staircase to the first floor, where Madame Walsh, lady of the house, stood waiting for them in the reception room.

'In the name of the one and indivisible Republic, we have come to search your house, citeness Walsh.'

She said nothing.

The Marats dispersed and began their search, gawping at the luxury in which these Grous lived: the velvet-covered armchairs, silk hangings, Aubusson tapestries, gold-framed mirrors, porcelain coffee service, glistening mahogany table and chest of drawers, marble-topped writing desk, marquetry chiffonier . . .

They found nothing.

'So, now you tell us what you've got hidden.'

'All I have is what you see here,' she replied.

'And the jewels, the silver, the precious stuff? Come on, enough pretending, down to business. We don't need to search – you've been denounced by good citizens. Come downstairs with us.'

A Marat started tapping with a small hammer at the walls by the foot of the stairs in a pantry on the lower floor. Part rang hollow. He reached for a sledgehammer and smashed through a plaster partition enclosing the space below the stairs, revealing chests piled one on the other.

'What have you got to say now? We are acting by virtue of a law which confiscates to the profit of the Republic everything we find hidden.'

'This was hidden last July,' said Madame Walsh heatedly, 'when the city of Nantes was under threat from invasion by the brigands. They would have looted everything. I took reasonable and legitimate precautions.'

'The law applies to every citizen of the Republic.'

'The law did not exist when I made this cache. I am a mother with a family, I was terrified by the threat of an army of brigands at the gates of Nantes. At the time, there was no law imposing limits on vigilance.'

'Why did you not take the partition down after the people of Nantes were victorious?'

'The threat of the Vendée brigands is still there. The law applies to those who bury their money to keep it from the needs of the state and public use. These people deprive the Republic of their fortune. But I have always given money voluntarily. You can verify that from our accounts.'

The Marats, meanwhile, were rummaging through the chests: a casket containing a diamond bracelet, rings set with precious stones . . . silver spoons, forks, coffee pot, candlesticks . . . dresses of silk, satin, trimmed with lace, embroidered cambric, silk and cotton stockings, skirts and petticoats, gowns of taffeta and muslin . . . At the bottom of one chest were seven chasubles, church linen, a missal: all suspect.

Madame Grou protested: 'They come from the chapel of Madame Grou, my aunt, who asked me, when she was still alive, to put them with the other things.'

'So, she was hiding refractory priests?'

'On the contrary: she was afraid that priests would be tempted to say Mass in the chapel in her country house while she was away. That's why she had them brought here.'

'So why hide them?'

'She was afraid that if she was found with them she'd be suspected of having Mass said here, at her house in the city.'

'We'll check to see if the church stuff appears on the general inventory of furniture in the Grou property.'

'You won't find anything there. They remain the property of the chapel which used them.'

'The facts are against you. We arrest you and impound your goods.'

Citizeness Walsh, her hands tied, was taken from her house to the Bon Pasteur prison, hitherto called the Sanitat. The Marats trooped behind with their booty, to the cheers of the crowd who had gathered to see the first of the rich fleeced by the forces of equality.

Three weeks later Carrier signed a warrant whereby 'the representatives of the people, in recognition of the diligence of the revolutionary company known as Marat, give orders for the payment of ten livres per day for the needs of each individual member. The quartermaster is instructed to make payment on the last day of each decade.'

At the time, daily earnings were fixed by the law of maximum on wages and prices at, for example: unskilled labourer, 1 livre 16 sols–2 livres; tailor, 3 livres; plasterer, employed by the day, 3 livres; cooper, 1 livre 17 sols–2 livres 10 sols. (A sol or sou equals 5 centimes; 20 sous equal 1 livre. Livre, 'pound', originally a pound of silver, derives from Latin *librum*.)

Carrier himself was impervious to the temptations of money. Born in the Auvergne in 1756, he had from early years been inured to a frugal life; he lived modestly and, like Robespierre, prided himself on being incorruptible, like the Roman republican prig Cato, unbribable.

His commission from the CPS was underlined by its spokesman, Hérault de Séchelles, who impressed on him the urgency of purging

Nantes without concern for humanity or legality. 'We will be humane,' he assured the former small-town lawyer, 'when we are assured of being victorious.' Until such time he must form no liaisons, risk no attachments with the people with whom he would have to deal; he must give the necessary job to men upon whom the responsibility for their actions would fall.

On 19 October Julien Minée, the constitutional bishop of the Lower Loire, which included Nantes, had denounced the prisoners, many of them priests, being held in the prison of Le Bouffay as being part of a plot to deliver the city to the enemy: 'they have received sharp-edged tools to accomplish their liberation'. He called on the representatives to save the people from the fury of counter-revolutionaries. The panic which had gripped Paris in September 1792 was reborn in Nantes a year later.

As soon as Carrier arrived in the city, which, in his view, was a sink of egoism, riddled with covert anti-republican sentiment, open federalism and collusion with the Vendean brigands, he set about the mammoth task of purging the dross. To extirpate such depths of rot called for drastic measures.

He secured the services of the coachbuilder Lamberty and the cooper Fouquet to adapt the local *gabares*, flat-bottomed lighters used to ferry in cargo to the city wharves from ships at anchor of too deep a draught to negotiate the shallower waters of the river. In quayside workshops near the slips, the two woodworkers cut square hatches 26 inches wide below the waterline in the deep-sided barges, then lidded them over with panels inside the hull.

On 12 November Carrier ordered the arrest of 132 rich men of the city who had been foremost proponents of the Revolution in the early days but represented a powerful body of opinion, even lingering influence, powerful enough to disrupt his radical programme of social cleansing. Not yet having the means adequate for their disposal, he sent them under armed guard, in the command of his milder colleague Francastel, to Paris, telling him, however, to tip them off into the river to drown at Les Ponts-de-Cé, just outside Angers. Francastel ignored the instruction and Carrier exploded: 'The fucking coward hadn't got the balls.'

On the night of 16 November the Jacobin club in Paris drew up a petition addressed to all the representatives of the people at present on mission: 'The Terror offers safety even to those cowardly enemies whom pity yearns to spare. So, representatives, continue, even in pity, to use the Medusa of the Terror.' (In classical mythology, anyone catching sight of the Medusa's head with its chevelure of snakes was instantly turned to stone.)

That same evening the popular society of Nantes, sister of the Paris Jacobins, set itself up in the church of the Sainte-Croix. Carrier ascended the pulpit and told the company that 'all the evils which beset the human race issue either from the throne or from the altar'. He told his rapt audience that he seemed to hear the departed shades of millions of slaughtered victims 'crying out for national vengeance on the priests' and so on.

The prisons of Nantes already held a large number of priests – 104 arrested for failing to take the oath recognising the civil constitution of the clergy.

Some hours after Carrier's republican sermon in the former church, some members of the Marat company transferred 90 elderly priests, because of their age exempt from deportation, many of them sick, from their temporary prison in a small galley moored to the quayside into the lighter modified by Fouquet and Lamberty. They told them they were being taken to better accommodation in the village of Chantenay, a short way downriver. They were led up on deck. In a throwback to an ancient privilege of perquisites accorded to executioners in the old regime, the prisoners were stripped of money and valuables, tied in pairs and manhandled down into the barge. Fouquet, Lamberty and others embarked in two-oared wherries alongside, let slip the moorings and, taking the barge in tow, headed downstream on the ebbing tide towards the estuary.

They entered the basin above Cheviré island, where the confluence of the two branches of the Loire extends some 350 metres from bank to bank. Lamberty and Fouquet's wherry came up and bumped the barge's side. Torches sputtered in the pitch-blackness, the freezing waters slapping against the hulls. With heavy mallets the two men knocked out the porthole lids; water poured into the flat-bottomed boat and rapidly filled it and, within a few minutes, the live freight of prisoners was adrift in the merciless torrent of the Loire and the first of Carrier's drownings was accomplished.

Twelve days later a letter from the representative in Nantes, read out in the national Convention, referred to 'an entirely new departure'. A line in one of the CPS registers reads: 'The priests have found their tomb in the Loire. Fifty-three others will undergo the same fate.' Hearing of this novel method of dispatch, the civil authorities in Anjou, south of the Loire to the east of Nantes, rounded up the refractory priests they were holding and transported them to Nantes. They went to their death in the dark, bitterly cold waters on 8 December.

'What a revolutionary torrent the Loire is,' said Carrier.

Wolves ranged the river banks where the corpses were washed up.

On 3 December the wife of the concierge of the Bouffay prison informed Goullin and the others of the revolutionary committee that six detainees were in league with the Vendée rebels and were planning to stage a mass breakout from the prison and then to set fire to the city.

At the order of the committee, a list of their names was prepared through the night and at 6 a.m. the next morning the local national Guard commandant, Boivin, received the list and an order to assemble 300 of his soldiers and proceed to the prison, where they should be ready to 'shoot them all indiscriminately, however the commandant thinks most convenient'.

Boivin read through the list but spotted several names of men detained for nothing more culpable than drunkenness. He made a formal protest to Goullin, who was required by bureaucratic procedure to pass it on to the departmental authorities. They, perhaps ashamed of their inertia and, anyway, caught up in the confusion and muddle between constituted authority and the limitless and ill-defined power of the representatives and his agents, congratulated Boivin on his scrupulosity and issued a covering order forbidding him to obey the order of the revolutionary committee as having no validity in law.

The next day Carrier himself intervened and rebuked Boivin, calling him a moderate. He proceeded directly to the revolutionary committee to order the drowning of all those of the Bouffay prisoners named on the list: they were guilty of conspiracy and acquisition of duplicate keys, and were ready to break out, kill the wardens and set light first to the prison and then to selected parts of the city.

On 14 December, towards 9 p.m. on a pitch-dark night, two Marats arrived at the Bouffay and handed the gaoler a packet of cord and told him to be ready for the transfer of prisoners to the offshore island fortress of Belle-Ile, where they would be set to building more fortifications. Thirty-four other members of the Marat company assembled under Captain Fleury at the revolutionary committee HQ. From there at 10 p.m. they marched to the Bouffay, where the gaoler insisted he had no written order; one of the men returned to the committee to get one; the rest of the company got stuck into some food and wine.

At 11 p.m., by the flare of torches, a posse of them followed the gatekeeper, Girardot, a sabre in his hand, along the corridors of the cell blocks. Consulting the list containing 155 names, they opened cell doors, thrust in the sputtering brand of light and told the occupants: 'Pack your things, children, above all your wallets, that's essential.'

In the courtyard of the prison, Ducoux and Joly, a foundryman, were busy tying up the prisoners in pairs as they were herded down. A final roll-call produced only around 100 – others on the list had either died or were in hospital or had been set free.

Goullin and Grandmaison, a leading Jacobin radical, arrived and were told of the shortfall. They said Carrier had asked for 155 and they would have to produce 155 because if they didn't they would be next. A full complement of names was needed, on the list or not on the list. The final tally, however, still reached only 129, of whom 34 had been convicted, 52 had not yet faced trial, 40 were due to be sent to Paris to appear before the Convention and three were recaptured escapees.

To one of the number, Julien Leroi, falsely accused of stealing a horse, a Marat said: 'You're dying of hunger in this place – we're going to take you somewhere where you'll be much better off.' Leroi, miraculously, survived the night.

As they left the Bouffay, Ducoux and Joly said goodbye to the gaoler: 'We'll be back soon to relieve you of another burden; today's lot is a nice little provider.'

The wretched procession wound its way down to the wharves, Grandmaison keeping order as they stumbled along, clubbing the hapless creatures across the head with his pistol butt and then, at the waterside, grabbing them by the collar and pushing them down into the barge, cursing them to speed things up. The barge pulled away. Joly, watching them from the quay, remarked: 'They told us we'd have a good breeze, we'll soon be there.'

Nearing Cheviré island, carpenters stove in the hatches. As the terrified prisoners tried to clutch on to the sides of the barge, to lift themselves away from the water flooding in, Bachelier, still on deck, hacked and cut at their hands and arms with his sabre. 'I was,' he said at his trial, 'intoxicated, drunk and scared, fighting to protect myself, fending off those who wanted to take me down to the bottom with them.'

Yet Bachelier, sobered, opposed Joly. Joly, who wanted to execute Leroi, who had escaped and been recaptured on the bank.

Goullin, the perfect revolutionary, rejoicing (he believed) in citizen representative Carrier's particular favour as a true patriot, harangued the popular society: 'Beware of letting in moderates, false patriots; you must only admit revolutionaries, patriots brave enough to drink a glass of human blood.'

Carrier's favour, or his capacity to terrorise them as much as their victims, intimidated them all. The members of the Nantes revolutionary committee claimed that they had been 'no more than the instruments of his cruelties and fury'; he it was who 'electrised their heads, guided their movements, despotised their opinions'. Despotised. It had been what the King did to his people but also, in one of the nastier paradoxes with which revolutionary rhetoric abounded, how Marat, their martyr hero, described the liberty which was the end of the Revolution. He called it a '*despotism of liberty*'.

On 19 December some 80 armed horsemen from the Vendean armies reported to a republican general and told him they regretted the rebellion and wished to make amends; they offered to ride as auxiliaries and to pacify their own parishes and even surrender their chiefs. Carrier, pressed to accept this surrender but baulking at what amounted to a pardon, retorted: 'Do you want me to get myself guillotined? It is not within my power to offer pardon to these people.'

Earlier that day Carrier had ordered the death of 27 prisoners, including four sisters from the La Métairie family – 28, 27, 26 and 17 – their servant, 22, and two other women, even though none had yet been judged. Jeanne Lallier, charged with informing them that same morning of their immediate execution, later said: 'The youngest of them, 17 years old, gave me this ring.' At the shock of the news, the four sisters slumped to the ground and cried out pitiably for judges at least to try them. Told that there would be none, they kneeled in prayer and, shortly before 9 a.m., were taken to the scaffold, at whose foot they waited for over an hour until, one by one, they mounted the steps to the bloodstained platform below the remorseless blade. The executioner, they say, died two or three days later from the horror, the chagrin, of having to guillotine these women.

To such horror Carrier was, or had made himself, immune. At his trial in November 1794, Renard, the mayor of Nantes, recorded how he went to see him, was blocked by a sentry who had nearly run him through with his bayonet but, pushing him aside, entered the room. In the course of their conversation, Carrier had said to him: 'My great kindness, my all too great weakness, will destroy me.'

On 21 December another 360 prisoners, victims of the 'vertical deportations', were dispatched in the 'national swimming baths', as Carrier dubbed the basin of the Loire where the lighters sank to the bottom. Within days vast number of Vendean prisoners began to arrive after their final near annihilation on 23 December at Savenay.

By 14 November the Vendean refugees had reached the Channel coast at Granville, hoping to find English ships ready to take them aboard. There had been word that the fleet would pick them up somewhere, but neither time nor place was specified. Granville stayed loyal, defended itself hard and, although part of the town was fired, the defences held.

The Vendeans, by now badly demoralised, ravaged with dysentery, fatigue and hunger, retraced their steps. Despite success against isolated republican forces, they encountered determined opposition at Le Mans: for two days, 12–13 December, the Blues vented a terrible fury on the rebels, soldiers, women, children, every living member of the royal Catholic army. The carnage in the street fighting was appalling.

When it was over and the broken Vendeans were in desperate flight, pursued by the Blues, the ground between Le Mans and Laval was covered with corpses, Westermann committing 'a disgusting butchery'; gunboats blasting at anyone trying to scramble into boats and cross the river.

Carrier received the news and reported that 'the defeat of the Vendeans is so complete that our guard posts kill, or take and lead them to Nantes in their hundreds. The guillotine is insufficient so I have decided to shoot them. I invite my colleague Francastel not to distance himself from this salutary and expeditious method . . . It is on the principle of humanity that I purge liberty's earth of these monsters.'

On 11 December he wrote two letters, one to the Convention announcing a defeat of the rebel leader Charette and assuring them there would follow 'total and definitive extermination'. To the CPS he sent a more detailed account but pinpointed the part played by women who, with the priests, 'have fomented and supported the Vendée war; they have shot our unfortunate prisoners, cut many throats, fight with the brigands and kill our volunteers pitilessly when they meet them singly in the villages', all of which justified a total purging of the soil. 'They must all be exterminated, everything burnt; truly republican soldiers can never allow themselves to be swayed by a false pity; nothing is finer than to know how to sacrifice all human feeling to the national vengeance.'

And on 25 December Francastel told the CPS: 'For my part, steeped in the duty which imposes true justice and the happiness of the people, I will always fill my mission with the same inflexibility. The Vendée will be depopulated, but the Republic will be avenged and tranquil.'

As the great Roman historian Tacitus said of the Empire: 'Everywhere they make a desolation and they call it peace.'

Because of the vast number of the accused, the process of law was parodied, reduced to what one representative, Lecarpentier, called a declaration of 'name, profession, down they go'.

By order of a commission under Antoine Saint-Félix set up at Les Ponts-de-Cé: 2–3 December – 124 Vendeans and (without judgement) 24 German deserters executed; 7 December – 69 shot; 8 December – 42 shot and 2 guillotined; 10 December – 69; 11 December – 32. By the middle of the month some 1,500 people were executed near Les Ponts-de-Cé, without judgement but with what Francastel called 'revolutionary legality'. On 23 December – 73 shot; 24 December – 75; 26 December – the prisons emptied,

203 shot. Before the end of the year this commission accounted for 1,169 victims, including 36 women. It resumed summary executions in February.

# NINE

# The Constitution of Revolutionary Government

4 December 1793
The CPS is charged with taking all the preceding measures
and of reporting each month to the Convention.

*Article 12*

CLAUDE JAVOGUES was born on 19 August 1759 into a respected
family of lawyers in the department of the Rhône and followed
them into the law. He was sufficiently esteemed locally to be made
a commandant of the night patrol in the bourgeois *milice*, the hated
civil guard of the old regime, charged with armed policing of the
community, and thus showed an early tendency to an essential
quality for the terrorist of the Republic: a cool predisposition to
getting fellow citizens into trouble. Elected to the Convention 14th
of 15 deputies from the department, he was probably a compromise candidate and had done nothing of note to date.

When he voted for the death of the King, Javogues' house in
Montbrison was daubed with blood in protest.

Appointed representative of the people, Javogues arrived in Saint-
Etienne on 14 October 1793, shortly after the fall of Lyon. The
department of the Haute-Loire (Upper Loire) fills a long, narrow
river valley, thinly populated, bounded on either side by uplands and
mountains – Beaujolais and the Lyonnais to the east, de la Madeleine
and Forez to the west, and a re-entrant south into upper Forez. Wolves
roamed the forests in greater numbers after the introduction of
restrictive laws on hunting. The people spoke a patois strongly influenced by French, a Franco-Provençal dialect or full Provençal.

In 1792 workers of the military and civil firearms factories in the large industrial town of Saint-Etienne rioted and nearly lynched two master artisans from Liège who were trying to introduce labour-saving devices in the treatment of iron. As with Lyon, Saint-Etienne's economic strength depended on the silk industry.

Three major roads crossed the department from east to west; only one major road ran north to south. Communications in the department were largely primitive: Javogues had been born in Bellegarde on the Montbrison–Lyon road, yet in September 1793, when pursuing some muscadins towards Lyon, he had to hire a guide in Bellegarde to show him the route east.

Speaking of that time of the early Terror, another representative, Sevestre, recalled: 'Each of us, in our missions, followed the impulses of our character; we had unlimited freedom of action to please or displease the people.' Not many of them obeyed to the strictest limit the austere description Saint-Just gave of the representative's role and duty, speaking of his own missions to the armies of the North: 'They must be fathers and friends to the soldiers; they must sleep under canvas and observe all military manoeuvres and training. They must not be too intimate with generals so as not to lose the soldiers' trust in their justice and impartiality. They should be prepared to listen to the soldiers day and night. They should eat alone. They must remember that it is they who are responsible for the public security and that the final defeat of kings is more important than brief spells of comfort.'

Fraternal care without fraternisation. But, in a war zone, the essential deterrent to unpatriotic and uncivic behaviour was constantly at hand: fear, in the shape of an enemy bent on blowing them all to smithereens. In the context of a battle against internal, unseen, enemies, promotion of that fear had to be by other, often less acceptable, means. The programme of state terror depended broadly on the willingness of citizens to implicate their fellows, and, in the provinces, more specifically on the readiness of the representatives to play the inquisitional justicer and martinet (named after Louis XIV's general and drill-master, Jean Martinet).

Javogues certainly followed the impulses of his own character and, in his foibles and excesses, embodied the potential inequities of a system which relied so heavily on the whim and unsupported judgement of its principal servants at the point of contact with ordinary citizens. So many of the representatives on mission left an indelible mark on the departments, cities and towns to which they were assigned. They wielded the instrument of summary justice with the same arrogance as any royal intendant and, more often than not, deserved the obloquy of those who suffered under their visitation. Whatever their inner motives, men like Javogues embodied the full oppressive cruelty of the reign of Terror in remote peasant communities whose only guilt had been geographical proximity to the acknowledged centres of counter-revolution.

Into these villages came men such as Javogues draped in the tricolour sash, wearing the big black hat with tricolour plumes and invested with immense powers: to arrest, to create revolutionary courts, conduct trials, erect guillotines; to nullify, extend or curtail the force of any existing law; to issue decrees and proclamations on any subject; to fix prices, requisition goods, confiscate property, collect taxes; to close churches and thus petrify the spiritual heart of the community; to purge any existing governmental body or dissolve it altogether and replace it with a commission filled with their own nominees. Through these Convention deputies on mission, so the theory went, all authority returned to the people, whose direct and immediate agents the representatives were. Denied all force of patronage in principle, their scope for patronage was, naturally, enormous, and tempting. Allegiance was a matter of favour, just as it had ever been. The practicalities of the job required them to depend on men whose reliability was often jaundiced by their own private agenda. Caught up in the inevitable conflict between parish-pump politics and the ukase from Paris, local interpretation of what constituted the true revolutionary spirit might easily cede more to long-standing local rivalries than any more high-minded aspiration to liberty, equality, fraternity.

Described variously as a bloodthirsty and cruel despot, an immoral thieving sot, by those with whom he had dealings in Montbrison, Saint-Etienne and Roanne, 'the most outlandish representative ever seen, an unbuttoned demagogue', his 'stupidity as insolent as it was ferocious, a cruel unapproachability, given to disgusting orgies, revolting language, incendiary threats as of a tyrant', Javogues was 35 years old, a gut forming, square shoulders, thick-set, imperious tone of voice, round head with short cropped hair, flinty, grey eyes, bushy eyebrows, wide mouth with thin, unsmiling lips; sallow cheeks framed by unkempt, shaggy side whiskers; in sum, one of those dog-like faces of which one says: 'he must be in bad shape'. A heavy drinker, a violent, choleric, excessive man. Verbal violence was a commonplace among terrorists. The foul-mouthed vituperations of *Le Père Duchesne* were the archetype. Fouché, in his memoirs, says they all ranted the same revolutionary cant and refers to 'the banal phrases in the language of the day which, in calmer times, inspire more a kind of fright and terror: the language of that other time was, so to put it, official and sanctioned'.

There is, thus, little significance in the fact that Javogues was wont to greet an unwelcome visitor with: 'Fuck off out of here right now. You're stained with aristocracy. Get the fuck out of here and jump to it.' Or in the jingle he chortled to his amusement: 'All for the pot, all for the pot', 'the pot' being his slang for the guillotine.

He was known also for his sudden rages and physical violence, which seemed to erupt from a pent-up frustration. A contemporary squib translated from the local dialect:

> Any petitioner made him see red:
> 'I'll bang you up or chop off your head'
> A fist in the face or a boot up the arse
> Was Javogues' way from first to last.

He certainly did tear up a petition delivered to him from some peasants, stamped on it and turned on them with a drawn sabre.

Javogues made it his business not only to carry out the orders he had been given, to root out and punish all traces of counter-revolution and federalism in the department of the Loire, but also saw it as his particular responsibility to impress on all and sundry, patriots and waverers alike, the awful majesty of the Convention, speaking for the sovereign people, and the CPS, to whose command he was immediately answerable and whose jurisdiction in every aspect of revolutionary law was absolute. Standing in front of a column of prisoners one day, he very publicly requisitioned a consignment of quicklime destined to consume their corpses.

Watching a convoy of condemned prisoners pass below his window that same evening he raised his glass to toast their good health.

Asked by the prison authorities for a delivery of bread for suspects being transferred to Feurs, he refused. 'What's the point? They've only got two days to live.'

He would argue that issuing an order to dig graves for those about to be executed was not an act of cruelty but merely an administrative detail; in the rule of reason, feelings had no real part.

Perhaps much of what appeared as cruelty was in fact a product of a maladroit, a macabre sense of humour. As he gloated over ropes destined to bind prisoners on the march, several of them fainted in his presence. He scoffed: 'These buggers are squeamish; you only have to wheel the guillotine in, that'll bring them back to life.' He told the judge of the local revolutionary tribunal how he would like to be in his position: 'I should love to savour the pleasure of guillotining all these bastards . . . and let not one of them go free.'

Yet all evidence points to his scrupulous personal honesty – integrity or sanctimonious rectitude? He kept receipts for all the gold and silver he collected, as well as detailed accounts, and obliged a commissioner, Jean Philippon, to return the 20,000 livres he had levied for unspecified expenses from the revolutionary committee of the commune of Chevrières.

His method was capricious: he obviously enjoyed toying with subordinates, keeping them on the hop, making play with a subtlety of terror so that no one felt safe because he was utterly unpredictable. Perhaps he saw such volatility as a necessary part of his role, if only to protect himself from any compromise by too close association with anyone. When the son of a local official was arrested for saying 'Javogues' orders weren't decrees and he shat on them', Javogues dismissed the matter – the remark was personal to him, no slight on the law itself – and ordered the man's release. Even this decision, at whim, spoke the fact that exercise of power was his and his alone.

When two chasseurs accompanying him heaped abuse on a prisoner, cut open his head with a broadsword and shot him in the leg, Javogues placed them under arrest.

This love of theatrical gesture, the predilection to strike attitudes, was not unusual in these men. The habit of power bred flamboyancy in them. And intemperance. When someone sawed through a Tree of Liberty planted in the small village of Bédoin in the Vaucluse, nearby, the representative Maignet, an apostate priest, ordered the massacre of 180 inhabitants and the torching of the place.

Albitte said of Javogues: 'I love and esteem him, but I do find he always acts on impulse, he never calculates anything, and his temperament prevents him from heeding reason at any time.'

Like all French revolutionary terrorists, Javogues knew himself to be a true patriot; thus his enemies were *de facto* the enemies of the Revolution. Such an analysis was incapable of subtlety: people were either totally good or totally bad and it behoved him to mete out punishment accordingly. He spouted the customary rhetoric: 'Blood will stream in [counter-revolutionary Montbrison] one day . . . like water in the streets after heavy rain' and 'Feurs will suffer the same fate as Sodom and . . . not one of its inhabitants will escape death'. And to those who dared suggest he acted intemperately he replied: 'What, you dare accuse me? Didn't I kill the King?'

Busson leaves a portrait of him in his account of levying revolutionary tax at Armeville:

He came into the Commune meeting room at 6 in the evening. The municipal officers were assembled and there was a large crowd of spectators. He was as grey as a Franciscan. He sat down, next to him a pretty young girl he had called in to sing a patriotic song. He demanded beer and told them to look in the cellar of citizen Vincent who was in prison. They brought him eight bottles of beer. They made several trips and he drank about 30 bottles, beer and wine, during the meeting. Javogues, the municipal officers and those who were our friends, ate *saucisson* with white bread taken from the baker . . . drank wine and beer in the face of the people muttering in their patois: 'Look, look at those bastards, all of them tight as ticks and us standing watching.'

The municipal officers and our friends threw little balls of bread at them for fun.

One of the spectators wanted to make some observations to Javogues about the arbitrary taxes he was drawing up and Javogues shouted: 'Holy fucking shit, arrest that bugger there, I'll have him shot.'

Citizeness Fressinette, an old spinster (who had led and still led an unimpeachable life) insisted that she was being taxed an amount she had no money to pay. She came to the meeting to make representations to Javogues, who screamed at her: 'You're a whore, a damned harlot, you've turned more tricks with priests than I've got hairs on my head; I bet your cunt's so wide I could crawl inside, whole.' He added, for good measure: 'All women are damned whores, damned harlots; they're our chamber pots . . .'

To the mayor's daughter, a girl of about 20, he said: 'You're a damned jade, a damned whore, but a good patriot for all that.'

He kissed the girl sitting next to him 100 times; when he fondled her breast she slapped his face hard and said: 'You're a representative of the people, you forget yourself.' He replied: 'Fuck, I tell you, there's more harm done stealing a penny than grabbing 100 tits.'

I do not believe that such exhibitions are at all the right way of regenerating our morals.

Javogues' time in the Loire highlights an aspect of the wider spread of the Terror which discredited it indelibly among people who, enthusiastic for the Revolution initially, came to see it as even more oppressive than ever was the rule of the King through his troops and agents. Whereas feudal law and dues had been curtailed within known limits and extenuated by that oddity of social conscience, *noblesse oblige*, the moral duty of the prosperous to look out for the indigent, the scope of revolutionary law was limitless and its apparent subordination of personal misery to political correctness inhuman. When a law existed that made every citizen a potential suspect, even the placid and unprovocative way of life in rural communities was open to intrusive, harrowing, merciless interrogation. The arrival of a revolutionary commissioner with orders from the grand potentate, the representative from Paris, backed by a few soldiers with itchy trigger fingers, intimidated timorous peasants as horribly as in the days of the dragoonings.

The representative Deville came to Ambierle, a small town northwest of Roanne, with an assistant, hunting for refractory priests. All five priests of the adjoining parishes had escaped. Deville threatened the villagers with reprisals: if the priests were not in Roanne gaol the next day, every member of the municipal authorities would be sent to the revolutionary tribunal. The mayor sank to his knees to beg for mercy. How could they know where the priests had gone? This law was too cruel. Deville was heard to say as he left: 'Unbelievable. Two men can make a parish tremble.'

From men like Javogues, local acolytes of the Terror took their convictions, a sort of moral carapace beneath which softer – politically unserviceable – sentiments could shelter. They all spouted the need to be pitiless for the sake of humanity, to use laws to shed blood in order to spare it: 'We cannot relax, may sleep flee from our eyelids; may laughter and games – sport and mirth – look elsewhere for idolators of pleasure; liberty and rest are incompatible until the Republic is cleansed of the last of the cat's paws of the aristocracy . . .'

These minor functionaries of the Republic, who basked in the reflected glow of power attached to the men from Paris, were not of a piece scoundrels, though the occasion for the paying off of local grudges, feuds, long-term quarrels, with which bucolic communities were as rife as they had ever been, was tempting to many of the brutish opportunists whom the Revolution released into a swaggering legalised power over the fellow citizens of their community. A mob is a mob, a genus apart, propelled by a physical and mental engine to commit acts which the individual caught up in the mass might always find abhorrent when not embroiled in it. But there is no reason to suppose that the poor, however they were sanctified by the sansculottes and reviled by the rest, were any more homogeneous during the Revolution than before or after it. Among the poor was the usual admix of good and indigent, cunning, decent, fraudulent, mendacious, naïve, salt of the earth and the essence of thuggery. The Terror did not always choose its servants: often they offered themselves, and whereas civic duty might be an excuse for all manner of brutality, it also inspired many simpler and less reprehensible motives.

A letter from a national agent of Saint-Jodard, by the banks of the Loire north-west of Saint-Etienne, written in halting phrases, unpunctuated and ill spelled – although such is a commonplace, French having so many elisions and a profusion of homophones alphabetised differently: 'Citizen being small farmer from birth and had a little education from the commencement of the municipality they nominated me lawyer despite the fact that I had never known anything in the law . . . It's enough that I am a good republikin but hearing that from lawyer they changed me to agent I understand the law even less than before you sent me lists to fill in to do with the Buttins [bulletins] of Law of the Republic these altogether are for me complete misery I don't understand a single thing I can't send you scribbles which you can't work out at all I can't find anyone in our commune to do it those who aren't obliged or not pressed to do it we do have a citizen clerk of the court who like me is a bit educated and has a little money as well as me and sick for a long time and in no state to do it.'

Marat stabbed in his bath by Charlotte Corday. '… anything was justified for the security of the nation. I killed one man in order to save a thousand … and I have never lacked that resolution of people who can put aside their personal interests and have the courage to sacrifice themselves for their country.' (Charlotte Corday at her trial.)

'From end to end of the nation there is one united cry: We want to be free.' Camille Desmoulins harangues the crowd in the gardens of the Palais Royal, 12 July 1789.

'The Aristocrat Hunt' – an anti-royalist caricature. The Revolution made hunting, formerly a privilege of the nobility, a perquisite common to all citizens.

Keeping the formidable market-women at bay – an officer of the national Guard remonstrates while his detachment of troops form a cordon round a cargo of sugar.

*Aux armes, citoyens.* The nation called to fight: recently recruited men of the national Guard of Paris march out from the city to join the army in September 1792.

Prison tribunal, 2 and 3 September: 'determined revolutionaries entirely ignorant of judicial procedures, intoxicated with wine and alcohol send prisoners hauled before them to their death.'

The trial of Louis XVI before the Convention sitting in the former riding school. Note the steep-raked benches of the Mountain.

Shackling prisoners at the infamous Bicêtre prison.

'The Republic or Death.' A membership card for the national Convention declares that its holder, F. Jouy, has been 'purged [ie examined for civic rectitude] on 27 floréal of the year II' (16 May 1793).

Small comforts – a woman bringing a basket of food supplies and a letter to citizen Aubry knocks at the outer portal of the gaol where he is held.

Antoine Quentin Fouquier-Tinville, public prosecutor of the revolutionary Tribunal.

A new peacockery: Jean-Baptiste Milhaud, deputy of the Convention, in the flamboyant uniform – sash, hat and plumes, of an all-powerful representative of the people on a mission.

BELOW Enforced idleness, wasted time and energy: some of Paris' vast gaol population at recreation in the Saint-Lazare prison.

The Incorruptible. Fresh-faced, elegantly dressed, the young lawyer from Arras, Maximilien Robespierre, newly elected deputy to the legislative Assembly in 1791, stands for his portrait.

'He carries his head as if it were the Eucharist.' The Angel of Death, Louis-Antoine Saint-Just.

'The old regime drove us to it [revolution] by giving us a good education without opening any opportunity for our talents.'
A portrait of Georges Danton.

24 April 1793. Marat is borne away in triumph by his supporters after being acquitted on charges of treason by the revolutionary Tribunal. They barge into a session of the Convention before reinstalling him as president of the Jacobins.

Breton rebels in the town of Fouesnant, south of Quimper, being marched off to prison by troops of the national Guard.

Transporting corpses – presumably casualties of rioting, self-evidently not of the guillotine.

The Pont au Change and the towers of the Conciergerie; laundry barges anchored in the river below.

The misery of retreat. After the decisive battle in Cholet, 17 October 1793, the broken Vendeans flee north towards Florent-le-Veil and thence across the Loire.

VUE DU PRÉAU DES FEMMES.

The women's yard in the Conciergerie (little changed to this day) – beyond the arcaded corridor to the right, the men's yard.

ABOVE The drownings in the Loire near Nantes – what Carrier dubbed the National Swimming Bath: scuttling flat-bottomed river wherries loaded with prisoners.

The Girondins condemned to death. Valazé prepares to stab himself through the heart.

'The zenith of French Glory: the Pinnacle of Liberty. Religion, Justice, Loyalty and all the Bugbears of Unenlightened Minds, Farewell.' A sansculotte perched on a *lanterne* gallows tramples a hanged priest and fiddles while Paris burns.

BELOW Tension and prevarication in the upstairs room at the Hôtel de Ville, during the night of 8–9 Thermidor, 27–8 July 1794.

*Here lies all France.* 'Having sent the entire French people to the guillotine, Robespierre guillotines the executioner.'

CY·GYT
TOUTE
LA FRANCE

BELOW The Festival of the Supreme Being, Paris, 8 July 1794. The Statue of Atheism goes up in flames to be replaced by the Statue of Wisdom.

In the Conciergerie, the last, dejected victims of the Terror await their doom; the poet André Chénier seated in the foreground.

The end of the Terror: Robespierre on the scaffold. Note the tilting plank to which the victims were strapped.

The rue Saint-Honoré: jeered at and taunted by the crowd, Robespierre and the others in the tumbrel bound for the place de la Révolution.

Was he a decent man? The sober fact is that the most intelligent – or sly – inhabitant of a village was in a position to dominate the rest and to wield a possibly pernicious influence. In the country of the blind, the one-eyed man is king.

Underscoring the mutual suspicions which inevitably accompanied the intrusion of the officers of Terror into remote communities was the age-old antipathy between townies and villagers. The sullen, monosyllabic villager might too readily be taken to lack revolutionary fervour; the militant terrorists, a small minority in rural areas, too easily reckoned to be on the make. The fact that so many of them *were* on the make did not help.

There was, too, the slow pace of the country, against which Javogues might froth and rage, but who knows how long is a country mile?

A Commission of Popular Justice was set up at Feurs on 7 November; for two weeks it did nothing – it had no guillotine. The machine arrived from Paris on 22 November but the place des Armes was too small to accommodate the 'national razor' and the crowds who would gather to watch it in action; the Commission of Popular Justice had to requisition part of a vicarage garden. On 29 November four rebels were executed before what officials called a huge crowd chanting 'Long live the Republic', but the machine was not working properly. Besides, the People's Avenger, as the public executioner had been dubbed, was out of practice, having had no one to execute for three years. The solemn process of revolutionary justice became something of a lash-up.

On 9 December the public prosecutor of the department remonstrated with the municipality of Feurs: it was bringing the law into disrepute. The Feurs guillotine had, that day, as on the previous occasion, failed to cut off the victim's head, being misaligned or blunt. Workmen were set to fix and sharpen the machine; without much success. The Feurs authority had been obliged to use a firing squad but the 'dignity of the People had been compromised' when several volleys were required and those under sentence had to wait while the soldiers ran around looking for cartridges.

Was this simply bucolic bumbling or sheer inadequacy to cope with the enormous, the extravagant demands of the directives from Paris? The volume and diversity of business conducted by Javogues himself, as by all representatives in the field, was staggering. Day in, day out, Javogues was trying to procure funds for the departmental treasury, authorising administrators to lodge in sequestrated houses, appealing to the population to pay taxes, annulling sales of national land made by federalist administrations, finding a successor to a hospital pharmacist, providing for the education of an abandoned child . . .

He received piles of letters from his own family asking for his sympathetic intervention on behalf of an arrested relative, for stable positions for his brothers, for advice whether to sell a house in Montbrisé (the revolutionary name for the canton of Montbrison): 'If you are plucking at so many different details', wrote one, 'you can surely do something for those nearest to you; the first need, following an ancient proverb, is to start with yourself.' Charity, in other words, begins at home.

Other individuals appealed to him as the highest authority in the department: dossiers of the revolutionary tribunal at Feurs contain 223 letters to him or on behalf of suspects and another 20 to people close to him, mostly pleas of innocence, pitiable demands for release and the *sine qua non* of such correspondence: the denunciations.

A musket-maker requires a loan for the purchase of metal, to be paid back when the weapons – ordered by the Republic – are made.

A baker seeks permission to sow grain in the drained pond of a suspect (now in prison) without interference from the municipality.

Disabled soldiers or the widows of men killed by the muscadins during the federalist revolt are still waiting for monetary relief.

Patriots must be rewarded – a gold watch 'for good and friendly services', a job for someone out of work. 'I must alert you to the intention of citizen Javogues,' writes one, indicating that he can pull the most important string of all, 'that is, that citizen Varenne should be given a position, at least as a court usher.'

The jockeying for position and office, the currying of favour with the people's representative, brought out the worst in them. One bitter-tempered, jumped-up officious terrorist, David of Montbrisé, was nick-named 'Javogues' little shark' and he was but one of the motley team, most of them married, small-town men avid for a bit of clout, seeing their chance with the backing of the all-powerful representatives from Paris. Emerging from the shallows of the backwater, they took their little place in the grander scheme of things, making a name for themselves locally in the hope that their name would be noised to the revolutionary government in whose service they placed themselves.

Some may have ardently and near selflessly believed in all this – those with limited focus and dull imagination, the bread-and-dripping clerks; others pitched in with an eye open to the main chance. Power was what counted. Whichever lot was in, savoury or unsavoury, better to join them than risk losing everything, even death.

Best, after all, to have the ear of the man from Paris and watch as others quailed at his voice. 'I know that there are among you those who have the heart of a goldsmith, who love gold. Beings untrustworthy and not fit for republican government. You will mount guard on the prisons, only that, until I arrive and you will answer to me on your own heads for all the prisoners in your care . . . remain at your post and pass no judgement lest my ears retain any more of your iniquities.'

Javogues and the terrorists of the department he reigned over believed that the justice of the revolutionary tribunal needed to be delivered with relentless speed to prove its efficacy. Javogues laid it down that 24 hours between a suspect's arrival in court and his burial was ample and necessary, to cow potential counter-revolutionaries and rid the countryside of rebels as well as to secure the release of those who were innocent and tainted with suspicion by malice or error.

Family bonds, friendship, neighbourliness, commercial ties, local nodding acquaintance, old loyalties, affiliation of shared need, all these at root compromised the absolutism of the Terror in the regions. The centre was too far away and, however diligent the representatives, their extreme application of terrorist demands would, after the first onslaught, be dulled by the intransigence of local custom and unwillingness to pursue militancy for long, if at all. Overheated heads cooled; Jacobinism might be kept fervently alive in Paris, close to the organs of power, but it was not so easily sustained in the provinces, certainly not in the village halls taken over as club premises wherein local disputes might always supersede the exigencies of pure revolutionary principles. As Swift wrote, not long before, of the gulf between capital and outlying corners: 'It is the folly of too many to mistake the echo of a London coffee-house for the voice of the kingdom.'

Local ties could bind terrorist groups into formidable solidarity; the revolutionary commission at Noirétable was called a 'family tribunal' because so many members were related. Club, family, friends dividing the community: for the Terror as against it; the same groups meeting in the same favourite cafés where they drank together before the Terror. One suspect from Montbrisé pleaded civism on the grounds that he had a paper signed by several terrorists which alleged, as a weighty argument in his favour, that he frequented Simonin's café with other clubbists, not the Café des Suisses.

(After the fall of Robespierre, Javogues did not surrender his extreme Jacobin affiliations. He kept his sash and plumes of the Conventional 'as a religious devotee might carry a relic' and said they were all he had left and he would carry them till he died. He was one of a small group of republican militants, including at least one former terrorist from Lyon, who walked into an ambush prepared by government troops in October 1796. Javogues escaped but was arrested next morning at an inn in Montrouge, just south of Paris. Condemned to death by a military council on 19 October, he was shot the following day in company with others. *La Gazette française* reported: 'They all died like cowards. Only Javogues sang as they went.' The 'Marseillaise'.)

In Nantes in the late autumn of 1793, the Abbé Julien Landeau of Saint-Lyphard, a town in the marshlands north of Saint-Nazaire, taken with others to the wharfside one night, was tied to an old monk and lowered into the lighter; once there, the boat cast off into the stream of the Loire, Landeau found that the rope tying him to the old man was loose. He worked at the knots, untied their hands; out in midstream, in the pitch-dark lit only by the flare of pitch torches, he heard the dull thud of mallet blows opening the ports; instantly, water started pouring in, the victims, maddened with terror, struggling to stay afloat, crying out. Landeau, a powerful swimmer, kicked away from the side of the sinking boat, took the old man in tow, fought his way through the dreadful turmoil of bodies half-submerged, drowning, flailing in despair. Uncertain where they were in the murky darkness, he breasted the surface of the water and saw men on boats alongside the lighters pushing priests down into the water with boat hooks, beating them with oars. He swam away with his right arm, supporting the old man in his left hand, out into the open torrent of river. The water was icy, the weight of the old man dragging at his depleted energies, his lungs rasping as he gulped for air, the effort merely to keep his head above water taking its toll. The old priest urged him to let him go and save himself. His strength was failing; the old man, stiff with cold, hung inert, a dead weight. Suddenly he had no more life in him, perished with the cold and shock: the clutching hands unclasped, Landeau let him sink. Floating briefly on his back to rest, he saw the silhouette of men aboard a boat chatting. He swam across and begged for help.

'A priest they've just thrown in to drown,' said one of the men.

'Black cowl? Plenty more where he came from.'

'Friends,' said the first man, 'if he were an enemy's dog we wouldn't let him die, let's rescue him.'

They pulled him into the boat, half dead and shivering uncontrollably with cold. There was some argument as to what to do with him. Finally, it was agreed: they pulled in to the right bank, left Landeau on the sandy beach and rowed away. Landeau lay some time in the pitch-darkness and recovered something of his strength. When he got up and looked around, he found he was near Roche Maurice, about five kilometres downstream from Nantes. He approached a hovel, knocked; no one opened; at another hovel, the peasants gave him food, clothes, a warming by a good fire. At dawn they told him how frightened they were – the surrounding villages were infested with patriots: the first house he had tried the night before belonged to one of the most ardent in the area.

They assured him that he must leave but they wouldn't abandon him. Their daughter took milk to Nantes each day and she would ask a Madame Lamy, who, like the Abbé, came from Queninen, a hamlet on the edge of the salt marshes near Guérande, to help. The peasants fitted him out in a pair of breeches, jacket, clogs, gave him a basketful of vegetables and bid him adieu. With who can guess what feelings, he set out on the road back to Nantes.

He made it to Madame Lamy's house at Port-au-Vin and from his refuge there sent a letter to one of his brothers at Queninen. The brother walked to Nantes to fetch him, wearing the broad hat, white jacket and loose breeches of the marshmen of the peninsula, their home ground. He brought a similar outfit for Landeau. As they approached a guardhouse on the city outskirts, Landeau was stricken with a violent trembling which he simply couldn't check. His brother pretended he was drunk – cursed him, cut his mule with a stick on its hindquarters and set the beast off at a trot.

Landeau spent the winter at Queninen alternating between two hiding places: one, in his brother's house under a truss of hay, another in a bosky hollow of the village. At night, he travelled the countryside, bringing the consolations of his ministry to the faithful. He kept a record of baptisms, scratching names with a nail on a brass plate which he buried in a field to be recovered in happier days.

Of the humble people eking out an existence in the remote marshlands, Madame la marquise de Rochejaquelin, wife of the Vendean leader, wrote in her memoirs: 'No one in that secluded spot had any idea of what was going on in France.' Yet, however far beyond oblivion lay the rest of the country, the local populace of the Vendée lived in constant in terror of the Blues. Landeau was often on the verge of being taken.

One evening at the village of Guérande, as the peasants gathered in his brother's house for Mass, he set sacred vessels using a table as an altar, footsteps were heard outside. It was a patrol of national Guardsmen. Someone must have talked. As they surrounded the house, the peasants stowed everything out of sight, bundled the Abbé out to the barn and hid him under the hay. The soldiers broke down the door and stormed into the house, shouting for them to give up the 'skullcapped gentleman' they were hiding. They rapped the walls with musket butts, rummaged through the stable, threatening to burn everything. One spotted the chalice ill hidden on the top shelf of a dresser. He said nothing, and surreptitiously tipped it behind other objects with the muzzle of his firearm.

Meanwhile, other Blues were in the barn sounding the forage and hay with their long bayonets. One of them lit on the priest but whispered, 'Don't move' and passed on among the bundles of hay as if pursuing his search, then went back outside and assured his comrades there was nobody there.

Landeau eventually decided to go back to his own parish of Saint-Lyphard; two local brothers, Charles and Jean Deniaud, offered to hide him in the little town on the fringes of the Grande Brière, a vast expanse of marsh beneath which lay a submerged oak forest, once sacred to the Druids; its trees still stand unseen, buried in slime up to their topmost boughs, bent, some say, by the west wind which had not blown on them for 1,000 years. Two days each year the Briérons were allowed by ancient right to dig out trunks of the bog oak, old and hard as ebony. One week per year, they were also permitted to dig peat from the marsh which they sold as turfs, a fuel used throughout Lower Brittany. The rest of the time, they fished for leeches, eels, pike or reared geese and cattle. In fine weather, the soil dries and offers grazing. Still, any stranger would run the risk of drowning if walking on it; the strands of dry ground are narrow and erratic, it is impossible for the untutored eye to see what is solid ground and what marsh, but the locals know every path.

The Blues dared not venture here and, 60 metres from the edge, a man could lie on the grass and be invisible. In these marshes the Abbé Goujon, Landeau's curate, who had stayed on as vicar of Saint-Lyphard, had evaded capture. Landeau joined him. Whenever a patrol approached, they took to the wetlands. One of their parishioners, Jean Lebeau, who had sent his son to fight in the Vendean army, acted as their guide, going ahead to knock at the window of a house and ask: 'Are there any strange sheep in the fold?' The code phrase. Answered 'yes' or 'no', as the case might be, they found lodging or not for the night in houses thatched with rushes from the marsh and embellished up to the roof ridge with bird's vine, a pretty plant with pink cups. [Landeau's own words]

(Landeau's health, broken down by incessant anxiety and physical misery and nights spent exposed in the cold, damp marshes, collapsed, and he died in Charles Deniaud's house on 24 June 1799, aged 55. New regulations said that his remains must be carried to Guérande, his home parish of Kernogan being in its district, and thrown into a common ditch. His parishioners, however, were determined that he should be buried in the cemetery in Saint-Lyphard; they carried his corpse by night to the hamlet of Crutier, scarcely 50 metres from Kernogan but part of the commune of Saint-Lyphard, and laid the corpse in the bed of an old man who had just died; him they carried off to Kernogan to lay in the common ditch. Guérande got a body and the cemetery of Saint-Lyphard received the body of its faithful priest who had survived Carrier's drownings and continued his ministry with such selfless devotion.)

Fouché's brief sojourn as representative of the people on mission in the Nièvre was marked by a brisk and furious bout of dechristianising, a particular enthusiasm of the sansculotte faction in Paris, which saw the eradication of all trace of sacerdotal influence and religious superstition as integral to the purity of the Revolution. On 10 November 1793, in the cathedral of Notre Dame, the Paris Commune authorities held a Festival of Reason, a public ceremony in the building which was now renamed a Temple of Reason: at the altar end stood a massive paper- and linen-covered wood-framed Mountain, a sort of obelisk to the new force of enlightenment, encircled by a parade of young patriotic vestals in virginal white, each wearing a crown of oak leaves. At the climax of the ceremony, solemn republican music, patriotic hymns and exhortations to revolutionary virtue, red bonnets and carmagnoles in place of priestly skullcaps and cassocks, a figure representing Liberty (played by Momoro's wife, an actress from the Opéra) emerged from the Mountain. Dressed in white, red bonnet and the sansculotte emblematic pike and all, she made obeisance to the sacred flame of Reason and then placed herself on a throne covered with plaited grass, on a bank of nature's wild bounty, whatever plants and flowers the season could muster. It was, said the official recorder, 'a masterpiece of nature'.

The congregation capered round the sanctuary of Reason, bawling out the republican hymn, the 'Carmagnole', men without breeches, women with bare neck and breasts, said one shocked bystander.

Two days later one of the city sections, Gravilliers, round the Temple tower, fanatical supporters of the extremist leader Jacques Roux, sent a deputation to the Convention festooned with sacred linen and cloths and loaded with 'ornaments from churches in the district, spoils taken from the superstitious credulity of our forefathers and repossessed by the reason of free men'; they announced that all churches in the section had been closed. However, the rabid anticlericalism of the Jacobin-dominated Paris mob was not widely shared. In the Brie region, for example, in the second week of December, crowds of peasants sacked the local Jacobin club, chanting, reminiscent of the Vendean rebels: 'Long live the Catholic religion, we want our priests, we want the Mass on Sundays and Holy Days.' The advent of the new republican calendar, with its strictly rational ten-day weeks and one rest day, the *décadi*, replacing Sunday, merely emphasised the soulless nature of existence, the endless slog of work, patriotic duty, fraternal banquets at which everyone had to mind their tongue or else be denounced for as small – but great – a crime as 'lack of enthusiasm' – and a vacuum of emotional and spiritual support in the vast wash of requisite civic 'virtue'.

Fouché, playing the extreme popular card, focused particularly on cemeteries, from which he removed all pious objects and mottoes; above the gates he had posted new signs proclaiming that 'Death is but an eternal sleep'. It accorded well enough with the trimmed-down philosophy of the Revolution; it did little to appease the profound anxieties and fears of people with an atavistic need for consolation, however committed they might be to the practical tenets of the new order. They wanted spiritual bread as well as the real stuff to fill their bellies. Grub first, ethics later. It was not a need which the intelligent cynics and rhetoricians of Paris could assuage.

Undoubtedly Fouché was playing the revolutionary game for all he was worth. Arrived in Lyon, he inaugurated a systematic removal of all Christian emblems and icons and, on the same day as the celebration in Notre Dame, he oversaw a solemn-ridiculous memorial parade for Chalier through Lyon.

After a cannon salute, the cortège moved off, led by a giant of a man with an axe balanced over his shoulder; on a catafalque, a coffin containing Chalier's body, the centrepiece of the procession (his head later went to Paris to be laid to rest, as had Marat's, in the Panthéon). Behind him, a detachment of infantry and young girls wearing floral crowns, a small group of men carrying a bust of Chalier, the town band, funeral music and a local choir, singing dirges. The model was the parades honouring the memory of Le Peletier de Saint-Fargeau and Marat. But, bringing up the rear, walked a sansculotte wearing a mitre and a cross, leading an ass draped with episcopal vestments belonging to Lamourette, the constitutional bishop, his mitre, a chalice slung round its neck and, tied to its tail, a Bible and a missal. Another sansculotte trailed a royal fleur-de-lis ensign in the mud. Behind the procession walked the three representatives on mission, Fouché, Collot d'Herbois and Laporte, swathed in their tricolour sashes of office.

The procession arrived at the place des Terreaux; here they sang a hymn to the glory of Chalier, and Fouché lambasted the martyr's murderers: 'Chalier, you are no more . . . Martyr of liberty, wicked men have made sacrifice of you. Their blood alone can serve as a lustration to appease your justly tormented shade. Chalier. Chalier. We swear before your sacred image to avenge your sufferings. Yes, the blood of aristocrats will be your incense.'

A fire was lit into which were tossed the Bible and the missal and the ass was given to drink from the chalice and a leading radical Jacobin, Grandmaison, in parody of the Mass, cried out: 'Take and drink ye all of this, for this is the chalice of the blood of kings, of the new and eternal testament of the republican communion.'

But the rain began to fall, grew heavier and the crowd dispersed.

On the eve of the atrocities for which Fouché and Collot would always be remembered, Fouché organised his own festival of Reason as the Supreme Being in the cathedral church of Saint-Jean in Lyon.

Collot, fretting at the legacy of what had become a new word in the Jacobin demonology, the *indulgence* left like a crippling malaise by Couthon's inadequate measures, complained bitterly of the inefficiency of the local revolutionary committees, one of which had had the unmitigated temerity to release from custody the executioner of the Jacobin saint Chalier. Indulgence, a softening of rigorous principle, was counter-revolutionary.

On 23 November Collot, Fouché and Albitte declared the Emancipated Commune to be 'in a state of revolutionary war' and resolved to increase drastically the rate of executions. 'That is still too slow for the justice of the whole people, who must blast with lightning all their enemies at once, and we will busy ourselves with forging the thunderbolt.'

Popular perception being most susceptible to the daily rate of elimination of enemies, Collot and Fouché determined to heighten the perception.

That very day the local authorities, in discussion with the representatives, agreed to execute the rebels *en masse* with cannonade – to economise on gunpowder and a very potent means of delivering the thunderbolt – with troops on hand, ready to dispatch those merely wounded in the salvo.

On 4 December 60 men were taken from prison, chained together and led through the streets across the Saône, whose course flows down the west side of the peninsula on which the old city was built, across the Rhône on the east side and out on to the open fields of the Plain of Brotteaux, where the execution squads and the long grave pits waited. The cannon were loaded with canister shot: thin-cased canisters packed with fragments of metal named after the English artillery officer who refined the munition, Henry Shrapnel. The percussive force of firing caused the projectile to burst and unleash a hail of jagged bullets at the target. Those of the prisoners not killed outright were dispatched with sabres or bayonets; some were buried hideously wounded but still alive. Some of the troops, forgetting how wasteful of powder it was, dispatched the survivors in their death agony with musket shot.

The following day, cheered by the success of the first experiment, the representatives sent out 211 to be mown down. They called it 'death by the fire of lightning'. Fouché apparently did not attend the executions, though some prints show him directing the fire.

Those killed included a few women; most of the men were mostly artisans and shopkeepers, domestic servants and workers.

On 6 December Fouché was already writing to the Convention, saying 'how difficult, how distressing, it was for us to carry out your orders. The city is short of food despite reiterated requisitions . . . the whole place inspires nothing but indignation . . . The administration is made up of worthy men because they were oppressed by the rebels but they are too disposed to shed their public responsibility, forgetting the bloody outrage committed on liberty, yielding to a personal desire to pardon. We are employing all the means imaginable to sow the seeds of a cruel pity in every heart and to paint ourselves as men thirsty for blood and destruction. Our enemies need to be taught a terrible lesson. Very well, we will give them one. The southern region of the Republic is, because of its perfidy, enveloped in a destructive tourbillion from which must come the thunder to crush them; all the allies they have in the Liberated City must fall beneath the thunderbolts of justice, their bloody corpses flung into the Rhône, washed on to both banks at the estuary beneath the walls of infamous Toulon and the eyes of the cowardly English fiends, a fearsome sight, image of the all-powerful French people.'

But the gulf between the abstraction of inhuman measures ordained in Paris and the stark reality of carrying them out in the provinces affected even the soldiers who were ordered to carry out their masters' will. Collot returned to Paris on 21 December to deliver a report in the face of mounting criticism. His self-righteous disclaimer may have satisfied the theoreticians in Paris; it did not wash with those who witnessed the result: 'We shot down 200 in a single instant and are told that this was a crime. How can anyone fail to see that this is an example of *sensitivity*? When 20 culprits go to the guillotine, the last one to be executed dies 20 times, but these 200 conspirators died together, all at once.'

Fouché added his own judgement: 'The sentences passed by this tribunal may frighten criminals but they reassure and comfort the people. Let none imagine that we have reprieved any offender.'

Their joint statement affirmed their steadfastness: 'To those who act according to the spirit of the Republic, all is permitted.'

Nevertheless, the soldiers required to carry out these massacres were sickened, and after the second cannonade not even the temporary commission set up to try and sentence the rebels had any stomach for more. It resolved 'to write to the representatives of the People that these methods did not produce the execution we would have desired and that they should find others more dependable'. There were, accordingly, no more cannonades, but executions by firing squad and guillotine continued apace. Altogether between 1,876 and 1,907 were executed in Lyon, 11 per cent of victims in the whole of France.

If the mass slaughter on the Plain of Brotteaux caused a blip of revulsion, thirst for the continued wreaking of vengeance on the muscadins and counter-revolutionaries who had brought such ignominy on the city did not abate. The Lyonnais Jean-Jacques Achard, administrator of the restored Jacobin Municipality, wrote to Claude Gravier, founder and leader of a very active radical club, on 7 December: 'More heads and every day heads roll. What joys you would have tasted had you seen, the day before yesterday, this national justice visited on 209 criminals. What majesty. What dignified style. Utterly edifying.'

Another of his Jacobin friends described 'the fire of the lightning' which belched from the cannon mouths as 'the festival of virtue' and one Pilot told Gravier that his health was improving 'thanks to the destruction of the enemies of our common patrie'.

The Jacobins' orthodoxy heartily approved of this insatiable enthusiasm for blood and it thus became a central tenet in their government's policy. The squeamishness of the men who ordered the savagery, of Robespierre in particular, who, until he mounted the scaffold himself, never saw any of it, was, to their shame, an obscure irrelevance. The killing had become an integral part of the policy, from the moment that Barère announced: 'Destroy the Vendée.' Whatever semantic arguments might apply to the precise definition of that aerated call for the Republic to come down like a ravening wolf on the rebel fold, there was a powerful practicality inherent in the very word 'destroy'. In Lyon, Fouché and Collot went by the letter. It was not only rebellion that must be obliterated but the inequities perpetrated by the rich.

In a decree to abolish mendicancy, Fouché, Albitte and Collot declared: 'Wherever there are people who suffer there are enemies of humanity . . . All citizens who are infirm, elderly, orphaned, needy will be given accommodation, nourished and clothed at the expense of the rich of their respective cantons, traces of misery will be annihilated.'

Collot stressed that 'by killing off criminals we assure the life of all succeeding generations of free men' and Achard seconded: 'The rich in Lyon killed the energy which ought to have given life to 60,000 indigent individuals, they have never ceased to crush with poverty and hunger the vital impulse which was carrying them towards liberty . . . this class of monstrous beings, vampires on society, leeches of the whole people, vile, contemptible beings going under the name of merchants.'

A German adventurer marching with the revolutionary army which arrived in Lyon on 22 January 1794 wrote: 'Whole ranges of houses, always the most handsome, have been burnt. The churches, convents and all the dwellings of the former patricians were in ruins. When I came to the guillotine, the blood of those who had been executed a few hours beforehand was still running in the street . . . I said to a group of sansculottes . . . that it would be decent to clear away all this human gore. "Why should it be cleared?" one of them said to me. "It's the blood of aristocrats. The dogs should lick it up."'

After a siege lasting three and a half months, the troops who had taken Lyon moved south to join those encircling Toulon.

On 17 December 1793 artillery captain Napoleon Bonaparte's guns drove the English and Spanish from the fortified heights above the harbour city with accurately ranged artillery fire. Seven thousand refugees, including most of the rebel leaders, crowded on to Hood's warships, which sailed out in the next three days under a barrage of republican gunfire. Jacobins released from the gaols set about identifying the large number of remaining rebels and, loosely applying the decree of March, some 800 were shot without trial as French citizens caught up in armed rebellion. A revolutionary commission set up by the representatives Barras and Fréron condemned 282 to the guillotine over the next month on charges of conniving at a revolt that had proclaimed Louis XVII and allowed enemy ships to tow off or destroy over two-thirds of the Mediterranean fleet. Toulon was renamed Port-de-la-Montagne. The changing of names effectively blotted the town out and marked its former existence with an indelible disgrace.

Fréron informed the CPS: 'Marseille is entirely beyond cure.' Since Marseille had been the first town of the Midi to rebel against the Convention, by decree of 6 January 1794, it was to be called provisionally 'Without Name'; the haunts of the federalist sections demolished; the Marseillais revolutionary tribunal to be quashed for letting the richest merchants go free, even though their wealth had sustained the sections.

The CPS had sounded a cautious note, writing to Barras and Fréron on 4 January that Marseille should be allowed to preserve its name, recalling past services of the city to the Revolution, including those Marseillais who had fought at Toulon. For 'the majority of people in Marseille are patriots; during the counter-revolution they were no more than led astray'.

But Barras and Fréron were not to be swayed. In their proclamation of 22 January in the city they declared: 'Marseille is the root and primordial cause of virtually every internal ill which has afflicted the patrie . . . Marseille will bow its arrogant head beneath the level of the Law or it will disappear from the soil of the Republic.'

Bayle, a local deputy and member of the Committee for General Security, defended his adopted town and decried the decree robbing it of its name. He advised the CPS to reject Barras' and Fréron's order. How could a city which, in its time, had defied Julius Caesar, the Goths, the Constable of Bourbon, the Emperor Charles V and Louis XIV bow its head permanently under the federalists? Not even the colonising Romans changed town names, merely Latinised them.

Barras upbraided him for intervening and, with Fréron, told the CPS from Marseille on 2 February: 'The importance that has been placed on conserving Marseille's name is probably the most powerful reason for changing it. The Marseillais instinctively consider themselves a people apart. The geographical position, the mountains, the rivers which separate them from the rest of France, their own language, everything nourishes this federalist view . . . they would prefer to have their own unique laws; they see only Marseille; Marseille is their patrie. France means nothing to them.'

It was a view with which, in less precarious times, most Marseillais would have agreed wholeheartedly.

In his journal Fréron wrote of 'a southern faction, intent, without cease, for five years, on making Marseille a state apart, independent of the French Republic'.

Marseille, in his view, had infected the whole of the Midi and was responsible for the revolt of Lyon and Bordeaux as well as the treason of Toulon. 'I believe that Marseille will never be cured save by deporting its entire population and a transfusion of men from the north . . .'

The arrival of the representative Maignet eased the situation and it was clear that even the political purists in Paris, perhaps influenced by saner heads and certainly by the pressure from a man of the inner circle, Bayle, had realised that the Republic could not afford to allow so important a commercial centre as Marseille to languish in the throes of purges. Maignet proved to be intent on cooperating with local patriots. He was constantly in Marseille; his inflammatory colleagues Fréron and Barras spent most of their time in Toulon. As a result of Maignet's intervention, the Convention agreed that Marseille should keep its name. Fréron and Barras saw this as a triumph for calumny and intrigue closer to home and resented the snub for a long while.

Maignet told the Marseille Jacobin club: 'Death to the conspirators, but protection for patriots. No confusion in punishment' and accused them of being too often the theatre of vindictive quarrels which forced law-abiding citizens to desert it, whereas it was properly the forum for true political debate.

But the Revolution had made a cat's cradle of ties of loyalty; nothing was so straightforward; jobsworth interests of self-preservation were to the fore. Jean-Baptiste-François Nicolas explained his acceptance of a post in the popular tribunal which had tried his fellow citizens during the rebellion: 'I believed it was my duty not to shirk the orders of the sovereign people nor the law of the strongest and I yielded to the large majority.'

Others caught up in the secession called themselves no more than the 'fifth wheel of the coach', a useless element, of no account in the greater scheme; 'I was a scrap of wood in the rebellion . . . I was a real sheep and there were plenty like me . . . I have no other motif for my defence than saying I was led by the nose . . . I was an imbecile to get involved . . .'

Men of every social class and profession were brought before the revolutionary tribunal of the city: the largest, 92 farmers of large and smallholdings, and 93 property owners, but the category was ill defined – some properties were very rich, others quite modest. Members of the city and section administrations suffered badly: of 219 office-holders judged, 147 were condemned to death, 12 to reclusion, confinement in a house of detention, until the end of the war, one to deportation, 13 to prison; nine trials did not reach conclusion and 37 prisoners were released.

Conditions in the overcrowded prisons with masses of inmates held waiting trial at the conclusion of the long and cumbersome legal process were horrible. And, in Marseille, this punitive work of the Terror pointed up the devastating impact it had, quite apart from the bloodletting on the scaffold. The Terror brought abject misery to many thousands: those in gaol reduced to penury and protracted emotional and physical distress, their families and those dependent upon them for work or support rendered destitute. The life of the city was paralysed; the social order infected with hatreds and suspicions which extended beyond political division and penetrated deeply the psyche of the populace. Where blasé Jacobins prattled that the 'patriot ought to be the spoilt child of the patrie', whole swathes of common people were ruined by what had promised to better their lives. Much employment was lost during the Revolution and many suffered from the fall-out of attacks on more obvious targets: workers in the manufacture of soap (a luxury item) and sulphur (used in the silk industry), and sugar refiners, all suffered from a dearth of raw materials; merchants saw their trade dry up; artisans were cast into lengthening labour queues; domestic servants and wigmakers, dancing masters, hairdressers, valets, cooks all lost employment as big households were reduced to poverty.

An illiterate poor worker, Joseph Sagnolles, was probably not atypical. With a wife and three children to support, he worked in a silk factory as a roller of ribbons. Having had no work for six months he suffered chronic depression; one day he got drunk and quarrelled with his wife, who reproached him for his feckless spending. Her taunts tipped the quarrel into a terrible slanging match. But, whatever his political leanings, Sagnolles joined the Lyonnais, who gave him five livres a day.

What choice did such humble men as Sagnolles have? Even at such a lowly level, to express discontent anywhere, most of all to the revolutionary tribunal, was to incriminate oneself.

For the net was cast wide. As the journal of the Jacobin club of Marseille warned in October 1793: 'Do not imagine that the *aristocrat* exists only in the once privileged class of the nobility. It is there, unquestionably, that aristocracy par excellence is to be found, but not exclusively. You would not believe how many aristocrats one finds among the valets of former nobles and the domestics of the bourgeois. One would be tempted to believe that this proletarian class idolises servitude and that the habit of going on all fours in antechambers has made it impossible for them to stand up. So, look for aristocrats everywhere because there are aristocrats in every class; some by principle and pride; others by self-interest, prejudice, sheep-like habit and every one of them by wickedness.'

And as far as the Jacobins were concerned, lynx-eyed and sharp-eared for every sign of grumbling disaffection, in Marseille even the warehouse porters, the sailors and workers were just as egoistic and aristocratic as the merchants.

The agents of the Terror preyed on this and used it as their justification. Fouché and Collot reported to the Convention from Lyon: 'We are convinced that the only innocent are those who are or have been oppressed or enchained by the assassins of the people and we gird ourselves against the tears of those who regret their folly. Nothing will dilute our severity. It is our duty, citizen colleagues, to tell you that mercy is a dangerous frailty, likely to arouse the hopes of criminals just when they deserve extermination. Some urge us to neutralise your justice. But the demolitions proceed too slowly; the impatience of the Republic requires a hasty end. Only the explosion of mines [a particular fad of Collot's] and the devouring by fire can fulfil the design of the all-powerful people. Its will cannot be frustrated like that of tyrants.'

The last of the victims to mount the scaffold in Lyon were, by Fouché's order, given in the vaguest of terms, those who had carried out, under his orders, the executions. In the Convention, Chaumette, the Hébertist public prosecutor of the Commune, praised their protégé Fouché's invaluable work in the Emancipated Commune: 'Citizen Fouché has worked the miracles of which I have spoken. Old age has been honoured; infirmity succoured; misfortune respected; fanaticism eradicated; federalism wiped out; iron production increased; suspects arrested and crimes punished in an exemplary fashion; swindlers and hoarders prosecuted and imprisoned. Thus everything has been accomplished by the work of Fouché as representative of the people.'

Praise from such a quarter had a double edge, for it placed Fouché firmly in the dechristianising sansculotte camp; not a comfortable place to be, given the suspicion of and aversion to it welling in the breast of the man who was slowly manoeuvring round the remaining factions: Robespierre. His opponents were doing little to extenuate his isolation. Whereas the zealotry of Hébert and the rest might be guaranteed to ruffle feathers, it was from much closer to Robespierre's own past alliance that the first hard criticism came. He was, by now, identifying atheism with the most pernicious brand of divisiveness: aristocracy.

On 5 December 1793 there appeared the first edition of a journal which Camille Desmoulins called *The Old Cordelier*, a frank appeal to the original values of the Revolution. Danton had told him to take up his pen and he had done so. Robespierre had seen the copy.

# TEN

# *Indulgence*

Today a miracle has occurred in Paris: a man died in his bed.

Camille Desmoulins, *The Old Cordelier*

WHEN THE JACOBINS in Paris heard of Toulon's surrender to the English, in early September 1793, Claude Royer declared his support for a petition from the popular society in Mâcon for 'a revolutionary army to range through the Republic and eradicate all the germs of federalism, royalism and fanaticism which still infect it . . .' He added: 'You have made terror the order of the day; what better way to ensure its success than to create an army of 30,000 men divided into flying columns to each of which is attached a revolutionary tribunal and a guillotine, the instrument of terror, to administer justice both to traitors and conspirators? . . . Once such an idea would have been dangerous [he meant it might be used as an instrument of federalisation] but now that the Rolandist faction has been defeated, the Republic's army is in Marseille, Lyon is on the verge of falling and Bordeaux has been made to see its errors, there is no longer any obstacle to our victory; liberty must triumph.'

In the Convention he pressed the demand: 'Representatives of the people, the Republic is in extreme danger, the remedy must be extreme . . . We call for the raising of a revolutionary army to be divided into a number of sections, each one accompanied by a tribunal and a guillotine to instil terror. This army should continue its work until the soil of the Republic is cleansed of traitors and every conspirator has been exterminated . . .'

\*　　\*　　\*

Backed and whipped up by the Paris Commune to further its own political aims, namely to wring more radical measures out of the Convention, the historic day of 4 September began at 5 a.m. in the Temple and Enfants Rouges districts north of the Hôtel de Ville: workers from workshops and building sites assembled in a mass demonstration. Another mob gathered near the Ministry of War on the boulevards. Calling for bread, the demonstrators marched on the place de Grève, where Hébert and Pierre Gaspard 'Anaxagoras' Chaumette, public prosecutor of the Paris Commune, delivered speeches.

Later Chaumette climbed on to a table to address workers who had packed the HQ of the General Council of the Commune: 'Now it is open war between the rich and the poor . . . they want to crush us, very well, we must stop them – *we* must crush *them* and we have the means to do it. We must demand from the Convention the immediate setting up of a revolutionary army to go out into the country-side to supervise the requisition of grain, to oppose the obstruction of rich egoists and to deliver them to the vengeance of the law.'

The next day, 5 September, having resisted similar calls for so long, the Convention buckled and decreed:

> The creation of an armed force of 6,000 men and 1,200 cannoneers in Paris, financed by the national treasury, to suppress counter-revolution, to execute revolutionary laws and measures for public safety decreed by the national Convention and to protect food supplies. (The sections had demanded an army of 25,000–100,000 sansculottes.)

This armed force to be organised forthwith on terms laid down by the law by the Municipality of Paris and the commander-general jointly with members of the CPS.

The pay of this revolutionary force to be the same as that of the national gendarmerie of Paris.

Support from popular societies across the country was vociferous, mainly because the raising of a *legitimised* armed force would enable local Jacobins to protect local interests, not least in the matter of food and provisions: in rich grain areas, for example Arles in the south-east, where a hard-pressed people was intent on prohibiting the export of precious harvests and wherever poor towns were also willing to use force to maintain supply levels against requisition.

On 29 September a small-town popular society in Arc-sur-Tille, in the Dijon district, sent a fraternal address to the Jacobins in Paris: all inhabitants of their commune were ready to form a revolutionary army. 'Soon the sowing season will be finished; during the winter we usually hunt boar and other wild prey. Instead, allow us to spend our time wiping out these hordes of slaves whom we hate worse than the ravenous wild beasts who ravage our crops and herds. Simply give us the word, citizen representatives, and we will set out on the instant, armed with our hunting guns and pitchforks . . . their human skin is not as tough as that of wolves and boars, our blows will strike home. We are used to frost and snow . . .'

Soon these popular armies were gathering 'in every corner of the Republic' and the argument for the dispersal of such an army throughout France bruited more widely: 'Before we rush to the frontiers to destroy the satellites of tyranny, first let us exterminate the traitors *inside* our borders by the most courageous means possible – the best method is by a revolutionary army . . .' So said the Swedish-born sansculotte Lindberg, from the Bonnet-rouge section (formerly Croix Rouge, in the south-east corner of the seventh arrondissement), in support of calls from the Caen popular society to send a contingent into every department.

A local man, Canby, countered that such a force would discredit the national Guard and was therefore not only superfluous but unworthy.

Lindberg replied that the creation of the revolutionary army in Paris did not dishonour the city but that there were enemies even in the national Guard. But the central government was always loath to oversee a dispersal of armed force so far from its control and battalions were still mustering across France when the law of 5 December concentrating power in the hands of the CPS disbanded them. The revolutionising 'picnic in the country' was over. The anarchic Terror was replaced by a policed Terror.

The problem, which these irregular forces aggravated, was that the prosecution of revolutionary government principles in the localities depended on local interpretation and the willingness of a few individuals to impose their will. Such an open-ended system was too open to unruly elements, uncontrollable violence and a tendency to stray from the tight grip of law as monitored and executed by the government agents, the representatives on mission who were directly responsible to the CPS, whereas the local gangs could not easily be made to answer to such direct governance. Proper justice was tainted by the playing out of ingrained local grievances and different notions of what constituted treacherous behaviour – leaning towards either the overzealous or the lenient.

There nonetheless existed private armies in the service of particular groups, local dignitaries bolstering their authority against protest, such as the so-called army of Lassay in the Mayenne, where three or four notables employed their heavies to sort out opponents in back alleys, paid for by the levy of fines and 'taxes' imposed on the rich and the 'fanatical'. So too at Dax, a gang loyal to the families who dominated the popular society and controlled the municipality and the revolutionary committee; thugs given drinking money by their bosses in return for intimidating support in the popular society and the streets and receiving wages from the Dax commune. In Sedan patriotic revolutionaries attached themselves to a small body of soldiers guarding prisoners and called themselves the revolutionary army of Mont-Dieu, subsidised by the prisoners, who had to pay for the not inconsiderable costs of their own detention. Armies of hired hands, bully-boys, simpletons . . . what was to distinguish between a private army and an extortion gang?

The CPS feared above all the overt intention of the revolutionary armies to further the work of dechristianising so close to the heart of the sansculottes. In a rough draft of a letter Prieur de la Marne complained, on 5 October, to Maure, a representative on mission in his native region, Auxerre, that revolutionary army horsemen had ridden through Coulanges-la-Vineuse, just south of Auxerre, and forced the locals to tear down all the crosses in the parish. 'This revolutionary army you have created is a faithless institution without loyalty to anyone; it should be discharged at once. A representative of the people's power is backed by public opinion. Resorting to bayonets is to copy despots . . .'

The CPS ordered Maure to 'check the unthinking enthusiasm of the revolutionary army trying to preach theories of government while brandishing weapons . . . reason will bring the downfall of Catholicism . . . The Committee feels obliged to point out that the revolutionary force, which is useful so long as it is under the command of and observed by the representative of the people, can become extremely dangerous and subvert liberty if allowed to act without constraint.' He was ordered to disband the army.

The Committee underlined their order: 'The true revolutionary force is public opinion; its lever is in your hands . . . the national Guard is at your disposal – you have only to purge its ranks . . . You will be supported by a decree which the Convention is about to pass.'

The Paris revolutionary army was put under the command of the former actor Ronsin, who surrounded himself at the army's head-quarters in the rue de Choiseul, near the Opéra, with cronies from the profession, all of whom had suffered opprobrium from the church, which regarded the theatre as a den of iniquity and its people with a very jaundiced eye as flagrantly immoral, perhaps taking too seriously the fact that hypocrite comes from the classical Greek for actor.

The activities of the revolutionary army sent from Paris to assist in the crushing of the Lyonnais rebels excited most of the revulsion heaped on these forces of the anarchic Terror and, almost certainly, led to their disbandment. The fact that they were the child of the extremist sansculotte faction and impelled by a violence and atheism most directly associated with the Paris mob discredited them with the CPS, even as it exerted a tighter grip on affairs. The proles had outlived their usefulness. Their leaders – Hébert, Chaumette, Roux – had over-stepped the limits of governed discipline as, from the beginning, they had outraged decency. Hébert's blasphemies, the stock-in-trade of his vulgar ranting in *Le Père Duchesne*, had become worse than an embarrassment to Robespierre: they had become subversive. Anti-clericalism accorded well with Voltaire's imperative to 'crush superstition'. Atheism conflicted with any proper view of the human universe: Rousseau's Supreme Being, the Creator and universal Spirit, must take his place in the republican cosmology. The desecration of churches was no more than the vandalism of an unruly mob, an offence to the purity of revolutionary principles, at odds with the reign of virtue towards which the Republic must be steered with a firm and unyielding grip. This grip Robespierre was applying as he countered the violations of the atheistic revolutionary armies, egged on by their irreligious sansculotte generals and the more reprehensible of their lieutenants, such as Louis-Reine Vauquoy.

Formerly a clerk in the administration of the royal tax farmers, he became secretary of the Jacobins and worked his way through the military administration. An extremist, he accompanied the revolutionary army sent to the Isère, as part of the mopping-up operations following the fall of Lyon. Like Carrier in Nantes, he fortified his anti-Christian zeal with wine – often of excellent quality – from priests' cellars, gulping it in great draughts from sacramental chalices. Standing before a congregation of peasants in one church, he glugged wine from a ciborium, blatantly mocking the central mystery of the Mass, the Eucharist, and shouted: 'If there is a God let him strike me down here and now in front of you all . . .' In another church, he cried: 'They say it's a sin even to touch a chalice and here I am drinking from one.'

Copycatting was symptomatic of these hard-nosed, loose-mouthed revolutionaries, marching south in their revolutionary sansculotte uniform, cockades and red bonnets, to teach the bucolic village idiots a lesson in patriotism. Vauquoy was not the only one to tope communion wine on altars, an obscene act of bravado to chivvy the mirth and stiffen the resolve of his band of dragoons. Iconoclasm, once started, gets easier, and these troopers of the true revolution delighted in stripping churches of sacred vessels, revelling in wilful damage and mock sermons. Whatever direct orders Vauquoy had, a lot of the time he acted autonomously and his company were seen as no better than pillagers. What possible reason did they have for behaving in this fashion? As the popular society of Bourgoin said of Vauquoy, he 'openly preached atheism, ridiculed the Jacobins in Paris, the insurrection of the poor against the landowners whom they called thieves, brigands . . . their goods were the patrimony of the sansculottes, the reign of the landowners had lasted too long and the turn of the sansculottes had finally arrived'.

They pilfered linen, sheets and blankets from the cupboards of rich farmers and handed them out to the poor of the village or their own soldiers. Vauquoy said, in justification of his pillaging: 'I am the delegate of the people's representative, therefore I am the same as a representative of the people.' He made arrests and ordered acquittals, levied taxes, confiscated and distributed goods. Curiously, given the brutality of his comportment, he did not line his own pockets. His task he saw simply as fleecing the rich and he mocked his soldiers when they complained of finding nothing in a search: 'You stupid bastards, you don't know *how* to search. When *I* go into a house I find plenty . . .'

Vauquoy eventually paid the price for his enthusiastic usurpation of powers, always ill defined, opened to him and many others by the brief sanctioning of the revolutionary armies. The day of the sansculottes did, indeed, dawn, to the great detriment of the established authority and the Convention so long cowed by the mob, but the day was short.

The revolutionary armies dispatched to Lyon left a trail of ruin in their wake: church towers stripped of bells, sacred vessels abused and smashed, a wanton parade of ugly despoliation, a crude efflorescence of sansculotte rage at the trappings, the trumpery of the old regime: a dechristianising mob togged out in bishops' mitres and cassocks piling into the Convention itself on 11 November and scattering church vessels over the floor. In October, in Reims cathedral, a representative of the people, Philippe-Jacques Rühl, supervised the smashing of a glass phial containing the sacred oil of Clovis, first king of the Franks (481–511), which had been used to anoint every succeeding king of France.

But all this was a brute bellow of formless anger at the invisible authority of the church, at the mysteries of religion, which held their so-called counterparts in the rural backwaters, the peasantry, the small-town burghers, in thrall; it had little or nothing to do with spirituality. The sansculotte thugs did in the regions what they had done best in Paris: they broke things up, as the Revolution had broken down so much of the intangible: privilege, law, social order, respect for authority, any authority, optimism. As a soldier of the armies complained: 'Under the old regime I was not free but I had food; now I have no food. Fuck the new regime.'

On 25 November Ronsin, general-in-chief of the revolutionary army, wrote to the Cordeliers in Paris from Lyon describing how they had marched into that 'guilty city':

Terror was etched on every face and the complete silence I made sure to require of our brave soldiers made the entrance still more terrifying, more menacing. Most of the shops were closed. Some women stood by the roadside, in their expression more indignation than fear. The men stayed hidden in the lairs from which they had stolen, during the siege, to murder the true friends of liberty.

The guillotine and the firing squad did justice to more than 400 rebels, but a new revolutionary commission has been set up, composed of true sansculottes. My colleague Parein is its president and in a few days the grapeshot . . . will deliver to us, in an instant, more than 4,000 conspirators . . . delay will arouse not the courage but the despair of traitors still hidden amid the debris of this impious town. The Republic has need of a striking example – the Rhône, reddened with blood, must wash along its banks and into the sea the corpses of those cowards who murdered our brothers . . .

Already the cowards have assassinated one of our revolutionary soldiers during the night. Decide, then, brothers and friends, if it is not time to use the most terrible and prompt means of justice . . .

For a brief while it had been in their apparent power to decide, but the gods of the central power thought otherwise.

Despite his self-proclaimed love of the sansculottes and his lip service to the vituperations of Marat, Philippe-Egalité went to the scaffold in November. Taken into the room of the pre-execution toilette at the Conciergerie, another victim, Laroque, a veteran soldier 73 years old, looked at him and said: 'I don't regret life any more, when the man who has destroyed my country is punished for his crimes. What humiliates me is being obliged to die on the same scaffold . . .' The former duc d'Orléans made no reply.

Encouraged by Danton to take up his pen, Camille Desmoulins wrote what would be a proleptic death warrant for them both. The first two editions of his *The Old Cordelier* – a pointed call to the values which had informed the earlier optimism, the wider, more humane possibility of the apparent consensus for liberty – caused a stir, but their appeal to men of sense to consider anew the state of things consisted, as many recognised, principally in voicing an opinion that was widely held but not broadcast. The Revolution had lurched perilously towards a dictatorship; the forthright resistance to such a state had been long since expressed as a dire warning: 'It is vitally important that no individual should emerge in the Republic . . . who draws into his own hands total power and, when he has it, employs it in destroying any who refuse to march under his aegis.'

Those words came from Robespierre. But his incensed reaction to Desmoulins' appeal for what became a poisonous jibe in Jacobin vocabulary – *indulgence* – marks the next stage in his ruthless eradication of the factions who opposed him, although he would say rather those who opposed his sanitised, uncorrupted model of revolutionary virtue. In this polarisation between the virginal purist man of law and the party of the indulgents whose horror at the giddy course the Revolution was taking gave them the moral force to wish to draw back lies the final crisis of the factional feud.

The nauseating impact of the policy of Terror was felt elsewhere than in Paris. From the Vendée, the adjutant-general, Rouyer, wrote to the minister of War, the sansculotte Bouchotte, suggesting the offer of amnesty – if, he stressed, that were compatible with the dignity of the sovereign people. Pardon for the defeated rebels would produce an almost universal defection among the insurgents. 'Our soldiers would fight with more courage if we took prisoners, as the Vendeans themselves demand of their own fighters, for, although we shoot everyone who falls into our hands, prisoners, wounded, the sick in hospitals, they send us back our sick whom we have been forced to leave behind.'

He received no reply.

Others were less squeamish. The sansculotte General Rossignol wrote to the CPS on 11 November: 'I am expending all effort to destroy everyone and everything which does violence to liberty but there exist, still, men of humanity: in my view, in a revolution, that is a failing.' He asked the chemist Antoine Fourcroy to work on mines, soporific gas or other chemical means to asphyxiate or knock out the Vendeans. Carrier proposed putting arsenic in the wells as an answer to the vexatious practical problem of mass extermination.

Robespierre, convinced that all theoretical problems could be settled with reason, eschewed passion, a messy, disordered condition of the human psyche. As a lawyer, he argued every case on evidence, on forensic proof, turning analysis into rhetoric before the bar of judgement, whether in the Convention, the Jacobins or the revolutionary tribunal. The Terror merely extended the legal process: its reach into every corner of life no more than a reflection of how deep-seated human corruption, *vice*, was. His young spokesman, Saint-Just, nicknamed the Angel of Death, fantasised on the implications of the *reductio ad absurdum* that the politics of Terror entailed. The revolutionary government owed its enemies death and death alone. The only citizens who can exist – that is, function in any healthy condition – in the Republic are republicans, with all the imposed civic and moral duty that implied. The principal qualification was virtue and, as he put it at his most chilly: 'Virtue is unaffected, modest, humble, often ignorant, sometimes vulgar; the natural birthright of the poor, the patrimony of the masses. Vice is lapped round by wealth, fortified with every lubricious passion to attract the sensualist and entrap the weak.'

To such sentiments Danton, the lover of life, riposted: 'Whoever hates vice hates humanity.' But, whatever their affiliation and friendship had fused between them earlier, he and Robespierre were fatally at odds in this dichotomy. No matter that Danton had called out in that great ebullient roar of his for terror, for the full punitive force of a Republic fighting for its young existence against its enemies; he knew, too, the difference between what a patriot might call for in a bout of rhetorical excess and the madness that it might lead to if taken literally and to its limit. Caught up in the gory welter of death yet, his fealty was to life. Life must go on and life, with all its frailties, moral impasses, compromise, all its *passion*, must be the driving motive, not some abstraction of *virtue* which had neither ethical nor practical value. Robespierre had no *life* as such. He was, as he had been in the Oratorian college, engrossed in study of one tiny detail of it: the belief that the infinite and troubling complexity of human existence could be managed by law. In Cicero's words, 'the highest law is the people's safety'.

To the detriment of actual *safety*, the supreme objective of all that the great Committee was required and directed to do, Robespierre made his objective the sacred inviolability of *law*. Thus he drew adulation, the adulation of Saint-Just's vulgar ignorant, who addressed him as 'incorruptible genius, enlightened man of the Mountain who sees all, foresees all, unravels all, who cannot be deceived or seduced'. Such nauseating flattery matched the kind of sycophancy that had been routine under the old regime. But, to the hideous cost of all those who died under the Terror, Robespierre actually believed it. Integrity is not a matter of circumstance. It ought to be an essential part of the moral process; but whereas opinion may flex according to circumstance, ideology cannot: it cannot read its own experience, whereas integrity takes account of experience and adjusts in its own growth.

Robespierre's ideas became ideals without any test of experience, a test which he avoided, just as he avoided being touched, a basic, animal aversion which mirrored his moral incorruptibility. But this made his ideals childish, stunted. The danger in him was that he lagged this crucial weakness of moral sense with an impenetrable layer of prickly disdain for all those who had not preserved the ideals of their first understanding. He had kept himself apart from the depravities of society, the pernicious influence which, said Rousseau, put men in chains. All round him he saw men enslaved to their lusts, their frailty, their willingness to compromise, their corrupt souls. He was the holier-than-thou child despising the stupid adults with all the formidable cunning and incisiveness of the practised orator whose advocacy is punishment, and only ever punishment.

The third issue of *The Old Cordelier*, dated 15 December, which he did not see in advance, provoked another burst of his fury, this time unleashed on those who had the temerity to observe what was happening, in the name of the people of France, and to cry: 'Stop.'

Desmoulins drew astute, but disturbing, parallels between the bloody treason trials which convulsed the reign of the second Roman Emperor, Tiberius, successor to Augustus, himself no stranger to the vicious practice of proscription – the lists of political enemies marked down for liquidation. Tiberius's infamous dictum 'Let them hate me, so long as they fear me' might have been taken by the CPS as a motto. His immediate successors stand high on any roll-call of cruel tyrants: Nero, Caligula, Domitian, who had the corridors of his palace fitted with mirrors so that no lurking assassin could jump out on him unseen.

Desmoulins makes his challenge boldly: 'There is, yet, this difference between the monarchy and the Republic, that the reigns of the most wicked emperors, Tiberius, Claudius, Nero, Caligula, Domitius [*sic*] all started happily. Each reign began in joy. The advantage of Republics is to improve and go on improving.'

This, manifestly, was not the case in France.

Before conducting my reader to the Plain of Brotteaux and on to the place de la Révolution, and showing how they are soaked with the blood which has flowed this past six months, for the eternal liberation of a people of 25 million and not yet washed by liberty and the public good, I am going to start by carrying my fellow citizens' eyes back on the rule of the Caesars and on that river of blood,

that sewer of corruption and impurity which flowed perpetually
under monarchy.

The point could not be mistaken: that feculent cloaca had still not
been emptied; the river of blood flowed yet, and in spate; and, while
Desmoulins assured his readers that they could 'count on the candour
of his pen and may derive a malicious pleasure in noting it as it made
a faithful sketch of the tableau of events of the previous week', the
pained anger of his cri de coeur was unmistakable. 'As soon as conversation became a crime against the state, from there on there was but
a step to making crime of a simple look, of sorrow, of compassion,
of sighs, even of silence.'

He referred to ancient Rome, but he had wept for the Girondins
and, in those tears, was substance of suspicion. The world had gone
mad under the terrible mask of reason, of considered public good.

In what he paraded as a direct translation from the work of Tacitus,
the acerbic republican commentator on the corruption of Roman
government under the Caesars, Desmoulins feinted at parallel with
cold irony: 'It is for those who, reading these vivid portraits of tyranny,
find in them a certain unhappy resemblance with their own conduct
. . . for no one will ever persuade himself that the portrait of a tyrant,
traced by the hand of the greatest portraitist of antiquity [Tacitus]
. . . could become a living portrait . . . and that what Tacitus called
despotism and the worst of governments, 12 centuries ago, could,
today, call itself liberty and the best of all possible worlds.'

The allusion to *Candide*, the satirical novel by one of the
Revolution's natural philosophical apologists, Voltaire, pointed the
irony sharply (the dopey Dr Pangloss warbling his mantra that 'all is
for the best in this best of all possible worlds'). Not long before,
Robespierre, speaking against the dechristianising tendency of the
ultra-revolutionaries of the Hébertist persuasion, had declared
'atheism is aristocratic' and concluded his attack by himself quoting
the great hero of liberty, Voltaire: 'If God did not exist it would be
necessary to invent him.' He would have done well to ponder something else Voltaire said, in another book (*Dictionnaire Philosophiene*,
1764): 'The best is the enemy of the good.'

Desmoulins and Danton were openly discussing the idea of setting
up a committee of Clemency, to investigate the cases of many awaiting

trial under the slimmest of pretexts. It would also counter the open invitation offered by the Law of Suspects to malicious incrimination. This move back to the sober intelligence of a revolution geared to reform rather than demolition, Desmoulins made the central feature of the fourth number of *The Old Cordelier*, which appeared on 24 December. Such a proposal was, inevitably, tarred with the disgrace of *moderation*. As Robespierre had it, deploying another revolutionary neologism of disgust: 'This moderatism they are preaching is a weapon more dangerous than the bayonet.' He darkened the attack with a gnomic utterance which said as much of his own spinsterish sexuality as anything: 'Moderatism is to moderation as impotence is to chastity, and excess resembles energy as dropsy good health.'

Others joined the condemnation, not least Collot d'Herbois, returned from Lyon to justify the butchery he had supervised there. In a barn-storming performance, Collot rounded on the Convention, smug in their seats, far from the harsh reality, the grim but necessary business of bringing down vengeance on the enemies of the people: 'When I left this place two months ago, you burnt with thirst for retribution on the infamous conspirators of Lyon. Now that I have returned, I scarcely recognise the prevailing opinion around me. Had I come back only two days after I did, I would have been arrested myself . . . Who are these men who reserve their sensibilities for counter-revolutionaries . . . who weep so copiously over the corpses of the enemies of liberty while the heart of the Revolution is being torn out?' And on 21 December in the Jacobins, one of the jurors of the revolutionary tribunal who printed all its forms, Léopold Nicolas, Robespierre's bodyguard, warned: 'Camille has been skimming the guillotine for a long time' . . . this Camille who was saying that the Revolution could have been carried through by the pen and with one guillotine.

The fourth issue of *The Old Cordelier* had made a direct appeal to Desmoulins' former school fellow Robespierre to acknowledge that compassion, a humane approach to the thorny problems of revolution, was wholly consistent with patriotism. This was a sentiment irrevocably linked with the moderate Girondins; Vergniaud had once said to Robespierre: 'We are trying to achieve the Republic through terror – I would have wished to do so by love.'

However, the committee for Clemency was actually set up and now

Philippeaux, Danton's close friend, pitched in for the indulgents, roundly denouncing the fanatical, sanguinary excesses of the revolutionary army under Ronsin in Lyon. Ronsin and his adjutant, Vincent, were arrested, together with Rossignol, another revolutionary army general, Hanriot, the reckless commander of the Paris national Guard, and Maillard, the self-appointed recording angel of the September Massacres: the government, the CPS, had spoken – no citizen must overstep the mark that *they* had imposed, even if this apparent scruple *after* the fact seemed to be at odds with the inexorable severity they had preached *before* the fact. The rule of Terror, from now on, was to be a matter of the strictest governance, from the top, *for* the people but no longer exploited by the worst elements *of* the people.

Since October the guillotine in Paris had cut off only 177 heads; it was cheated of that of the extremist Roux, who, arrested in August, released and rearrested on 5 September, committed suicide in his cell in October. He had assumed the mantle of the people's friend, Marat, and, days after his funeral, snarled at the Convention: 'It is only by instilling terror in the soul of traitors that you assure the independence of the patrie.' His impatience with the fine words that buttered no spinach was central to the continuing resentment of the poor: 'Liberty is but a phantom when one class of men can starve another with impunity. Liberty is but a phantom when the rich man, through monopoly, possesses the power of life and death over his fellow man.' One abiding problem, however, was the total lack of sympathy between Paris and the surrounding parishes.

Why should a butcher, 15 kilometres from the Pont Neuf, drive his cattle to the city to be sold at a ruinous loss? As the pseudonymous spy Raoul Hesdin puts it: 'All Paris ate meat under the old regime and the quantity of foreign meat imported then from neighbouring countries is proved by the difficulty of obtaining it now . . . The bread shops are generally cleaned out and shut by 9 or 10 a.m.; only too frequently half those waiting have to go away empty. How the poorest class live, God knows.' Bread was being made of dried pease and the general lack of staple supplies was being called 'the Republican Lent'.

Roux and the others had a point. In the sections where government offices were situated, restaurants were more numerous and much better supplied than elsewhere; the deputies ate well, none in the CPS or the CGS ever went short, and the grocers and dealers who supplied them and the eating houses got their deliveries first 'by every species of bribery and fraud'. Police, set to supervise food queues, gave out numbers as people arrived; but for a bribe would move latecomers to the head of the line. Hesdin records two incidents: 'A peasant's cart arrived at one of the city barriers, laden with butter, eggs and vegetables from the Bourg-la-Reine road, at six in the morning. The Blues on guard were asleep or drunk, but a crowd of women inside undid the grilles with the keys which they stole from the sleeping men. The instant the cart was inside, it was invaded by the women . . . the villager, a stalwart, was flung in the mud and the whole contents plundered, the women fighting like starving tigresses for the fragments.' Food also came in by river, to be unloaded at the wharves near the Ile de la Cité: 'As for any order being kept by the Blues at the ports and barriers, it's absurd. I saw a most entertaining scene not long ago on the Tournelle: a boat coming down laden with wine was pillaged and sunk in the shallow water; the guards themselves taking part and rushing into the water up to their knees, broke open the tuns with their pikes.'

Vapouring about 'the general will' and the innate virtue of that airy abstraction 'the people', Robespierre and the others, all well fed and removed from the bitter plight of the poor, could dismiss the furious Roux and his supporter Varlet as little better than ruffians who manipulated the people by appealing to the base demands of their bellies. They were an embarrassment, an inconvenience, an awkward self-seeking irritant to the business of keeping the holy Revolution on course, where necessary by making 'terrifying examples' of those who perverted the truth, such as the fact that good and honest people had been subverted and misled by malign authorities. Among them, corrupted men of the ultra persuasion such as Roux.

More palatable to the Incorruptible were the young heroes of the Revolution, such as Barra, 'whose beautiful actions have honoured the war of liberty against tyranny': ' . . . this young man aged 13 years performed prodigies of valour in the Vendée. Surrounded by brigands who, on one hand, offered him death and on the other called for him to cry, "Long live the King", he died crying, "Long live the Republic". This young boy supported his mother with his wages, sharing what he owned between filial love and love of the patrie. It is not possible to find a finer example, a more perfect model to excite in young hearts the love of glory, the love of patrie, the love of virtue, and to prepare the way for the prodigies which the coming generation will perform . . .'

Robespierre demanded 'the honours of the Panthéon' for the young martyr; David painted an iconic tableau, *The Death of Barra*. The fiends of the Vendée would meet their nemesis soon. First, there was corruption closer to home to deal with.

The Foreign Plot and the scandal of the Indies Company scam implicated a number of deputies and officials and, inevitably, the elusive baron de Batz, flitting through shadows from mischief to misdemeanour.

More had come to light on his activities. A policeman, Burlandeux, gave testimony that he had been offered a million livres by Batz to aid and abet the Queen's escape from the Conciergerie; this was confirmed by Chabot, and when the escape attempt failed Chabot denounced Batz as a 'corrupter of state functionaries'.

Rougeville (the man who had entered the Queen's cell and given her the letter advising her of the escape) later gave an account of getting her through the two main internal doors.

Batz, realising that he was going to be exploited without any advantage to the Queen, mistrusted Burlandeux. The CGS's spy Sénar confirmed his misgivings in a report that the gendarmes in the Conciergerie had been bought; when the guard changed on the night of the escape attempt, one was missing – the man detailed to wear two overcoats, one to give to the Queen so she could get out. He must have been warned off, presumably by Burlandeux.

Batz knew he would be the first to be denounced and taken to the CGS unless he escaped. He decided to present himself there two days later. 'I went to see the president of the CGS and eventually got to the man himself; I did not ask him what possible reason there could be for public surveillance directed at fitting me up as a spy and I offered to give an account of my conduct. This candour was salutary. A few days later I was called by this same president of the CGS, who said: "You were to be arrested this morning; the warrant is signed; commissaries and gendarmes were all ready . . . Stay calm: the warrant is false. One of the Committee's spies followed Burlandeux, won over the brigand's confidence and we know everything. Burlandeux intended to implicate you. Having failed to ensnare you in his first trap he concocted this false warrant against you; the Committee's spy helped draw it up: the plan was to put on a show of embroiling you and to scare you into buying your liberty at any price." A few days later [Batz continues] Burlandeux extorted 26,000 livres from a businessman Hoffman by threats to him and his family . . . As for Burlandeux, I heard he had said of me: "He's rich, I shall make it my business to charge him 100,000 écus [1 écu equals 5 francs silver] for his head."' Burlandeux was arrested that day.

If his plans to save the Queen and restore the monarchy were to succeed, Batz needed somebody of influence in the Convention. The most likely candidate, a man of audacity and known propensity to enjoy backhanders of money, Danton, seemed disgusted with politics, spending much time at Arcis with his new young wife, who absorbed all his energy. Batz's two contacts in the Convention, Delaunay (of Angers) and Julien (of Toulouse), suggested Chabot or Bazire. Batz fastened on Chabot.

Chabot was a stocky, nervous man of small stature, fiery temperament and deplorable moral cowardice. Thirty-four years old, a Capuchin monk since the age of 15, trammelled by one of the most ascetic of monastic regimens, he had thrown off his cowl impatiently. Very popular in the legislative Assembly, he had become drunk with his success as a revolutionary leader, spouting opinions on everything with superficial facility in high, know-all style – war, politics, finance, interior affairs, diplomacy, agriculture. Figuring himself that paragon of men, a sansculotte by merit, he mimicked the fashion statements of the slovenly populist Marat and, in flagrant affectation of cynicism, attended the Assembly in unbuttoned chemise, legs half bare, stockings rolled down, red cap.

He lived with a maidservant in the rue Saint-Honoré.

Enter Junius (with reference to Marcus Junius Brutus) Frey (Frei, originally von Schönfeld, or Dobruszka), calling himself a Jewish banker from Austria, and his brother Emmanuel. Arrived in Paris, both joined the Jacobins to ingratiate themselves with the revolutionaries, as two friends of liberty; they claimed to have left Vienna because they were no longer prepared to sweat under the yoke of the tyrant Emperor. They took up with Chabot – whose peasant mother had ground coarse bran bread with her own hands in the remote limestone plateau of the Causses in the department of the

Lot – and played on his appetite for good food and wine with sumptuous hospitality at their hotel on the corner of the rue d'Anjou
and rue du Faugbourg Saint-Honoré, close by the Champs-Elysées.
He marvelled at these lavish dinners of men who spent 40–50,000
livres per annum on food and drink; at a time when there were
food riots in Paris, Chabot seemed entirely unfazed by the contra-
diction. At these and other dinners at Batz's house in Charonne –
now 148–50 rue de Bagnolet, in the 20th arrondissement, east of
Père Lachaise – Chabot joined Bazire, Delaunay, Julien, other
bankers and Batz's mistress, Marie Grandmaison: here was sophisticated society, monied, seductive.

Amar, of the CGS, reproached Chabot: 'You mean to tell me you
know these corrupt individuals and you still keep company with
them?'

The Freys pressed Chabot about his housekeeper and when he
admitted that she had become his mistress, they warned him off: she
was a hussy, a jade, she could compromise him, she wasn't worthy of
a man of his integrity. They gave him money to pay her off. He left
her pregnant.

They proposed that he marry their 16-year-old sister, Léopoldine,
in return for a dowry of food and lodging in their hotel for five years
plus 4,000 livres for out-of-pocket expenses.

Now Delaunay was sent to bell the cat. He found Chabot in the
antechamber of the Convention next to its statue of Liberty – the
young Republic trampling underfoot the ignominies of the old
regime. A few days later Chabot, who, with Bazire, had been the
scourge of bankers and men of commerce, proposed that the
Convention should lift all seals it had lately put on bankers' houses.
The seals were soon lifted. Chabot, it seemed, had accepted, by
default, Madame Roland's cynical view that 'democracy is no more
than an auction of government, a sort of fair'.

Poverty, the former monk turned man of the world might have
said, was its own reward. In the Jacobins on 30 September he proposed
a measure to take care of foundling children, who, like any other
children, deserved the love and birthright of their parents. They
listened to him coldly. Dufourny stood up: 'Before your plans for
marriage, you chose a companion who has become a mother . . .
what have you done for her? Why have you abandoned her? In taking
a foreign wife you desert, you repudiate a French scion.'

On 3 October Chabot announced his marriage at the Jacobins. 'I believed that it was my duty to give an example of all virtues . . . People reproach me as a womaniser, and I believed it was to eliminate this calumny that I should take a wife whom the law accorded me and whom my heart has cleaved to for a long time.' He launched into a toe-curling history of his love affairs and then read out his marriage contract, justifying the dowry. (Not the least unattractive trait of these Jacobins was their promptness to make intimate confession a tool for self-justification.) No priest, he declared, would taint the ceremony and he invited a deputation from the club to attend the marriage – at 8 a.m., so that he would not neglect his duties at the Convention (something his wife-to-be had insisted on) and a banquet, all to be finished by 9 a.m.

He finished, looked up, expecting a thunder of applause, to be greeted with glacial silence. Dufourny said, drily, that the society could not attend a marriage and a meal in person.

Ten days later Chabot was married shortly before the Queen was taken to the revolutionary Tribunal bench for cross-examination. That evening, in *Le Père Duchesne*, Hébert referred to Léopoldine Frey as 'Chabot's Austrian woman', playing on the hated Marie-Antoinette's nationality.

Delaunay confronted Chabot: the CGS, in the persons of Panis, Amar and David, was planning to denounce him because of his marriage to an Austrian alien; moreover, her fortune was a figment, and it was known that Chabot had handed over to her 200,000 francs, the fruits of his speculation in the Indies Company.

Chabot made a strenuous denial: his brothers-in-law detested tyranny and had left Vienna to live a free life in France, which they loved.

Delaunay disabused him: the brothers had never had either name or fortune. They were Moravian Jews, their name was Tropuska, they were unknown in Vienna except for a mountain of debts; they had been hanged in effigy following various unsavoury escapades and the details had been given to the CGS. As for Léopoldine, they had bought her as a child from a hetaira in the Emperor's harem.

Chabot was hooked.

Delaunay assured him that his friend Batz exercised strong influence over the CGS, but if speculation in the Indies Company failed, Chabot would have lost his strongest defender; worse, if his wife had no dowry, Chabot was up to his neck in deep trouble. Luckily, a banker in the circle, one Benoît, had offered to put up 100,000 livres to avert suspicion from Chabot.

The original Indies Company, operating under royal patronage, enjoyed a monopoly of trade east of the Cape of Good Hope. In August 1792 the legislative Assembly, seeking to redress the grave imbalance between the depreciating revolutionary paper money, the assignats, and a prosperous stock market, in the control of rich commercial interests, decreed, with special reference to the Indies Company, the registration of and taxation on all transferable stock. The Indies Company evaded the tax by calling in all its stock and substituting a register of holdings and carried on with its business in defiance of the law, but with the connivance of Clavière, the Finance minister in Brissot's Girondin government until it fell in June 1793.

On 16 July Delaunay charged the Indies Company in the Convention with evading taxes, cornering stocks and profiteering; the company's warehouses were duly sealed and the entire business liquidated. Delaunay and Fabre d'Eglantine, former president of the radical Cordelier Club, now led the assault on the speculators behind the fraudulent dealings of the Indies Company and the combine of bankers, several of them foreign nationals, all embroiled in the vast conspiracy funded by Pitt in England, including Batz, Benoît, Proly, Dubuisson.

'The aim of Pitt and his agents in speculation is to lower the exchange and to raise the price of food, raw materials and commodities, thus making it impossible for us to prosecute the war, and to exhaust our people by sowing divisions by the effects of high prices and poverty.'

Following the liquidation, a group of speculators bought up as many of the much-devalued shares as it could, certain that they would rise again and deliver a fat profit. Ringleader of this cabal: Delaunay.

On 8 October Delaunay proposed a second decree in the Convention which allowed the administrators of the Indies Company – which, he said, had foundered as the result of royal brigandage and corruption, the iniquity of the old regime – to carry out its liquidation, and thus provided a pretext to the company for carrying on business. Fabre d'Eglantine actually opposed this decree, insisting that the government should seize all merchandise belonging to the company and put seals on all its papers so as to find new proofs of corruption.

Delaunay, who had so far relied on Fabre's complicity, was thunderstruck. He told Batz, who said: 'Fabre? I'll buy him too.'

Fabre's amendment was carried but Delaunay altered the drafting, expunged the provisions of the amendment and got Fabre to countersign this falsified version, adding a corollary attesting that it had also been signed by other members of the committee investigating the matter.

On 10 November Philippeaux addressed the Convention: it was time for the masks to fall. Each member of the Convention should, within ten days, declare the state of his fortune before the start of the Revolution and, if it had increased, by what means. Any member who did not satisfy the dispositions of the decree should be declared a traitor to the patrie and prosecuted as such.

Bazire opposed the motion: he was the poorest of them all; crime invents all sorts of ruses, and criminals assume different names while the honest man has placed on his head the fruits of his labour. These denunciations, these calumnies of honest men, don't spring from patriotism but from counter-revolutionary intentions. Don't snatch so greedily at this hook which the criminals offer us so as to tear us apart. 'I know what fate awaits my speaking so candidly at this tribune but when one knows how to speak thus one knows how to die . . . the loss of my head will be the price of my courage, but I have learnt to risk death.'

Uproar. Montaut, calling upon the President to restore order, said: 'The Convention strikes only conspirators.'

Chabot intervened: 'If the Convention adopts Philippeaux's measures, which virtuous deputy will want to occupy himself with the affairs of the Republic if he can be struck down at the very moment when he is devoting himself to it? Death cannot frighten me: if my head is useful to the Republic let it fall. What is important is that there should never be but one opinion about decrees. Who told you, citizens, that counter-revolutionaries are not counting on sending your heads to the scaffold? One of your colleagues was overheard recently: "Today it's so and so's turn, tomorrow Danton's, the next day Billaud-Varenne's, we'll finish with Robespierre." This must terrify republicans. Who told you that somebody will not come with a forged letter to seek a decree against the best patriots?'

He was in a seizure of fear each time someone approached the tribune: was he going to be denounced?

Bourdon: 'And the Girondins, Chabot? Were the Girondins heard?'

Bazire, another sweating on his own safety: 'As to them, public opinion condemned them. Today it is the true friends of liberty who are being attacked on vague facts . . . I support Chabot's measure. May it be adopted.'

Chabot's decree was adopted but in the face of vitriolic opposition of Terrorists to what they called a very *indulgent* measure. Billaud, especially, claimed that 'our zeal will be smothered only in the tomb: either the Revolution triumphs or we die'. Barère added his powerful voice and the following day Chabot's motion was overturned.

Chabot made a run for it. Soon afterwards he went to see Robespierre at dawn and squealed on the conspiracy 'to save the patrie'.

It was not enough to save him. Chabot and those he denounced were arrested at 8 a.m. He had asked the CGS to come at 8 p.m., when he would deliver Batz and Benoît, Delaunay and Bazire, with whom he had a rendezvous; the Committee agreed, and said they would arrest the guilty men and Chabot the innocent, for show. Batz's informer, the spy Lavicomterie, warned him of the treachery and it was Batz's idea to tell the Committee to go at 8 a.m. and arrest Chabot alone at his hotel on 12 January. On the evidence of the falsified decree, Fabre d'Eglantine was also arrested; with him Delaunay and Bazire.

Batz, once more, melted into invisibility.

# ELEVEN

# *The Infernal Columns*

It is not killing innocents as innocents which destroys society,
it is killing innocents as guilty.

*Chateaubriand*

O N 17 DECEMBER Carrier sat in a fiacre, a four-wheel hackney
carriage on the place du Bouffay, as 24 Vendeans waited at the
foot of the scaffold. A month earlier, following the practice of
reducing rebel territories to a sort of shameful anonymity, the Vendée
had been renamed, with tabloid punch, the Vengé, the Avenged.
Carrier, growing impatient, told Naux, of the Marat company, to seek
out the judges and the public prosecutor. They sent one Lamarie to
tell Carrier that among the prisoners were two children, 14 and 13
years old, hence the delay. Carrier 'cried out in a rage, "ye gods what
country am I in? . . . just like all the rest . . ."' and delivered an order
for summary execution to proceed.

Nantes was stupefied with fear and suspicion. No one dared admit
to any friendship, acquaintance or relationship. Everyone was a potential informer. 'If you met your brother you didn't dare acknowledge
him for fear of seeming to have bad intentions.' A chief of battalion,
Binet, always carried two pistols: one for anyone coming to arrest
him, the other to blow his own brains out. Carrier painted a different
picture of the glazed smiles, the rictus of dread, on every face:
'Everywhere I saw the people embrace me, full of calm joy.' Goullin
of the revolutionary committee walked in dread of Carrier; Goullin's
malign presence touched them all.

Everyone in Nantes knew about the drownings but even to show distaste was perilous. Lying, dissimulation, self-protection smothered every humane reaction, any visible sign of compassion. In the end the authorities made no effort to conceal what was happening: drownings took place quite openly at 3 p.m. and were dubbed 'bathing', 'coral fishing', 'vertical deportation'.

Rémy Brejot watched lines of prisoners chained together filing below his window: 'I could have seen the victims fall except for a hedge of spectators which blocked my view.'

The Entrepôt was a warehouse built on the waterside just west of the city, for colonial produce. After the final collapse of the Vendean rebellion it was used as a prison and so crammed with prisoners that there was an outbreak of pustulent typhus. Georges Thomas, a doctor: 'Entering this frightful butchery, I found a large number of corpses scattered about; I saw infants trembling or drowned in buckets of human excrement.' Having established pregnancy in some 30 detainees, he returned some days later, but the 'bathings' had done their work.

Two men in charge of the drownings, Lamberty and Fouquet, were accused of taking women out of the Entrepôt for their sexual diversion.

Marie Ervin, a woman merchant, said of the Entrepôt: 'I saw an incalculable multitude of children; in one hall there were more than 300 simply waiting to die', incommoded by 'fetid exhalations'. She prudently stayed at the entrance, whence she tried to draw them out, telling them she meant them only well. 'Only six came, they could hardly move. Shortly afterwards, I went back; there were no more children; they had been drowned.'

On 24 January 1794, when the Entrepôt had been emptied of all but 20 captives, mostly girls and children too young to be tried, Carrier went to the president of the military commission, Gonchon, who was charged with meting out punishment on the captured Vendeans: 'So you old rogue, you old good-for-nothing, you want to try them? Go ahead, judge them; if the Entrepôt isn't empty within 24 hours I'll have you and your colleagues shot.' The following day the commission sent 26 victims to their death and Gonchon collapsed and died, assuredly from an apoplexy of fear.

\*    \*    \*

On Nantes, Carrier visited a sort of biblical wrath. The cosmopolitanism and riches of a city fattened on commerce, the slave trade, colonial import and export, was incompatible, in his eyes, with pure citizenship. 'Liberty does not compromise. We will be able to be human when we are assured of being conquerors.' He was doing no less, he thought, than what the CPS had ordered him to do: to wreak the national vengeance on a miscreant city. However, the strong meat of bloated rhetoric does not always suit a delicate stomach.

The young Marie-Antoinette Jullien came to Nantes to investigate Carrier's activities and wrote to the CPS on 3 February: 'I have just left Nantes, and in Carrier I have seen a satrap, a despot, an assassin of public spirit and liberty.' He speaks of how Carrier 'submerged in the Loire all those filling the prisons of Nantes' and 'Justice must be rendered to Carrier – he has in his time there destroyed trade.' It was rather too late. And, although what pitiable remnants of the military threat of the Vendée had been crushed at Cholet and stamped out to oblivion at Savenay and Le Mans, the CPS now ordered the final retribution, demanded by Barère in August and supposedly completed during the autumn: the destruction of the Vendée.

Reports from the region were contradictory, but the CPS was inclined to believe the gloomier scaremongering assessments. Isidore Broussais, administrator of subsistences, wrote a typically mixed message to the minister of War from Niort: 'I heartily wish this wretched war in the Vendée was over but there will be bands of brigands at large all winter compelling our troops to keep on the move and one must not believe anyone who says that the Vendée no longer exists. There are 3 or 4,000 men who can murder our men at their posts for another three months if they don't stay on their guard . . . I repeat, citizen Minister, the Vendée war is not wholly terminated but *there is no cause for anxiety.*'

There were, however, still prisoners in the gaols of Nantes to be mopped up. On 23 February, a week exactly after Carrier left the city, the coaster *Destin,* moored at Paimboeuf, a town on the left bank of the Loire 11 kilometres from the mouth, took on board 24 women, ten children aged five to ten years, five babies at the breast, two men, of whom one was blind and nearly 80 years old: all supposedly insurgents. The aim was, supposedly, to take them upstream to Nantes, but the captain had an order written by the adjutant-general, Lefèvre, and countersigned by Foucaud, a Marat present at most of the drownings.

Once out at sea, the live cargo was pushed overboard as 'rebels, outlaws'. Carrier had gone. Who could have given such an order? At his trial Foucaud claimed that, as for himself, he had only ever obeyed the orders of a superior. He had received the order from Haxo and Turreau, two men whose names are indelibly linked with the awful fate that awaited the Vendée.

General Turreau had first received the order to 'destroy the Vendée *within three weeks*' on 1 October, the Convention reiterating the earlier injunction following Barère's resonant speech. Similar hysterical demands flew periodically west from Paris and excuses for failure to implement them fully flew back. To 'destroy the Vendée' seemed a simple enough task, given the will to apply the match and ply the bayonet under the considerable weight of military force deployed in a rebellious region 'dominated by ignorance and fanatism'. A simple matter of cutting down forests, battering down hedges, toppling embankments into ditches and burning all combustible matter; of rounding up rebel women and children – spies, every one – herding them into captivity and slaughtering the rest; of commandeering harvests garnered by the local population; of seizing cattle. For, as Carrier argued, 'a department whose citizens should be shot, to a man, does not need food'.

Louis-Marie Turreau de Linières was born at Evreux in 1756 into a family of minor nobility. A professional soldier, he was friends with Bouchotte, who became minister of War in April 1793, and, though eager to assure his political masters of continued zeal for and attachment to the Republic, he remained modest about his own talents. Appointed to command of the armies of the West in late November 1793, he professed surprise: Kléber was the obvious choice. Of the Vendeans, he was frank in admiration: 'The Vendeans fought in a hitherto unknown and inimitable way, uniquely appropriate to the country and the genius of the inhabitants. They were unshakeably attached to their political ideals, possessed unlimited confidence in their chiefs and kept their promises with a loyalty which could serve as a substitute for discipline. Their courage was indomitable, proof against danger, hardship and privation. These qualities made the Vendeans formidable enemies – they deserve to be ranked with the foremost warrior peoples.'

He was particularly impressed with their skill and dexterity with firearms – hunters and poachers who never fired without taking aim (a swipe at the erratic, trigger-happy Blues) and rarely missed their target; marksmen capable of delivering a withering onslaught of fire, not in volleys but in such rapid shooting that the hail of bullets never flagged. Their intimate knowledge of the fields, hedges, woods, thickets, ravines, gullies and byways gave them a crucial head start on the floundering republicans. 'They attacked and pursued with inconceivable fury and speed . . . firing all the time. They load their muskets as they march or even at the double and being on the move does not detract from the rapidity or the accuracy of their fire . . . a successful general arriving in the Vendée with ten frontier campaigns to his credit will find it very difficult to operate successfully in this region.'

Turreau was chosen more for his political adroitness than for his military abilities. His Hébertist sympathies made him a natural ally of Bouchotte in the jockeying for place which followed the destruction of the Vendean army. Turreau had studiously avoided the intrigues, the jealousies – between sansculotte and professional generals – which had so rent the army. He was well aware of the propensity of generals to puff their own achievements, their 'desire to have a small place in the newspapers . . . pompous accounts in periodicals about small gains won by officers in the army I command of which I would have remained ignorant for a long time were I not to have read them in the public press'. He assured the CPS that he would 'sacrifice all other interests, including my own, to the truth'.

He behaved much as any political representative of the people, regarding his duty to the literal interpretation of his orders as uppermost. Told to destroy the Vendée, he wrote: 'If the measures I have taken are well supported, within two weeks there will be not a house, nor food, no weapons, no men in the whole of the Vendée except those hidden in the depths of the forests, given that, according to the general [Haxo], they could not be burnt down. He proposes to have them cut down and sold at auction with the proviso that buyers will be given a time limit for clearing the ground.'

The preposterous idea that entire tracts of dense, sodden forest could be burnt down in the depths of winter gives some measure of the incompatibility of commands and obedience to them.

Another letter outlined Turreau's plan for 12 columns of soldiers to converge on the Vendée and sweep the region end to end: 'All brigands found bearing arms or convicted of having taken them up in revolt against their patrie will be bayoneted. This will also be done with girls, women and children answering the same charge. Persons no more than suspect will not be spared but no execution will be carried out except by prior order of the general.'

This final caution was entirely consistent with the muddle inherent in most of the dealings between central government and men on the ground. Carrier told the CPS in early December that he had ordered generals Haxo and Dutray to 'kill them all, both sexes, indiscriminately, burn everything . . . for it is as well for you to know that the women and the priests have fomented and supported the war in the Vendée, that the women have shot our luckless prisoners . . . and have fought with the brigands and killed our volunteers pitilessly when they came on them in the villages'. Fatuous misconstruction based on hearsay. Yet, on 16 January, Turreau had requested of the representatives in the region clarification of the order with reference to women and children: 'If my orders are to bayonet them all, I cannot execute such an order without a warrant which covers my responsibility.' There was no reply. He wrote to the CPS and attached the letter as evidence that he had, at least, informed the authorities of his intentions.

The order for the assembling of the 12 columns followed the next day. Two weeks later Turreau received a sort of response from the CPS: 'You complain that you have not received from the Committee formal approbation of your measures. They appear to the Committee good and your intentions pure; but, far removed from the theatre of operations, it awaits substantial results before pronouncing on a matter on which it has already been let down so many times, so too the national Convention.'

Six generals were put in command of 12 columns of soldiers armed with muskets and bayonets; no artillery trains to slow their progress; minimal rations; swift, ruthless attack must be the *modus operandi*. General Haxo had already begun the work of reprisal: four of what were soon called 'infernal columns', had descended on 700–800 rebels under their leader, Ripaultoé la Cathelinière, in the forest of Princé, 16 kilometres south-west of Nantes; hit from both sides, the rebels fled in terror, hotly pursued. Haxo announced that he was moving on south and east to clear the forests of Machecoul, Touvois, Grandes Landes and Rocheservière. The general of brigade, Grignon, encamped at Argenton on the eastern edge of the Vendée, reported that as well as conducting daytime operations his patrols were also carrying out nightly searches of smallholdings, hunting down rebels who had returned home and recommenced their work. Grignon appended a request for shoes: half the soldiers in his columns were barefoot. (Many soldiers were marginally luckier – shod with brown paper.)

Turreau's commission was complicated by the failure of one of the column commanders, Marceau, to keep him abreast of progress with campaign reports and the refusal of Westermann's Mayençais regiments to collaborate with him. Westermann, bragging wildly and without basis, informed Paris that 'the Vendée is destroyed – in a very short time we have exterminated to the last man the 80,000 combatants who remained'. Having rebutted this nonsense, Turreau was further harried by fears of an English landing, a belated reinforcement of the rebels. Since this had not happened when the Vendeans were at full force, the likelihood now that they were spent was remote. However, Turreau received warnings from the minister in Paris, Bouchotte, that a 12,000-strong invasion force was mustered on 'the English islands' with 60 transport vessels and frigates. Had he, they asked, organised mobile furnaces for the manufacture of red-hot bullets?

The infernal columns had another deleterious effect: rebel forces were reforming to defend their territory and their people against these entirely vindictive reprisal raids. Rochejaquelin, Stofflet and Charette stood, once more, in the front line, Rochejaquelin with his trademark red handkerchief tied round his head. At the battle of Fontenay the Blues had been told to aim at the red handkerchief, after which all Rochejaquelin's men sported the bandana to divert the danger from their leader. When the republicans marched into a small settlement in the bosky Mauges of the southern banks of the Loire, 1,000 peasants sprang out of cover, scattered and chased the Blues towards Sainte-Christine, which had just been set on fire by the 26-year-old General Cordellier. They pressed them on further, to Chemillé, where the young republican General Moulin, trying to rally his troops, was hit by a musket ball. About to be taken by the rebels, he turned his pistol on himself. On the way back, four days later, the Vendeans ran into a large body of republican forces; Rochejaquelin was killed, although his death was not bruited abroad for two weeks.

However, the reactivated Vendean resistance perforce changed Turreau's plan. In February he addressed different imperatives. The Vendée was no longer a docile tract of vanquished territory awaiting systematic desolation, but a nest of brigands whose legendary courage was now overlaid with a terrible desperation. The one hope of safety left to the vanquished is to surrender all hope of safety. To the task of exterminating the 'wicked race of people inhabiting the Vendée' was added the need to harry new rebel groupings, search forests, defend positions under attack, guard convoys taking grain and cattle to military supply depots.

The bell tower in Saint-Aubin-du-Plain was, once again, flying two flags – the tricolour and the black and white rebel standard. Grignon's men corralled the 69 inhabitants they could find, made them dig their own grave and bayoneted them. Use of the bayonet was enjoined to economise on powder.

Boucret, 29 years old, directing operations in the central area, found Châtillon already destroyed, put to the torch by Westermann's Mayençais; he moved on and 'yesterday I burnt all the mills I saw and today, without running any risk, I can burn most of Maulévrier'. When his general complained that burning woodland was hampered by rain, Turreau advised them to cut the trees down – 'leave them nowhere to hide'.

The slaughter went on relentlessly, any sensibilities still dormant in the reprisal squads thoroughly benumbed: typical, the massacre of women and children in La Poitevinière, a report of a child stuck on a pike and paraded through the town as a trophy. When Turreau ordered the shooting of two prisoners in Cholet, the town's surveillance committee, voicing a revulsion many felt but few were in a position to evince, complained to him, insisting that they be taken for trial before the military commission: 'Citizen general, your soldiers call themselves republicans and give themselves up to debauchery, the destruction of property and to every horror to which not even cannibals are prone. The carrier of this message will give you all the evidence you need for repressing this destructive fury and punishing the guilty.' And an agent for military provender and supplies, Beaudesson, said (under oath): 'The eyes could not but see everywhere bloody images; everywhere fields covered with victims whose throats had been cut. Wishing to establish for myself whether there were any foodstuffs still to be found in houses scattered here and there only half burnt, I entered several. But what did I find there? Fathers, mothers, children of all ages and both sexes, swimming in their own blood, naked and in postures which the most heartless soul could not gaze upon without shuddering. It upsets me even to think of it.'

The soldiers became inured to the horrors they were perpetrating. Many of the reinforcements had come from the eastern frontier and, told that they were marching against the Vendean brigands, the royal Catholic scum demonised in Hébert's journal, 'their joy, their happiness were indescribable'. Pumped up by the obscene ranting of *Le Père Duchesne*, swallowing whole the raw syllogism that since anyone with property was an anti-patriot, taking, or destroying, property was a simple act of justice, they further dulled their senses by emptying the wine cellars at every place they marched into. And, since all the Vendeans wore the same clothes – loose trousers, clumping wooden clogs, broad-brimmed hats, neckerchiefs, how could they distinguish between rebels and patriots when they were flushed out of their sneaky hidey-holes like rabbits out of burrows?

The Blues were occasionally joined by the local militia fighting as part of Ronsin's revolutionary army. Jean Pinard, a 26-year-old illiterate drunkard farmworker, had for some months commanded a troop of gendarmes bent on profiting from the general destruction. Led by Pinard, they pillaged the Château de Careil, carried off cartloads of property and, given 800 livres by the family not to set light to the house, Pinard pocketed it and burnt the place down anyway. This was but one incident in a trail of havoc he wrought, a rampage of pure thuggery. On 18 February, by now in command of a large company, he captured seven young female brigands, 'beautiful as goddesses', whom he handed over to 600 men. 'In one day, each of the girls received 100 men. Afterwards they could no longer walk, turned imbecile, and, a few days later, they were shot.' (Testimony of Cormeray, a mirror-maker.)

The resurgent rebels were fighting with unwonted savagery; the tactics of the Blues had removed all calls for clemency. Three thousand of them, only half armed with firearms, pushed Cordellier into hapless retreat as far as Nantes, where Carrier excoriated him for turning tail 'without firing a shot . . . It's astonishing, it's humiliating that republicans have abjectly fled a bunch of brigands without artillery and most of them without firearms. Punish, punish, I say, the traitors and cowards with justice, severe justice.'

This defeat changed everything. Turreau's plan for what was called 'cleansing' was now dead. He needed a united front, not least because 'one legitimate cause of anxiety was the absence of ambulances [carts following the army – a recent innovation] with the army so that the troops fear that if they are wounded they are left without help and a prey to the enemy's fury'. For the Vendeans had thrown off their earlier innocence: the viciousness of the war had imposed on them its own woeful, iniquitous laws of engagement. General Prévignaud, wounded and taken back to the hospital in Niort, wrote to Turreau: 'I have witnessed Grignon's columns massacring indiscriminately, mothers, fathers, children, all wiped out. This behaviour has swollen Charette's army. Patriots have been forced to join with brigands. This was decidedly not your intention.'

Charette's army had recently given General Duquesnoy's column a pasting quite close to Nantes, only to turn and flee when the Blues made a last desperate rush. The rebels hurled their clogs at them and, firepower exhausted, ran. Duquesnoy reported that 'some 800 have bitten the dust. Night stopped us and having neither bread nor cartridges I was forced to bivouac on the highway and await your orders.' (A bivouac was originally a night watch mounted by an army in the field; its use for a makeshift encampment was a recent innovation.)

Still Turreau voiced frustration with the misinformation which abounded, writing to the CPS a formal denunciation, to be read out in the Convention, of the 'ignorant, the wastrels, the plotters, the traitors who don't cease to falsify the true situation in the Vendée'.

Still the killings went on. Boucret gave notice that he intended to go to La Gaubretière 'to burn this town, to kill everyone I meet without compunction because it is a refuge of brigands. I have never occupied a territory where it was possible to encounter so many evil people, women as well as men. They will all go by fire and the sword.' At the news of his approach the old people, the women and children took to the spinneys; the men barricaded themselves in the church. His men broke down the doors and cut the refugees to pieces. It was the third time in six weeks that La Gaubretière had been hammered by the Blues. In all, some 500 victims died. Two locales near the town were subsequently renamed in bitter memory of the massacres and mutilations: the Valley of Howling . . . the Field of Ears.

On 18 February Cordellier's columns descended on the small town of Clisson, where the ancient castle perched atop a rocky bluff over-hanging the confluence of the rivers Moine and Sèvre. The Blues sacked the town and broke into the castle, where a number of inhab-itants had taken refuge. In the central stone-paved courtyard of the keep stands a deep well rimmed by a low parapet wall. Into this well the republicans tipped as many bodies as the shaft would hold.

Cordellier, under overall command of Haxo, moved on in the direction of Les Lucs – two villages, Grand and Petit, straddling the valley of the Boulogne – on directions from the two representatives Hentz and Garrau, who told him that 'Charette's brigands are in Les Lucs or in the surrounding forests'. They advised an attack at dawn, the cavalry encircling the whole area ready to cut down anyone who tried to escape. Les Lucs occupied a position of considerable strategic importance on the Nantes–La Roche-sur-Yon axis, and a major junc-tion on the main route between the flatlands stretching from Machecoul to the west and the dense bocage of the interior. Grand Luc stands on slightly higher ground than Petit Luc down in the densely wooded valley.

Several towns in the Vendée suffered a heavier toll of massacre than Les Lucs, but the strategic position loaded the slaughter there with a heavier symbolic significance: this was a devastating strike at the very heart of the Vendée, at a crossroads of its communications. Turreau had planned the attack for the night of 23–24 February, but Charette had, as ever, slipped the noose. The pursuing Blues were caught in the thickets and tangles of the bocage and went in constant terror of ambush.

The carnage inflicted on Les Lucs occurred on the last day of February and the first day of March 1794. Nearly a month later the Abbé Barbedette, a refractory priest, came to Les Lucs and found, scattered in the open, the rotting corpses of 564 inhabitants of the two villages, among them 127 children less than ten years old. Working through the parish registers, he recorded every name.

Jullien wrote to the CPS deprecating the excesses of Carrier and the anarchy which obtained in the conduct of the Vendean war: 'It is a proven fact that there would be no longer any war in the Vendée if the generals had been of good faith in wanting to end it . . . you gave orders for them to burn the brigands' refuges . . . They have burnt whole communes whose inhabitants were armed with pitch-forks, sickles and firearms and were themselves arresting brigands to hand over to the republican army. Would you credit it that under the pretext of following your orders they have murdered women, children and, following a civic banquet in honour of a division of the army, the municipal officers who held it? I have seen poor unfortunates in despair, having no prospect other than death, either from the republican army or from the royalist horde . . . Everything is given up to pillage and fire.'

Carrier was recalled. Barère told the Convention that 'the CPS ordered the destruction and burning of brigands' refuges, *not* of the farms and houses of good citizens'. But contrary reports still muddied the situation. Hentz and Garrau told the CPS, at the end of February, that 'the race of men inhabiting the Vendée is evil, made up of fanatics, federalists, Messieurs. The proof of this is that there are so few good men who have not supported the rebels . . . We must have a telling example, we must teach the malevolents that the national vengeance is severe and that a region which has cost the blood of so many thousands of patriots must not serve as a refuge for those in revolt against the government.'

On 10 March Hentz and the new representative Francastel warned Turreau that, having been given all the necessary resources, he had no excuse for failing to render the region at peace over the past two months. 'You must neither quit the army, nor sleep nor rest as long as there is a gathering of rebels in the Vendée . . . there is no other reply you can make to this letter than to tell us, forthwith, that you can scatter all brigand groupings within eight days at the most . . . and that Charette and Stofflet or any others no longer command an army in the Vendée. Beware: whatever path you take, anything, except victory, exposes you to a far from illusory responsibility and to dangers whose consequences you can foresee.'

The generals, many of them as feckless and inebriated as the soldiery and most of them heavily influenced by Hébertist attitudes, certainly wanted to prolong their activities in the Vendée: this rich granary keeping much-needed grain and foodstuffs from the starving poor of Paris, and a people who put King and Church before the Republic and still kowtowed to the aristocrats who held sway over them. Turreau, caught between orders and threats from Paris and orders and threats from the representatives in the Vendée, and amid the interminable confusion as to what precisely 'destroy the Vendée' did or should entail, responded to intelligence from Haxo that his orders were being obstructed by the municipal authorities in Challans, who had complained to the Convention, through the representative Laignelet, about the 'devastations which are ruining them'. He reminded the patriots of Challans that their efforts to impede his destruction of brigands' hideouts was in flagrant breach of orders from a much higher authority. He had been commanded to destroy or confiscate and 'each of the generals whom I have the honour to command has received from me a positive order to execute these rigorous measures and to ignore any protest even from constituent bodies . . . I bid you not forget that, having been ordered specifically by the CPS to finish the war in the Vendée, I do not have to account to you for the means I have adopted to achieve that.'

He was replaced in mid-May and arrested in the autumn and imprisoned with most of the generals who had commanded his infernal columns and the representatives Hentz, Francastel and Laignelet, not to be released until late December 1795.

From prison he wrote to the CPS, after an amnesty for the Vendée was voted on 2 December 1794: 'France will doubtless learn with interest and surprise that this Turreau accused of ferocity proposed an amnesty similar to that of today, an amnesty which, after the defeat at Savenay would have been as humane as politic . . . but he received orders *if within 8 days everything in the Vendée is not totally annihilated, consider you responsible . . . the scaffold awaits you. The scaffold, again the scaffold and always the scaffold.*

'Finally, citizen representatives, I appeal to your hearts. Innocent, I have languished too long; blameworthy, you have delayed striking a criminal too long. I ask for a response. Only tyrants stifle the voice of the accused – under the empire of liberty it must be heard. Do you hear me?'

At the start of the Vendean war the population of the region stood at around 400,000. Of approximately 200,000 victims of the war, perhaps around 40,000 perished at the hands of the infernal columns. The population of Les Lucs, 2,150 in 1787, was fewer than 900 ten years later.

Lequinio, a representative at the time, instigator of another if shorter chapter of horrors and author of an account of the Vendean war, vindicated Turreau: public safety had demanded draconian measures. He condemned only gratuitous cruelty. 'In wiping out these entire generations for the good of the patrie, nothing could induce toleration of barbaric, inhuman, wicked measures, carried out by a single individual. These frightful actions, necessary as they were to consolidating the Republic, should have been carried through with more pity, more compassion, so as not to add to their misery by heaping upon them the stain of remorse.'

# ✤ TWELVE ✤

# *The Need for Rigour*

> . . . there cannot a greater judgement befall a country than such a dreadful spirit of division that rends a government into two distinct people and makes them greater strangers to one another than if they were different nations . . . a furious party spirit which rages in its full violence . . . fills a nation with spleen and rancour and extinguishes all the seeds of good nature, compassion and humanity.
>
> Joseph Addison, *Spectator*

RAOUL HESDIN RECORDS THAT:

It is absolutely necessary, either by bribery or by secret influence, or by an affectation of extreme patriotism, to possess one's self of the little card or paper on which, together with a description of one's personal appearance, a note is made of one's dwelling place, age and employment. The paper is obtained first at a section meeting, signed by the president and secretary of the same and then forwarded to the Town Hall in copy. Any person who has been continually resident since 1789 must produce proof of having served in the Blues, paid all taxes including those so ridiculously called 'patriotic [that is, enforced] gifts', signed no monarchical petitions, been rejected at no republican club; not have held more than one office or received more than one salary from the Republic at the same time, and the like. By strict law, seven signatures of members of the section revolutionary committee are necessary but such are hardly ever present to give force to it. A man is at all times liable

to be called on to present his certificate of civism to any agent of
the government or to any person representing himself to be such.
It is a favourite device of the municipals for the extortion of money
to summon a whole family to the bar and then, cancelling their
certificates without assigning any reason, to leave the dread of being
suspect hanging over their heads. It is the fashion to wear one's
certificate in the hat band.

Hesdin lost his certificate of civism to a pickpocket who returned it
to him by post, with a note attached saying that though regretfully
obliged to 'borrow the assignats for my necessities, I would not for
the world disquiet so brave a sansculotte respecting his citizenship'.

The award of certificates was another case of extraordinary power
wielded by a small caucus. In each of the Paris sections were about
3,000 electors, of whom probably about 100 attended meetings at
which business was managed by a nucleus of some dozen activists,
the 40-sou patriots drawing the pay decreed in Danton's measure.

Since the certificate was issued only to those who attended section
meetings regularly and were approved by the issuing committee, the
caucus exercised a ready means of excluding their opponents of whatever class.

The section reports joined the morass of paperwork generated by
the machinery of surveillance, police operations and judicial process,
and the invasive culture of suspicion and delation. The character references drawn up after interview came on printed forms with columns
for: name/age/marital status/children; the place where the interview
was held; professions before the Revolution; earnings before and after
the Revolution; relations and liaisons of the subject, as evidence of
patriotism or shady dealing and opinion; an assessment of the subject's
moral character and political opinions as manifested on the historic
days: May, July and October 1789, 10 August 1792; the flight and death
of the tyrants; 31 May 1793; the crises of the war; has the subject signed
any liberticide petitions or orders?

Paramount were the qualifying credentials for anyone wanting to
claim pedigree as a sansculotte, which, during the Terror, were, variously: never to have missed a historic day, a wound sustained at the
Tuileries; attendance at the section general assembly every time it
met; to have been to and enjoyed the great patriotic Festivals; to have
denounced three royalists, five fanatics and seven hoarders, or secured

the arrest of a refractory priest hiding in a cupboard; always to have upheld respect due to the national Convention, the revolutionary tribunal, the revolutionary government, the holy law of the maximum, the Revolution; marriage to a brave working woman; eschewing all luxuries and idle pursuits – gambling and billiards, over-drinking – never to have doubted official news; always to have read the Declaration of the Rights of Man to his children at bedtime . . .

And, since the true sansculotte could be recognised by the inflammatory style of his language, larding his outbursts with the words that made up the ABC of Jacobin vengefulness – carnage, blood, death, vengeance – he must employ the cannibalistic metaphors which were the common coin of Hébert's acolytes: I'd like to eat an aristocrat's liver . . . open his stomach and eat his guts . . . I'd like to eat the head of a bourgeois . . . let's eat a good dish of aristocrat's lights . . .

Smoking a pipe was regarded as another must for the earnest sansculotte – the tax farmers were accused of putting water in the tobacco to increase their profit on its sale and smoking became a visible act of solidarity with the proletarian struggle for fair trade. Hesdin remarks on the consequences: 'I walked this evening to the Tavern of the Guard at the barrier on the Orléans road [south]. It is a pleasant place with a pretty garden; but the disgusting habit of smoking tobacco in all the coffee houses poisons me. It was formerly the mode to do so only in the lowest cabarets [public house]; it was regarded as a mark of Dutch vulgarity and boorishness. I find many of the patriot fashions difficult to assume, but this one impossible and shall no doubt soon become suspect in consequence. All the Mucios [*sic*] Scaevolas were puffing their pipes there this evening.'

The day after the taking of the Tuileries on 10 August 1792, sansculotte vigilantes began to demand presentation of a passport from anyone seeking to leave Paris and passports (temporary documents indicating height, complexion, name, residence of the holder and stating time of egress and ingress) were not issued without a certificate of civism. The Law of Suspects had made the requirement of the certificate general throughout France. Anyone who failed to present one was liable to arrest and imprisonment.

The comte de Paroy, outlawed at Fontainebleau in 1792, took refuge in Bordeaux and was an engraver of some talent. He offered to design a new civism card to be issued to the members of his section in return for his own card. He went to the printers with the president of his section but stayed behind when the president left, ostensibly to supervise the finer points of finish. The printer went off to dinner and, in his absence, de Paroy ran off 50 extra cards and filled in 20 for friends who, like him, were living in hiding and fear of arrest.

But everyone lived with fear of arrest: the stall-keeper selling lemons who eked out a living by selling newspapers on a street corner, arrested for distributing counter-revolutionary propaganda, was acquitted only when the police discovered that he couldn't read . . . the road-maker regarded as an aristocrat by his section largely because he worked on the new rest days, the décadis, while continuing to take Sundays off . . . the unfortunate bystander in a crowd hauled in on suspicion of wearing some ribbon or other token which might be taken as a rallying sign – a man or woman sporting a sprig of oak, a flower, a piece of paper on which a slogan might be written, a faded cockade in hat or hair or pinned to a jacket or dress . . .

Most held their tongues; exasperation drove others to reckless incaution. The Paris stable boy overheard saying that he didn't give a toss for the Republic. A voice in a crowd overheard by Mercier: 'Let the French die so long as liberty triumphs.' The candle-maker of Rochefort who supplied the navy with candles made not with wax but turpentine and grease, which burnt for 21 minutes as against 24 hours. The baker in Alsace who snapped and said: 'The Republic will go to hell with its partisans just as Lucifer was destroyed by the Almighty.' The gardener in Arras who predicted that 'a beast with seven horns will come to devour the patriots'. A cutler of the same town who boasted that he had 'enough knives to slaughter the patriots' and would take care to 'put an edge on the sabres of the aristocrats'. François Lemaire, merchant of Béthune, who expressed the belief that 'one day the patriots will be eaten up by lice'. Jean Vatelle, volunteer in the 92nd Battalion of Haute-Saône, had served the King and had money; now he served the Republic and had none: 'I shit on the nation. I haven't got a tricolour cockade in my hat, I'd rather be hanged than wear one for the nation.'

Careless talk cost lives but many people had got to the weary point where they couldn't care less. The country was bankrupt, the Revolution was bankrupt and all promise of change, liberty, equality and fraternity was bankrupt. Millin de Labrosse, a former captain in

the army, was sitting on a street corner in the north-east of Paris reading
a newspaper. Turkey had just declared for France in the war against
the coalition of foreign tyrannies. He opined: Turkey would have done
better to join Austria. A man, hearing this, one Joly Braquehaye, an
informer for the CGS, took Labrosse to task; they scuffled; Labrosse
demanded satisfaction and next morning arrived at the rendezvous
with two swords under his coat, to be met by Braquehaye in company
with three gendarmes who arrested him.

Labrosse was confined in the gaol at the Hôtel de Ville for 51 days
without being interrogated. On 13 January 1794 he wrote to a friend
of his mother: 'My last linen is filthy, my stockings have rotted away,
my breeches are threadbare, I am dying of hunger and boredom . . .
the world is an abomination. Farewell.' Worn out, he wrote to
Fouquier-Tinville begging to be brought to trial. Sentenced to death,
he wrote to him a second time, a full month later, pointing out that
he was leaving behind a cardboard model of an air balloon of revolutionary design and begged two hours' grace in order to explain the
theory behind its construction to the revolutionary committee of his
section. He took the liberty to propose this and asked Fouquier to
pass the note on to the CPS if he deemed it necessary. 'I am resigned.
I shall die resigned. I am not simply trying to prolong my life but I
admit that I am thinking of how I might ensure that my name should
be remembered when this time of fury is past. I greet you respect-
fully. Alas there is no fraternity any more. Millin Labrosse. PS Citizen
Harny is acquainted with my air balloon and I appeal to his
conscience, though he bears me a grudge. I have no more paper.'

The fifth issue of *The Old Cordelier* castigated the radicalism of Hébert
– the pig's swill of his rants, the excrement of his spuming nastiness,
the intemperate profanity of his tub oratory. It also blasted the
inherent cruelty of Robespierre's dogmatic law-making, the lurch into
a police state; it appealed to the original defenders of revolution, the
liberators of the nation whose honest endeavours had been trampled
on by the self-seeking scum who dominated the Commune and
packed the juries of the revolutionary tribunal. It defended Danton,
Legendre and Fabre d'Eglantine against charges of indulgence
levelled at them in the Jacobin club.

On 7 January Robespierre broke cover. He told the Jacobins: 'Some
time ago [14 December] I undertook to defend Desmoulins against

charges made here in the Jacobins. I allowed myself some reflections on his character; that was acceptable in friendship; but today I am compelled to adopt a very different tone.' Camille Desmoulins was, as he had said on that earlier occasion, a spoilt child with a sunny disposition but he had been led astray by bad company. 'Now we must apply rigour . . . I demand that all five numbers of Camille's journal be burnt in this Society.'

At this, Desmoulins burst out: 'All very well, says Robespierre, but I reply to you, as Rousseau once said: *To burn is not to answer.*' Robespierre paled. Desmoulins gave ground, recalling how he had read the journal to Robespierre in his lodgings and asked for his comments. Robespierre said he had seen only one or two numbers. Danton proposed a reading of the journals and the following day, after Momoro had read out the third issue to the Jacobins who listened 'in a profound silence' to such sentiments as: 'Do you really believe that it is women, old men, the feeble, the "egoists" who are dangerous? Of your true enemies, only the cowards and the sick remain . . .', Robespierre demanded the right to speak. 'It is pointless,' he said, 'to read out the fifth number of *The Old Cordelier* because opinion about Camille must already be formed. You see in his works the most revolutionary principles juxtaposed with maxims of the most pernicious moderatism . . . Desmoulins is a bizarre composite of truths and lies, of politics and absurdities, of healthy views and chimerical private projects. On top of all that, whether the Jacobins persecute or protect Desmoulins is of no importance – he is nothing but an individual.'

He then turned on Fabre d'Eglantine, whom he had had prevented from leaving the room: 'I demand that this man whom one never sees without a lorgnette in his hand and who knows so well how to unravel the intrigues of the theatre, be good enough explain himself fully here.' That lorgnette, through which Fabre peered so supercilliously; that lorgnette, such an affectation, an aristocratic opera-house trumpery that made Robespierre, in his old-regime silk coat, breeches and stockings, his powdered wig and green-lensed spectacles, bridle.

Fabre's attempts to exculpate himself from the imbroglio of the Indies Company scandal were howled down by a chant of 'To the guillotine'. He was excluded from the Jacobin club and Desmoulins would have followed him into that dangerous exile two days later had not Robespierre, playing another turn of cat and mouse, not intervened on his behalf, taking the opportunity to dilate piously on his own disinterestedness: 'Because *I* have exercised in the CPS a twelfth part of the authority, people call me dictator . . . *my* dictatorship is that of Lepeletier, of Marat. [Applause]. You have misunderstood me; *I* do not wish to say that *I* resemble such and such a man; *I* am neither Lepeletier nor Marat; nor more am *I* the martyr of the Revolution; *my* dictatorship is the same as theirs, that is to say, the daggers of tyrants.' Wild applause. And the evangelist of those who sought to murder him was Desmoulins and his libels.

The following day, 12 January, Robespierre fell ill and that very night Fabre was arrested: it was a heavy blow to the indulgent cause, especially given the nature of the charge.

Desmoulins' wife wrote to his and Robespierre's old schoolfriend Fréron, now overseeing the bloody punishment of the rebels in Toulon: 'Come back, Fréron, come back quickly. You have not a minute to lose, bring with you all the old Cordeliers [that is, men of the same persuasion] you can find, we need them desperately . . . Robespierre, your guiding compass, has denounced Camille in the Jacobins . . . All through two meetings he thundered and shouted at Camille . . . Danton is no longer heard, he is losing courage, he has become feeble. D'Eglantine is arrested and sent to the Luxembourg. Was he not a patriot, then?'

Two weeks later Desmoulins (whose father-in-law had just been arrested) was bold enough to produce a sixth issue of *The Old Cordelier*, showing no sign of any climbdown in his opposition to the government. Shortly afterwards Robespierre reappeared at the Jacobins, where Léonard Bourdon demanded that 'the red general', Ronsin, arrested on the denunciation of Fabre d'Eglantine on 17 December, should be set free. Robespierre was opposed but Paris was starving, he and the CPS could well do without any more riots and on the night of 2–3 February Ronsin and Vincent were released by the CGS for want of evidence. A week later Robespierre withdrew once again from public life: he remained absent for a month, from 11 February to 12 March. On 13 February Saint-Just returned to Paris from the armies of the North and a week later was elected president of the Convention.

Before he left for the army he proposed to the CPS a method for dealing with suspect and arrested nobles: 'For 1,000 years the nobility have oppressed the French people by their extortions and feudal exactions of every kind. The feudal age and the nobility are finished. You need to carry out repairs to the roads in the frontier regions for the passage of our artillery and the convoys of our armies. All the nobles who are held in prisons should do forced labour and carry out the work on the roads.' The other members were horrified: to apply such a punishment – a revival of the corvée – to detainees was obscene, it smacked of the tyranny of a king. 'Very well,' retorted Saint-Just. 'I wanted to test the will of the Committee. You are not strong enough to fight against the nobility since you do not know how to destroy it. It is the nobility who will devour the Revolution and the revolutionaries. I withdraw from the Committee.'

Once with the army in Alsace, Saint-Just applied the same rigour to more malleable subjects. He instructed the commune of Strasbourg: 'Ten thousand of our soldiers lack shoes. You will at once confiscate the shoes of all aristocrats in Strasbourg and, by ten o'clock tomorrow morning, 10,000 pairs of shoes must be on their way to our headquarters. The overcoats of every citizen in Strasbourg are hereby commandeered. They must be handed over to the military commissariat of the Republic by tomorrow evening.' His colleague and friend Philippe le Bas wrote to his wife from his headquarters in the city: 'I hope that the bliss of our reunion will be doubled by the news of a lasting victory for our army. Saint-Just and I are working ceaselessly to achieve this, supervising everything to the last button. He is almost as impatient as I am to return to Paris. I have promised him that you will cook him one of your delicious dinners. I am so pleased that you are well disposed to him. He is a really good man; every day my love and admiration for him increases. He mentions you frequently. I really think he values our friendship a great deal.'

Barère, his colleague in the CPS, was less complimentary: 'Saint-Just was autocratic, imperious, cutting. He had a mind of fire and a heart of ice. His conviction was almost mathematically precise.' On one occasion Robespierre was getting heated about some points of law with which he disagreed. Saint-Just said to him: 'Relax. Authority resides in him who remains cool.' That coolness of his did not, it seems, hold in the face of physical danger.

He accompanied Levasseur, an officer, on a reconnaissance of the enemy lines – they could see quite clearly the gunners putting tapers to the cannon. Levasseur said: 'The people's representative ought not to view the battle from such a long way off – shall we go down there in the thick of it?' "To do what?" he said. One of the other officers in the party laughed. I smiled and said to Saint-Just: "I see the smell of powder disagrees with you" and galloped off and left him to it.'

The next day Saint-Just called to see Levasseur, who was busy with letters. While he wrote, Saint-Just picked up Levasseur's carbine and fiddled with the hammer. Unbeknown to him, it was loaded; it went off and the ball flew straight past Levasseur into his valise, which was on a chair about two metres away. He stood up. Saint-Just went as pale as death, let go of the gun, staggered over and slumped in Levasseur's arms. 'What if I'd killed you?' he croaked. Levasseur replied: 'You'd have done me a bad turn – if I'm going to be shot I hope it'll be by an enemy.' The room filled with officers, drawn by the report of the gun. Levasseur mused on the chance of Saint-Just being accused of murder, following the chance remark of the day before.

The writer Charles Nodier describes a meeting with the man they called the Angel of Death: 'I was very young at the time. I was arrested at 6 in the morning and taken to see this terrible Saint-Just about whom everyone spoke so menacingly. My heart beat violently; I felt my knees go weak when I entered his office. He did not look at me. He had his back turned. He stood in front of the mantelpiece, flanked by two candelabra filled with candles; he stared into a mirror, adjusting the folds of his voluminous stock, high round his neck. His head was raised up, as Camille Desmoulins scoffingly remarked, like the sacred host in a monstrance at the Mass, motionless.

'I could see that the arch of his eyebrows was not rounded but almost a straight line; his eyes were large and pensive; his complexion pale and unhealthy, probably from fatigue, his lips soft and sensuous. He was not so handsome as his portraits make out but he was good-looking in a statuesque way. While he folded his cravat he dictated to a secretary in laconic and almost brutal phrases – orders, decrees, sentences from which there was no appeal. I cannot bring to mind without a shudder the constant repetition of the cruel word *death* with which they all ended, like the sting of a scorpion.

'Finally he turned to me and asked my name, where I came from, my age. Suddenly he darted forward and tugged me into the light. "He cannot be more than 11 or 12 [actually 13]," he said, "he looks like a young girl." He shook with anger. "A warrant of arrest for a child? I will make them pay for their murderous accusations. They dare to threaten me because I will give them no blood? Very well:

they will have blood – I shall bathe these new tyrants who enslave our France in blood."

'In spite of his heightened emotion, Saint-Just remained calm on the exterior. His hand was clenched on the paper and I shiver as I write this but he spoke coolly as if reading the words out.

'Dismissing me, he asked me what I was doing in Strasbourg. "I came to study Greek, citizen [Nodier lodged with Eulogius Schneider, the notorious Jacobin governor of Alsace, a noted Greek scholar]."

'"What good is Greek?" he said. "The Spartans wrote nothing." He paused and then said: "Go" with a chilling smile. "If I thought you were being made to learn anything else, I would sign a death warrant."'

Back in Paris, Saint-Just presented two measures, the Laws of Ventôse, the windy month (on 26 February and 3 March): the first required that 'the goods of persons identified as enemies of the people and the Revolution' should be sequestered; the second that all surveillance committees should draw up lists of those detained since 1 May 1789 in order to make provision for redistributing their property to 'needy patriots'. A further decree set up popular commissions to investigate the lists and decide which of those named should be declared enemies of the Revolution and have their property confiscated. And, although the CGS was in overall charge of police matters and remained junior to the great CPS, the Ventôse laws also made provision for the establishment of a new police bureau within the CPS 'for the inspection of authorities and administrations' – that is, directly pinpointing government officials and usurping the functions of the CGS.

There was no great enthusiasm for these decrees; their principal objective was to outmanoeuvre the radicals of the Commune and to press home the attack on the indulgents. Danton drew Saint-Just's oblique scorn: 'There is someone here who, in his heart, nurses the aim of making us go backwards or of crushing us.' Perhaps Robespierre had reported the acrimonious exchanges that passed between him and Danton when the leading indulgent visited him one evening at the Duplays' house in the rue Saint-Honoré, where he lodged, to seek some measure of rapprochement. He taxed Robespierre with the inflexibility of a law which swept up the innocent with the guilty; the Terror exercised no discretion. Robespierre rounded on him: 'Whoever told you that a single innocent person has died?'

Danton, shocked at so blatant a disregard for the verity of what was happening, angrily left the room, saying bitterly: 'And he says not a single innocent being has perished.'

Having overseen the triumphs of the Rhine army, Saint-Just sought to replicate the victory over the backsliders and the Parisian anarchists.

Hébertists and indulgents were trading insults. Desmoulins railed against the suppression of freedom: he was being prevented from bringing out further editions of *The Old Cordelier*. Hébert clamoured for a new insurrection, a re-emphasis of the sansculotte revolutionary programme – he and Carrier, returned from Nantes, veiled the bust of Marat in the Cordeliers, the signal for an uprising. Paris seethed with discontent. The black marketeers thrived. Crowds jostled at food stalls trying to buy basic supplies. An unemployed labourer was arrested for shouting at a grocer: 'Call this liberty. It's all for the rich. The only war they're fighting is on the poor.'

Ronsin and Vincent, supported by Hébert, called for purges of the corrupt authorities. Collot d'Herbois urged the Jacobins, now closely identified with the central government, to rally the Cordeliers, whose affiliations to the Paris Commune separated them from the Mountain in allegiance much as the river separated them physically.

The Convention voted the renewal of the CPS's authority on 11 March. Two days later, strengthened by Robespierre's return from illness, they struck. Saint-Just advanced to the Convention tribunal. Holding his paper quite still in one hand, with the other he gestured metronomically up and down like the blade of the guillotine, as he read: 'I announce to you that there exists in the Republic a conspiracy conducted by foreigners.' Foreigners infiltrating a faction composed of the Hébertists who were themselves in league with the indulgents, both parties 'meeting together by night to concert their daytime assaults'. He played the Robespierre card – pessimism to prick consciences: 'What friends do you have on earth if it is not the people, so long as the people is free, and hemlock when it has ceased to be free?' (Hemlock was the poison of capital punishment in ancient Athens, fed to Socrates by the despotic oligarchs of the city.)

Saint-Just continued, anguished by his failure to understand why Desmoulins, Danton and, he knew too well, many others, wished to call a halt to the Terror, addressing pained rhetorical questions to these fallen stalwarts, ruined by mildness: 'What do you seek, you who want no virtue for your happiness? What do you seek, you who want no terror against criminals? What do you seek, oh you who, without virtue, turn terror on liberty? You will perish, you who run after fortune, you who seek a happiness separate from that of the people.'

From the Convention, Saint-Just walked with Robespierre the short distance up what was then the rue du Dauphin, along the rue Saint-Honoré to the Jacobins, where the members greeted the two patriots back in the fold with tumultuous applause. Robespierre addressed them, thanked them and bid them mobilise against this new 'odious plot' and added: 'Thanks be to God, my physical strength was equal to my moral strength so that today I should have the power to confound the traitors.'

That night, 13–14 March, the police of the CGS knocked on the doors and took into custody Hébert, Momoro, Vincent and Ronsin. The following day they took in Marie-Jean Hérault de Séchelles of the CPS, noble-born, handsome, rich, a man of brilliant and effortless intellect, a womaniser, an atheist. From the age of 18 a king's attorney in the Paris courts, he was good-hearted, amiable, a flamboyant speaker, a man of charm and wit. He had, from the start, been something of an oddity in the CPS: the man to whom things came, or seemed to come, easy could not be taken seriously by those who expended enormous effort and conviction on the minutest detail. Horace Walpole, in 1776, said that this world is a comedy to those who think, a tragedy to those who feel; the macabre achievement of the men who directed the Terror was, somehow, to reverse it and make the comedy of feeling outside the strictures of reason a very black comedy indeed.

The urbane, aristocratic Hérault de Séchelles had been implicated in the Indies Company scandal, suspected (by Robespierre) of protecting the ring of foreign bankers. Now that the dross of Hébert's associates was being trawled in, Hérault could finally be picked off. His arrest was followed by that of Chaumette, the public prosecutor of the Commune, a malignant atheist, proponent of the dechristianising which Robespierre so abhorred.

Condemned with Chaumette was the 26-year-old Lapalus, an agent of the CGS and in cahoots with Javogues in the Loire, who boasted that he had sent to their death no more than 7,000 men in the departments round the Emancipated Town, but that there were 400,000 federalist heads he could have lopped off, just as easily.

As they awaited trial in prison (according to another inmate, Laboureau), Ronsin, 27 years old, evinced a wholly pragmatic acceptance of his fate, an indifference to danger tempered in the pugnacities of soldiering. As the Momoro scribbled away, Ronsin taunted him with the realities: 'What are you writing? All that's useless; this is a political trial; all the time you should have been doing you were talking to the Cordeliers; ingenuousness, indiscretion, has destroyed you; you must know that sooner or later the tools of revolution get broken. You had one chance left and you missed it. However, don't worry: [here he turned to Hébert, Momoro and Vincent] time will avenge us; the people will call our judges to account and have justice for our death. I have an adopted son – I've inculcated in him the principles of a liberty without limit; when he's grown up he will remember his adoptive father's unjust death: he'll kill those who brought us to our death; he'll need no more than a twopenny knife for that.'

Whatever else Momoro wrote, he sent this letter to his wife shortly before he went to the scaffold: 'Republican, guard your character, your courage, you know the purity of my patriotism, I will conserve the same character till death.

'Bring up my son in republican principles. You cannot maintain the printing press, send the workers away. Greetings to the citizenesses Marat, to the republican. I leave you my memory and my virtues, Marat has taught me to suffer. Your husband, Momoro.'

To one of the prisoners reading Hébert's *Le Père Duchesne* Ronsin said: 'Verbiage. Get ready to die – I swear you won't see me flinch.'

When Hébert bemoaned the fact that 'liberty is lost', Ronsin replied: 'You don't know what you're talking about. Liberty can't be destroyed now; the party sending you to your death will follow in its turn and it won't be long' and, with plain reference to Robespierre: 'I realised a long time ago that you were being watched and dogged by a man who is fearful, cunning and dangerous; he took you by surprise because you didn't mistrust him enough.'

Their trial took place on 21–24 March. The accused were charged with fomenting insurrection, manipulating food supplies to create shortages, implication with the foreign plotters who joined them in the dock and the wife of General Quétineau, defeated in the Vendée, who had tried to organise his escape from prison. Robespierre forbade the presence of shorthand writers.

The revolutionary Tribunal assembled in what was once the Grand Hall of the Parliament but had been renamed the Hall of Liberty, adorned with busts of Marat, Brutus and other heroes of republican virtue. In the centre stood a table at which the notaries sat, and another for the public prosecutor, Fouquier-Tinville. The president of the court and three other judges sat on a raised platform in front of which stood the accused in a half-circle, each guarded by a Blue standing behind them. There were counsel allotted for the defence, 'a pitiful set of low attorneys [Hesdin remarks] who would not dare to show their faces at an English sessions and even in them it needs some courage. If they show the least skill in argument or sympathy for their clients, the women and children in the galleries hiss them. Nothing but the allotted 18 livres per day could tempt such wretches to their task.'

Fouquier read out the indictment, affirming, to huge applause, that 'never has there existed a conspiracy against the sovereignty of the French people and its liberty more atrocious in its aim, more wide-reaching, more numerous in its contacts and purpose'.

Accusing the Hébertists of 'organising a false famine to starve the people and reduce them to despair', he made sure of alienating the Commune, their natural constituency, against them.

After three days of evidence Fouquier asked the jury pointedly whether they found the case clear. Not having read his script, the jury answered no, they needed to hear another witness. Since the result of the trial had never been in doubt, this was supererogatory. The president of the court, Pierre-André Coffinhal, at once launched into the accused: 'Did you not form the barbarous project of starving the people? Did you not try to debase the national representation? Your intelligences with the enemy are surely not in doubt? Vile creatures, you will die – your punishment has been postponed too long . . .'

The jury got the message. The legal process ended, the defence lawyers were not called upon to speak, the guilty verdict was delivered on 19 of the 20 accused. One man, a CGS spy, planted in prison to report on their conversation, was acquitted.

On 24 March a huge crowd lined the route to the place de la Révolution, for the first time in ages, to bray and hoot their derision.

It was said that all the windows of the rue Saint-Honoré, last stage of the Calvary, had been let for a week to people eager to see their erstwhile heroes pass in the carts: the very people who had excoriated the class enemies and called for a clearing of the prisons, 'a new September'.

Ronsin had not been popular. 'The Paris cannoneers declared that they would take pleasure in conducting their general to the guillotine, that he had never shown his patriotism save under the influence of copious wine.' The Paris sections had no doubt that he and the rest of the greedy scoundrels of the rue de Choiseul had machinated with the foreign bankers riding with them in the tumbrels. Worse, there were mutterings, without foundation (but so what?), that Ronsin was plotting to overthrow the CGS and the CPS, organs of the fatally corrupt Convention, and establish a military dictatorship. The agents provocateurs and rumour-mongers of the CGS had done their work.

The singular focus of the watching crowd's most scabrous mockery was Hébert himself, 'a patriot, but for money', in the pay of 'the minister of War who allowed the mothers and wives of men defending the patrie to die of starvation while he handed over 100,000 livres, 125,000 livres to Monsieur Hébert, who wants us to sleep with his fucking *Père Duchesne*.'

In the last issue he wrote: 'I cannot repeat it too often: the cause of all the troubles which afflict us stem from the indulgence which has been introduced into the punishment of traitors. One step backwards would destroy the Republic. Fuck it, let us swear, then, death to the moderates as to the royalists and the aristocrats. Unity, courage, constancy and all our enemies will be floored, fuck them.'

He wept and snivelled the whole way, his body convulsing, his hands straining at their bonds. The crowd heaped contempt on him. He was dragged, moaning with terror, on to the scaffold. Not even Madame du Barry, they say, Louis XV's mistress, guillotined the previous December, screamed louder than Hébert. The executioner caught the mood of the crowd and feigned the drop of the blade to provoke one last screech from the gutter of Hébert's misery.

Of Momoro's wife, who had played the goddess of Reason in the dechristianising festival in Notre Dame, Laboureau wrote: 'The goddess of Reason has been very far from reasonable all day; she wept and wailed at the fate of her husband.'

Grammont, another former actor brought into Ronsin's revolutionary army staff, tried to embrace his son at the foot of the scaffold. The young man pushed him away: 'It's you who have brought me here,' he said.

The Hébertists eliminated, it could not be long before the indulgents had their own collar felt. And Danton had, it seemed, given up. 'Can power be worth the effort I observe all round?' The men grasping at power 'have given me such a hatred of these days we are living through, that I sometimes mourn the days when the whole of my weekly income depended on a bottle of ink.' Leaving the Convention hall one day, he heard Vadier, of the CGS, saying: 'We're going to gut that fat slob.' Danton snapped back: 'Tell that bastard that if he makes one move against me I'll eat his brains and shit in his skull.'

Whatever else it was about Danton which drew down Robespierre's enmity, his coarseness made the Incorruptible's skin crawl. Sick, one day, of Robespierre's vapouring about virtue, Danton scoffed with vulgar raillery: 'There's no more solid virtue than what I do every night with my wife. How can a man to whom every idea about morality is alien be the defender of liberty?'

Nevertheless, Danton made a last attempt at reconciliation; he went to see Robespierre, but his nerve was gone, he came without poise, his petition was one of despair and Robespierre knew it. Danton implored him to put aside the whisperings against him of Collot and Billaud, former associates of Hébert and the Commune. 'Let us forget our differences and consider only the needs and interests of the patrie.' Unity was what counted; harmony and consensus within France. The divisive politics of Terror had shattered the common agreement about liberty. Let them work to bring the people together, not continually to drive them apart by punitive laws. 'Once the Republic is respected beyond its borders men inside its borders will love it, even men who now work to undermine it.'

Robespierre brushed the appeal aside: 'Someone with your principles and your morals would never find any criminals to condemn.'

'And would you regret that? Would you be sorry not to find any criminals to send to the scaffold?'

Danton had asked for the release from prison of 73 deputies with indulgent sympathies. Robespierre refused point-blank. 'The only way to establish liberty is to cut off the heads of such criminals.' Danton burst into tears. Robespierre's anger was surely laced with contempt for this man before him, once so large a presence in the Revolution, now crumbling like a woman. He noted later that Danton 'made himself ridiculous with melodramatic posturing and tears'.

Danton tried to embrace him as he left but Robespierre shrank frostily and remained 'as cold as marble'.

# THIRTEEN

# The Titan of the Revolution

Yes, I dreamed – the earth in full career under me, like a
wild horse bolting, I clung to its mane with giant arms, dug
my knees into its ribs, my head craned over its neck, my
hair streaming out over the abyss of space. Then I cried out
in terror: 'September.' And I woke up.

Georg Büchner, *Dantons Tod*, II v

SPRING CAME EARLY to Paris; trees in blossom fully six weeks before
their time, lilacs blooming in the Tuileries gardens, writes Hesdin,
'as if the smile of Nature meant to mock at the Horrors of mankind';
those trees that had survived the foraging for fuel. A huge tranche
of the Bois de Boulogne had become a woodyard. Armourers under
government contract worked in forges set upon the esplanade of the
Invalides and in the Luxembourg gardens, turning out pikes, cannons
and metal components for firearms. Such government plants
produced about two-thirds of weapons manufactured in the year from
September 1793. Close by the open-air forges, beds of potato plants,
manure heaps for the harvest of nitrates for saltpetre. Government
agencies occupied the old chateau of Meudon outside the city and
were believed to be engaged on secret experiments in the manufacture of war munitions, rumours of an incendiary cannon ball for the
navy, flying machines which could drop shells into besieged towns.
French chemists had refined the chemical composition of steel.
Deputies from the provinces had recently been brought together to
learn about the manufacture and safe distribution of gunpowder at
government factories.

As much of Paris had been converted into a munitions factory, so much of Paris had become a penal colony. The vast population of the city's prisons might have been the spectral phantoms of Robespierre's persecution mania, the unceasing nightmare of conspiracy, the Jacobin complex, the civic 'I denounce' which filled the gaols in Lyon, Toulon, Nantes, Bordeaux, Marseille, the Loire, Arras, the Incorruptible's home town, in the Breton towns of Lorient and Brest, main base of the Atlantic fleet, where Jeanbon Saint-André of the CPS had conducted a major overhaul of the navy. And this spring had been set for the embarkation of a combined operation of fleet and army.

The marine service, as riddled with old-regime officers as the military, was not, however, susceptible to a radical clear-out of the royal commissioned professionals. Where the revolutionary army could dispense with the rigid programme of parade-ground drill (the legacy of General Martinet) which licked the King's armies into shape, the sailing ships of whatever tonnage had to be handled by experts whose skill came neither swiftly nor surely. Perhaps the very conservative nature of the navy, the sailor's necessary acknowledgement that, whatever superficial discipline of human invention may be imposed on a ship's company, there was a natural tyranny of wind and tides to which they were all subject, captains and tars alike, assisted the transition from the despotism of a royal marine to that of a republican. A change in emphasis.

Saint-André, therefore, imposed republican ideals: officers were deprived of traditional luxuries – no more pastries, special cooks and shore-based ovens cooking wardroom feasts; parcels of Jacobin newspapers were delivered on board, and schoolmasters to teach sailors to read and write and conduct republican propaganda; lessons in seamanship were given to recruits produced by the levy en masse. Two principles preached by Danton informed this approach: audacity and education. To the Assembly in September 1792 he said: 'To conquer the enemies of the patrie we must show boldness, more boldness and always boldness.' And to the Convention in August 1793: 'After bread, education is the people's primary need.'

Brest had been put on a wholesale war footing, dockyards and workshops at full production round the clock and a strict military law imposed on the arsenals and shipyards for citizens and mariners. Saint-André spouted the politician's morale-boosting maxims – 'To work in the manner of despots does not suit republicans, the negligence of a sleepy tyrant or of somnolent ministers does not agree with our principles' – but the workers did not always get paid and chronic arrears of wages caused more than one violent riot of enraged dockyard artisans being required to live on patriotism and thin air.

As to the major naval offensive scheduled for this spring of 1794, Saint-André's CPS colleague Prieur de la Marne directed it against the enemy, whose stratagems the streamlining of the navy in Brest must be geared to defeat. In a speech to the Jacobins of Lorient, Brittany's second port along the coast, he gave their struggle a global reach: 'London must be destroyed and London shall be destroyed. Let us rid the globe of this new Carthage. Then we shall have peace, then we shall be masters; no, not masters, but avengers of a world oppressed. We shall chase from the Indies and from Bengal these ferocious English so insatiable for gold that in selling necessities to the people of these countries they demand such high prices that a mother has often been seen to give up her child for a handful of rice . . . everywhere in short is the triumph of Pitt's despotism and of gold. Very well, we will make a triumph of courage and of iron . . . all the arrangements for the project are ready [an invasion force of 100,000 troops]; we shall go to visit the banks of the Thames. Those who wish to be in the expedition must ask priority of inscription. Meanwhile, let us show Pitt how a free people deliberates. I move that a sentence of the guillotine be dispatched to Pitt.' The Jacobins of Lorient greeted this with shouts of joy.

But Brittany had a long coast, much of it difficult to patrol, the roads crossing the interior were poor, the Bretons, speaking their own Celtic language, evinced little affection for the rest of France; they had enjoyed a certain provincial liberty under the kings; as with their neighbours in the Vendée, their clergy and nobility were influential, they accepted the leadership of gentlemen and priests. Republicans dominated in only a few seaboard cities and towns and the great harbour of Brest.

Prieur de la Marne had been busy in the towns along the south coast of the department of Morbihan, arresting suspects, purging local authorities, purifying and invigilating the political clubs. Of Vannes, for example, he noted a general disaffection: 'In a city of 12,000 only 200 accepted the constitution . . . the countryside is given over to fanatism . . . the poor hide themselves to shed their tears . . . the despotism of wealth and rank still presents the hideous image of the old regime.' From Nantes to Brest, the town gaols filled.

Jacques-Claude Beugnot, born in 1762, was arrested and sent to La Force on 26 December 1793 and thence taken to the Conciergerie 'for reasons [unspecified] of general security' but, being ill, with an order that he be taken directly to the infirmary.

Arriving in the Cour de Mai in a carriage, he saw the steps of the Palais de Justice lined with women as if seated in an amphitheatre waiting for a play. Then he noticed the death-cart at the gate waiting to take two unfortunates to the scaffold. He got out of the carriage and the whole audience of women stood and gave a long cry of joy, clapping their hands, stamping their feet, convulsed with laughter and 'the fierce pleasure of cannibals at the arrival of a new victim'. As Beugnot crossed the courtyard to the refuge of the wicket gate, the harridans hovering about the Palais de Justice like vultures at a feast of carrion pelted him with rubbish.

The gaoler's office inside was partitioned in two during the daytime – one side for registering new prisoners, the other for those waiting to be taken for execution. A newcomer might talk to them if he had the courage, a macabre exchange across a flimsy screen which stood as a reminder that there was but a single step between them and the scaffold.

This office was at the centre of the coming and going in the gaol: 'Women with their husbands, mistresses and their lovers sit on benches along the walls [said Bailleul, a deputy imprisoned there]. Some exchange caresses with as much assurance and frivolity as if they were in a rose arbour. Others, yielding to emotion, weep . . . through one window one sees, lying sick and in pain on a bed, a wretched woman, pale-browed, awaiting her call to execution, guarded by a gendarme. Gendarmes crowd the offices. Some take out the prisoners for the scaffold, hands tied, and push them into the carts. Others call out names of prisoners for transfer, tie their hands and lead them off while an ill-tempered usher with a haggard expression barks out brusque orders and thinks himself a hero because he can heap abuse with impunity on unfortunates who can't answer him back with blows from a cudgel . . .'

Two men were waiting when Beugnot arrived: they had been to

the toilette, the collar of their shirt cut off, the hair on their nape shorn. They sat expressionless, hands not yet tied, trying to look proud, disdainful. A pair of mattresses on the floor indicated that they had passed the night there; on the table, the remains of their last meal, a harking back to the final banquet offered to the gladiators, 'those about to die' – stuffed down by the men who resigned themselves to fate, picked at by those who knew that fighting lean, mean and hungry gave them a better chance of survival. No such option in the Conciergerie. The men's jackets and coats were tossed on the floor, perquisites for the gaolers; two candles guttered at their stump, shedding a funereal light in the daytime. The door opened, grating harshly on the big hinges, and in trooped gendarmes, turnkeys, executioners. The prison clerk had been occupied with paperwork relating to the two condemned men, so that Beugnot and three other new arrivals were kept waiting on the bench.

One of them, 'an idiotic fop', walked up and down, affecting a grand air, humming an Italian tune, stepping on feet, apologising. His name was similar to Beugnot – the clerk got them muddled, the fop, charged with forging assignats, was taken to the infirmary, housed below the revolutionary tribunal, and Beugnot, in his place, to the criminal cell, 1.4 square metres, dimly lit through a hole cut in the door. This was already home to two other prisoners: a matricide, 40 years old, lead-grey complexion, squint, twisted mouth, lips twitching constantly; and a 25-year-old man with agreeable open features; surely not a criminal? Perhaps, like Beugnot, confined on grounds of general security.

After three days Beugnot told the turnkey that a mistake had been made and that another two days in this fetid hole would surely kill him. The turnkey, to whom such errors must have been routine, decided that Beugnot must be the minister of the Interior's man Paré (actually Parey), former clerk of Danton. Beugnot had never spoken to this Parey in his life; nevertheless, he was moved to the infirmary and called it the most horripilant place in the world, resembling the palace of hell he had seen in a performance at the Opéra: a room 7.5 by 30.5 metres, iron grilles at either end, a high-pitched vaulted ceiling; walls of dressed stone, long flagstone floor, the whole cavern looking as if it had been hewn out of living rock. The fumes of charcoal from stove and lamps lent a sombre hue to the room. Daylight seeped in from two very narrow shuttered windows cut into the soffit of the vault.

Forty to 50 squalid mattress beds lined the walls of this narrow, airless hall, two, even three, invalids to a mattress. The straw was never changed, the covers never cleaned; it made, said Beugnot, a turbine of mephitic and corrupt odours. Mildew sprouted on the paving, to walk on which, even at its driest, filthied one's shoes. A row of slop buckets were set in the middle; there was no means of steadying oneself when using them and they were wholly inadequate for the number of prisoners – they overflowed and spilled – and so people used corners, anywhere. Often invalids who'd tried to reach the buckets but couldn't make it fell exhausted, sprawled on the floor in their pain and mortal distress.

Over this so-called hospital ward ruled Dr Thierry, protégé of Robespierre, who recommended him to Fouquier for this job: a charmless, brutish man with never a word of consolation for patients enduring such privations. His visits lasted about 18 minutes, never more than 25. In this time he made his round of 40 sick inmates; the sole remedy he prescribed – tisane.

A sporadic ululation of plaintive cries and groans. A poor wretch persecuted by a frightful dream emitted cries which froze Beugnot with horror: in the lunatic tirade, Beugnot distinguished a repetitious descant of words such as 'blood', 'executioner', 'death', 'words which went the rounds of the funereal beds' and, in lugubrious counterpoint, hour after hour, the bell's nocturnal tolling parcelled up this eternity of suffering. Dogs howled in answer to the chimes of the clock, the tintinnabulation of time running out. 'You who have never passed a night there in the midst of this gathering of horrors, you have yet to be tried, you have suffered nothing in this world.'

Sickness offered no dispensation from the grinding millstones of the law. A priest from Autun, given no more than 12 hours to live, was nonetheless dragged before the Tribunal and died even as he was being put into the cart. 'In the presence of such crushing, such profound misery,' wrote Beugnot, 'I blushed to have been born a human being.'

The courage of many who died in those last months derived largely from relief, resignation, even lassitude, a sort of freakish contentment that their sufferings had come to an end. As one Birion told Beugnot: 'These people have been harassing me for a long time; they are going to cut my neck but at least it will be finished.' And Aymar-Charles-Marie de Nicolay, 47 years old, a former noble, offered medical attention in the Conciergerie for a pain in his shoulder, brushed it aside: 'No need for a doctor, the pain is too close to my head – the one will remove the other.'

Beugnot was moved from the infirmary to what was called the small pharmacy – its doors, five inches thick, strengthened with iron and provided with three locks. Two windows, one firmly sealed, the other plastered with posters, as was every bit of the walls, placards acclaiming Liberty, Equality, the Rights of Man, the Constitution – on every side Liberty or bars, Equality or heavy iron bolts.

The male prisoners went down to the men's courtyard for exercise in the morning; the women somewhat later to their own yard. Their mode of dress had imprescriptible rules which even the confines of this hellhole could not bend: clad in a saucy negligee, a light gown worn for the toilette before getting fully dressed, they showed no sign of having spent the night on a low bed on putrid straw. At midday they re-emerged, coiffed and trim in their dresses. In the evening they appeared in déshabillé, the languid nonchalance of the boudoir. Those who possessed only one dress laundered it in the fountain first thing in the morning.

Women and men took full advantage of the shadows in the dim crepuscular light of the courtyards hemmed in by the high walls of the surrounding buildings, to come to the assignations they had made earlier by wave or wink, the tick-tack of amorous sport. At this late hour, the wine in the guardrooms had begun to flow, the guards were tired, less watchful, indifferent, deaf to the twilight murmurs out in the yard; most of the prisoners had retired, and those who hadn't were discreet and 'at this time of peace, the prelude to night, we more than once blessed the improvidence of the artist who designed the grille'.

A 40-year-old woman, still lively of nature, beautiful features, trim figure, was condemned to death with her lover, a young officer in the army of the North. They came back from the revolutionary Tribunal around 6 p.m. and were separated for the night. The woman seduced her gaoler to be reunited with her lover, their last night together, and they were torn out of each other's arms only when mounting the tumbrel next morning. They and others were ennobled by their defiance of the squalor – material and moral – to which they had been subjected, saying, in the warmth of their humanity and mutual affection, to the glacial judges of their so-called treason: 'You will kill us when you like but you cannot stop us from being decent.'

Straitened by summary law and justice, the currency of corruption and what, given the nature of the justice, may ironically be termed its perversion, was, as it had ever been: sex, money and information.

Reservations about the unhinging effect of the guillotine on the victims of the poorer classes, not born to the dignified self-control and emotional stiffness of the nobly born, proved to be entirely unfounded. Beugnot himself saw only one man evince any faint-heartedness and him an aristocrat: the marquis du Châtelet, a colonel of a regiment of French Guards, condemned to death at the age of 66. He arrived from the Madelonettes prison hopelessly drunk. The turnkeys threw him on his bed unconscious for the night. The next morning he traipsed round moaning and complaining, visibly and pathetically astonished that no one sympathised with his plight, as if he were alone in this misfortune. He approached the grille next to the women's quarters and wept miserably. A girl, scarcely more than a child, went up to him and said: 'Shame on you for weeping. Let me tell you, sir duke, those who don't have a name before they come here soon get one in here and those who *do* have a name must learn how to merit it.' A name. Precisely the original meaning of the word 'noble' – somebody *known*.

Beugnot took the young woman to be an aristocrat by her bearing and manner and asked her who she was. She told him: she shared lodgings with a street prostitute, a woman despised by the moral pygmies of the revolutionary Tribunal but a creature of dignity who had comported herself throughout more heroically than any of the nobility, the virtuous peers and émigrés in the salons of Koblenz. One curiosity of the Revolution: however many of the poor it scythed down in the name of liberty, many of those poor took on the dignity and self-control previously associated exclusively with rank. This was a very marked revolution in popular morale.

Beugnot's interlocutor was a young prostitute, about 20 years old, known as Eglé. She had lived for two years in the rue Fromenteau, between the river and the Palais Royal (a quarter much frequented by prostitutes), having quit a garret in the Faubourg Saint-Antoine, and did a brisk trade, her spirits undiminished. She detested the revolutionary order and made no bones who knew it; she voiced seditious ideas with perfect disregard. The police arrested her together with a companion whom she had instilled with what the authorities called her 'aristocratic' fury.

Chaumette had the idea of bringing the two of them before the revolutionary Tribunal at the same time as the Queen and sending all three to their death in the same cart. The majesty of France with a couple of whores – nice joke. It was typical of the man but it was not agreed to. (As a member of the insurrectionary Commune following 10 August 1792, Chaumette had been delegated to visit prisons and arrest suspects. An ardent social reformer, he secured the abolition of corporal punishment in schools and the suppression of brothels and obscene literature.)

Beugnot, reflecting on this, mused: 'If you had been executed with the Queen you'd have appeared equal.'

Eglé replied with spirit: 'Yes, but I'd have cheated the villains of that. Halfway to the scaffold I'd have flung myself at her feet and neither the executioner nor the devil would have made me get up.'

Three months after the death of the Queen, Eglé and her friend might have been forgotten but Eglé was irrepressible; she had not thought that advertising her opinions was shameful and Fouquier determined to have done with her.

Before the revolutionary tribunal she said: 'I, a poor girl who earned her living at street corners, would not have believed myself fit to approach even a scullion of the King's kitchen; *that's* the class of person who is worthy of a bunch of good-for-nothings and imbeciles such as you – a kitchen boy.'

She was actually acquitted. Some of the jury supposed she was drunk; others had known her for a long time and seized on the excuse of her inebriation to let her go. Eglé would have none of it: if anyone in the room was drunk it wasn't her and to demonstrate the clarity of her wits she started to rehearse word-perfect the process of the trial. The president rebuked her and gave her a severe warning to sit down and shut up. Her companion accepted the charge of inebriation to save herself. Eglé railed at her for her weakness; pandering to these snivelling wretches dishonoured her – and *they* dared to label them trollops? No, let her remember the qualities that marked them out in this place of moral decrepitude: truth and courage.

Eglé's remonstrations induced her friend to forswear her momentary lapse: she wanted to show that she was equally capable of sangfroid. Eglé was sent to the scaffold as an incorrigible aristocrat; her companion was condemned to the Salpêtrière prison for 20 years.

As the president of the court read out the judgement, Eglé smiled at the depositions which found her guilty of counter-revolution and condemned her to death. When it came to the article confiscating her property, she addressed the president: 'Ah, you thief, that's what I was waiting for. I tell *you* that what you don't eat doesn't give you indigestion.'

Her one fear was that in going to her death she was 'going to sleep with the devil'. The good abbé Emery, formerly superior of the seminary of Saint-Sulpice, a man of serene, gentle cheerfulness, the angel of this prison, reassured her that this would not be so and she jumped into the cart as lightly as a bird.

Robespierre was compiling a dossier of notes, a character report – character assassination – on Danton; this he passed to Saint-Just as the basis of a charge sheet. One of his animadversions on the man whom he had once called friend: 'Danton never spoke with energy on any subject other than himself. His silence during serious discussion can be explained only by his big physical size and his indulgence in sex . . .' The man was prissily obsessed with revolting priapic appetites and Danton's scurrilous definition of virtue had already condemned him morally. As to the silence, Danton himself had already expressed his weariness with the internecine feuding; it was, he might have said, a basket of crabs. He was under no illusions about his own fate.

Robespierre had taken steps to obviate any chance of a popular uprising in Danton's favour: loyal Jacobins, among them Lescot-Fleuriot as mayor, were installed in the Commune, replacing Hébert and his cronies.

Saint-Just once again acted as Robespierre's front man; while his incorruptible *éminence grise* hugged the shadows, he would deliver the indictment. A few days before he did so, Robespierre and Danton attended the performance of an obscure tragedy at the Théâtre Français. A member of the audience recalled that: 'Robespierre sat in a box; Danton sat in the stalls in company with a large group of his friends. When an actor spoke the line "Death to the tyrant", Danton's friends stood up and broke into wild applause, then turned to stare at Robespierre and shook their fists threateningly at him. Robespierre went pale, his face twitching nervously, swaying like that of a snake. He waved his small clerk's hand in a gesture expressing his fright but menace, too.'

Danton was urged to escape while he could. Like Socrates he demurred. 'You do not wear patriotism on the soles of your shoes,' he said and rebuffed any suggestion that he might mount a campaign to overthrow Robespierre: it would mean more blood and there had been too much shedding of blood already. 'Yes, it is time to break the scythe of death.' Better to be guillotined than to guillotine. What Saint-Just said was true: the practice of government produced nothing but monsters.

On the evening of 30 March Robespierre called an emergency session of the two committees, whose combined signatures were required for the issue of an arrest warrant. Twenty men attended. Saint-Just read out the deposition he had prepared demanding the arrest of Danton and Desmoulins. Lindet of the CPS, in charge of subsistences, refused to sign; he was there to feed citizens, he said, not to put patriots to death. So too did Rühl of the CGS, loyal to his friend Danton. Carnot, surely mindful of the many times Danton had unleashed that great roar of his, 'the patrie in danger', to stir the people to its patriotic defence, deliberated before adding his name; he warned the others to think long and hard. 'A head like Danton's will bring down many others with it.'

Saint-Just proposed that instead of issuing the warrant to the arresting authority, the Commune, straight away, he should read out the list of charges against Danton in the Convention the following day and compound the ogre's humiliation in the presence of so many of his indulgent friends. This was foolish and Vadier of the CGS, a bitter enemy of the man they called the 'titan of the Revolution', knew it. '*You* may run the risk of being guillotined,' he said, 'if that's your pleasure; however, I wish to avoid the danger of that by having them arrested right now, because we must not have any illusions about the course we are taking; it all comes down to this: if we don't guillotine them, we'll go to the scaffold ourselves.'

Robespierre, with no stomach for such an eventuality or any confrontation he could not master in advance, acceded. Saint-Just, thwarted of his chance to play the hero Hercules delivering the *coup de grâce* to the evil Hydra, threw a tantrum. His interpretation of staying cool was, on occasion, distinctly flexible.

The warrant, drawn up on a sheet of wrapping paper and signed by 18 members of the CPS and the CGS, was issued and later that night the civilian municipal officers, wearing the holy tricolour sash of their authority, accompanied by patrols of gendarmes, thumped on the doors in the Cour du Commerce to arrest, in the name of the Republic and the people, Georges Danton and Camille Desmoulins.

Rühl had sent a messenger to forewarn Danton. He found him sitting in an armchair by the fire. Danton evinced no surprise and showed no inclination to avoid what he saw as the inevitable. He was resigned. When the patrol arrived, heavy hobnailed boots clattering on the stone paving of the street, Danton went to wake his wife. 'They've come to arrest me.' She wept; he kissed her and told her not to be afraid; they would not dare kill him.

They took him to the Luxembourg, where he was joined by Desmoulins, who bore up strongly enough when taken away from his wife and young son, but once in prison his stoicism gave way to a vortex of emotions.

The shocking news of the arrests broke next morning. Danton? So many had claimed to speak *for* the people, but Danton's voice bore the unfeigned accents of a real man *of* the people, his charisma charmed them all. And Desmoulins, the voice of clemency? Danton's belief that they would not dare kill him was widely shared. But there could be no doubt that this was an endgame: a Danton brought before the bar of the revolutionary Tribunal must certainly pose a considerable threat to the government, a poisonous embarrassment, were he allowed to mount the sturdy defence they must expect. Yet, having arrested him on whatever trumped-up charges, how could they conceivably risk an acquittal?

In the Convention, Danton's friend the sansculotte butcher Legendre came to his aid. (A member of the CGS, a coarse, violent man, one of the three who arrested Corday, Legendre was not, in this climate, a wholly desirable friend to have speaking out in public on one's behalf.)

'Citizens, last night certain members of this Assembly were arrested. Danton was among them. I demand that the members of the Convention who were arrested be brought to the bar of this

Assembly to be accused or absolved by us. I am convinced that Danton is as pure as I am.' This last comment played heavily on Legendre's sansculotte credentials, which, given its track record with resistance to mob petition by force, the Convention was by no means yet ready to discount. Legendre was even bold enough to hint that Danton was the victim of certain 'private hatreds'.

This evoked scattered – perhaps tentative – cries of 'Down with the dictatorship.'

Tallien, president that day, was about to put Legendre's motion to the vote when Robespierre entered the hall and hurried to the rostrum. His power rested on the inexplicable confusion into which his very appearance at the rostrum threw his opponents; he somehow contrived to project into others his own paranoid fears. He stared round at his audience, 'letting his eye rest for the space of two heart-beats on those whom he mistrusted'. A deathly stillness in the room. Robespierre lowered the green-tinted spectacles and, in what must be taken as a defining moment of the Terror, picked Legendre to pieces. The accused were 'ambitious hypocrites': 'As for this turmoil which, unrecognised for a long time, dominates this Assembly, it is easy to see that it centres on a great party interest and that a small group of men are about to foist this chaos on the patrie. Legendre has spoken of Danton apparently because he believes some privilege attaches to this name: no, we have no desire for privileges. [The word 'privilege' implies 'standing outside the provisions of the law', a private legitimacy, so to speak.] We will see this day whether the Convention knows how to break an idol, for so long false and corrupt, or whether, in its fall, that idol will crush the Convention and the French people. [He turned his gaze on those occupying the benches in the Plain, the flat level of the chamber over which the raked tiers of the Mountain's benches towered.] There are not many who are guilty – a few traitors who must be struck down in the name of the patrie. The moment has come to tell the truth.'

Now, using the rhetorical trick that concentrated all the dangers of the counter-revolution on him, sole prophet of the dangers that beset them all, now, like an assassin's dagger, pointed at his heart, he concluded, fixing Legendre: '*I* say that whoever trembles at this very moment is guilty. Innocence has never feared public scrutiny. Danton's friends have pestered me with their arguments. They believe that the memory of a former liaison will make me soften my zeal and my passion for liberty. I say to you, no such motive has grazed my soul with the slightest impression. I was Pétion's friend [the mayor of Paris who ordered soldiers to fire on the Champ de Mars]: as soon as he was unmasked, I cut with him. I also had links with Roland; he committed treason, I denounced him. Danton wishes to take their place and he is, in my eyes, nothing less than an enemy of the patrie.'

A heavy silence.

The blood drained from Legendre's face; he stammered: 'If Robespierre thinks that I am capable of sacrificing liberty for an individual, he mistook my meaning. Those who have proof in their hands know better than we do the guilt of the men who have been arrested . . .'

Barère stepped in, as ever, with the cooling voice of reason and the hinted reminder that having been malleable on other occasions they were in no position to assert moral indignation now: the rights of law were common to them all. Had they heard the federalists at the bar, or Chabot or Fabre d'Eglantine? No, there must be no privileges.

It was Saint-Just's moment: he mounted the Tribunal and read the indictment in his metallic tone of voice. Of Danton he said, addressing him as if he were sitting there in their midst: 'Every time you saw storms in the offing, having intrigued with everyone, you withdrew to Arcis-sur-Aube; we did not see you again till after the victory. During the stormy debates here, we were indignant at your silence and your absence, while you talked of the pleasures of the countryside, solitude, idleness and then came back from your life of leisure to renew your intrigues. Your harangues at the Tribunal began like thunderclaps to peter out in compromises.'

He topped the charges with a peroration straight out of the revolutionary's solemn liturgy: 'There is something terrible in the sacred love of the patrie; it is so utterly exclusive that it sacrifices everything to the public interest, without pity, without fear, without consideration of humanity. It takes some courage for you to speak further of severity after so much severity. The aristocracy says of us, "they are going to destroy one another". But the aristocracy lies in its very heart: it is that mendacity which we are destroying.'

At 7 p.m. the decree of accusation was adopted. Lumped in with Danton and Desmoulins were Lacroix and Philippeaux, Hérault de Séchelles, General Westermann, the corrupt deputies Chabot, Fabre d'Eglantine, Delaunay and Bazire and several foreigners implicated in the Indies Company scandal, including the Frey brothers and the Spanish banker Guzman. Danton and friends were being tarred with the same brush as the insider dealers.

From the Luxembourg prison, Desmoulins could see the gardens where he and his beloved Lucile had so often walked. He wrote to her: 'Seeing them recalls so many memories of our love . . . then I fall to my knees and stretch out my arms to embrace you . . .' and: 'I sleep and heaven takes pity on me for in sleep I am free once more. A moment ago I saw you as in a dream and held you in my arms again . . . I married a woman of celestial virtue. I have been a faithful husband, a good son; I would have been a good father . . . I enjoy the esteem and the sorrows of all true republicans. For five years I have walked along the precipices of the Revolution without falling into the abyss. I rest my head in tranquillity on the pillow of all that I have written, all filled with the same compassion and the same desire to lead my fellow citizens to happiness and freedom.'

If only it were true; but he, as many others, had been infected with the same bile and aggression which so embittered the struggle between opposing factions. Still, Desmoulins spoke for many in a quite different way; he voiced his own pangs of misery at parting from the woman he loved and thus voiced the terrible sorrow of thousands riding to the scaffold on mere pretext: 'O my darling, my Lucile, we will be together again . . . can this death which delivers me from witnessing such crimes be a misfortune? The shores of my life recede. I see you again, Lucile, beloved. My bound hands embrace you and when my head falls into the basket, my dying eyes will rest upon you.'

After only two days in the Luxembourg, Danton and the rest were transferred to the Conciergerie, death's antechamber, and the trial began on 2 April, a day on which the CGS arrested two women sans-culotte agitators, Pauline Léon, who had called for a woman's regiment of pikes, and the actress Claire Lacombe, founder of the Republican Revolutionaries' Club.

In the Conciergerie, Riouffe, who had little sympathy for Danton and the others – had not Danton called for Terror to be order of the day, that demented decree that had put them all in prison? – nonetheless recorded what he overheard, Danton's final ruminations.

This very day a year ago [he was out by nearly a month] I set up the revolutionary Tribunal; but I ask pardon for it of God and men. It was not intended to be a scourge on humanity, but to prevent a recurrence of 2 and 3 September. *Let us be terrible so that the people do not need to be.*

When factions attack men who have rendered the patrie service, one may imprison them provisionally until material proof of their crimes is assembled. We must enshrine this great principle: that a patriot must have committed three errors before one can deal harshly with him.

I leave everything in an appalling mess: the entire government is completely at odds. In the midst of such insanity, I am glad not to have put my name to certain decrees – people will know I wanted nothing to do with them.

Not one of them knows the first thing about government. A pity I can't leave my balls to that eunuch Robespierre and my legs to the cripple Couthon . . . But Robespierre will follow, I will drag him down.

They are all the brothers of Cain. Brissot would have sent me to the guillotine just as Robespierre has.

The proof that that bastard Robespierre is a Nero – he never spoke to Camille Desmoulins in such terms of friendship as the day before he was arrested.

In revolutions, authority rests with the worst criminals.

The fucking animals, they'll be shouting, 'Long live the Republic' when they see me go past.

And, Riouffe says, he spoke unceasingly of trees, the countryside, as did another titan of nature, the dying Falstaff, who 'babbled of green fields'.

April 2nd, 1794, 10 a.m. The great hall of the Palais de Justice, where the Parlement of Paris used to meet; gilded ceiling, marble floor. The tapestries stripped from the walls, the carpet embroidered with the royal fleur-de-lis rolled up, the King's throne and Dürer's painting of Christ gone. At the wooden table which serves as a bench, the judges and, at a small table in front of them, Fouquier, all garbed in dark clothes and hats with black plumes. To the left, chairs and a table for the seven jurors only, the most dependable of the dependable. The rest of the room and corridors outside packed with spectators craning for a view, ears pricked.

When the prisoners were arraigned, Westermann asked the court president, Herman, to be included on his old friend Danton's indictment. When Herman replied that that was a mere formality, Danton chimed in that their very presence was a mere formality. Asked for his place of residence, Danton retorted: 'My home will soon be in nothingness; my name you will find in the pantheon of history. Danton an aristocrat? France will not believe that for long. Me, bought? A man such as I cannot be bought.' While he could not be bought, he had certainly had no compunction about taking money. It's what they did under the old regime, it's what men in any sort of government did and, at worst, no more than a peccadillo, in truth the oil that lubricates the machinery of government, whatever form it took.

The very idea of incorruptibility was at odds with the management of human affairs, the organisation of such a disparate conglomeration of beings as mankind. Incorruptibility was for cloud cuckoo land, that preposterous utopia for the birds dreamed up by Aristophanes to satirise the crazy imperialistic ambitions of the warmongers who endangered and then destroyed the Athenian democracy. But that was the central flaw in the hero of what may be called the high point of the Revolution in which he believed, or affected to believe: the overthrow of the monarchy in August 1792. For he did sway in the breeze; he called for Terror and three months later wanted no Terror. His principles were tailored to the moment. As open-hearted and generous as he was in spirit, as open-minded to the point of lackadaisical, his championship was never consistent, as great an impact as he had on the events of his brief glory. He summed himself up: 'Let my reputation perish before that of my patrie.' France's honour before Danton's. In that indifference, at least, there was no posturing.

Asked his age, Desmoulins replied: 'Thirty-three, the same age as the sansculotte Jesus Christ when he was crucified.'

Fouquier and Herman were well primed: a frontal attack on Danton would expose the flimsiness of the case; they concentrated, rather, on the Indies Company peculation, a lengthy report which consumed most of the first day of the trial. Whenever Danton tried to interrupt, Herman rang his bell furiously to drown out his voice.

'Can't you hear my bell?' he cried.

Danton scoffed: a man fighting for his life laughs at bells.

The dread moment arrived when Danton was called to account and must unleash his stentorian voice. 'Danton, you are accused of favouring the traitor Dumouriez and sharing his plots to murder liberty by marching on Paris with an army to destroy the Republic and to re-establish royalty.'

Danton launched in. The voice which had so frequently spoken for the people would brush such calumnies aside with ease. He called on the Convention to set up a commission to investigate the dictatorship he would denounce to them, a dictatorship he, Danton, would unmask.

Herman took fright and tried to call Danton to order – 'your audacity is the hallmark of crime, innocence remains calm' – but Danton was not to be checked. How could he rein in his indignation when such unjust charges were levelled at him?

Once more Herman intervened: it was not by insolent attacks on his accusers, who enjoyed public esteem, that he would convince the jury. Danton roared back: 'A man accused as I am being accused does not answer to a jury; I stand before it and I defend myself, slandering no one. I have never acted through ambition or greed. I have devoted myself to the patrie and I made the sacrifice gladly. Now I must speak of three base cowards who have perverted Robespierre, and here I will reveal important facts . . .'

Herman cut him off. The various accusations were advanced one by one and Danton rubbished them in turn, lambasting the deceit, the malice, the total lack of substance contaminating them. The crowded courtroom applauded: this was the best prize-fighting they had seen in a while, the big fellow Danton wading into the high and mighty judges in their hats and sashes and giving them a rare pasting. There were even rumours that he might be acquitted, the so-called evidence against him was so ludicrous, so flagrantly outside any legitimacy. At one point Herman scribbled a note to Fouquier informing him that he was 'going to suspend Danton's defence in half an hour'.

When he did so, Danton met the illegality head-on and declared that he might as well forfeit any thought of rebutting the charges. He knew that they had long since torn such holes in the law that it could never be any kind of safety net, not for him, not for anyone. They would all, inevitably, plummet down through the gaping loopholes these justices had cut in the law, once the safety of the people. Turning to the bench, he as it were translated for them the clamour of the crowd at his back, and said: 'The people will tear my enemies into pieces within three months.'

Fouquier and Herman were losing grip of the trial. Fouquier announced that the court was being made mock of and he intended to submit the judgement to the national Convention. That meant, of course, its central committee, its Cerberus, the CPS. He told them that 'the accused are behaving like madmen; they call for witnesses, they appeal to the people and ignore our refusal. In spite of the resolution of the president their incessant demands are causing disorder and disruption: they simply will not be quiet. We ask your advice; our judicial powers are not adequate to what we are being asked to do.'

The CPS and the CGS had made contingency plans. A letter from one Laflotte, a prisoner in the Luxembourg, was produced in court. Lucile Desmoulins had been observed in the vicinity of the prison, carrying their infant son Horace in her arms; she was known, in her despair, to have sought help for her husband from a number of people in Paris. Laflotte's letter revealed the existence of a plot among the Luxembourg prisoners, drummed up by Danton and Desmoulins, to overthrow the revolutionary tribunal. By order of the public prosecutor, therefore, the trial was suspended until the Convention had deliberated. The conspiracy had been unmasked, the conspirators identified, and, to Desmoulins' horror, his wife named as its leader.

Once more the CPS had come to the rescue of the Republic in danger. In the Convention, Saint-Just called for a law which denied 'every accused person who resists or insults the national justice the right to plead a defence'. The Convention passed it; Amar of the CGS took the notice to Fouquier and told him: 'This should make your job easier.'

Danton vilified them: they were murderers, they had not called a single witness, they had produced no documentary evidence; were the accused to be sentenced without a hearing? But he was crying out, solitary in the desert. In the manic jangling of Herman's bell, it was over. David of the CGS cried out: 'We've got them at last' and Herman ordered the prisoners to be returned to the Conciergerie for immediate execution of the sentence which was to be read out to them *in* the prison. For form's sake, he read it to the empty benches like a bored priest mumbling the first office of the day in a vacant church.

On the way to the place de la Révolution, Desmoulins, in an access of nervous distraction, cried out to the crowd as if a protest of innocence could deliver an act of last-minute pardon: 'They lied. They are killing people who served you. My only crime is to have wept.' Danton calmed him. 'Quiet, now. Pay no heed to that vile rabble.' The 'they' of Desmoulins' lament were stool pigeons of the mob lining the route. Danton knew it; Robespierre, with his apostrophising of the noble, the holy, the sovereign people, would never dare consider the blasphemy of it.

They were taken in three red-painted tumbrels. The route skirted the café where Danton had met his first wife, past the reptilian David, sketching his quondam friend Danton as the cortège went by the Duplays' house, its blinds drawn. They reached the scaffold at about four o'clock in the afternoon. The crowd watched in silence as, one after the other, they mounted the steps. The turnkey in the Conciergerie was right: it was 'big game today'. Hérault de Séchelles went first. He turned to kiss Danton; the executioner pulled Hérault on to the steps. Danton rebuked him: 'You won't be able to stop our heads from meeting in the basket.'

Desmoulins went third; Danton last of all onto the abattoir of a scaffold over which had poured some five gallons of fresh blood, spouts from severed necks: the platform and plank on to which the victims were shoved awash with gore, the spray spattering those who waited below, the steps spattered with the overspill, in the 20-odd minutes of the blade's work, the rusty reek of life-blood infecting the ghastly altar of the Revolution.

They say he nearly broke, muttered involuntarily the aching sadness of leaving his wife behind, but suddenly reproved himself, told himself to hold firm and stepped up, head high, and, knowing that only the head of someone notable would be held up and flaunted, 'Behold the head of a traitor', bid the executioner: 'Make sure you show them my head – it'll be worth it.'

\* \* \*

His body and head joined the 17 others in the cart.

A little over a week later, on 13 April, Lucile Desmoulins made the same journey with 18 others, including Hébert's widow.

Lucile wrote to her mother a brief, poignant last note from the Conciergerie: 'Good night, dearest mother. A tear falls from my eye, for you. I will go to sleep in the tranquillity of innocence. Lucile.'

# FOURTEEN

# *The Revolution Iced Over*

The Revolution is iced over; all its principles are enfeebled;
there remain only red bonnets worn by intrigue.

*Saint-Just*

TWO DAYS AFTER the execution of the Dantonists, the Convention,
on the proposal of Couthon of the CPS and Vadier of the CGS,
voted, in taut silence, a decree that 'each deputy should deliver,
within a month at the latest, a moral report on his public conduct
and the state of his personal fortune'. There was no outbreak of the
ecstatic applause which customarily greeted each noble and liberating directive of the CPS. The Dantonists had enjoyed no privilege
of exemption from scrutiny and it was right and proper that they
did not. For a long time the Jacobins in clubs up and down the
country had been conducting their own internal 'purging scrutinies'
of members; none could be thought too exalted to submit to the
same grilling.

The very evening of their executions in the Jacobins, Robespierre
drove the point home – no one was safe now from the closest probe
of character and action: 'Since we are agreed that we have just
witnessed an event of interest to liberty and that the sublime workings of the Convention have, once more, intervened to save the
patrie . . . I demand [French does not readily distinguish between
*ask* and *demand*] that conspiracy be made the order of the day, so
that if any good citizen wishes to reveal the hideous circumstances
which derive from this conspiracy, in acquainting us with important
details as yet unknown, he should be able to mount the tribune and

make known to its very depths the wickedness of the conspirators who wished to drag us down over the precipice where they have fallen . . . It is by going straight to them, it is by attacking them face on and relentlessly; it is by plunging into their heart the dagger of justice that we deliver liberty from all the criminals who seek to destroy it.'

Robespierre, dilating about confrontation? It was not two hours since the heads of the latest batch of his enemies, Danton et al., had tumbled into the basket. Already he was reminding those hidden others, the tail of the conspiracy still twitching after the decapitation, that here spoke the authentic voice of the Revolution; disagreement with it would not be tolerated.

A few days later the faithful Saint-Just underlined the message in a report on behalf of the CGS and the CPS, 'On the national police, justice, commerce, legislation and factional crimes', in which he repudiated the dead Danton, 'this horrible man who lived for carnal pleasure', and warned any of those alive who adhered to similar turpitude: 'Ambitious men, go and walk an hour in the cemetery where sleep the conspirators and the tyrant and make your decision . . .' He developed a portrait of the true revolutionary: inflexible, judicious, frugal, eschewing luxury and false modesty; the irreconcilable enemy of all lies, indulgence and affectation; averse to insult, quick to enlighten; jealous of his purity; claiming never to be equal to the authority of law, but on a par with humanity, especially those who are unhappy or unfortunate; an honourable man; civilised without being insipid, candid and at peace with his own heart and so on and so on. Marat, he said, 'was mild when at home, he ought to terrify only traitors, Jean-Jacques Rousseau was undoubtedly a revolutionary and in no way impudent: I conclude that a revolutionary is a hero of good sense and probity'.

The Revolution was now tightly hoppled by men who idolised these story-book paragons.

Four days after Saint-Just delivered this creed for revolutionary saints, Robespierre once more absented himself from public life. Between 19 April and 7 May he made no appearance at either the Convention or the Jacobins. Paul Vicomte de Barras describes a visit he made with Fréron to see Robespierre at the Duplays' house around this time: 'Robespierre was one of the few who still dressed in the pre-revolutionary vogue, even when the red cap of liberty came back in fashion and all the Jacobins wore it. With his hair dressed and powdered, he looked just like a tailor of the old regime.

> He was standing in his room, swathed in a dressing gown; his hairdresser had just finished combing and powdering his hair. He wasn't wearing the spectacles he usually wore in public and, piercing through the powder covering his face, already so pallid, his eyes, dim and myopic, fastened on us in a fixed stare. His face was mean-featured and ghostly pale with veins of a greenish hue; it worked constantly. His hands, too, clenched and unclenched as if from a nervous tic; his neck and shoulders twitched spasmodically.
>
> We greeted him in the informal republican manner. He made no response; he went to his toilet glass hanging by a window over-looking the courtyard, then to a mirror on the mantelpiece. Taking his toilet knife, he began to scrape off the powder, careful not to muss his hair. Then he removed his dressing gown and tossed it on to a chair so close to us that the powder came off on our clothes. He washed his face from a small dish which he held in one hand; then brushed his teeth and spat out several times right by our feet as if he didn't even know we were there. Even when the ritual was over, he made no attempt to open the conversation.
>
> Fréron [who had been at school with him] introduced me at some length; Robespierre maintained a supercilious silence. Fréron, thinking that the reason for his stiffness was our use of the familiar *tu* – standard mode of address during the Revolution – reverted to the more formal *vous*. Still Robespierre said nothing, did not even offer us a seat. His face revealed no trace of emotion at all. I have not seen a marble statue or the cold face of a corpse more impassive.

The new police bureau set up to scrutinise government officials, which met on the third floor of the Palais Egalité, sifted evidence and laid possible charges for consideration by whomever of the CPS they had available – allowing for pressure of time or work or the need for secrecy without any reference to the CGS. In fact, its business was controlled by the three central committee members – Couthon, Saint-Just and Robespierre – who took it over from the beginning. If the case against any suspect was deemed to be solid, it was to be turned over directly to the revolutionary tribunal. The bureau had been briefly in the sole charge of Saint-Just; towards the end he managed it with Couthon; Robespierre controlled it alone for five weeks during May and June 1794. Its very existence reinforced the impression that the essential power of government was concentrated in the hands of a small stronghold within the CPS, a close triumvirate, and, with fatal consequences, it further subordinated and marginalised the lesser CGS, whose junior status to that of the CPS had always rankled.

The purges which followed the Ventôse laws spread ever more dismay. The members of the national Convention, to whose authority the CPS was, in theory, required to defer and in whose name it acted, grew increasingly alarmed at its effectively absolute power. The faction of deputies opposed to this intransigent executive body directing the policy of state terror, more and more threatened, became more elusive and dispersed, hiding opinion, daring no open confrontation, splintered in small cells. Its leading men, Fouché, Tallien, Barras, Fréron, each of whom, at the bidding of the CPS, had wreaked terrible vengeance on the rebellious cities of Lyon, Bordeaux, Marseille and Toulon, feared investigation of their conduct. They had had no written orders; had merely been told that if they did not do what was required of them, as representatives of the sovereign people, that abstract of republican unity to which Robespierre ever referred, that fiction of his ideology, the scaffold awaited them. Their opposition to Robespierre and his supporters was known and marked out as had been the Hébertists and Dantonists, first isolated then accused.

Even within the CPS, Collot d'Herbois, a former associate of Hébert, bore the stigma of ultra-revolutionaries detested by the purist Robespierre, and Lindet had been close to Danton. Such friendships could be mortally dangerous.

One day Carnot and Saint-Just were in the green room of the central committee room arguing furiously about some military matters; Prieur de la Côte-d'Or arrived, in company with a munitions contractor. The startled man heard Carnot calling Robespierre and Saint-Just absurd dictators. He had to be pledged to silence. And yet, whatever the vituperation behind the closed doors, so long as there were foreign armies camped on the French frontiers the inner circle of the CPS – three of its members were permanently on mission with the armies and never in Paris, others intermittently absent on official business – somehow kept its internal hatreds secret and acted in concert.

Lazare Carnot was a mathematician of some standing who had served as an army captain of engineers. A sober, austere man whose preoccupation with work, though it spoke of the dedicated professional, made him seem at times somewhat chilly. This masked a kind heart. His organising genius marshalled the 14 sansculotte armies against the half a million troops of the foreign coalition ranged against France during the Revolution; soldiers who, in many cases, marched almost direct from their hearth to the battlefront. (Carnot's revolutionary principles were unimpeachable. When Napoleon seized power in 1796, he voiced his opposition and was banished. 'I am,' he said, 'an irreconcilable foe of all kings.') He was indifferent to the squabbles of factions and to the nervous suspicions which preyed upon Robespierre, who had hated him from the first, perhaps envious of his expertise in matters so alien to the prissy lawyer from Arras. This envy for Carnot's gifts must also be overlaid with jealousy of his natural authority and the high regard in which he was so evidently held by the many who respected him. Robespierre was feared, he was not greatly respected. Respect demands a certain liking. Carnot remained cool, aloof, impervious to the infighting; only Saint-Just's intemperate outbursts could, and often did, provoke him, Saint-Just the haughty ideologue presuming to tell his business to a man who knew it inside out.

Robespierre, blinkered egoist, assumed that, because his own method of achieving his ends was to drive splits between his enemies and then, by patient nagging, widen them, this must be common practice. Moral ignorance made him incapable of believing anyone capable of behaviour better than his own. Seeing Collot d'Herbois hugger-mugger with Billaud-Varenne, he at once suspected it was him they were talking about, that it must be a plot they were hatching, a subtle manoeuvre afoot, that they looked *guilty*. The filthy Hébert dead, they must be forming a new faction against him.

Robespierre's contempt for Collot d'Herbois was commonly known. A citizen of Lyon, where one of Collot's theatrical ventures had failed, wrote: 'Robespierre detests Collot. He can scarcely bring himself to look at him in the CPS. He only tolerates him because of the strong links he has with the Hébertists who have such sway over the Commune, on whose backing Robespierre so depends.'

Jean-Nicolas Billaud-Varenne had been a radical from the start. His metaphor of a gangrened limb for moral corruption became a commonplace in the political clubs and spread like a contagion through French revolutionary politics for five years, a flippant justification of the surgical work of the guillotine. Remorse had no place, pity or mercy no place. 'The only cry to be listened to is that which takes for its devices Conscience and Truth,' said Collot.

As Barère records in his memoirs, the CPS was divided in three: the professional experts Carnot and Prieur de la Côte-d'Or, military engineers, and Lindet, a lawyer and extremely able administrator; the high hands, Couthon, Robespierre and Saint-Just; the true revolutionaries, Billaud, Collot and himself. Divisions among those who attended most of the meetings, conflicting opinions on the direction of the Revolution, were deepening.

(Barère, Lindet, Carnot and Robespierre all lived in the rue Saint-Honoré, within a short walk of the Jacobin club in the place du Marché Saint-Honoré.)

Of the leading figures in the CGS, Rühl, Bayle, Amar and Vadier were prominent dechristianisers and, as such, Robespierre's natural enemies. They even pressed for a policy of enforced dechristianisation. The CGS had been to the fore in creating the revolutionary armies and the official disbanding of these (the Parisian army apart) on 27 March, three days after the execution of the Hébertists but long after suppression of most of their activities, had been more than a calculated snub, rather a dire warning to the dechristianisers. It effectively distanced the CPS from the often lawless, generally violent work of those who had, under their auspices, even if nominally as agents of the Convention, repressed 'egoism, fanatism, indifferentism' in the departments.

The revolutionary army in the Lower Rhine had been nicknamed 'the guard of honour' of the public prosecutor its revolutionary court the godless former Capuchin monk Euloge Schneider, a sanguinary brute who delighted in the mental torture of his victims and conducted summary execution of victims in front of their farmhouse and families. He is reputed to have used the threat of the guillotine to force an aristocrat to give him his daughter in marriage. Saint-Just sent Schneider to the guillotine and, as his secretary wrote to Vincent: 'Detachments from the revolutionary army behaved despicably . . . they tried, unsuccessfully, to carry out the most audacious enterprise . . . I mean the sudden and complete destruction of all forms of religion which the robust stomach of the Revolution has happily digested . . .'

One example may suffice: the first units of the revolutionary army arrived in Auxerre en route from Paris to Lyon, on 11 November, the feast of Saint Martin, with mounted cannon, wagons, flags, banners, drums. They were met at the Saint-Siméon gate by a patrol from the Auxerre national Guard, and lodged and provisioned at the citizens' expense. They left the following morning. A second detachment arrived on 13 November and was welcomed likewise. However, these men had already wrought considerable damage along the way – smashing down church doors, demolishing altars, toppling statues and images of saints. On the chapel of Sainte Marguerite they unleashed an orgy of wanton destruction and then paraded a copper crucifix from the altar round the streets on a cart, pressing passers-by to spit on it. 'Thus did they repeat the insults of Jews on Jesus Christ at the time of his passion.' When a quarryman some distance from the chapel refused, one of soldiers sliced off part of his nose with a wild blow from his sabre.

The Parisians went on the rampage, pushing over and hacking at every stone and plaster cross they could find; they even clambered on to church roofs and towers to seize the finial crosses. That evening they harnessed four horses to an ornate sculpted cross in the square in front of the church of Saint Pierre. The paintings which decorated the nave of the church, as well as the bells, had been removed two weeks before their arrival as a precaution. The great abbey of Cluny, to the south, misread the impending emergency. All the paintings, wooden statues, papers and deeds of the abbey church were piled up in the public square and burnt in an auto-da-fé by the revolutionary army iconoclasts to the howls of the populace.

On this issue of religion much now hinged and the men associated with seeking to eradicate Christianity, those who agreed with commissioner Chaix in the Nièvre that God was too old, that he was an aristocrat and needed to be replaced, were marked as the Hébertists had been. Chaix had mounted the pulpit in Bazoches on a Sunday morning and preached atheism: 'For the first time, you are going to hear the truth spoken in this place . . . you have been told there is a god, a paradise, a hell, and you believed it, well don't, it is all a fabrication of priests and church – you haven't seen god and nor have I, it's pious tosh, ditch it, you don't need it any more.'

Vadier, an energetic representative on mission in the Ariège of his birth, in the Low Pyrenees, one of France's remoter regions, had acted as public prosecutor to a military commission which arrested a large number of priests and their parishioners in Saint-Girons and district in the Ariège. Others, zealous Jacobins, men of the Mountain, such as Javogues in the Loire, Carrier in Nantes, 'Iron-arm' Taillefer, who had terrorised the Lot region, had called on local bully-boys to enforce the law from Paris and now Paris washed its hands of them and their excesses and recalled them to answer. Others, like Fouché and Collot, the scourges of Lyon, and Fréron and Barras in Toulon, proved more elusive and, although they could not be described as a faction, they all had dangerous things in common: a detestation of Robespierre and an entirely cynical belief that surviving the Revolution was more important than serving and dying for it. The CGS continued to use the 252 infantrymen of the Paris army, at the time of the Ventôse laws stationed in the Ecole Militaire awaiting posting, for policing.

The new police – rather 'secret police' – bureau was staffed by placemen: Lejeune, the director of operations, was a friend of Saint-Just from Soissons; the wooden-legged Simon Duplay, whom Robespierre employed as a secretary; Claude Guérin, charged with surveillance of suspect persons and producing a 'detailed daily report to the CPS [read 'Robespierre'] on information he has gathered on intriguers, thieves, conspirators , their manoeuvres, their hideouts'. Within two months the bureau had grown into a formidable rival to the CGS.

The day after the Dantonists went to the guillotine, Couthon announced, to great applause, 'a project for a festival each decade [that is, every tenth day, on the *décadi* or rest day] dedicated to the Eternal being, the consoling idea of whom the Hébertists could not deprive the people'. A week later, when the ashes of the high priest of reason, Jean-Jacques Rousseau, were installed with solemn pomp in the Panthéon, Payan proclaimed in the Commune that 'Reason was none other than the Supreme Being'. Payan, an artillery officer of noble birth and ardent partisan of the Revolution, had recently been sent by the municipality of the Drôme to deliver an address to the Convention when he was but 26 years old. Robespierre liked him and put his name forward as a juror for the revolutionary tribunal, whence he progressed to become national agent of Paris, replacing the disgraced Chaumette.

These pronouncements on the Supreme Being were preliminaries to the report prepared by Robespierre during his detachment from public business and read out by him to the Convention on 7 May, in the name of the CPS.

Robespierre, so long schooled by the Oratorians, confirmed the veracity of the boast made by the Jesuits: 'Give us a boy till he is seven and he is ours for life.' He said grace before meals, accused the Encyclopaedist enemies of Rousseau of judging human relations to be no more than a battle of cunning and himself considered the existence of a god an essential to good government. Belief in a Supreme Being he deemed necessary to human existence, the only corroboration of virtue. These beliefs he had adumbrated already but on 7 May he expatiated on his ideas about the relationship between republican precepts and religion and morality. He drew much on the critique Rousseau presents in Book IV of *The Social Contract*, 'Of religion and the state'. To speak of a Christian republic is an oxymoron. The Roman, that is, Catholic, version of Christianity 'is a bizarre religion which gives men two bodies of law, two masters, two patries, subjects them to contradictory duties and prevents them from being both devotees *and* citizens . . . one can call this the religion of the Priest'. The chapter concludes with a paragraph on intolerance: 'Those who draw a distinction between civil intolerance and theological intolerance are, I believe, in error. The two intolerances are inseparable. It is impossible to live in peace with fellow beings whom one believes to be damned; to love them would be to hate God for punishing them; one must absolutely either bring them back into the fold or torment them.' A crux which Robespierre interpreted all too literally.

Whereas, Robespierre said in his dissertation, the arts, sciences and technology had made significant advances, man's nature had not shown similar improvement; humanity remained benighted, even bestial. His ethical sense was crude and callow; his appreciation of rights and obligations no better than embryonic. Rulers manifested this sorry infantile moral vacuity at its worst, in their egregious selfishness and lust for power, and ruthlessly squeezed out the thinkers and philosophers who might have instilled some moral code and balance into governance. Robespierre didn't mention a sense of humour.

He proposed a decree to establish the worship of the Supreme Being and recognition of the immortality of the soul, a worship best reinforced by a sense and practice of civic duty, which included the hatred of tyrants and traitors. Festivals marking the glorious passage of the Revolution were to be held on 14 July, 10 August, 21 January and 31 May in commemoration of the Fall of the Bastille, the overthrow of the monarchy, the execution of the King and the first anti-Girondin uprising in Paris. The décadis would celebrate ideas and ideals: the human race, equality, liberty, patriotism, truth, justice, friendship, maternal tenderness, heroism and so on. Musicians and poets were requested to submit civic hymns and songs for which they would be paid. Freedom of worship was guaranteed and the report outlined arrangements for a great Festival of the Supreme Being to be held on 8 June to concretise Robespierre's stated belief that 'the idea of the Supreme Being and the immortality of the soul is a constant recall to the notion of justice'.

The report was larded with the habitual vagaries, reference to 'the voices of wisdom . . . prosperity . . . the stability and felicity of the Republic' and a swingeing attack on 'the factional chiefs', of whom Danton was 'the most dangerous of enemies of the patrie . . . ringleader of all crimes, bound up in every plot, promising the criminals his protection while he swore fidelity to patriots'.

That evening of 7 May in the Jacobins, Lequinio who, during his mission in the west of France, had sponsored a frenzied programme of dechristianisation and terror, delivered an overblown and unctuous eulogy of Robespierre's speech to the Convention as a prelude to Robespierre rehearsing the whole tract.

The following day the revolutionary tribunal sent to the guillotine 28 tax farmers, including the great chemist Antoine-Laurent Lavoisier.

Lavoisier, 'the father of modern chemistry', was a man of extraordinarily wide accomplishment, though his fame rests principally on his discovery of the secret of fire and his naming of the essential ingredient (which he himself did not first discover) *oxigène*.

In 1778 Lavoisier set up a model farm in Fréchine to demonstrate the advantages of scientific agriculture. Over nine years, thanks to his methods, produce from the farm doubled. The patent success of the scheme led to Lavoisier's appointment to the government committee on Agriculture, where, as secretary, he drew up reports and instructions on the cultivation of crops and the efficient running of national agriculture.

Chosen as a member of the provincial assembly of Orléans in 1787,

Lavoisier advanced subventions of money to the towns of Blois (in whose commune he held his estates) and Romorantin for the purchase of barley during the famine of 1787. He had already commenced a major overhaul of the social infrastructure of the region, applying the same meticulous attention to detail in the human sphere as in the laboratory. It was an early and striking example of the application of altruism to rigorous economic method: enlightened intelligence allied to social conscience.

He proposed savings banks for workers; insurance societies; national pension schemes; plans to improve the canal network for greater efficiency and speed in the transport of essential commodities; workhouses for the security of the homeless, jobless poor. Was this simply a case of the honest civil servant acquitting himself with due sense of official responsibility or genuine charity sprung from the principle of noblesse oblige? He had become a full, titular member of the royal tax farm in 1779 and, by his direct intervention, had revoked a specific, punitive tax on the Jews of Metz – known contemptuously as 'cloven hoofs' – which had survived from the Middle Ages. A small blow for equality before the Revolution made equality an excuse for scything everyone to the same common level when Revolutionary Law began to bite hard.

But it was his scientific work which proved so revolutionary. Lavoisier lived at a time when false theories and surmises about natural phenomena abounded. He was one of the few who recognised that supposititious ideas handed down from the past exercised a compelling influence on current thinking largely because of the weight of tradition. Their authority had something of holy writ about it. He would have none of that. 'It is time,' he said, 'to lead chemistry back to a stricter way of thinking, to strip the facts with which this science is daily enriched of the additions of rationality and prejudice, to distinguish what is fact and observation from what is system and hypothesis. We must draw no conclusions beyond the warrant of facts.'

His rigorous approach to experiment and proof was quite as inflexible as any Jacobin's attitude to law, and the old regime of belief which he overthrew centred on the idea that fire depended on a mysterious theoretical substance called phlogiston. Theoretical because no one had identified it, seen it and therefore been able to weigh it – an essential process in determining what happened during combustion. Marat, himself a failed chemist, described fire as 'an igneous fluid' in a report he delivered to the Royal Academy of Sciences: Lavoisier was one of the Academicians who rejected Marat's hypothesis and thereby earned further vitriol from the people's friend, who denounced him as 'the chorus-master of charlatans . . . this little gentleman with his income of 40,000 livres whose only claim to fame is that he enclosed all Paris in a prison by cutting off the fresh air with a wall . . .' Marat's diagnosis of current ills was simple: they were due to prostitution. 'Princes prostitute power; ministers prostitute authority; magistrates prostitute justice; the rich prostitute wealth; scientists prostitute science; philosophers prostitute reason. The members of the Royal Academy are to be numbered among our street entertainers, magic tricks men, like the most zealous disciple of Mesmer [inventor of the quack mesmeric panacea based on animal magnetism]; it is false enchantment.'

And Lavoisier was nothing but the 'putative father of every discovery which is acclaimed. Having no ideas of his own he grabs those of others, but, since he doesn't have a clue what to make of them, he tosses them aside as lightly as he picks them up; he changes his opinions much as he changes his shoes.'

It was against this kind of wild aspersion and inexactitude that Lavoisier set his every scruple of intellectual energy.

In 1791, when the tax farm was abolished, Lavoisier found himself co-opted to the new public treasury as a commissioner in charge of producing a full statement of accounts. He did this work as meticulously as he did all his work. 'Nowadays both good and evil are described in such extreme terms, as if they were seen through a distorting glass, either too close or too far away to be assessed in proper proportion. Therefore I thought it useful to address myself calmly to the situation and submit the state finances to rigorous mathematical analysis.'

The accounts he produced were not only comprehensive and lucid, they were delivered on time. It had never happened under the King. The new government had found a trustworthy accountant. Lavoisier was asked to draw up a new scheme of taxation; he had already undertaken the job of regularising the chaotic system of weights and measures to establish a uniform standard, including the new metre (from Greek *metron*, literally 'measure') and centimetre; he even researched into qualities of paper and typeset and advised on the printing of assignats.

On 12 November one of Lavoisier's research collaborators, Bailly, went to the guillotine and two days later the net closed round Lavoisier himself when deputy Bourdon from the Oise region stood up in the Convention and bellowed: 'This is the hundredth time the affairs of the tax farm have been brought before us. The farm has been swept away but those who have grown fat on its iniquities walk free. They continue to rake in profits by putting water into our tobacco. [A popular accusation this: the addition of water to tobacco to increase its weight allowed less to be sold for more than its worth.] In the name of the people, I demand the arrest of the bloodsuckers. I demand the restitution of the 22 millions they have extorted. I demand that they be arraigned before the revolutionary Tribunal.' The Convention decreed an order for the arrest of all the former tax farmers.

Lavoisier was taken to the Port-Libre prison, where he shared cell 33 with his wife's father, Jacques Paulze, who had proposed him for membership of the tax farm. He worked on his memoirs, in which he wrote a credo: 'To warrant well of humanity and to serve one's country as one ought, it is not necessary to engage in public service in the public eye, concerned with the organisation and regeneration of empires. The physicist, working in the silence of his laboratory or his study, can do patriotic work. He can hope that his labours may lessen the mass of ills which afflict humankind; and to increase humanity's joys and contentment and if, by the new avenues of possibility which his researches open up, he does no more than extend human life span a few years, even a few days, he may aspire to the glorious title of benefactor of mankind.' He also made a forlorn appeal to sense and reason: 'Legislators: education made the Revolution; let education be still your palladium of Liberty.' Lavoisier, like so many caught up in the horrors, simply could not believe that sense, reason, calm would not overrule the excess.

He wrote frequently to his wife, Marie-Anne, letters which reveal ever more candidly the dreadful strain, the nagging uncertainty that haunted them both. 'It's a hard time you're having to endure; you are giving yourself much mental and physical anguish which I cannot share with you. Take care of your health: to lose that would be the worst misfortune of all. My life's work has been a success; I have had a happy life since I found my true direction and shared my life with you. You have contributed to that success and happiness every single day, by your affection, by the endearments you gave me. I will never forget the consideration you showed me, the esteem you paid me. My work is finished. But you have a right to hope for a long life. Do not give that up. When you came yesterday, you seemed very miserable. Why? I am resigned to my fate. They cannot take away from me anything of what I have achieved. Besides, it's not absolutely certain that we won't be reunited. I may be released. Meanwhile, my greatest happiness is when you visit me.'

While Lavoisier was in prison, the Bureau de Consultation des Arts et des Métiers requisitioned a report on his work. If he had any hope of survival it lay in recognition of his importance to the young Republic as a scientist; even, for her revolutionary armies, as the best fabricator of gunpowder in Europe. But the association with the detested and reviled tax farm counted so heavily against his chance of release that Marie-Anne went to one of the Convention deputies, Dupin, to intercede: 'I have not come to plead my husband's case: he is innocent. Only someone with no moral principles could accuse him of any crime. He has been charged along with all the other ex-members of the tax farm. To make his own case distinct from theirs would be dishonourable. None of them is guilty of any crime. They have only aroused bitterness because they were wealthy. If they die, they will die innocent.'

Dupin was unmoved. He went to the CPS and said: 'I demand the restitution of the 22 million livres stolen by the tax farmers from the people of France. I demand that the farmers be brought before the revolutionary Tribunal. Let the Tribunal judges distinguish between them if they can.'

It can only have been sheer volume of work which kept the tax farmers out of the dock for so long and they were, finally, taken to what everyone knew to be the last port of call: the Conciergerie.

Lavoisier knew the place well; under the auspices of the Royal Academy he had headed a royal commission to inquire into the state of prisons, by order of the first minister, Necker, and wrote a full report, dated 5 April and 6 September 1780. Of the Conciergerie he remarked: 'In the middle of the prison there had previously been a drystone well from which emanated a morbid stench. We re-channelled rainwater from every possible inflow to cleanse this water source and to siphon off all the impurities into the river. Since which time there has been no foul odour.'

Lavoisier was walking in the courtyard when the news came that the tax farmers were to appear the following day before the revolutionary Tribunal. Time had finished now. He had to go and tell the others the news. In the perverse anguished relief of knowing that the end must be near, one of them, who had somehow held himself together during the ghastly strain of waiting, broke down and stabbed himself to death. Lavoisier's recorded reaction is typical of the man: 'Why go out to meet death? Knowing that the death we face will be unjust, did he think it shameful to be killed by someone else's hand? The very fact that it *is* unjust effaces all shame. Our real judges are not the Tribunal to which we are summoned, nor the people who insult us. Let us leave an example behind us which others can follow.'

And news came of another suicide. The distinguished mathematician the marquis de Condorcet had slipped out of Paris and was heading for safety. He stopped at an inn in the village of Clamart, south-west of Paris, on the evening of 29 March 1794: he asked for an omelette. The woman innkeeper squinted at him; suspicion of any stranger was instinctive in those fretful hag-ridden times. Or perhaps his hands looked uncommonly soft. She asked him how many eggs he would like in his omelette. He had never made an omelette. Few men in France, one imagines, had ever made an omelette.

He replied: 'Oh, a dozen?'

An aristocrat's omelette. She reported him; he was arrested and, taken to the prison in Bourg-la-Reine, he was found dead next morning, either from nervous collapse or poison.

Shortly afterwards a deputation from the Lycée des Arts, founded in 1793 and of which Lavoisier was a charter member, came to the Conciergerie to crown him with a wreath in honour of his invaluable contribution to learning. And the report for the Bureau de Consultation des Arts et des Métiers was finished. It concluded: 'This summary of achievements and work covers such a rich and varied scope of interest that it is scarcely credible that they come from one man alone . . . Citizen Lavoisier deserves to be enrolled among those whose work in advancing human knowledge have done most to enhance the science and the glory of the nation . . .'

The document was not used at his trial.

Lavoisier wrote a final letter to Marie-Anne: 'I have had a long career, I have enjoyed my work and I think it will carry some glory with it. What more could I wish for? What is happening to me spares me the troubles of old age. I will die in perfect health. This will probably be the last letter I can write to you. They may not allow me to write tomorrow. Thinking of you now in these last hours of my life, of you and those I hold dear, is a consolation which brings peace to me.'

He kept from his wife the piercing dread of what he, like the others, faced. He touched on it in another letter, to his cousin, Angez de Villiers: 'Whatever I have done of importance for the nation in the interests of science and human knowledge cannot save me from this dismal end. I must die like a guilty person. I am writing to you today because they may not allow me to write tomorrow and because there is some consolation in thinking of you and those who are dear to me in these last hours. Remember me to them who love me and to whom this letter is sent to share. It is probably the last I'll write.'

At 1 in the morning of 8 May 1794 Lavoisier and the others were woken and handed the papers, drawn up by Fouquier, on which were enumerated the charges against them. At dawn they were roused again, searched and informed that they would each be allowed 15 minutes with their defence lawyers before trial. At 10 a.m. they were taken to the revolutionary Tribunal. This had been established on 10 March 1793, and judges and jury had wept when they condemned to death their first victim, a man called des Maulans. They had grown more pachydermatous over the intervening year. When Lavoisier's lawyer advanced the argument that his achievements as a scientist would make his death a national tragedy, the presiding judge, Coffinhal, snarled: 'The Republic has no need of scientists; justice must run its course.' And, when the lawyer protested, Coffinhal snapped back at him the rebuke which had become a catchphrase: 'Shut up, you have no leave to speak.'

(When he came, in his turn, to mount the scaffold, the jeering mob chanted gleefully: 'Coffinhal, Coffinhal, you have no leave to speak.' He had had wind of his impending arrest and escaped, but was betrayed while on the run.)

At five p.m. Lavoisier and the others boarded the tumbrels in the courtyard. The heavy gates opened and they began the melancholy ride to the place de la Révolution through streets lined with people yelling insults, spitting, howling abuse at this loathsome remnant of royal subjugation. At one point the press of the crowd brought the procession of tumbrels to a halt. One of the prisoners, Papillon, standing next to Lavoisier in the sickly transport, looked down at the faces of their tormentors, twisted with hatred, and remarked: 'A sorry bunch to bequeath the world to.'

The crowds milling round the scaffold were dense. They fought to get close enough to hear the hiss of the falling blade, 'the whisper of the axe', as someone described it.

Lagrange, the great mathematician, said of Lavoisier's miserable end: 'It took them only a moment to cut off that head and it may take 100 years to produce the like.' Above all, though, in any reflection on the remorseless passage of a mania perversely disguised as the legitimate business of government, it is the hideous waste of life, of talent, of honourable feeling and behaviour that strikes one to the heart. Asked what he had done during the Revolution, the Abbé Sieyès said: 'I stayed alive.' It was as much as many could do.

# FIFTEEN

# *Blood and Judgement*

Our prison is really a tomb where people still in their death
throes wait for the scythe to terminate their existence.

*Anonymous prisoner*

JOSEPH LEBON, constitutional priest and deputy for the Pas-de-
Calais, sent to his home department in October 1793 on mission
by the CPS, set up a revolutionary tribunal in Robespierre's home
town of Arras. Its members, wrote another representative, with the
army of the North, Chaudieu, in a letter to his wife, 'behaved more
like public executioners than judges'. Lebon traversed the region
trailing the guillotine and a reputation for apoplectic savagery.
Although a decree of 19 April 1794 suppressed all such Tribunals in
the provinces, the CPS excluded Lebon's from the order. He had just
transferred his Tribunal to Cambrai, at the request of Saint-Just and
Le Bas, with the army of the North, when he received an order to
return to Paris 'as quickly as possible'.

He went back, cringed suitably and after two days returned to
Arras, taking Charlotte Robespierre with him. Guffroy, another
deputy for the Pas-de-Calais, truculently opposed to both Robespierre
(with whom he had been at school) and Lebon, wrote to Robespierre
on 19 May: 'You said recently [15 May] in the Jacobins that in our
desire to establish the rule of virtue we should not use persecution.
I think you believe what you say. Why then are you shielding the
priest-persecutor Joseph Lebon who has killed patriotism in Arras
and established the rule of debauchery and crime?'

Nothing was done. Not long afterwards the CPS set up another extraordinary instrument of the Terror, the infamous Popular Commission in Orange, on 10 May, the same day that the King's sister, Madame Elisabeth, went to the scaffold.

Whereas the savagery of the Terror had been largely extinguished outside Paris, the majority of victims executed in Bordeaux, Orange and Nîmes, Arras and Cambrai died during the last two months of its course. In Orange 332; Arras 343; Cambrai 149; Nîmes (from December 1793) 136; Bordeaux (from October 1793) 299.

In Paris wax and tallow had disappeared, so there was a shortage of candles and section meetings closed early. One evening, as the days lengthened and the candle famine was less onerous, Hesdin went a long way round via the quays on his way home. He felt 'sick and weary of life and wished to God my head was in the basket. The very paving stones smell of blood and the river seems to run blood. Not a group of chatterers tonight but there were two or three government agents listening for the least sign of sympathy with an accused person.' The fashionable suburbs were nearly deserted; the Faubourg Saint-Marcel still bustled with a medley of trades people and artisans; the Quai de l'Hôpital (to the east, by the Salpêtrière prison), an insalubrious district, was now teeming with life. An English visitor commented on the 'narrowness, dirt and stench' of the city's streets and Hesdin remarks that the filth was as great or greater than ever 'but the splendour that was hard by the filth is gone. Even the great chestnut walk in the Elysian Fields, once the resort of all that was gay and gentle, is encumbered with ordures. The old city magistrates did little enough to keep Paris clean but it did not allow pigs to be killed in the streets and their blood to swill into the kennels, nor heaps of dung to accumulate for weeks at the corners.'

As if there was not already enough blood splashing on to the pavement.

In the holding prisons life still had something of the same routine as on the outside. The marquis de Nicolaï, former president of the audit office, detained in the Luxembourg, never went past an open door if he met someone without an 'after you . . . no, please, after you' tussle of politesse as to who should pass first. There was no such parlour politeness in the purgatory of the Conciergerie, where all custom, all manners had been levelled to a real, maybe surreal, egalitarian order.

In the Conciergerie there was no restraint, no ceremony: all feelings burst out, no one hesitated, reflected, pondered. As one of them said, there often reigned in that prison 'a considerable gaiety', particularly when they had had some wine and liqueurs to drink and 'overheated with drink we vied with each other to behave outrageously'.

But the swings of mood were violent. One prisoner, the Parisian editor Claude-François Beaulieu, took comfort from the rack of anxiety about the fate that awaited him, in the possession of a small dose of opium, given him by a cell mate. 'From the moment when I realised that my destiny lay in my own hands, I breathed again and waited with a truly unimaginable calm the last blow of tyranny, quite certain that I could escape it at the very instant it should fall on me.' He hid the sachet and, even when the storms of the Revolution had blown themselves out, kept the souvenir as a reminder 'to maintain a serene, a tranquil outlook in every circumstance of his life in future'.

When Beaulieu was removed from the horrors of the Conciergerie to the Luxembourg, he thought he had gone to another world: the inmates were quite unlike the impetuous people he had been with and they were suspicious of him, treating him as a spy. For some days he regretted the grim cell which he had left in tears, knowing that he would never see the comrades of his confinement there again.

For, bizarrely, the prisons became a rendezvous of good company. The prisoners played all sorts of games, flipping coins to dislodge coins balanced on a cork, dice, backgammon, vingt-et-un, crowded games of ball in the garden or courtyard. Musicians, many of them former dancing masters, accompanied dancing, particularly the lively traditional triple-time carmagnole brought to Paris from Provence, and the singing of hymns and songs to violins, cello, viola to lift spirits, and it was this good cheer which somehow helped to reduce any moping, any dwelling on what might otherwise have seemed the incurable sadness of their situation. A prisoner in the former English Benedictine convent says that these lazy days of eating, drinking, aimless mooching, sleeping, 'wasted valuable time which might have been spent in the service of our country' but he stressed that the detainees behaved with great politeness to one another.

In short, the prisons became the sole refuge of that French urbanity which dared not show itself any more in public for fear of being taken as mischievous frivolity. Ducourneau wrote to a friend from prison: 'If I contemplate the moment of my death with sangfroid it is because of what happens all the time in here, this is death's antechamber. We live with death. We dine, we laugh with our companions in misfortune; they have the fatal order in their pocket. The next day they go before the Tribunal; a bit later we hear they have been condemned; they congratulate us and reassure us of their courage. Our routine of life does not change because of this, it is a mixture of horror at what we see and a sort of ferocious gaiety; for we often joke about the most frightful things to the point where the other day we showed a new arrival how that works, with a chair that we see-sawed and tipped over; then someone chanted: "No more getting up his nose when he to the guillotine goes."

'To show you how we harden ourselves – a condemned woman has just come up to me in great distress to ask my help: "My tears have dried up," she said. "Not one has escaped my eyes since yesterday evening. The most sensitive of women is no longer susceptible to any feelings; the affections which made my life happy have been exhausted. I regret nothing, I regard the moment of my death with indifference." Her name is Madame Laviolette de Tournay [executed 7 January 1794]. She had spent huge sums of money for the cause of liberty, kept open house to commissioners, army officers; had her portrait painted with her hand on a skull, unhappy omen. Filled with lessons so august:

> Yes, my friends, we face death so
> As did many famous just
> Such as Brutus, such as Cato.
> If in spite of calumnies
> We continue to draw breath
> We will drink life to the lees
> As gustily as we face death.'

Laviolette had, in fact, left her husband to live with one Madrillon but he had been caught spying and compromised her. They went to the scaffold together on 8 January 1794 with two others. Someone who saw them in the tumbrel from a café in the rue Saint-Honoré remarked how 'they were all laughing at the citizen cart-driver taking them to the guillotine and the public looking on. The spectators were saying: "They've got the real air of traitors and former nobles; if anyone seemed to be moved to pity, they mocked us."

"'You see,' said one citizen, "how they mock our justice, laughing as they go to the scaffold, and that's a fact.'"

A fellow prisoner, Riouffe, records that Ducourneau also took part in some macabre high jinks in the Conciergerie.

Cell number 13. A row of 18 beds, separated by high wooden partitions, between which each individual is isolated as if entombed. On each bed sits a juror. The accused mounts a table in front of them; the bench consists of the clerk of the court and the public prosecutor. We usually began our séances at midnight when, under our gloomy vaults, the doors bolted for the night, we were almost certain not to be disturbed.

The accused is always condemned – how could it be otherwise, since this was the revolutionary tribunal? The prisoner once condemned, the frightful machinery of law swings into action: his hands are tied and the victim is laid on a wooden bed, a plank over his neck to receive the stroke of the sword on his neck.

By one of those turns of events so commonplace in the Revolution, the public prosecutor himself is accused and, consequently, condemned. He suffers judgement but suddenly returns, draped in a white sheet to terrify us with a tableau of the torments which he underwent in Hell; he tells off the list of his crimes, foretells what will happen to the jurors – they will be carted off in tumbrels awash with blood, shut up in iron cages and revolt society with the horror of their sufferings as they had disgusted them with the unparalleled cruelties.

In our dormitory was a man called Lapagne, from the Faubourg du Havre [the eastern edge of the eighth arrondissement, near the Gare Saint-Lazare] where he had been sent by the Jacobins and, at this time, very worthy to do them service since he had been ringleader of a gang of thieves and condemned to be broken on the wheel for murder under the old regime. His face was scarred and lined with heavy wrinkles; the muscles on his arms like iron and broad, broad shoulders; every sign of murder imprinted on him, head to toe; a raucous terrible voice. Our ghost seizes him by the collar and, rebuking him for all his crimes with terrible curses, he drags him off to hell. 'Lapagne, Lapagne, Lapagne,' he keened. Lapagne trailed behind him, disconcerted, frightened. His terror gave the scene, lit by one single candle, more colour, the shadows playing gently on the walls of our cell from vault to floor. This ghost was me. And thus we joked in the womb of death and thus in our prophetic games we spoke truth amidst spies/informers and executioners.

Our constant refrain in their midst was Liberty, Equality, Fraternity; we had even consecrated this oath by a sort of religious ceremony which owed its origins to quite pleasant circumstances.

One of our company was a pious Benedictine, a most enlightened man, his hands forever folded on his breast as in the portraits of Saint Benedict, particularly tormented by the passion for making converts.

A likeable young lawyer from Bordeaux, Pierre Ducorneau, full of spirit, talent and good humour, later murdered [guillotined on 17 March 1794] for the crime of federalism, was the devil tempter for this new Saint Antony. Ducourneau had disguised himself as a Satanic creature in black, hunchbacked, one-eyed, limping, the lame horned Devil in person. He creeps up, grabs the monk by the ankles, drags him off the bed shrieking that he has been condemned to the flames of the eternal bonfire, damned without remission, for having turned the Creator of the Universe into an envious being, a wicked drunkard, an enemy of love and joy.

'Ah, ah,' he howled horribly, scarce able to muffle his giggles, 'you old Buddhist, you have preached how God enjoys seeing his creatures languishing in penitence and abstaining from the most precious gifts he has given them. Impostor. Hypocrite. Whited sepulchre, squat upon nails and eat eggshells for all eternity.'

At which point, he could no longer contain himself, and dissolved in hysterics.

Then, no sooner than he had snatched his breviary than Saint Antony chased after the devil with a broom handle; he knocked the candle over; he made as many circuits of the room as the Devil made temptation of Saint Antony; the saint chanted psalms, the devil descanted a ribald song. But the holy man did not falter; he never stopped praying, always on the look-out, one eye on his breviary the other on Ducorneau.

To counter his endless sermonising, chanted prayers and psalms, they invent their own cult, hymns and incantations. The saint despairs of their salvation but peers at one or two of them as being made of better stuff and more apt for conversion, calls their god

Ibrascha and starts to work on the Spaniard – imagine the joy, the blessing of leading a renegade Spanish soul to the bosom of the church. The Spaniard rallies: 'Long live Ibrascha.'

The monk pretends to sleep as they start their office, then springs up, chants the *De profundis* at the top of his voice – 'Out of the depths I have cried to Thee, O Lord; Lord hear my voice' [Psalm 130] – heaps curses on them, tries to break down their altar . . . In spite of all our bad jokes we loved and respected him. We wept sincerely for him when he went to the scaffold.

One man who had taken part in these macabre antics, Adjutant-General Boisguyon, as he climbed into the tumbrel in the courtyard of the Conciergerie, on his way to the scaffold, remarked to Sanson, the executioner: 'Today we do it for real – you'll be amazed how well I am rehearsed.'

A grenadier from the regiment stationed in Artois, Gosnay, 27 years old, was arrested by Ronsin in Chalon-sur-Saône for a suspected attempt to escape across the border. He fell for a pretty young woman who came to visit her asthmatic uncle in the Conciergerie; she cared for her uncle, then went to Gosnay to minister to him, including some small pleasures. Gosnay promised to marry her after his release but in fact was determined to die.

Handed his indictment, he twisted the sheet of paper into a taper and lit his pipe with it. His friends were horrified – such folly to hasten to death when he had good grounds for a defence. Before being taken before the Tribunal, he drank white wine and ate oysters with his friends, smoked a pipe and discussed the lost hope of the times they lived in. 'That's not all,' he said. 'Now that we have had lunch, we must look to supper and you will give me the address of the best restaurateur in the next world so I can prepare you a good meal for this evening.'

When they read out the list of charges against him in the Tribunal he affirmed that all the main counts against him were true; his defence lawyer said he must be out of his head. He responded: 'My head has never been so lucid as at this moment even if I am on the verge of losing it. Officious defender, I will not stand for your standing up for me – [and turning to the judges] let them take me to the guillotine.'

Condemned to death, he crossed the courtyard and greeted his comrades with his usual good cheer, the expression on his face not a jot altered. In the hall of the condemned, he drank and ate with appetite; he was as he had always been, as if the certainty of ending his life gave it firmness of purpose again.

Mounting the tumbrel, he spoke to one of the turnkeys with whom he had become quite pally: 'Friend Larivière, we must drink a tot of kirsch in your cup otherwise I'll bear a grudge against you till the day I die.' Larivière brought the liqueur and Gosnay appeared to drink it with pleasure. As they crossed the courtyard several people booed and hissed him; he replied coldly: 'Fucking cowards that you are, you insult me? Ha. Will you go to your death with as much courage as I do?'

At the foot of the scaffold he cried out: 'Here I am, just where I wanted to be' and calmly delivered his head to the executioner.

The CPS and the CGS employed prisoners as spies to compile lists which were sent on by the committees to Fouquier. Boyenval, a tailor by trade, was supposedly in the Luxembourg prison for royalist leanings. Prisoners had confidence in him, gave him clothes to mend. Boyenval took advantage of this sodality to probe their beliefs, sound their opinions, find out who they were and about their family.

One day Boyenval met an unhappy suspect from Toulouse walking down the long gallery of the prison in a pair of red Moroccan slippers. Boyenval looked him up and down and walked on, thinking: only an aristocrat could have slippers like that. He put the name of the man on his list and the next day the Tribunal condemned him to death.

A young woman of good family, a talented painter, won permission to accompany her husband to the Luxembourg to console him and to paint. She had a reasonable expectation of her husband's being released – he had been caught up in a few silly brawls in the section, a crime hardly worth remark – but those placid days in the most relaxed of the holding prisons, the hours spent in the garden, were a precious advantage of peace and quiet, which outweighed the more disagreeable aspects.

It was false calm. She found out that Boyenval, at the prompting of another spy less obtrusive than him, had put her husband on the list. She searched him out and begged him to remove the name; her husband was a simple man without much money and possessed of neither the will nor the strength to be a counter-revolutionary. Boyenval listened, considered and promised to save her husband on one condition. She blushed, went pale and then gave herself to him.

Her husband went to the scaffold the following day.

One of the most active spies, the Comte de Ferrières-Sauveboeuf, was known to be a snitch in the pay of the revolutionary tribunal and the CGS; he received 500 livres per month and, presumably, his keep in La Force, where he spied, eavesdropped outside doors, kept a detailed diary of all he heard and saw and sent innumerable inmates to the revolutionary tribunal. The wonder is that he could boast that he was among people who did not fear him. Family connections gave him invaluable inside information as to the whereabouts of fugitives, property, money, and most of the 'infamous villains' whom he betrayed were nobles and wealthy bourgeois.

Dinner in the Luxembourg, for which the prisoners were charged 50 sous, consisted of undrinkable soup, half a bottle of sour wine, a dish of vegetables swimming in water and always pork mixed with cabbage, plus one and a half pounds of ration bread. The meat was often bad and full of hairs, dirt, maggots, the vegetables dry. Those who complained were told they would be given haricots and potatoes if they made a fuss.

Since there were between 800 and 1,000 people confined in the prison, there were three sittings: 11 a.m., noon, 1 p.m.; prisoners brought their own bottle for wine and a plate for food. Gaolers stood guard; agents on visits took the opportunity of having everyone gathered in one place at mealtime, to ask names, ages, professions.

Maxims painted in big letters decorated the walls of the refectory:

'The free man cherishes his freedom even when he is deprived of it.'
'Events [illegible word] do not alter his heart; liberty, equality, reason are the divinities which cense him constantly.'
'Morality, virtue, candour, these are the principles of the true republican.'
'Nature, patrie, reason, these are his cult of worship.'
'In liberty are enshrined the rights of man, namely reason, equality, justice.'
'The Republic renders society happy; it ranges all men under the banner of the common interest.'

The police administrator Marino, believing that 'the rich must expiate their wealth', adopted a straightforward approach to the matter of equality and was popular with the prisoners, one of whom, Coittant, recalls seeing him arrive one day dishevelled and unshaven. Various prisoners approached him with requests; he ignored them, singled out a rich prisoner and took him by the arm to where a group of the poorest inmates sat.

'Right, my boy,' he said, 'these men are from my section, you've got to look after them, you understand what I'm saying?'

'Yes, citizen.'

'Sit yourself down.'

'Yes, citizen.'

Marino tapped him on the cheek: 'You pay for the food, OK?'

'Yes, citizen.'

'The room, the expenses, the wine.'

'Yes, citizen.'

'So, this is the president [pointing out Jousseran], he'll keep an account of all the costs, all right?'

'Yes, citizen.'

'You've got money, they haven't got any, so it's for you to pay, see?'

'Yes, citizen.'

'You take care of everything.'

'Yes, citizen.'

'Gigot with garlic, potatoes and salad.'

'Yes, citizen.'

Marino gave him another light biff on the cheek and went off whistling.

Eight nuns were found in hiding and interrogated. Pressed to take an oath to liberty and equality, they refused: how could they take an oath to liberty when they were prisoners? As for equality, they were not living in times of equality, seeing that the man who had arrested them had behaved with such arrogance. Threatened with the revolutionary tribunal, they said they would go with pleasure. Asked if they would renounce their living, they said no, because it represented all the goods that had been taken from them.

'But the law forbids payment to anyone who refuses to obey it, so how will you live?'

'Providence will take care of us.'

'But Providence won't give you bread.'

'We ask nothing of anybody.'

'Since the Republic does not nurture enemies in its bosom, you will be deported; where do you want to go?'

'France, which is our patrie.'

They were guillotined as fanatics.

At 8 a.m. on the morning that the tax farmers went to the revolutionary Tribunal, a considerable force of armed men wearing tricolour ribbons mustered in the garden of the Madelonettes convent, rue des Fontaines-du-Temple. It transpired that three prisoners had been caught with knives, scissors, razors, and the entire prison was to be ransacked and searched.

At 3 p.m. the tocsin rang and all prisoners were sent to their bedchambers; all communication was forbidden. Coittant burnt all his 'fugitive verses', hid his journal in the ashes of the fireplace behind a large log at the back so that it wouldn't burn, and his scissors, watch and razor in holes in the chimney.

That night, there were 100 men on guard patrolling the prison corridors.

The next day the commissioners were still searching, confiscating knives or blunting their points. New men replaced them when they became exhausted.

All the windows were kept closed; the atmosphere inside the building was stifling. As each room was searched, the prisoners were allowed out into the garden.

The commissioners, full of swagger and tricolour pomp, arrived at Coittant's cell; the search took an age, but nothing was found.

There was a roll-call every day; since most of the gaolers were scarcely literate, hard put to it to decipher the ill-spelled, scrawled lists of names, and frequently drunk, the *appels* were grim, tedious, frightening affairs. A name is called, no one answers, the gaolers, guard dogs straining at the leash, 'swear, rage, threaten; they call the name again: we explain, help them, finally work out who it is that they're calling for. They do a head count of the rest of the flock; they get the number wrong, and, more and more furious, order everyone back into the yard; we go back, we troop out, they get the number wrong again and sometimes it takes three or four attempts before, in their befuddled state, finally they're sure they've got everybody.'

\* \* \*

The more ingenious a tyranny in its persecutions, the more imaginative in their evasions those whom it torments. The authorities had imposed no prohibition on telescopes and a brisk exchange in them sprang up – prisoners slipping gaolers money to purchase them so they could be passed round. The friends and family on the outside also bought them and a new system of signals for communication developed. But someone found out and denounced this hideous new conspiracy and the gaoler made the round, collecting them up, save those that were spirited away and hidden.

Although communication with the outside world was strictly forbidden, tiny objects of consolation were smuggled into the prisons ' . . . in a folded handkerchief, a pigeon's beak, the hem of a necktie'. These arrived in parcels of food and clean clothing. Boilleau wrote to his wife on 23 April asking her to do her very best to bring 'a goodly well-seasoned salad or else the making, we have bowls; but try to see that it is fresh and decently dressed . . . We have salt but bring a little pepper. Try to do this service for us today if possible, I will be most obliged and bring as much oil as you can, I will be most obliged and kiss you with all my heart.'

Citizeness Fournier, anxious for her husband, sends him 'a pigeon, some redcurrants, some apricots, a bottle of wine. I am not sending any linen because you do not ask for any. I kiss you with all my heart, I would so like not to say it but to embrace you in earnest. I do not know when I will have that pleasure, I await it with great impatience. I am your beloved and wife, Fournier.'

A note hurriedly scribbled at the prison gate and passed to one of the gaolers with a basket of food informs citizen Maisonneuve: 'A pigeon, an artichoke, a bottle of wine, a handkerchief. If Catherine finds any figs she will bring them for you . . . your little [female] cousin, if it please you.'

Bourget writes to his wife at the lemonade seller's house, rue des Poulies, near the place du Louvre: 'I wrote to you the day before yesterday and waited for a reply yesterday but heard nothing. It is that you have given birth? If so, tell me and let me know whether it's a boy or a girl. I asked you for a basket of cherries, my comrades will pay for them and I will pass on the money to you. I need a handkerchief, a pair of stockings, some thread and a needle to repair my breeches; I have no more tobacco. Your husband, Bourget.'

Etienne-Pierre Gourneau (1773–93) from Bordeaux, where he

worked as a clerk to a notary, arrived in Paris at the beginning of 1793 and entered the ministry of the Interior on the recommendation of his uncle. A bumptious and ill-advised youth, he made no secret of his contempt for the institutions of the republican government and his letters to friends in Bordeaux were no less imprudent.

One such, intercepted by the surveillance committee of the department of Paris, occasioned his arrest. Following interrogation he was taken before the CGS on 3 July and asked to explain the opprobrious terms of the contents: he wrote disdainfully of two representatives on mission to Bordeaux, Treilhard and Mathieu, ridiculed Marat as well as describing 'the blabber-mouth cut-throats of the sections who could hardly even speak French'. Moreover, he painted a scabrous picture of life in Paris and just how disagreeable he found it.

On 6 July his rooms were searched, papers seized, the dossier sent to Fouquier and he to the Sainte-Pélagie prison. Interrogated by the revolutionary Tribunal on 9 August he was quizzed particularly about a letter baldly comparing the national representative assembly to the frogs in La Fontaine's fable derived from Aesop, where the frogs are in thrall to a dead log half-submerged in their pond to which they defer as their king. He also signed a parody of the Marseillaise as 'an émigré who doesn't give a toss for the guillotine and is not afraid of his property being stolen'.

After three weeks in prison, Gourneau was condemned as counter-revolutionary by the revolutionary Tribunal. Neither the efforts of his father, former lawyer to the Parlement and recorder of its Chancellory, second highest in France, nor his youth swayed the verdict.

He addressed his last letter to his family:

To citizen Gourneau
Cloister Saint-Merry no. 452

My dear father and family,
I send you my last adieus. My sole regret in leaving this life is not to be able to embrace you. No other affection holds me: he who has never committed any crime, who has never harmed anyone, who has been a decent, sensitive and generous human being, dies in peace. I had hoped to work in the service of the Republic when it had been firmly established. I have always desired the good of my patrie. I have abhorred despotism and adored liberty. Today I am

the victim of an indiscretion, of an imprudence committed at twenty years of age and I die without fear.

I had hoped to become, together with my elder brother, a support for the old age of our good parents who brought me up with the utmost care and who, during the years of our childhood, evinced the most tender feelings towards us. I am cheated of this hope.

Hello, you, true brother, honest friend, in my absence, be a bold defender of the rights of humanity. When you have rendered service to the patrie, take care to give our younger brother a start in life, so too our only sister and do not waste any more tears of friendship than are necessary to erase the memory of a brother who adored you and who, in a few hours time, is going to be happier than you . . .

I leave a prison which is a real preparation for this act of eternity. I was crammed in there, on straw, with forty poor devils, all waiting, as I waited there, for the same lot. I no longer know if I can believe in presentiments, but I have pondered for several days on what has happened to me and to the lot that awaited me. When I realised that I was being hustled out of Sainte-Pélagie I said: 'It's all over for me.'

My cousin Dupuy may wish to go to Sainte-Pélagie to retrieve the things he loaned me.

Herewith my order authorising the transfer:

I ask citizen Boucherot, concierge of the Sainte-Pelagie house of detention to remit, or have remitted by a room-mate to the bearer, my cousin, items belonging to him:

1. a trestle bed 2. a mattress 3. the works of Crebillon in three volumes 4. my mathematics, by Surin, in five octavo volumes 5. a refracting telescope.

I have sold the remainder of my books to my cell-mate who also loaned me some money.

Etienne-Pierre Gourneau

I bid all my friends, and all those of my family, a sincere goodbye and kiss them for the last time. I ask that my father conserve this letter and bequeath it to his heirs to remind them of my existence and that I perished on the scaffold, victim of my opinions, 14 frimaire, old style 4 December 1793, year II of the French Republic, between noon and 1 p.m., or 11 a.m., in the place de la Révolution.

Once more adieu *in vitus eternam* (Into eternal life) Father, Mother, Brothers, Sisters, Uncles, Aunts, Relatives, Friends, Cousins all dear to me and whose acquaintance is death because of the friendship we have known.

*In vitam more datus* Gourneau, second son, this 4 Xcember 1793, 4 frimaire.

In an office of the Palais de Justice, above the prison and adjacent to the revolutionary Tribunal, Fouquier attended to the enormous drift of papers which accumulated without cease on his desk. Denunciations, police reports, notes from informers, pleas from the wives of men already in prison, a request from the chief gaoler for the trial of a dead man – Heurtault de Lammerville – to proceed, nevertheless, so that he could legally confiscate the man's possessions, the legitimate perquisites of the prison officials.

Fouquier was the man for the task: a meticulous, pedestrian bureaucrat, he checked everything scrupulously, ploughed through masses of paperwork leaf by leaf. As a measure of how he regarded the high importance of his office, in his indictments he used the pompous, stilted style of the old Parlements, the grand verbosity of the royal servants.

His dogged competence was not only his own raison d'être but also the justification of, and excuse for, his role in the Terror. He was, too, punctilious in the matter of eating. He dined daily at 3 p.m. in a small restaurant near the courts, run by Anne Maurisan, who asked him one day: 'Very busy, citizen?'

'Yes, very.'

'You look really tired.'

'Ah, what a cruel job. I'd rather be a labourer.'

The fatigue sometimes served a good turn. When Bligny, the public prosecutor of the Paris Commune, asked Fouquier for pardon for someone, he replied that he couldn't do anything, he took only those they sent him, as Bligny well knew.

'But not this one – you know he's done nothing.'

'Every man charged is suspect. If the man is not guilty, the Tribunal will acquit him.'

This was a fiction they all parroted as if somehow it vindicated use, now obsolete, of the word 'justice'.

Bligny pressed the matter. 'Allow yourself, why not? the joy of saving a life.'

Fouquier muttered protest, cut the conversation off but furtively slipped the dossier under a pile of papers and forgot it. The gesture represented a life and, with him, there was never any suggestion of hatred, of personal animosity; after all, one life was no different, in his eyes, from any another.

The corridors of the Palais de Justice were thronged with petitioners. One such, Mademoiselle de Monty, managed to gain access to Fouquier. The young woman modestly dressed, reserved, pale, her hands tightly clenched, asked Fouquier to release her father, a farmer from Nantes: he had committed no crime.

Fouquier laughed. 'Ah, as simple as that. You know they have sent me 100 suspects from Nantes.'

'I know, citizen. There were 132, now only 95 are left – the others died on the journey or could not bear the life in prison. My father is still there.'

'He is innocent?'

'I swear it.'

'You want me to set him and the others free?'

'All of them – it will be justice done.'

He stared at her from under his thick, bushy eyebrows. 'Very well, I will examine the dossiers. Leave, now. I will see. Come back in a few days.' As she left, he whispered: 'Be in the garden of the Tuileries tomorrow evening at 6 p.m., by the water. I will give you my answer.'

The next evening, at nightfall, he appeared in a dark frock coat, a broad-brimmed hat shading his face. The young woman waited, trembling with fear as he approached.

He beckoned. 'Sit next to me on this bench. Who sent you to me?'

'Ouvrard [a wealthy banker].'

'You know him? Yes – he likes pretty young girls.'

'I am not interested.'

'Nevertheless, he's rich.'

'I don't need money. My father told me that only you can save him. So I came to you.'

'What feelings do you impute to me?'

'I hope you are just.'

Fouquier took her hands in his. They sat in silence, then abruptly he said: 'I will do what I can for you. Be discreet. Remember, if you say anything you will lose them all. Wait a few days. Don't worry.'

He kissed her forehead and very softly said: 'Since you believe in God, pray to him occasionally for Antoine-Quentin Fouquier-Tinville.'

Two days later, on recommendation of the doctor in the Conciergerie, Salmon de Monty was, for reasons of health, transferred to the convalescent house of Dr Belhomme in the rue de Charonne. The dossiers of the 95 Nantais were put into the bottom of a drawer and forgotten, to be found again in late summer 1794, when Fouquier himself was in prison. His successor sent the accused to the regenerated revolutionary Tribunal, whence, after a three-day hearing, they were discharged for lack of proof.

There was a handful of escapes from the Conciergerie, prisoners were missed at roll-call, and Fouquier, by a nice irony, involuntarily colluded in one. He occasionally stepped into the prison as night fell. One evening he saw a turnkey padding noiselessly along a corridor and hailed him. The startled warder explained that he was just going off duty for a short break. Fouquier asked him if he knew who he was.

'Who doesn't know the eminent public prosecutor of our Tribunal?'

'Do you know where I live?'

The turnkey had once taken a note to the house in the place Dauphine behind the Palais de Justice. Fouquier asked him to go and give his wife a message not to wait for him as he had business to attend to and would be late for supper. The turnkey replied timidly that at this late hour perhaps they wouldn't let him leave the building. Fouquier conducted him to the main gate and told the guards: 'Let him through, official business.'

As Louis Larivière, the warder who recorded the incident, remarks, none of the gaolers recognised the turnkey but supposed he was a new man.

When Fouquier got home, his wife was agitated: she'd waited and waited, hadn't wanted to eat without him, kept the soup warm. The message I sent? No messenger had come.

The next morning Fouquier learnt that a young woman accused of complicity with émigrés had just disappeared, on the eve of her appearance before the Tribunal; the chief gaoler, Richard, said they had searched for her everywhere. Fouquier told them to 'search for that traitor of a warder and try to cheer up'.

The turnkey was not to be found but one of the gaolers reported the loss of his best uniform. The conclusion was clear. Fouquier, 'boiling with suppressed rage played Tartuffe [the sanctimonious hypocrite of Molière's eponymous play] and dismissed the affair: "After all, she wasn't so guilty and I would probably have acquitted her."'

Held responsible after the fall of Robespierre for all the serious irregularities in the performance of his office, Fouquier was arrested and held in a windowless prison without candles for over a year before he was examined and tried. He wrote to his wife: 'And so I wait to be sacrificed to the opinion of the public, stirred up against me and wholly exaggerated; I will not be judged . . . I will die for having served my country too zealously and with too much energy in conformity to the wishes of the government, my hands and heart pure. But, my dearly beloved, what will become of you, you and my poor children? You are going to be given over to the horrors of the worst affliction; this will at least be proof positive that I have served my country with the disinterest of a true republican; but what will become of you, all of you? These are the sinister thoughts which torment me day and night. I was, then, born for unhappiness; what a frightful idea. To die like a conspirator . . .' He bids her farewell and writes in a postscript: 'The sole pledge of my affection which I have still in my power is a lock of my hair which I beg you to keep.'

So many other prisoners had done a similar thing the moment they thought death was certain, and tried to pass on a small memento: a lock of hair to twist round a medallion, a portrait sketch to send to wife, children, mother, dearest friends; one man his collar stud and every article described as 'all I have left to leave you' – all that they retained when the gaolers had taken their perks. And with what care, what precaution they tried to smuggle out these precious, sad presents.

Tried and condemned to death, Fouquier wrote one last letter to his wife: 'I have nothing to reproach myself with; I always conformed to the law; I was never the creature of Robespierre nor of Saint-Just; on the contrary, I was on the point of being arrested four times. I die for my patrie without reproach, I am satisfied; my innocence will be recognised one day. A.Q. Fouquier.'

The signature is revealing: he rarely styled himself Fouquier-Tinville, which would be instantly recognisable, whereas Fouquier was fairly common.

On his way to the scaffold, the crowd greeted him with a hail of abuse. Riled, he shouted back: 'Starvelings, all of you – I'm going to the guillotine with a full belly – your bellies are empty.'

Fouquier's legacy cast a longer poignancy. The last letters written from the prison to loved ones, family, friends, final messages on the eve of extinction; pleas to wives to remind the children they once had a father who loved them, the pathetic gifts, the messages, the details of bequests were never delivered: everything emanating from condemned prisoners was deemed to be the property of the Republic and removed and retained on the order of Fouquier as possibly incriminatory, certainly as evidence.

# SIXTEEN

# The Supreme Being

French republicans, it is up to you to purify the earth which
has been contaminated and recall the banished Justice.
*Maximilien Robespierre*

HENRI ADMIRAT, born in a small village near the Puy de Dôme
in 1744, had done service at court and served in the 6th
Battalion of the national Guard of Paris, the Filles-Saint-Thomas,
which fired on the mob storming the Tuileries on 10 August 1792.
He and a close friend, sergeant Pierre Balthazar Roucel, escaped,
exhausted and dismayed. His counter-revolutionary work was not,
however, finished. His friend the Abbé d'Alençon, a constitutional
priest, convinced that any hope of restoring the monarchy depended
on English support, maintained close contacts with several English
secret agents in Paris, among them his mistress, Arabella Williams.

The Abbé, 32 years old, with a long face, freckled and bearing
smallpox scars, deep-blue eyes, reddish hair and beard, a gloomy
expression, was a rather ugly man. She, an indefatigable agent for
the English, had blonde hair, a round pretty face, small mouth,
comely bosom, shapely figure and frequently disguised herself as a
man, in blue jacket and trousers and a billycock hat, to all intents
a young cabin boy. As a woman she wore the red and white of Saint
George. They lived together at 666 rue Helvétius in the Le Peletier
section, near the Bibliothèque Nationale, as did many English
nationals.

In pursuance of the law of October 1793 against foreign nationals
residing in Paris, many of the English residents of the rue Helvétius

were arrested, Arabella Williams among them. Cast in prison, she arranged for a transfer to the du Plessis (formerly a college, rue de la Bourbe) to be with her close friend, the elderly widow Blondel.

By one of those miracles never explained, both Blondel and Williams contrived to be liberated.

D'Alençon was denounced on 30 November 1793 for lending 3,000 livres 'to an Englishwoman, in whom he was interested who had close contact with Pitt'. Clearly Arabella Williams. He produced evidence that he had resided in Paris since the beginning of the Revolution and was of open patriotism. Several neighbours in the section spoke in his favour, among them Admirat.

A law of 16 April 1794 compelled former nobles to quit Paris. D'Alençon pleaded poor health and acquired a false certificate of indisposition, signed by three members of the CPS, Barère, Carnot and Billaud-Varenne, which gave him leave to stay until 26 April. His father, meanwhile, had been condemned to death and at the mere instance of the name d'Alençon on the list, the CGS issued a warrant for the priest's arrest on 5 May. Higher forces intervened. The warrant was issued not in the city but outside in the Paris department. Thus d'Alençon could evade being taken at home by the police commissaire of his section, Thomé, a public exposure it would be hard to cover up; moreover, five days elapsed between the issue of the warrant and its execution. D'Alençon took refuge just south of Paris, in Arcueil, where, three days later, the police arrived, not to arrest him but to deliver into his safe keeping the widow Blondel, to whom Louis XVI's confidant Malesherbes had given the original copy of the will dictated to him by the King and a secret codicil. D'Alençon organised her passage across the Channel to England.

It is generally agreed that this d'Alençon was none other than the Baron de Batz. Although he later denied categorically that he ever put on disguise, Batz was almost certainly lying. Changing identity had become instinctive, a habit. A woman walked past him in the street, knew it to be him, but could not at first see what was different about him. He had looped a fine string under his nose and over his head to tilt his nose up at a sharper angle. And one day a man saw him, recognised him, cried out: 'There is Batz.' A man near Batz stopped, turned round, looked anxiously to see who had called out, the very image of startled guilt, and was arrested. Batz didn't flinch, kept walking, evaded, once more, his pursuers.

Malesherbes, arrested along with many former ministers of the King and known royalists whose sympathies were against the Republic, was guillotined, together with his daughter, a granddaughter and her husband, on 22 April. His daughter had been charged with conducting treasonable correspondence with the enemies, internal and external, of the Republic. Malesherbes had been denounced by a nark of a revolutionary committee: when his sister, the Comtesse de Senozan, wrote to tell him that the grapes in her vineyards had been destroyed by frost, he welcomed the news: no wine meant the peasants would have to stay sober and if they had stayed sober there would have been no revolution. This was read as conspiracy against the liberty of the French nation and Fouquier condemned him as an archetypal counter-revolutionary.

The 73-year-old Malesherbes, who had admired and corresponded with Rousseau, and whose wife had shot herself in the woods near their home, waited his turn at the foot of the scaffold as the other three members of his family were executed before him. So too a batch of the old nobility, including Madame Elisabeth, the Princesse de Lubomirski, the duchesse de Châtelet, the duchesse de Grammont and three former deputies of the old constituent Assembly, Huel, Thouret and d'Eprémesnil.

Furthering his efforts to plant the idea firmly in the public perception that Robespierre was aiming at dictatorship, Barère enlisted the services of a professional police informer, Marie-Suzanne du Plessis de Lamartinière from Poitou, who had for some time been acting as his contact with d'Alençon. She was part of a large circle of royalist sympathisers undermining the work of the police. She was unscrupulous, hard up – most of her former wealthy contacts had been rounded up and were in gaol.

Lamartinière was very willing to sell her professional discretion and skills at intrigue to the highest bidder. She was, indeed, entirely to Barère's pleasing and soon became a frequent visitor to his soirées at the Clichy house where he remunerated her services handsomely. At Barère's prompting, d'Alençon funded her and put her in touch with another counter-revolutionary who was short of money, Henri Admirat, with orders to persuade him to make an attempt on the life of Robespierre. Admirat was a hothead, a drunk, of violent and uncertain temper; the perfect stooge for such a job; he would be protected. Lamartinière, who claimed to have met Admirat independently at an auction on the Champs-Elysées, seduced him and he agreed to the assignment.

At a sumptuous dinner party attended by d'Alençon and Lamartinière, there was a sombre mood: another 15 members of the Filles-Saint-Thomas battalion had been arrested and called to the revolutionary tribunal. D'Alençon said that it was time for the royalists to act – better to strike and die in the process than to wait around for the inevitable nocturnal knock on the door.

Admirat lived at 4 rue Favart, near the Opéra Comique, established in 1757 by Charles Favart, in the same building as Collot d'Herbois; indeed, he pointedly bragged of it to Lamartinière. 'This is where my friend Collot lives, a good patriot. If there were 40 like him in the Convention things would be fine.' Such public manifestations of 'good patriotism' were run-of-the-mill among closet royalists. Collot later denied having any acquaintance with Admirat or Lamartinière and it is almost certain that he was privy to the plot. Tormented as he was by fears of what might be held against him for the terrible events in Lyon which he and Fouché had supervised, it was of pressing interest to him to see Robespierre removed from the political arena.

Some time before the assassination attempt, Admirat was dining in a favourite restaurant owned by one Dufils and during conversation announced, quite openly, that he had an assignation with a noblewoman, citizeness de Lamartinière, and that he was 'fucking her a lot better than a certain deputy living in the same building as him'. For a man whose income as an office messenger was no more than 600 livres per annum, Admirat was spending lavishly: nearly four livres a week on lunch alone, not counting wine; betting on billiards in company with one Roussel, an accomplice of the Baron de Batz.

On the morning of 22 May Admirat walked about a kilometre south to the Duplays' residence and asked a fruit seller at what time the deputy Robespierre tended to leave home. She directed him to the house, where he was refused admittance: the deputy was too busy to see anyone. Admirat waited a while, then repaired for lunch chez Roulot, near the terrace of the Feuillants and close by the Tuileries. He ate and drank copiously, after which he walked the short distance to the Manège, where the Convention session had opened. From there to the Tuileries and the long corridor outside the room where the CPS met. Under his frock coat he carried two pistols.

Robespierre did not appear. Late that afternoon Admirat went to Lamartinière's apartment on the rue Chabanais, five minutes' walk away. There, in a state of despondency, he said: 'If you're ready to die you have only to say the word – I'll kill you and I have another pistol for myself.'

She replied: 'Are you mad? I'm in no hurry to die yet.'

At 7 p.m. Admirat went to the Café Marie for a drink; he moved on to the Café Gervoise, where he met commissaire Thomé, who was being handsomely paid by the CGS and, in tune with their wishes, was entirely devoted to the anti-Robespierre cause. Admirat was by now quite drunk; Thomé warned him that he was being watched and that there were patriots ready to put a bullet in his brain. He also let slip that Lamartinière was Collot's wholly compliant mistress. Thomé left and Admirat went back to Dufils' restaurant to dine. He drank a bottle of wine, two glasses of Málaga and one of eau de vie. When he asked for a second bottle because he hadn't slept for a fortnight, despite taking opium, the waiter refused.

Admirat returned home, three sheets to the wind and in a jealous rage. Towards one o'clock in the morning he heard Collot's housekeeper descending the stairs to meet him. He followed her down from his room on the fifth floor and, seeing Collot, yelled: 'Swine. Breathe your last' and loosed off one pistol; the powder was bad stuff, it misfired; so too the second. Collot crying, 'Help, help, I'm being shot at and murdered', Admirat, in a panic, fled upstairs, grabbed an old hunting gun and ran on to a room at the top of the building. He said he put the muzzle of the gun in his mouth and tried to commit suicide but the trigger jammed. Down below, Nicolas Horgue, an architect and corporal in the section guard, and François Rion, a wigmaker and fusilier, heard the rumpus and ran down from the corner of the street and into the building, where they found Collot cowering at the foot of the stairs. They were joined by several neighbours, including a locksmith, Geffroy, who ordered Collot sternly, 'in the name of the people', to take cover. Led by Horgue, the rescuers pelted up the stairs, knocked on the door and told Admirat to give himself up.

'Come on, you low-lifes, come and get it.'

They burst into the room, the gun fired, Geffroy was hit in the shoulder and Admirat was wrestled to the ground and taken to the guard post in the rue de Ménar [now Ménars]; the captain, Nailly, said to the would-be assassin as he arrived: 'You're a bold bastard. I suppose you're proud of yourself.'

Admirat looked at him coldly. 'Well, captain, the little window for me,' he said, meaning the lunette of the guillotine.

Interrogated until 1.30 a.m., he said that, having waited in vain for Robespierre outside the CPS for four hours, he decided to go for another tyrant and reiterated that he deeply regretted his failure: it would, said Admirat, have been 'a beautiful day for him and he would have been loved and admired throughout France. It was only bad luck that he had bought a brace of pistols for 90 livres and they had let him down.'

Other citizens of the quarter were in no doubt that the pistols had been primed with bad powder on purpose. 'The pistols were bought more than six months ago and they will have been sold to him by trusties of people in on the plot.'

To other prisoners as he was taken into the Conciergerie, Admirat said: 'If I told you why I did what I did, you'd never believe me.'

Fouquier wrote to the Convention that morning that it was his intention 'to judge this criminal this very afternoon at two o'clock' but the CGS had other ideas. It was Amar's idea to link Admirat's attempted assassination, in which they had colluded, with another – that by one Cécile Renault which, it transpires, had arrived by sheer coincidence.

The following night the police hammered on Lamartinière's door and took her, protesting bitterly, to the Conciergerie, where she was manacled and put in a secret cell.

A neighbour of Admirat, Elisabeth Mouttonet, remarked: 'What are we supposed to think about this attempted murder of Robespierre and Collot? It was a put-up job by the CPS pure and simple to enhance its own importance and reputation.'

Saint-Just claimed that 'for over a month we have known about the man guilty of this action, l'Amiral [*sic*] – he is a madman of violent temper and he was a tool being kept ready for a given moment'. He had been ready to assassinate Saint-Just at the instigation of his enemies, alluding to Barère and his associates, Collot among them. The attempt on Collot, he said, was a sham; Collot had undoubtedly been forewarned and all precautions had been taken to ensure failure. What, then, was to come of this tragedy? If its purpose was, as there was reason to believe, to install Robespierre and his friends in the Tuileries with a Praetorian Guard, to set him apart, safe from the 'daggers of assassins sent by Pitt-Cobourg', he, Saint-Just, would prove his own adherence to the principles of democracy and equality by coming out at once at the head of those who opposed tyranny.

Barère, addressing the Convention, said: 'The people are alert, the Convention deliberates, and the revolutionary government acts.' He then quoted from letters purporting to come from Pitt: 'We greatly fear Robespierre's influence. The more concentrated the French republican government is, the stronger it will be and the more difficult to overthrow.'

He reported on Geffroy's wound – it was serious but not fatal and 'thus,' he ended, 'it was upon Robespierre that the blow was intended to fall. The counter-revolutionary assassin tried to get into his house; he looked for him here in the Convention.'

Uproar.

The Convention decreed:

1. The revolutionary tribunal to pursue Admirat's accomplices.
2. A letter of commendation to be sent to Geffroy.
3. A daily bulletin on the progress of his recovery to be read at the tribune.
4. A pension of 1,500 livres to be awarded to him and his family.
5. The text of the decree to be sent, along with the medical bulletin, to all the armies, departments, districts, communes and popular societies throughout France.

One of Barère's cronies, Legendre, proposed that citizen Robespierre should be given a bodyguard. The motion was rejected and that evening in the Jacobins Couthon pooh-poohed the idea roundly. Only despots had and needed bodyguards, whereas 'it is Virtue, it is the confidence of the people and Providence which watch over our lives; we have, too, friends who are there to come to our aid'. Robespierre endorsed his friend's view. Bodyguards tend to isolate individuals, those that rely on them lose esteem and bring on themselves 'all that hatred can devise'. He then confessed to be astonished that a man 'who appears only rarely in the society of Jacobins' obstinately persisted in forever presenting 'insidious motions'.

Although Robespierre and Couthon rejected the proposal to assign them official bodyguards, Robespierre himself never went anywhere inside the city limits on his own; moreover, walks in the fields apart, he rarely went anywhere other than home, the Jacobins and the Tuileries, all within a 200-metre radius. Nevertheless, he and Couthon were hard at work shaping the law which defines the Great Terror. To that extent, both men are indirectly responsible for the ghastly bloodletting of the six weeks leading up to their own execution. Direct responsibility lies on their enemies inside the government and the CGS, for both men were absent from public business for the whole period.

From prison, Lamartinière wrote a letter to Barère, of which Fouquier took charge. She had no money for food, her last cash having been spent on a filthy straw mattress 'on which to lay my revolutionary frame'. She swore that she had not been seduced by Admirat and that she would never strike or harm a republican soul, a Brutus. In conclusion she said: 'I depend fully on justice, on truth and on your fairness. Greetings and fraternity. Your fellow citizen.' The tone was unmistakable: the threat of blackmail but thinly veiled. But she was too late: anyone who might corroborate her story was being rounded up by an army of snoops and spies, eavesdroppers and informers which Thomé had mobilised in the locality of the Palais Royal. Sixty-eight suspects were brought in and 18 sent without formality of charges, to the nearby Hôtel de Talaru, a former mansion at 62 rue de Richelieu now being used as a prison.

The cover-up engineered by Barère, Collot, Vadier and the CGS and Fouquier was being executed ruthlessly.

In the late afternoon the day after Admirat's arrest, Charlotte Boucher, daughter of a pastrycook in the Ile Saint-Louis, entered the stationery shop run by Antoine Renault to buy a couple of pens and overheard his daughter, Cécile, a young woman of 20, talking to a dressmaker of the same quarter, Barbe Cruel. Cruel had called to collect a piece of muslin and an Italian blue taffeta dress which needed alteration and Cécile said that she would bring the linen shift to complete the ensemble and the ribbons to garnish it the next day. As Cruel left, Cécile light-heartedly urged her to have the dress ready on time 'because these days you never know what might happen – I might be going to the guillotine'. This kind of bitter gallows humour had become something of a cliché, an indiscreet cliché nevertheless.

The following afternoon, some time between 5 and 6 p.m., Cécile folded the linen shift and ribbons in a small packet, walked along the rue des Deux-Ponts, which crosses the Ile Saint-Louis, and stopped at a shop run by citizeness Julle, where she bought a small mirror, and then on to number 25, citizeness Cruel's dressmaker's. Cruel was not there, so Cécile left the packet with Payen, the proprietor of a café next door, with instructions to deliver it when the dressmaker came back.

Cécile was a rather giddy naïve creature; as vain as any young woman of her age, she lived for dresses and ribbons and furbelows and trinketry. Her father, a widower, allowed her only small sums in pocket money, and both he and her brother tended to keep a close eye on her; she very rarely strayed from the quarter and had no interest in politics; of the by now famous, infamous, deputies of the CGS and the CPS, she could not name one.

That afternoon the talk among the throngs crowding the street of the busy neighbourhood was all of Lamiral [*sic*], Robespierre and the tyrant and the CPS's people in the streets. Everywhere for the past week, anonymous posters called on the people of Paris to be on their guard against the tyrants who filled the Committee, in particular its president, Robespierre. These meant nothing to Cécile – she was illiterate – but, hearing his name mentioned so frequently, she asked one of the firemen lounging outside the station guardroom who this Robespierre was, what did he do, did he behave like a tyrant? The man informed her that he was president of the CPS, to which she replied, offhand: 'Then he's a king' and then asked where he lived.

It was enough to rouse suspicion. The section police were called, Cécile was arrested and taken direct to the CGS's headquarters in the Hôtel de Brienne, in the rue Saint-Dominique. The time was about 6.30 p.m. Other officers collected the packet she had left with Payen.

At the CGS the political police grilled her mercilessly. Simon-Edmé Mounel saw her in a room there, bewildered, a lost expression on her face as if she simply did not understand what was going on. Led into the main room, she looked resigned, there was no sign of heightened emotion in her face. Amar conducted the interrogation and when he asked her age and the names she answered to, she replied in a trembling voice: she clearly understood nothing of any of this. Amar then asked:

'What was your intention in going to Robespierre's house?'

'I didn't, I didn't see him.'

'We know that, but what was in your mind?'

'I thought a deputy was always accessible and ought to be . . . I wanted to see him. Isn't he the one who presides over one of the Committees and directs the Convention which governs us?'

'France has neither a king nor a dictator. What you say is counter-revolutionary.'

'I wanted to assure myself . . . I'm a republican. In some people's eyes he's a tyrant. I wanted to see him.'

Elie-Lacoste of the CGS, present at the questioning, remarked that nothing about her, up to this point, suggested any guilt or culpable intentions and Bayle added that 'nothing suggested even the idea of crime'.

Did they rely on suggesting that she had been traumatised by the constant flow of tumbrels emerging from the big gates of the Conciergerie not far from where she lived? Or that she was one of those women who cried out 'Long live the King' as the victims passed with no other motive than to be free of the debilitating horror of living at such times? There was, after all, a sort of crowd contagion like vertigo on the brink of a cliff or a precipice, a maddened impulse to go to the guillotine like all the rest.

Meanwhile, a CGS agent, Châtelet, was ordered to produce a false testimony that Renault had been found in the courtyard of Robespierre's lodging house, 398 rue Saint-Honoré, in an unfamiliar district at least half an hour's walk away from where she lived, asking to see the deputy urgently, at 9 p.m., that is, around dusk. This deposition was countersigned by two other citizens. If Admirat's assassination attempt had been well planned, the delivery of Renault was a happy chance.

No one could possibly mistake the resonance with the arrival of another young virgin, Charlotte Corday, asking for the people's friend, become the people's martyr, Marat.

A woman called Lamotte was called in to search Cécile. In her basket were found, among the bits and pieces, two small knives, as for sharpening quill pens or snipping thread. These were seized and labelled '[attempted] murder weapons' – hardly the chosen weapons of a determined assassin. (Julius Caesar had been struck down at the base of a statue to Pompey the Great with metal styli. Clay tablets and pens aroused no suspicion.)

Asked why she was carrying a light shift around with her, Cécile is said to have replied that 'expecting to be taken to prison and then to the guillotine I made sure to have some clean linen with me' but added 'when you've done nothing wrong you have nothing to be afraid of'. According to the official record, she also declared that 'under the old regime when you asked for an audience with the King they let you in straight away'. And, when pressed to say whether she would rather live under a king, she replied: 'I would pour out all my blood to have one. You are nothing but tyrants. That is my opinion.'

Bidden sign the text of this farrago of lies, she refused even to mark it with a cross.

On the evening of 23 May the CGS signed her arrest form stipulating that the transcript of her interrogation, the material evidence and the (false) declaration made by Châtelet and Cécile herself, should be handed over to Fouquier. He now took it upon himself to plump this non-event into a full-scale conspiracy. He issued orders for the arrest and secret confinement of Cécile's father, brother and elderly aunt. Police were also sent to the Ile Saint-Louis to root out new proofs of Cécile's guilt. It was just the sort of lazy, shabby fabrication that Fouquier was best at.

Citizeness Cruel, brought in at 5 p.m. on 25 May to give evidence, repeated, in a state of terror, what Cécile had said about going to the guillotine. This amounted to further clear proof that the 'crime' was premeditated.

That evening in the Jacobins, Collot, playing the role of the hero who by a miracle had survived a dastardly attempt on his life, like the old ham actor he had been, addressed the assembled patriots, the true guardians of pure revolution: 'From the depths of this emotion at the same time gentle and powerful which penetrates my soul, I bring to mind that truism: the fact that anyone who has courted dangers on behalf of the patrie finds himself infused with a new strength by the brotherly concern which all republican hearts bear for him; it is a new seal of unity which seems to renew itself between all those strong souls and which for ever consolidates the puissance of the principles of liberty and virtue. Already these principles divert my attention from the particular circumstances of an event: they direct all my meditations towards the common good.'

Not a dry eye in the house.

On 6 June Fouché, a man to whom manoeuvre and intrigue were

second nature, was elected president of the Jacobins and thus carried his opposition to Robespierre, who had denounced him in the club a month before, right into the duelling ground.

On 8 June, also Whit Sunday, the seventh Sunday after Easter, festival of the Pentecost, when the Holy Ghost descended, the Festival of the Supreme Being proposed by Robespierre in his address to the Convention on religion a month before was celebrated throughout France. There was little instruction on what form the festival should take: some communities lugged out the cardboard mountains (now, for the men of the Mountain, the chosen symbolic feature of all such celebrations) and triumphal arches already used for republican junkets; others took the opportunity to have Mass said for the first time in ages.

In Paris, the architect of state ceremonial and civic art, Jacque-Louis David, of the CGS, organised another jamboree on the Champ de Mars, now renamed the Champ de Réunion. He designed and had fabricated a huge mountain, dotted with rocks and trees, from painted plaster, cardboard and canvas on a wooden framework, topped with a spreading tree of Liberty and, beside it, atop a 15-metre column, a colossal statue of Hercules holding a diminutive figure of Liberty in his left hand. A long procession marched to the site from the Tuileries, headed by the members of the Convention led by their president, who happened, at the time, to be Robespierre. The route passed by way of the place de la Révolution but there was no unsightly instrument of death on its stained scaffold to be seen: the guillotine, on Robespierre's orders, had been removed (and, this festal day, draped with rich velvet hangings) to the empty patch of ground where the Bastille had stood. There it accounted for three days' worth of victims before the vociferous denizens of the Faubourg Saint-Antoine kicked up such an outcry against the reek of blood that it was newly positioned on the outskirts of the city by the barrier of the Throne, now renamed the Overturned Throne, Trône Renversé.

There was glorious sunshine, a crowd of thousands, banks of roses, countless young girls dressed in white carrying baskets of fruit and flowers, boys bearing oak wands, choral groups to sing republican hymns, the 'Marseillaise', a newly composed hymn of the Supreme Being, 2,400 choristers all told.

Robespierre, in a silk coat of robin's-egg blue, jonquil-yellow breeches, tricolour sash and plumed hat, made a speech heralding the dawn of a new age of liberty and virtue in the French Republic and, in a grand theatrical gesture, took a blazing torch and set fire to a papier-mâché image representing Atheism, Egoism and Insincerity, from inside which shakily arose a slightly scorched figure of Wisdom, with the words: 'This monster that the spirit of kings spewed forth on France has gone back to nothingness.'

That afternoon the procession made its way to the Champ de Réunion; a cart laden with symbols of triumph, a printing press, a plough, drawn by a team of oxen with gilded horns; a cart of blind children singing a hymn to Divinity; a troop of mothers carrying bunches of roses; fathers and sons armed with swords (mimicking the Horatii brothers of David's painting, those early heroes who, according to tradition, went out from Rome to engage in mortal combat with three opposing champions).

The deputies of the Convention, carrying sheaves of corn, walked up to the summit of the mountain, martial music played, the choirs rose to a great crescendo, and then silence, and in the silence Robespierre descended the mountain to a crowd of some 300,000 people, who swamped him with a well-managed storm of applause: 'Long live the Republic . . . long live Robespierre.'

Thuriot, a friend of Danton, muttered: 'Look at him – it's not enough for the bugger to be king, he has to be God as well.'

Having proposed the establishment of a religion without a priesthood, how else could Robespierre appear but as a priest in this sacerdotal role as guardian and of the laws (fulfilling exactly the King's role as font of justice) descending from the mountain? And, in a state whose head had been chopped off by the sacred blade of *law*, how else could he seem, this fatherless orphan, but as a claimant to the sole arbiter of *virtue*, as surrogate father of the orphaned patrie? For wasn't that at the core of his psyche, the abstraction from the everyday, the muddle and mess of normalcy, the chaotic state of multifarious humanity, this early bereavement? Charlotte, his sister, says of that loss: 'We lost both our parents when we were young. It is impossible to describe what an impression their death had on Maximilien. He changed completely. Until then, like any boy his age, he had been carefree, naughty, playful. But when he became head of the family, being the eldest, he grew staid, serious-minded, ponderous. He would speak to us gravely; if he joined in our games it was to tell us what to do.

'He had an aviary in which he kept sparrows and pigeons. My sister and I were keen to have one of these birds for ourselves; for a long time he refused to give us one. One day, though, he gave way and let us have a handsome pigeon. My sister and I were enchanted. He made us promise solemnly to let it want for nothing and we swore a thousand times on oath to look after it carefully. One night, during a storm, the pigeon died – we had left it out in the garden. When we told Maximilien, he wept and reproached us bitterly, and he swore he'd never give us another of his beloved birds.'

And, in the construction of his ideal world, everything in place and in order as he disposed it, to eliminate the frightening contradictions and disorder of reality, came the belief that it was indeed possible to force unanimity and consensus by cutting out dissent with surgical precision. Beware the man who believes in Paradise.

In the Saint-Lazare prison the police administrator Bergo, who spent most of his time drunk, was in a crapulous rage. Accustomed to a copious lunch at the start of his day's work, Bergo, this day of the Festival of the Supreme Being, selected a celebratory vintage and found it so delicious he indulged himself even more liberally than usual, slumped into a stupor and didn't wake up until it was evening. He unleashed a furious tirade on the doxy with whom he had lunched and post-prandialled for not waking him so he could get togged up and swagger off to the fête.

The Convent of Canonesses stood on the rue Picpus in a tranquil, sweet-smelling quarter in east Paris known as Bel-Air because of the number of gardens and trees in the vicinity and the salubrious air, so very different from much of the rest of the city, rank and unventilated. Closed in 1790 after the anticlerical legislation, it had been made the property of the nation in the spring of 1792 and rented out that autumn to a citizen Riédain. At the beginning of spring 1794 Riédain sublet it to a citizen Coignard, who turned it into a sanatorium and house of detention – a sort of halfway house between liberty and prison. Prisoners with money bribed officials attached to the revolutionary tribunal to be transferred to such so-called convalescent homes, of which there were a number in Paris. It was well known that a certain Delainville, state counsel for the defence, took substantial sums for these transfers, exploiting his position to persuade the police administration to release, for example, a lottery administrator and a banker into a sanatorium. In such evident rude health were they that the gaoler initially refused to let them go. The next day, however, new orders came through. The men went their way.

Delainville charged a sick elderly Englishman 1,400 livres for such a transfer. So long as they could pay the reprieve of ready money, the wealthy detainees were safe; when the money ran out they were pronounced cured and released. Into the Conciergerie. There were some 12 such nursing homes doing good business in the districts of Saint-Antoine, Saint-Jacques and Montmartre; the most celebrated, that run by Dr Belhomme in the rue de Charonne, a few streets north of Picpus. When he was denounced, Belhomme became one of Coignard's first 'patients', together with the marquis de Sade.

On the night of 13 June one of Riédain's servants hammered on his master's door and reported disgraceful goings-on in the orchard at the bottom of his garden: a mob of men, about 30 of them, with spades and trenching tools, had broken in, demolished part of the wall, cut down plants, torn up vines and pear trees and marked out two huge plots. They were even now digging the place up under a great ring of flaring torches. Riédain rushed down in a fury, confronted one of the men, who seemed to be in charge of the gang, protested that this was his property and produced his lease duly signed by the authorities. The man, Rique, replied flatly: 'This land is requisitioned by order of the Republic and the municipal architect Poyet.' Riédain argued. Rique snapped: 'If you don't want to be the first one in the hole, I advise you to get lost.'

The first ditch was some nine metres long, five wide and seven deep; the second, 11 metres long, seven wide, eight and a half deep. There were orders for a third, larger still. When filled, the three would be able to hold a total of 9,000 corpses.

An anonymous pamphleteer sent a *New Means of Supplying the Nation with Food Proposed to the CPS, Messidor 1794*: 'To those patriots slaughtering their fellow countrymen, I suggest they eat the flesh of their victims and, considering the state of famine to which they have reduced the nation, they should feed those people they allow to live on flesh from the same source. Why not even set up a national

Butchery – designed by the great artist and patriot David – and pass a law obliging all citizens to buy meat from it at least once a week on pain of being imprisoned, deported or having their throat cut on suspicion of conspiracy. I demand also that at every patriotic festival one course should be served of this meat; this would be the true communion of patriots, the Jacobin Eucharist.'

# SEVENTEEN

# The Red Mass

When I was fifteen, I went into battle for my king. I am now nearly 80 and go to the scaffold for my God. I am not unlucky.

*Maréchal de Mouchy*, executed 27 June 1794

BARÈRE AND VADIER made full propaganda use of the Admirat and Renault cases, linking them as unarguable evidence of a widespread conspiracy targeting Robespierre.

On 10 June 1794, two days after the Festival of the Supreme Being, the Convention heard details of a new law on which Robespierre and Couthon had been working for some time. Its measures were radical, shocking, revolutionary: it created a perverse new privilege by enshrining exemption from the ordinary force of law, a privilege quite as divisive and illiberal as those of the old regime.

Several deputies leapt to stall it.

Ruamps: 'This decree is a serious matter; I demand that it be printed and an adjournment on the debate. If it is adopted without adjournment, I will blow my brains out.'

Lecointre: 'I support the motion for an indefinite adjournment.'

Several voices: 'No. No.'

Barère: 'When a law entirely to the benefit of patriots is proposed, a law which assures the prompt punishment of the conspirators [*the* conspirators – there could be no doubt about their existence] our legislators must speak with one voice. I demand that the adjournment should last no longer than three days.'

Lecointre: 'We ask an adjournment of only two days.'

Robespierre advanced to the Tribunal, unfolded his papers and began to speak: 'There is no position so delicate, no situation so perplexing in which one would wish to put the defenders of liberty which might force them to dissemble the truth. So, I would say that although the liberty to ask for an adjournment is incontestable, although it may be overlaid with perhaps specious motives, it could not, however, compromise the safety of the patrie less.'

Two opinions ran concurrently: one for the severe punishment of those who obstinately sought to revive old plots and to instigate new conspiracies; the other, the cowardly criminal view of the aristocracy that the conspirators should be offered an amnesty.

'For the past two months you have been asking the CPS for a law more sweeping than the one it presents to you today. For the past two months the national Convention has been under the swords of the assassins; and the moment when liberty seemed to achieve a ringing triumph was the moment when the enemies of the patrie were conspiring with greater boldness. For over two months, the revolutionary tribunal has been denouncing to you the obstacles which arrest the march of national justice.'

There was, he knew, no one present who had voted with enthusiasm for other laws proposed to the Convention who would hesitate over this law. Why did he make these reflections?

'Is it to impede the adjournment? No. I have wanted solely to pay homage to the truth, to alert the Convention to the risks it is running. For, be sure, citizens, everywhere there appears a sign of demarcation, everywhere division announces itself, there is something which concerns the safety of the patrie. It is not natural that there should be schism between men equally smitten with love of the public good.'

Applause.

'It is not natural for a sort of coalition to arise against the government which devotes itself to the safety of the patrie. Citizens, they want to divide you [cries of 'No, no we will not be divided' from all sides]. Citizens, they want to frighten you. It is as well to remember that it is we who have defended part of this assembly from the daggers which wickedness and sham zeal sharpened against you. We expose ourselves to assassins of our persons in order to pursue assassins of the people. We are quite ready to die so long as the Convention and the patrie may go safe.'

Vigorous applause.

'We will face perfidious insinuations made by those who would wish to tax with undue severity measures prescribed by the public interest. This severity is deadly only to the conspirators, only to the enemies of liberty.'

Applause.

There was no adjournment: the debate on the 'law of blood', the law 'instituted for the punishment of enemies of the people', would go on till they were done, even till nine o'clock at night.

They all knew what Robespierre had required of them: agree or be suspect. 'For us or against us' had become 'for me or against me'. Every human activity and thought had now to pass into the public domain, including the interrogation of the accused and the deposition of witnesses. Robespierre now spoke not for himself but for the sovereign will of the people. The nation must be cleansed once and for all of its impurity. 'Victory,' he told them, 'is within our grasp; there remain only a few serpents to crush . . . If we weed out the cheats and intriguers from our midst, they will be unable to divide us. Thus will the divine charm and virtue of friendship unite us.'

The Convention said nothing; Ruamps did not reach for his pistol; he remained, like the rest, locked tight in silence. They voted the decree and renewed the powers of the CPS for a further month.

The CGS had not been consulted on this law of 22 Prairial which inaugurated the official French Bulletin of Laws, the legal codex still in use, and sent the last victims of the Great Terror to the guillotine, the People's Axe, the Scythe of Equality – 1,306 in six weeks, from an overall total (for Paris alone) of 2,300. At the time of its passage, there were 7,321 suspects imprisoned in Paris, and many others held in provincial gaols. The law detailed a comprehensive list of enemies of the people – brigands, royalists, spies, traitors, propagandists, corrupt officials, speculators, embezzlers and so on, concluding with a vague catch-all: 'Finally, all those identified in preceding laws relating to the punishment of conspirators and counter-revolutionaries and those who, by whatever means they may choose, shall harm the liberty, the unity and the security of the Republic or else strive to impede its consolidation.'

The law suppressed all other courts and established the revolutionary tribunal in Paris as the supreme court before which all enemies of the people should be tried. Of the 50 jurors elected to serve on it, over half were adherents of Robespierre, chosen by him although approved by the trio of Barère, Collot d'Herbois and Billaud-Varenne, whose opposition to Robespierre was hardening but who took care not to show it. His friend Coffinhal was appointed president. Fouquier, his enemy, remained in post as public prosecutor. The procedures of the Tribunal were radically pared down: all prisoners brought for trial were deprived of the right to defending counsel on the grounds that the pure, the innocent, could have nothing to fear and that the guilty delivered themselves. In such circumstances 'the right to speak', to make a plea of innocence, was irrelevant. The indictment which brought prisoners into the dock was sufficient evidence of guilt.

Further, the Prairial law overrode all existing legislation and whereas before it the courts had been empowered to impose penalties of deportation, confinement in irons, detention pending more evidence, from now on one penalty served all crime deemed to be against the state: death. There was, said Robespierre, no article in the Prairial law which was not founded on justice and reason.

Robespierre's twin intention was to streamline the process of law which the six popular commissions set up in March had so signally failed to do and by exerting a tighter control of the revolutionary tribunal to diminish the power and influence of two of his principal enemies: Vadier, leader of the CGS, which provided the bulk of the arrest warrants feeding the prisons, and Fouquier, the public prosecutor, both of whom, in Robespierre's view, were dragging their feet in the vital work of establishing the rule of Virtue. To this purpose, the uncompromising law of Prairial and the reconstituted revolutionary tribunal were directed. No doubt by this time Robespierre's manically narrow focus, his obstinate, inflexible summary of moral distinction, the bigotry of his method, were seriously warped by fatigue. Certainly the Manichaean character of his assessment of what was wrong with society and the means of correcting it had set him dangerously apart. His incorruptibility further alienated him within a governing circle of venal men more and more inclined to corruption. That corruption was about to plumb new depths of cynical manoeuvre.

In the CPS that evening, Billaud-Varenne rebuked Couthon and Robespierre for failing to consult the rest of the Committee about the decree. When a member of the Committee could present a decree on his own responsibility without reference to his colleagues, liberty had become the will of an individual. To which Robespierre might have responded that he saw very well that he *was* alone, without support, surrounded by enemies – yes, even Billaud-Varenne himself, because he supported Robespierre's opponents against him. It was classic paranoia and persecution complex. Success, he insisted, was within their grasp; it needed only the extirpation of the last remaining vipers who threatened liberty.

The following day a nervous group of deputies, headed by Bourdon de l'Oise, demanded a guarantee of the immunity of all members of the house: Danton had been arrested without any decree from the Convention. The article denying them such immunity was, in Robespierre's absence, voted out. Late that afternoon the jurist Merlin de Douai framed the objection: 'the exclusive right of the national representatives of decreeing any accusation against its members and of submitting them to judgement is inalienable'.

That evening at the Jacobins, Fouché, in the chair as president, received a deputation from the popular society of Nevers who had come to Paris to vindicate his work of eradicating religion in the district. Robespierre approached the rostrum and accused Fouché of being an accomplice of the 'monster' Chaumette, the atheist who, with Hébert, had been the arch proponent of the dechristianising faction. Fouché, he said, was, like the rest of them, a dissembler, a closet counter-revolutionary, a hypocrite: 'There are others who seem to be afire to defend the CPS but who are sharpening their daggers. The enemies of liberty are just as bold, they have changed not one jot; they absolutely do not want to be seen apart from patriots; they praise them and they flatter them; they are even capable of vague imprecations against tyrants and they conspire for their cause.'

Fouché was the first of his opponents that Robespierre identified so publicly; he had effectively thrown down the gauntlet, the game was afoot. Fouché had been fingered but he had no intention of being cornered. He lay low and began to organise in secret.

Robespierre, Couthon and the rest of the CPS returned to the Convention to deal with the impertinent puppies who had tampered with the bill. Couthon accused Bourdon of insulting the members of the Committee by annulling the article of immunity. If they were innocent, what had they to fear? Bourdon defended his actions – he was as much a patriot as they were. Charles Delacroix, deputy for the

Marne, asked, referring to a phrase in Article VI of the decree, what was meant by 'depraving of morals'. Robespierre, hot with indignation, dressed him down: 'Citizens,' he said, 'is this the time to be asking what we mean by depraving morals when the wounds inflicted on the public morality by the Chabots, the Héberts, the Dantons, the Lacroix, still bleed?'

Pressed, he refused to elaborate: the Convention, the Mountain, the Committee (no reference to Committees) were one and the same. Pressed further, he said: 'There could be but two parties in the Convention, the good and the wicked, the patriots and the counter-revolutionary hypocrites.' And, with heavy, self-pitying sarcasm, he added: 'Who would have been the first victim of calumny and proscription, without the happy chance of the Revolution? I dare to say to you that it was I. No, I am wrong: not I; it was the phantom impostor they put in my place, in a faction of our wayward colleagues, in France, in the Universe.' He defended the Mountain, which occupied 'the heights of patriotism', the better to denounce the 'intriguers' (a clear reference to Bourdon) for seeking to inveigle some of its members into becoming leaders of another faction.

Bourdon expostulated: 'I demand proof of this; I have been accused of being a scoundrel . . .'

'I demand,' rejoined Robespierre, 'in the name of the patrie that my right to speak be safeguarded. I have not named Bourdon: misfortune to him who names himself.' Did he consciously allude here to the ancient formula of commination against the enemies of princes, *Honi soit qui mal y pense,* 'Evil be to him who evil thinks'? Despite Bourdon's protests he added: 'Yes, the Mountain is pure, it is sublime, and the intriguers are not of the Mountain.'

A voice called out: 'Name them.'

'I will name them when it becomes necessary.' He then urged all in the Convention to lay upon *him* the care of braving all dangers and, with homiletic ardour, appealed to the sublime notion of unity, in the name of the CPS: 'If the truths which I have just advanced have been heard, we will continue our labours with courage. Consider how sometimes we have need of encouragement, that there are those who have done all they could to make our life in office difficult. It is enough to have had to struggle against conspiring kings and against all the monsters of the Earth, without finding enemies right alongside us. Come, then, to our aid; do not allow us to be separated from you, for we are a part of you and we are nothing without you. Give us the strength to carry this burden, so immense as to be almost beyond human power, which you have imposed upon us. Be always just and united in spite of our common enemies.'

Couthon concluded the session with a report on the working of the revolutionary Tribunal: 'Our every idea, in the diverse departments of government, has been to reform': all measures framed to combat treachery, despotism or a bizarre mix of imposture and truth. He bruited the swiftness with which justice would, from now on, be administered. 'Any delay in punishing the enemies of the patrie must be no more than the time it takes to recognise who they are. It is less a case of punishing them than of annihilating them ... Indulgence towards them is an atrocity, clemency is parricide.' The definition of treason, originally applied only to infringement of the majesty of the King's person, had been at a stroke extended to an assault on the sovereign people, and the crime likened force of the killing of a member of one's own family.

At dawn on the day the Convention passed the Prairial law, the artillery of the French army encircling the Belgian town of Fleurus opened fire on the allied Austro-Prussian forces of the coalition. The ensuing battle lasted 16 hours. The French General Jourdan became the first army commander to use aerial reconnaissance – from a hot-air balloon, and news of the last great victory of what may be called the sansculotte army was brought to Paris on 29 June by Saint-Just. The day before Fleurus, he had been on hand with the forces besieging the town of Charleroi, garrisoned by a mere 3,000 troops. An officer approached from the beleaguered town with a written agreement to terms signed by the garrison commander.

Saint-Just repulsed him: 'I don't want paper, I want the town.'

The officer argued that, by surrendering at discretion, the garrison must necessarily put itself at the mercy of the republican army, and so dishonour itself.

Saint-Just replied frostily: 'We can neither honour nor dishonour *you*, just as *you* have not the power to honour or dishonour the French nation. There is nothing in common between you and us.'

The officer returned and the garrison commander surrendered at once, shortly before the Austrian commander-in-chief, Coburg, arrived with his main force to relieve them.

Not long before this, Saint-Just had received a letter from the other members of the CPS dated 25 May:

> Dear Colleague
>
> Liberty is exposed to new dangers; the factions are waking up in more alarming guise than ever. Mobs clamour for butter in greater numbers and more turbulent than ever, when they have the least pretext; an insurrection due to break out in the prisons yesterday, and the intrigues which manifested themselves in the time of Hébert, have combined with several attempts at murder on members of the CPS; the rest of the factions, or rather the factions which never die out, redouble their audacity and their treachery. The greatest of the perils which menace liberty is in Paris. The Committee needs to reunite the perspicacity and the energy of all its members. Calculate whether the army of the North, which, by your puissant contributions, you have set on the road to victory, can do without your presence for a few days. We will replace you, until you should return there, with a patriot representative.
>
> [Signed] Robespierre, Prieur, Carnot, Billaud-Varenne, Collot.

The representative with the army in Belgium, catching the mood, wrote to the CPS: 'I shall be careful to exercise the right of seizure established within the borders of the Republic. I shall also take notes on persons in these countries who have distinguished themselves by their hatred of the French Revolution and I shall not fail to have them arrested and arraigned before our revolutionary courts.' Terror spread in the wake of the armies.

Shortly after Saint-Just's return to the green table, tensions snapped. He and Robespierre quarrelled violently with Billaud and Collot. They branded Robespierre dictator to his face.

Robespierre stormed out of the room and, for a month, absented himself from the CPS and the Convention, as did Couthon. He kept to his rooms, occasionally sallying out to the Jacobin club, where he delivered speeches riven through with self-righteousness and morbid self-pity. Lines from one of his verses: 'The sole torment of the just man at his last hour and the sole torment which will rack me, is to see, with dying eyes, the pale and sombre envy distilling on my brow the opprobrium, the infamy of dying for the people and of being abhorred.'

He must have thought himself invulnerable; the grip of his supporters on the revolutionary tribunal seemed secure; the Commune was packed with his placemen but he had gravely miscalculated. This monumental and very public fit of sulking bracketed him, in very public perception, with those uncivic loafers who agitated vociferously while refusing to shoulder the patriotic burden of office. Saint-Just called to see him occasionally at night, but, like Achilles in his tent, the absent champion of the true revolution was, to his cost, less involved in the last convulsions of the Great Terror than some of his enemies. On 10 July, at the apogee of the slaughter, his confidant and personal guard Payan told him in a letter that the factions 'are profiting from our mildness and generosity . . . But the time of indulgence will pass.' Sycophancy masked the truth. The terrible days of the 'batches' may have been managed by Robespierre's enemies, but his absence would never be read as *indulgence* for it was his directive which compiled the batches.

Two anonymous threatening letters accused him of aiming at dictatorship and of killing liberty. One author, letting drop that he was a deputy in the Convention, menaced, as had been Danton, said: 'You think yourself a great man and you believe you have already triumphed, but will you know how to foresee, will you know how to avoid the stroke of my hand or those of 22 others, as determined as I am and as were Brutus and Scaevola? Yes, we are determined to take your life and to deliver France from the snake who seeks to tear her apart . . .' (Brutus, the assassin of Julius Caesar. Gaius Mucius Scaevola, 'Left-handed', who, having failed to kill the Etruscan tyrant Lars Porsenna, and hailed before him for punishment, demonstrated his indifference to physical pain by holding his right hand in the fire. Republican heroes both.) The author also says: 'I loved you once . . . I still love you, despite myself, but fear a jealous love, a furious love . . .'

The second would-be assassin warned: 'Every day I am with you, I see you every day; at every hour my raised arm points at your breast . . . oh, most wicked of men, live a few days more so as to think upon me; sleep so as to dream of me; may memory of me and your fright be the first instruments of your torture.

'Adieu . . . even this day, observing you, I shall rejoice in your terror.'

\* \* \*

On 15 June, wishing, as he put it, to forget the guillotine for a day – the people's axe had severed 32 heads the day before – the public executioner Sanson had delegated his duties to an assistant, Martin, and was taking his two young nieces for a walk in the fields beyond the Clichy barrier to the north-west of the city.

The meadows were enamelled with poppies and cornflowers; along the hedges trailed eglantine. The little girls ran ahead, picking stems for a nosegay. Sanson records how he saw, coming towards them, a large dog followed by its owner, a man wearing a pale blue coat, who greeted the children and started to help them make their posies, picking the blossoms they could not reach and handing them down to each of them in turn. They stood on tiptoe to kiss him and 'the three of them came over to me, the girls chattering gaily, the man smiling. I had already recognised him: it was Robespierre.'

One of the girls offered the kind citizen her bouquet; he took it, fastened it with great care in his buttonhole and asked her what her name was. 'The poor child told him first her baptismal name and then, quite unnecessarily, her family name. I have never seen a human face change so utterly so abruptly. He recoiled as if he'd trodden on a snake; his brow creased with deep furrows, his eyes blinking, he stared fixedly at me; his pallid complexion blushed earth-red. In a parched voice, with a haughtiness I hardly expected to encounter in the apostle of equality, he said: "You are . . ." using the formal *vous* of the old regime rather than the familiar republican *tu*. I bowed, he remained stock still; he was evidently struggling with a repugnance he could not master. As for me, I could not make up my mind whether to laugh or cry at the horror this man who ordered the killing felt for the axe which did the killing for him.'

Robespierre and Couthon having absented themselves from public life, as much as anything to disentangle themselves from the snares of the Barère trio drawing tighter in on them, the CGS began work on the massive show trial whose main purpose was to discredit Robespierre and isolate him and his supporters publicly. Triggered by the arrest of Admirat and Renault, the trial, of foreign conspirators and the 'assassins of the fathers of the people', spread a wide net and used false documents and decoy papers leading to entrapment, all supplied by Vadier and Fouquier.

Elie-Lacoste, of the CGS, concocted a long report on the under-hand intrigues and scheming of royalists, lumping in scores of names under that of the chief culprit, their ringleader, the shadowy Baron de Batz. This report he read to the Convention – neither Robespierre nor Couthon attended – and urged that all persons named should be judged without delay, for they were 'charged with being accomplices of Baron de Batz or of the foreign conspiracy and had desired, by murder, by famine, by the distribution of false assignats, the depraving of morale and public spirit, by uprisings in prisons, to cause civil war to break out, to dissolve the national representation, and to re-establish the monarchy or some other tyrannical domination'.

While Batz remained at large and elusive, his 'accomplices' could be taken. Madame d'Eprémesnil was denounced by the prison spy in the pay of the CGS, Ferrières-Sauveboeuf. She had given Batz asylum in her Château de Marefosse, outside Le Havre, and, perhaps, secretly her daughter Désirée's hand in marriage. Marie Grandmaison, an actress at the Théâtre des Italiens, now the Opéra Comique, had been Batz's mistress and there were murmurings that she had also been the mistress of Charles-Marie-Antoine de Sartine, a 34-year-old former *maître des requêtes*, [lawyers who processed pleas for justice and redress from the King] husband of the 18-year-old Emilie de Sainte-Amaranthe, and loved him still. Both, together with Emilie's mother, Madame de Sainte-Amaranthe, and her brother Louis, 17, were arrested on the orders of Saint-Just and had been held in prison since 31 March.

Madame de Sainte-Amaranthe, a widow, held a lavish riotous gambling salon in her house on the rue Vivienne, a rich quarter in the centre of Paris. She was host to supporters of Philippe, duc d'Orléans, cousin of the King but a staunch republican, who was executed on 6 November 1793, and to men of the Gironde and others of the more moderate right. Emilie, married to Sartine, a son of one of Madame de Pompadour's ministers, attracted the attention of several leading Jacobins; it was whispered that she been Saint-Just's mistress. Her mother did not hide her royalist leanings; she defiantly kept portraits of the King and the Queen in her salon. This was risky, but she was a woman of immense charm and her daughter's liaisons with prominent patriots would, surely, keep her safe until the storm blew over. Augustin Robespierre, younger brother of Maximilien, was a frequent visitor and through his protection they remained in prison, without judgement, until June. Did Emilie repulse Maximilien's advances? Had he, one evening of careless talk with her, seeking to impress her, let slip secrets, the seductions of power? Did Saint-Just, flushed with jealousy, denounce her?

Grandmaison's maid, Nicole Bouchard, was condemned for having taken her mistress a meal. She lived in a garret under the eaves and though she was 18 she could have passed for 14. The CGS informer who came to arrest her went back to the Committee and told them they couldn't guillotine a child. They, by some impenetrable logic which linked the young servant of a friend of a wanted suspect with the arrest of a putative assassin, replied that one could not treat lightly an attack on the person of Robespierre.

The day after Nicole's arrest the main gate of the Sainte-Pélagie prison in the rue du Puits-de-l'Ermite, west of the Jardin des Plantes, burst open and two carts rumbled into the cobbled courtyard as the prisoners were coming down to the refectory for the evening meal. A great din erupted – guard dogs barking, the clank of weaponry, gendarmes clattering over the pavement, shouting to the prisoners to go back immediately to their cells. Fifty prisoners, already seated at the dining table, were hustled out by the prison warders and pushed up the stairs. There was near panic: was this to be another prison massacre?

Quickly the word went round: 'They've come to look for the secret prisoners.'

Gazing down from the windows of the cells, they could see ten men being led to the first cart: they were pale, haggard, emaciated, bearded – their razors had been confiscated. For the past month they had been kept confined in another part of the prison and never seen by the other detainees. Six more followed into the second cart, then four women, some carrying a bundle of clothes. Charles-Marie-Antoine de Sartine was led out from the open cells to join them.

The nearby convent of the English Benedictines, the Anglaises, had been requisitioned as a prison under the law of suspects, 3 October 1793, and the entire community of nuns confined for holding religious services in secret. In the Anglaises, with her mother and brother, was Sartine's wife. All four had been named in Elie-Lacoste's list.

The carts rumbled in at 11 p.m., the noise of them each time they came, said one of the prisoners, like a stab of the dagger. The gendarmes came for the Sainte-Amaranthes. According to one of the other prisoners, Foignet, Madame de Sainte-Amaranthe said to them: 'What's this, you pity me? I think I am happier than you. If they are only putting the guilty to death, I have nothing to fear. If, on the contrary, everyone has to be sacrificed, indiscriminately, I am less unhappy to be one of the first because I will have fewer regrets about those who went ahead of me.' Women like Madame Jeanne de Sainte-Amaranthe showed a courage and tenderness quite beyond the expectation of many who reviled the aristocrats for their heartless insensitivity.

Emilie and her brother, realising that they were to be taken as well, embraced her and said: 'Ah, mother, we're so pleased, we are going to die with you.'

Foignet and their other friends in affliction kissed them goodbye 'despite the impatience of the barbarous turnkey Bignon' and they were driven directly to the Conciergerie, where they joined a large number of others, a job lot drawn in from various prisons and detention houses, clustered in the corridor outside the records office, waiting to be registered. Among them was a man called Jardin, protesting that the authorities had got the wrong man, he was a simple postilion, not Etienne Jardin, former groom to the King, and it wasn't the job of justice to make errors. The wrong Jardin was released. And Jean-Baptiste Michonis, lemonade seller, former police administrator, feverishly revising and polishing a deposition of defence he planned to read before the Tribunal. It was futile: his complicity in the escape attempt of the Queen from the Conciergerie had nailed him. Burlandeux, who had hoped to deliver Batz to the CGS. Ozanne, already condemned to ten years in irons for allowing Julien to escape. A citizeness Lemoine-Crécy, overheard and denounced by her valet when she reacted to the news that Robespierre had been murdered: 'My God, so much the better.' The elderly marquis de Sombreuil, former governor of the Invalides, whose daughter had saved his life during the September Massacres was resigned: 'My daughter,' he said, 'has written to Fouquier . . . there's no saving a man twice.' Citizen Lescuyer, a violinist by profession, had managed to keep hold of his instrument; he stood to one side, clutching it, the reminder of his life as it had been. Citizeness d'Eprémesnil, still in widow's weeds, mourning for her husband, guillotined two months earlier, sat contemplating miniature portraits of her three young children.

Collot d'Herbois and Billaud-Varenne of the CPS had sent a request by letter to Fouquier to interrogate Devaux, Batz's secretary, whom a juror, Châtelet, had recognised among the detainees in the Conciergerie. He was ordered to offer a pardon to Devaux conditional on his telling them where Batz was hidden. Devaux, 29 years old, happily married, supporting a father who was blind and without money, parried all Fouquier's questions. Finally, it was put to him: 'Tell the truth, tell us where Batz is hidden and you are free.'

'I am innocent,' he said, 'and I do not know where Batz is.'

At midnight Fouquier left the Palais de Justice for the CGS. Corporal Falempin, drafted in from the Bondy section to the far north of the city, stood guard by the Pont Neuf, at the westerly tip of the Ile de la Cité. Not recognising Fouquier, he challenged him and demanded his security pass. Fouquier was dumbfounded and stared back in outrage, at which Falempin shouted in his face, thumped him in the chest and jostled him into the guardroom, to the consternation of the regular watch, to whom the sinister public prosecutor was all too well known. Falempin was arrested, interrogated and escorted to the Luxembourg prison.

The CGS was in full session, grilling one of their more prolific informers, the former Comte de Ferrières-Sauveboeuf: they needed more 'conspirators', he wasn't working hard enough, he needed to chivvy his spies and deliver more charges, more information. Above all they wanted him to produce a report of a conspiracy in La Force. 'I've tried everything I can,' he said, 'and Aniel, the gendarme who was keeping a watch on me, can bear witness to how I persisted, but there aren't any plots in La Force.' This seemed to satisfy them; he was reinstated.

When Fouquier entered the chamber, the members of the Committee greeted him. He told them: 'I'm sending 39 to the barrier of the Overturned Throne today and tomorrow there will be 60.' They cheered: 'Bravo.'

At eight o'clock that morning Fouquier returned to his office in the Palais de Justice and opened his mail, which included letters from Sombreuil's daughter, Jardin and the former Comte de Fleury, plus a small packet of papers – a certificate of civic rectitude and civic attestations to the character of the banker Théodore Jauge. His plea for release ended: 'Citizen public prosecutor, here is the moment when a virtuous man of irreproachable honesty must make himself known . . .' Fouquier spat: 'Enough.'

The letter from Sombreuil's daughter elicited: 'She won't stop till Sanson shuts her up.'

As well as the letter to Fouquier, Jardin had sent a letter and a petition to the president of the Convention which Fouquier intercepted: 'If we listened to them, there'd be nobody guilty left.'

Citizen Gastrez was a neighbour of René Dumas, the president of the Tribunal – they lived in the same apartment building – and asked him if he might come to the trial of Renault. A short wait in Dumas' office, and Renault herself passed through on her way to the office of the clerk of the court. Dumas was handed a letter, folded like a billet-doux, from the former marquis de Fleury, confined in the Luxembourg. Dumas read it under his breath and then aloud: Fleury wrote in the tones of a man eager to die as soon as possible; he heaped on Dumas insults which only a desperate man would shy at his executioner: that he and his judges were butchers; that day after day they made judgements dictated by hatred; they had killed all his friends and he wanted to share their lot. When Fouquier came in Dumas handed him the 'love letter'. 'I do believe,' he said, 'this happy chap is in a hurry.' Fouquier, reading it through, replied: 'He is, isn't he? I'll send someone to fetch him.'

The last letter Fleury himself received in prison ended: 'Be bold, men of blood, in dreaming up new conspiracies to send to the scaffold the remainder of honest men who have nothing with which to reproach themselves.'

The hearing opened at 10 a.m. The first to be led in were Fleury and four police administrators, former associates of Hébert: Froidure, Soulès, Dangé and Marino, who assumed that they had been called as witnesses. Froidure smirked and obsequiously asked the Tribunal bench how they could be of assistance. In reply, Fouquier read out the charges against them and the Tribunal moved immediately to the prosecution; each of the accused, standing on the tiered steps of the dock, heard his or her indictment, one after the other. When they had all been read out, Dumas said: 'You have each heard the charges against you. I now call upon you to answer yes or no on the principal fact.

'You, Admirat, did you make an attempt on the life of the representatives of the people Robespierre and Collot d'Herbois?'

'Yes, and my one regret is that I did not finish off that criminal Collot.'

The rest replied: 'No.'

Fouquier turned to Dumas: 'Citizen, you have heard the responses of the accused; it is for you to take due consideration as to motive. I invite you to base your opinion solely on the fact that this is the gravest case ever to have been brought before the justice of the Tribunal. In consequence, I put my faith in your patriotism and your customary wisdom.'

Dumas: 'Citizen jurors, the accused standing before you are foreign agents. The national Convention has sent them to the Tribunal so that you may decide their fate. Their denials will not sway you. I believe it is otiose to remind you that the people demand vengeance on the monsters who sought to deprive them of two representatives whom they cherish. You will fulfil expectation in pronouncing on the questions that I am going to put to you.'

The jury retired, Dumas ordered the gendarmes to bring the accused up to the bench. There was uproar in the dock, prisoners weeping, crying out for justice and justification, appealing to the spectators. Dumas called for order; the gendarmes complied. Half an hour later the jury filed back, answered 'yes' to every question Dumas put, such as, Is their guilt proved? Does their guilt merit death?

As Dumas coldly read out the sentence of death, there was a renewed outburst – certain prisoners, knowing nothing of the provisions of the Prairial law, demanded to be allowed to speak in their own defence. Dumas droned on. Others protested that this trial was a sham, absurd, unjust, but the crowd, the old lags of the Tribunal gallery, howled them down with 'Death to the traitors . . . death to the assassins . . . Long live the Republic.' Amid the hullabaloo, Cécile Renault pressed against her aunt, yet 'the imminence of death had not marked her face at all. Her expression as she looked round the courtroom was serene.'

According to the court secretary-copyist, Breton, there was not enough scarlet material to make shifts 'to cover the poor wretches from neck to ankle. We hurriedly procured remnants of serge – purple and other shades of red – from nearby shops. This motley selection of colours produced the most hideous effect, to the enormous pleasure of the multitude.'

The last time the murderer's red tunic had been seen was that worn by Charlotte Corday as she made the journey to the scaffold *alone*.

Most of the prisoners were petits bourgeois – four domestic servants, merchants, priests, a notary, five ex-nobles, a cavalry gendarme, a banker, a wood merchant, a janitor, two young men described as living on inherited money, a schoolteacher, a musician, a painter of porcelain, a grocer, the elderly marquis de Sombreuil's 26-year-old son, Stanislas, accompanying his father. They were all conducted to the basement of the Conciergerie, where Sanson, his brother Martin and two assistants, Larivière and Desmorets, carried out the toilette.

When the young maid Nicole Bouchard was brought to the outer room of the prison office in the Conciergerie, Larivière, as he tied her hands, turned to Desmorets, and said: 'This must be a joke. Is it?'

'Oh no. For real.'

The crowd gathered on the far side of the courtyard railings to watch the prisoners as they climbed into the eight tumbrels was dense. The women mounted first and, when Nicole Bouchard stepped into the cart, there was a loud murmuring among the women spectators: 'No children. No children.'

(The youngest victim of the scaffold in Paris was Armand Bourrée de Corberon, former noble, 16.)

Madame de Sainte-Amaranthe, so far proud and resolute, suddenly faltered. Her daughter, Emilie, tried desperately to raise her spirits: 'Look, mother, aren't these red dresses pretty? We look like cardinals.'

The scene in the courtyard as the prisoners were led out was familiar: friends, relatives, gathered to touch them at the railings, to kiss them, weeping, trying to master the nauseating emotion, clutching at their clothes, or in taut silence, the grief too general to burst forth. The gaolers, the gendarmes, the executioner and his assistants were inured and, perhaps some trickle of humanity encroaching, ill disposed to comment or take note of these unpatriotic displays of sympathy for convicted enemies of the people. They did their duty briskly, the leave-taking was limited to the time it took to load the tumbrels.

One day, however, Fouquier, watching from his office window, suddenly screamed and pointed: 'There, him, that man in the black, take him.' Jean-Baptiste Louvatière was shaking the hand of the young de Nicolay, being taken to the scaffold two days after his father. Louvatière was incarcerated and three days later executed.

And this day, from his window overlooking the courtyard where the victims boarded the tumbrels, Fouquier slavered at the sight of the women, their cleavage exposed by the flimsy shifts, the palpitations of their breasts as they walked with firm tread across paving, mounted the cart and sat calmly without a sign of anguish. He said to his secretaries, this man whose routine revolved round mealtimes: 'Look at those jades, the effrontery of them. I've got to go and see them mount the scaffold, see if they can keep their nerve there, even if it means missing my dinner . . .'

At 4 p.m., under a blazing sun, nine carts started out on the journey to the scaffold, some prisoners weeping inconsolably, others prostrate, numb with fear, all emotion bludgeoned, others haranguing the crowd, paying back jeers with cries of defiance. The crowd was shocked not only by the repellent sudden brutality of this lurid blaze of red but also by the number of women in the carts. The mournful cavalcade took three hours from the Conciergerie to the guillotine's new site in the place du Trône Renversé (today the place de la Nation). Over the Pont au Change, lined with moneylenders' booths, right along the rue de Rivoli into that sector of the city from which the mobs had so often poured to turn up the violent heat of revolution: rue Saint-Antoine, Bastille, rue du Faubourg Saint-Antoine. Outriders armed with cavalry sabres were posted guard along the line of the cortège. Notes passed daily from Fouquier to Hanriot, commander of the national Guard, requesting detachments to accompany the dead marches, reinforcements for the big batches, forces 'sufficient for the day's executions'.

People along the way watched the long line of tumbrels, this dreadful cropping, pass in appalled silence, though Voulland, a member of the CGS, with that pithy wit affected by true patriots ('rich bastard, lost his head over a woman'), remarked to the friends standing with him: 'Let's go ahead of them and see this Red Mass celebrated on the high altar.' The blasphemy – an obvious prearranged catchphrase for this macabre spectacular – was not new. Hébert, married to a former nun, had apostrophised the Holy Guillotine and was wont to quote Christ in justification of its remedial work: 'If thy hand or foot offend thee, cut them off.' The offence he meant was the scourge of anti-patriotism, of counter-revolution.

Ahead of the cavalcade, CGS spies laced their own voices with those of the dense crowds lining the route: 'Here's the Red Mass . . . Death to Robespierre's murderers.'

Gazing down from their windows in certain streets, women shouted as some had shouted in the courtyard of the prison: 'No children. No children.'

There were other murmurs of dissent, but murmurs only; never too sure who was listening, but the horror of such a carnage to come bore in on many and they whispered: 'So many victims for one man? And he wasn't even harmed.' And where was he? Taking a solitary walk with his dog Brount in the tranquil Marbeuf gardens by the Champs-Elysées or strolling in the Montmorency Forest, way to the north, beyond the fetid confines of the city; Montmorency, favourite haunt of his sainted idol, Rousseau.

When the cortège arrived at the scaffold, the line of tumbrels halted, the outriders formed up inside the hollow square of infantry guards marshalling the crowd. Each tumbrel disgorged its passengers and they sat on benches to wait their turn. One by one they were brought to the foot of the steps, their hands tied behind them.

In front of the machine, part of the framework, was a pivoting plank. To this, in the upright position, the victim was tied; the plank, swung to the horizontal, made the first of three clunks as it hit its base, leaving the victim's neck in the circular aperture called the peephole, the window giving on to the last look at the world. The upper section of the peephole dropped. Clunk. The third clunk followed the hiss of the blade in its grooves down on to the neck. The head dropped into a bran basket from which the executioner might extricate it and hold it up. This he did not do every time but rather reserved it as a morbid privilege, of rank, or abhorrent foulness of crime.

The body was manhandled into the waiting straw-lined cart by the executioner's assistants even as the next victim mounted the steps.

The prisoners dismounted from the carts to sit facing outwards on benches grouped round the scaffold to wait their turn; a slight glance over their shoulder and they might see the hideous work going on behind them. The first died but once; the last as many times as those who had gone before, albeit the executioners were efficient, working quickly. They say that Sartines turned to his wife and, smiling, spoke a line concluding an opera: 'Even death is a favour because the tomb reunites us.'

The young Nicole was the ninth to go; a strapping young man who had watched head after head fall impassively, seeing this child pushed against the plank, and hearing her whisper to the executioner: 'Monsieur, am I doing it right?' fainted clean away. Sanson himself went white and one of his assistants, Marin, said: 'You're sick. Go home. I'll do it.'

Sanson made no reply, descended the scaffold and, without a backward glance, hurried off.

When Emilie de Sainte-Amaranthe mounted the platform, the executioner tugged the red shirt away from her shoulders and so imposing, so radiant was her beauty as she stood there that the guillotine claque, paid to applaud and rev up the crowd, fell silent. But, as with every one, she was manhandled unceremoniously on to the plank and swung into position under the machine, already drenched in blood, and the blade fell.

Admirat died last; the whole business had taken 28 minutes.

And perhaps there were those in the crowd watching the Red Mass who wondered how many more sacrificial lambs the godlike Incorruptible required on that altar of the guillotine to punish the supposed intent to murder him with a penknife. He who had once said: 'It is better to spare 100 guilty men than to sacrifice one innocent' was sending the small people in droves to the slaughter. The entire Renault family for the imagined guilt of the daughter. Not even the old regime had been so vindictive, terrible as its punishments were.

Batz was in the crowd and wrote of the frightful, the deathly silence broken by the shock of the blade falling. 'The blood spouted out over those in the front row; soon the scaffold was awash, the ground inundated, running over their feet . . . each mounted to repeat the dreadful spectacle . . . and then the baskets, the corpses piled up . . . the disgusting, the impious intimacy of ages, sexes, of crime and innocence . . . this sacrilegious mingling of impure blood and . . . ah, my task is done, I have said everything, this is how they perished . . . those whom I have not the strength to name.'

Sanson wrote: '29 Prairial. Terrible day. The guillotine devoured 54. My strength went, my heart failed me. That evening, sitting down to dinner, I told my wife that I could see spots of blood on my napkin. Someone has shown me a caricature going round town in which I'm depicted guillotining myself in the middle of an open plain, the surface lost to view, covered over with headless trunks and disembodied heads. It needs only my head to choke the guillotine and the caricature will be true. I don't lay claim to any sensibility I don't possess: I have seen too often and too close up the sufferings and death of my fellow human beings to be easily affected. If what I feel is not pity it must be caused by an attack of nerves; perhaps it is the hand of God punishing my cowardly pliancy to what so little resembles that justice which I was born to serve.'

A news-seller arrived at the garden of the Luxembourg prison with a batch of papers and cried out in stentorian tones: 'Here's the running order of all the ceremonies observed today at the Barrière Renversée [the gate near the place du Trône Renversé]. Here's the list of winners of the lottery of the most holy guillotine. Who wants to see the list? There were 60 today, give or take.'

Following the ghastly exhibition of this day, the women of Paris took a peculiar revenge; a new fashion was born, the Nemesis, in memory of Emilie de Sainte-Amaranthe: a red scarf thrown coquettishly across the bare shoulders . . . to the fury of the Jacobins.

As Hesdin says: 'Every fresh female execution, I notice, if it is not that of a former noble, rouses more and more secret hate against Robespierre. The peculiar horror of cutting off the head of a young and beautiful widow, Lucile Desmoulins, than whom a gentler, simpler creature never breathed, whose only crime was to speak to her husband in prison, can be due only to him.'

# EIGHTEEN

# The Tigers are Quarrelling

Pallid Death kicks in the door of the pauper's hovel and
the royal palace alike.

Quintus Horatius Flaccius, *Carmina*, I iv 13

D URING THE SUMMERS of 1789 and 1790 the people of Paris
'literally lived in the open air'. Street orators, street singers,
idlers gossiping, players putting on alfresco comic and satiric shows,
and sellers of lemonade, fruit, newspapers, political pamphlets,
speeches, squibs, thronged the city thoroughfares but now, in the
baking heat, the suffocating days of late July 1794, 'it is the silence
of the grave'. So wrote Hesdin, moved to tears, galled by 'the contrast
to my youthful recollections of Paris . . . Nothing but the eternal
white dust of the streets seems the same.' And, daily through that
dust, the processions to the eastern periphery of a city stunned by
an incapacity of grief.

The trooping of this booty of Terror evoked largely horror and
the unpitying, remorseless spectacle of Robespierre's bloodstained
reign of virtue more and more repugnant. It was vile. It was cannibalism. Yet even to be solicitous to the victims was dangerous.

Some apprentice printers watched the condemned go by.

'My God,' said one, 'when will we have had enough blood?'

'When we've run out of anyone guilty.'

'A man's death doesn't cost much.'

'If they guillotined you for thinking,' said another, 'how many
would they have to kill?'

'Don't talk so loud, someone might hear us and . . . *nicked.*'

For the victims in the cart, the pall of suspicion, the dread of arrest was far away. As the Maréchal de Mouchy had said before going to the scaffold: 'We were living in fear; now we live in hope.' One man cried out from the tumbrel in rebuke of the crowd: 'Cowards, imbeciles, they want the Republic and they have no bread. But I tell you, *I* tell you, before six weeks are out you'll have a king and you will have us to thank.'

There were even those in the crowd who muttered that the victims were fortunate, being 'no longer obliged to spend all their times waiting outside the butcher's and other merchants selling vital commodities'.

In England, *The Star* carried an account of a masked ball recently held in London. A woman disguised as Charlotte Corday stepped out of a catafalque brandishing a bloody dagger and for the rest of the evening pursued a man representing Robespierre, threatening to 'make a Marat' of him in due course.

Robespierre played heavily on the London connection. 'In London, he told the Convention, 'they denounce me to the French army as a dictator; the same calumnies are repeated in Paris – you would tremble if I were to tell you in what place. In London they say that calumny has succeeded in France and that patriots are split. In London they produce caricatures, they paint me as an assassin of honest men.'

The carts heaped with corpses were driven under escort of horse gendarmes armed with sabres the short distance – avenue de Saint-Mandé, rue Picpus – through the new breach in the curtain wall, now filled with heavy wooden gates, into the Picpus garden and there tipped on to the ground, where employees of the municipality performed the final indignity and stripped the dead of their clothes. Clerks keeping an inventory in large registers installed themselves in a small grotto built by the canonesses as a place of prayer. There were no jewels, no coins, not even a pair of spectacles to loot: all precious objects were taken during the last toilette in the Conciergerie. The top clothes taken from the corpses – dresses, overcoats, breeches – were bundled up and sent to the administration of hospitals, to be cleaned and reused. The rest – stockings, shoes, neckerchiefs, underclothes – were legitimate perks of the graveyard workers.

The work generally went on all night, the hot, stifling nights of a torrid summer; bottles of wine went the rounds. A burst of rain snuffed out the torches. Relit, they illumined the ghoulish scene once more; the trampled ground dark with blood, littered with headless cadavers, at one side a separate tumble of leather sacks containing the severed heads in bran. The stripping done, the litter of corpses was tipped into the first of the three trenches, bodies stacked first, heads filling the gaps between, and then the last of the batch was in place, the fresh layer covered with a thin scattering of soil from the heaps left over from the excavation.

Whether they knew of the existence of the Picpus ditches or not, the crowd seems to have confined its voyeurism to the executions, not the sordor of the mass burials, to the moribund not the dead. However, the 25-year-old daughter of André Paris, *did* follow the blood-streaked carts to the graveyard. Her father had, for 30 years, served as groom to the duc de Brissac, Madame du Barry's last lover. He and his son, François, were denounced and arrested on the same day. For two years they were held in prison, and for two years Mademoiselle Paris tried in vain to see them but never did see them again, except in the tumbrel.

On 10 July, the temperature 26 degrees and a light breeze blowing, she walked behind the cart ferrying her father all the way from the Conciergerie to the scaffold and then to the Picpus garden. Five days later she did the same for her brother. When any gesture of grief, any facial expression of dismay or repugnance was tantamount to complicity with the condemned, this was reckless behaviour. But she said with the indefeasible plain talk of the innocent, of the devoted: 'I saw my father and my brother guillotined and if I was not killed on the spot, it is because God came to my aid.'

She had nearly passed out with the shock of seeing her father put to death and came to only when the carts had left for Picpus. She hurried after them and recognised him only by the clothes, as the stripping crew did their work, and then watched as his naked corpse was lobbed into the pit.

One of the men who died on 6 July had been languishing in prison since the previous autumn, on charges of suspected royalism, counter-revolutionary activities and supporting priests in defiance of the anti-clerical laws. On 17 October Guillaume-Joseph Baudus, commissioner of prisons in Cahors and lieutenant to the King's regional governor, in civil and criminal law, wrote from prison, the eccentricity of the spelling of his original by no means uncommon:

Praised be Jesus Christ            Greetings to our good angel.
I want, my dearest wife to take and share with you this morning, some moments of mutual consolation in this our separation. May he alone be just who has reunited us in the sacrament which has sanctified our lawful alliance, let him separate us when it pleases him, for it is no accident that he grants so long an existence on earth to those, such as us, whom he has united by the ties of a marriage which, by his favour, has seen the passage of 40 years. It is, therefore, a trial that he imposes on us; let us take advantage of it to dispose ourselves better for our reunion for ever throughout the long duration of eternity. Let us be consoled, you and I, my dearest wife; men can separate us bodily, but they cannot divide our hearts which will always be united . . .
   I do earnestly hope that your health is as sound as mine, thanks be to God . . . I am going to list some things which I need here:
   a little soap for shaving
   my third wig
   a pair of sheets
   a pair of dancing shoes.
   My daughter will bring me enough assignats tomorrow together with the livre I asked her for a basket of grapes.
   I have tisane for today.
   I also need some tobacco: you could check all the bottles where I kept it: if there's none left, you will have to buy two pounds . . .
   I wish you all manner of comfort and I kiss you, so too my daughter with all the tenderness of your good husband and father.
   Yesterday evening, eight more detainees arrived here.
   To citizeness Baudus, née Malartic, in Caors [*sic*].

At the foot of the page, in another hand: 'Suspicious letter.'

The surveillance committee of Cahors denounced Baudus to the public prosecutor of the department of the Lot on 30 May 1794: 'Before the Revolution, Baudus was a Tartuffe and, since the Revolution, he has done much to impede its progress by fanaticising the people. This is the opinion of the sansculottes.' On 13 June the prosecutor asked the commandant of the national gendarmerie to take Baudus to Paris under heavy escort. He and three others left Cahors on 15 June, arrived in the capital a month later and Baudus was condemned – 'this monster in human form, fanatic and immoral, who has seduced so many people since the Revolution' – by Fouquier.

In the airless heat of a torrid summer the stench of the daily flux of blood congealing on the wooden scaffold and the pavement beneath most eloquently spoke for the revulsion at this daily mass slaughter which was hardening, even among extreme radicals. A cartoon shows Robespierre on the scaffold: behind him, crowding into the distance, a copse of guillotines marked with letters; a pyramidal obelisk topped with a spike on which is impaled, upside down, a red cap of liberty, stuffed in it, a burning scroll, smoke streaming away, as of incense from a ritual vessel. On the obelisk an inscription: 'Here lies all France.' Robespierre wears the tricolour sash, black hat with tricolour plumes, of a representative of the people; his right foot planted on the Constitution of 1793, left foot on the Constitution of 1791. Below the victim strapped to the plank stands the open basket, the feet of a corpse poking up over the rim. In his right hand Robespierre holds the cord which will release the blade. The caption reads: 'Robespierre guillotining the executioner, having guillotined the entire population of France.'

Hideous things had been done elsewhere in France but it was in Paris that the villainies of the Great Terror were enacted. Whatever repressive measures the CPS had required of the representatives they sent on mission to the cities and regions most deeply infected with the cancer of counter-revolution, or, at the very least, sanctioned by their silence, it was in Paris that the full shock of the perversion of justice was felt. The Prairial law embodied Robespierre's paranoid vision of virtue and terror; his own persecution mania seeing hydra-headed conspiracy everywhere. He had never left Paris; having, one by one, eliminated his political enemies, he dominated the CPS, the Convention, the Jacobins.

The people of Paris, the mob, were his theoretical heroes, the saints of his political canon, the paragons of true patriotism and revolutionary purity. They had stormed the Bastille, they had brought down the monarchy, at every turn they had demanded, through the cannons' muzzles, zeal of the cowardly, the inert, the malleable, the nation's legislators, zeal and more zeal. And it was Paris that was worst infected with intrigue: if none but he, Robespierre, could see that, then it was his melancholy, his terrible duty, to instruct. His megalomania prowled the margins of Paris, as Satan prowls the margins of Hell, and Paris, when it rose up again, would rise up against him. That it did so by doing nothing is as eloquent a measure as any of the intestinal horror he had spread.

As early as April one Frossard had observed: 'Robespierre cannot govern or live like this for long.'

The obscurity of most of the wretched victims in the tumbrels made even the innocent tremble for their own safety. Innocent? In these days of summary arrest, trial and execution, for the citizens of the one and indivisible French Republic there was no such thing as innocence. Police spies and informers in the pay of the CGS, as well as Robespierre's own agents, were everywhere, mingling with crowds, listening to street orators or singers, ears open for muttered comments, studying facial expressions of dissent or gloom, eavesdropping on conversations in cafés and bars. At the compulsory Fraternal Banquets held every ten days in the section assemblies, wine loosened tongues, indiscretions followed. Neighbour denounced neighbour. Careless words cost heavy. A young carpenter's apprentice, Jabin, playing cards in a café, cursed a bad hand he had been dealt. One of the other players rebuked him sanctimoniously: 'Good patriots do not use bad language.' Jabin flared up: 'Fuck good patriots.'

Arrested, tried, executed.

A simple-minded woman called Germaine Quetier was heard to say she could do with a spinning wheel – *rouet*; a malicious witness misheard and reported her to the police for complaining that France needed a king – *roi*. She went to the guillotine. A deaf and dumb couple were denounced for fostering anti-patriotic sentiments. When it was tentatively pointed out that, given their disabilities, such a charge had flimsy grounds, the informer justified himself by replying that they *looked* anti-patriotic.

Julie Hermanson, 24, a laundress, was arrested but defied the arresting officers pugnaciously; she refused to walk or ride in a carriage. Told to move herself she said: 'Fuck you all. Long live the King.' Taxed at the revolutionary Tribunal with the danger she had put herself in, she responded that she was not afraid of the guillotine and, as proof that she was not drunk but in full command of her senses, she said: 'Only honest people get guillotined.'

Colonel Lavergne, the 50-year-old commander of the garrison at Longwy who had surrendered to the Prussians, was tried for cowardice and treason. When the charges were read out, a young woman in the court rushed up to the judges' bench crying out: 'We need a king, yes a *king*. You judges are nothing but butchers. They're killing the whole world. I want to go to the guillotine with my husband.'

Arrested and interrogated, she proved to be Lavergne's wife, 26 years old. Her husband was already in the cart, knowing nothing of what had happened to her. When suddenly she climbed in alongside him, he fainted and slumped in the straw at her feet. The jolting of the tumbrel as it started out over the cobbles loosened the ties of her bodice and exposed her breast. Her hands bound behind her back, she asked one of the executioners to take one of the pins fastening her neckerchief and secure the bodice for modesty's sake.

When Lavergne regained consciousness she comforted him: 'Don't be alarmed. It's your beloved. You know I could not live without you. We are going to die together.' Lavergne broke down in tears. The crowd caught wind of this small drama and, as the tumbrels rumbled slowly by, voices cried out: 'Pardon her. She hasn't deserved this.' She turned to them and called back: 'My friends, it's my fault I'm here. I did not want to abandon my husband.'

At the foot of the scaffold they bid tender adieus and, when she climbed the steps, her courage radiated. She received death, they said, like a favour.

Dumas, the president of the revolutionary tribunal, went everywhere armed with two pistols, and laid them on the table in front of him when he took his seat in the principal courtroom in the Palais de Justice, the Hall of Liberty. Dumas thought himself somewhat droll. When the elderly abbess of Montmartre, Marie-Louise de Laval-Montmorency, was brought before him he asked her: 'Are you in the conspiracy?' She did not hear the question and answered: 'What?' 'Condemned,' he said. 'She was conspiring deafly.'

At a performance of a play in the Comédie Française one night – all Molière was banned, too old-regime, Voltaire bowdlerised, too indelicate – an actor spoke the line 'and the most tolerant are the most pardonable'. A Jacobin in the audience stood and shouted: 'No tolerance, in politics tolerance is a crime.' He was yelled down but at once left the theatre for the Jacobin club and there denounced this unpatriotic dramatic farrago of a play. The CGS was alerted and officers arrested the entire cast and the author. They were saved by the end of the Terror. When someone urged the celebrated playwright Ducis to write a tragedy he replied that merely stepping outside his house he was up to his ankles in blood. 'And so adieu to tragedy. It is poor drama when the people turn into the tyrant and the only ending can be to land in Hell.'

One day Fouquier told an usher to bring the Biron woman before the Tribunal. The usher left the room, consulted his list, went back and told the prosecutor that there were two women of that name in the prison. 'Take them both: it all amounts to the same.'

Within the vast bureaucracy upon which the mechanics of the Terror depended, such anomalies, often lethal, abounded. A woman called Mayet was confused with the homophonic Madame de Maillé and went to the guillotine. Fouquier was indifferent. Her very presence in prison, right name or not, was indication of guilt. Suspicion had put her there and suspicion sufficed.

The ushers were not infrequently nonplussed by contradictory or inexplicit orders. On 15 June, when an usher called for Gamache two men presented themselves, each around 50, both former nobles. The list merely gave names, neither profession nor forename. Which Gamache was required? Claude-Henri or Denis-Eléonore-Michel? The usher brought both men before Fouquier, who, thinking it a waste to have dragged a prisoner out of the holding prison in vain, sent both for the hearing and both were condemned, guilty of having the same name.

Given that many of the guards were illiterate, like many of the prisoners, and that spelling varied widely anyway, such errors were not uncommon, despite the almost fanatical obsession with paperwork that is the shocking characteristic of the police state. All papers were handwritten, often the scrawl near illegible. Is it Gribauval or Grihauval? Gauthier or Gautier? And the frequency of some names: 52 Girards, one of them a police spy, but the rest? The man Admirat who shot at Collot is still variously registered as Lamiral and Ladmiral. By the error of an usher, a young man of 17, Bertrand de Saint-Pern, appeared in court with his mother, though it was his father who had been accused. The Tribunal acknowledged that the innocent son stood before it in place of the father, presumed guilty. Nevertheless, with no accusation levelled at him, Bertrand was condemned for the imputed crimes of his father and went to the guillotine on 17 July. When the executioner's assistant took his hand to guide him up the steps, he said: 'OK, young 'un, don't be afraid.' The boy replied: 'I'm not afraid, it's you who are afraid – your hand is trembling.'

There were happy mistakes. Prisoners detailed for appearance before the Tribunal were marked out with a chalk cross on their cell door. Thomas Paine, the Norfolk man whose republican pamphlet *Common Sense* (1776) was of such inspiration to the American Revolution – which he had joined and then crossed the Atlantic to add his humanising weight to the French Revolution. He wrote *The Rights of Man* (1791–2) as a riposte to Burke's scathing *Reflections on the Revolution in France.* Indicted for treason in May 1792, but before the trial, he was opportunely elected a deputy for the department of Pas-de-Calais in the national Convention in Paris – his ideals and reputation flew before him – and hustled out of England by the poet William Blake and so across the Channel. Because he neither spoke French nor understood the dreadful difficulties of the Revolution he incurred the deep dislike and mistrust of the Jacobins. Suspected by Robespierre of intrigue with the foreign plot, he was arrested and marked for execution. Allegedly, however, when the gaoler with the list came round, Paine's door stood open. The cross was drawn on the inside and, next morning, when the psychopomps of the Conciergerie visited, the door was shut. No cross. They passed by. In *Common Sense* Paine wrote: 'Government, even in its best state, is but a necessary evil; in its worst state, an intolerable evil.'

On 2 June a convoy of wagons under guard set out from Saint-Malo transporting 29 prisoners to the revolutionary tribunal in Paris, a journey of some 450 kilometres which would take up to a fortnight. On 18 June they stopped at Villers-Bocage, a small village near Caen. There being no gaol, the prisoners were confined overnight in the inn. One of them, Pierre-Rose Turin, as they were led into the building, spotted a small window overlooking a side street. It offered a chance to escape. He was determined. Then, to his bitter chagrin, he discovered that to reach this window he would have to pass through a large room where the gendarmes were sleeping.

By great good luck the prisoners were left unfettered. Turin waited till the early hours, when there was a low hum of snoring, crept through the large bedroom and made his way along the landing to the tiny window. He looked down into the street – deserted? No. A sentry just below. He felt a rancid convulsion of despair. He was 32 and going to the guillotine. Suddenly a huge crack of thunder and seconds later a burst of torrential rain. The sentry below the window cringed from the downpour and then, duty thrown over for a dry room, made a dash for cover. Instantly Turin opened the window and jumped. Hurt in the fall, he was nonetheless free and ran and ran to a copse of trees at the edge of the village and hid. It was near dawn. The skies were pale with new light. He was too close to the inn. They would search. Surely they must find him.

The next morning, at about 10, he watched the convoy leaving the inn, search parties fanning out to either side of the road, but they missed him. He waited the long summer day till nightfall and set off west. For 18 days he lay up in cover by day and stumbled on through the short nights until he reached his mother's house in Tinténiac, in Brittany, where he lay low until 9 Thermidor. He married in 1799 and died in his sleep aged 85.

In the carts on 17 July went 16 Carmelite nuns arrested in their convent in Compiègne in mid-June. They had been denounced by the local postmaster, who reported certain suspicions he had regarding their correspondence. Compiègne, where Joan of Arc said her last confession, was very close to the border with the Netherlands and the ranged armies of the coalition.

When the sentence of death was pronounced, one of the sisters fainted. Not wishing to have anyone say that the women lacked courage, the prioress bartered a fur-lined coat for a cup of chocolate for each sister, to fortify them before they went to the scaffold; and, so that the executioners would not lay hands on the women, she cut their hair herself. They received absolution from a priest in the prison and went out to the carts dressed in their white habits. Along the way, their own *Via Dolorosa*, they sang the *Miserere*, the *Salve Regina*, the *Te Deum*. At the foot of the scaffold they chanted the *Veni Creator*: 'Come, creating Spirit of the world . . .' and the *Magnificat*: 'My soul doth magnify the Lord and my spirit hath rejoiced in God my Saviour.' Their dignity, the steady comforting power of their singing, quelled the usually raucous crowd; their serenity commanded silence. Even the celebrated *tricoteuses*, making a public display of their sansculottism, knitting patriotic woollens for the brave boys at the battlefront, were subdued by them.

The prioress asked to be taken last and, to each of the sisters as she mounted the steps, offered a tiny figurine of the Virgin Mary for them to kiss, and each in turn as she mounted the scaffold chanted the *Laudate Dominum omnes gentes*, 'Praise the Lord all ye peoples'.

On 7 Thermidor (25 July 1794) a guard walked along the corridors of the Saint-Lazare Seminary, now being used as a holding prison, and sang out the names of the day's victims, a procedure jokingly referred to by the warders as handing out the evening paper or the travel warrant. Among the names this day 'Loizerolles'. There were two detainees called Loizerolles, a father Jean and his son François, but only one – François – on the list. He at once ran to his father's room to find the guard ordering the old man out. He said: 'My dear boy, console your mother, live for her. They can butcher me but they cannot demean me.' François made to embrace his father but the guard pushed him away and, when he burst into tears, the turnkey scoffed: 'You're behaving like a baby. It'll be your turn tomorrow.'

Jean Loizerolles and 30 others were brought before the Tribunal the following day, Coffinhal presiding. As the indictment was read, there was some confusion: instead of a young man of 22, this Loizerolles was a white-haired 60-year-old. Coffinhal, a colossus of a man with a mournful bass voice, merely substituted the name 'Jean' for 'François', crossed out 'son' and replaced it with 'father' and changed the son's prison number 22 to the father's, 61. Loizerolles said nothing. He and a clerical error had saved his son.

In the six weeks between the first of the exsanguinary batches, the 32 on 14 June to the last, the 44 on 27 July, 1,306 men and women, old and young, went to the guillotine. On 7 July, 67. On 9 July, 60. There were four days only when the axe did not fall: three décadis and 14 July, the anniversary of the Fall of the Bastille.

The first Picpus ditch filled, the second began to fill; they remained uncovered, a few planks stretched across as walkways. The stench of the rotting dead in the stinking heat of that June and July grew intolerable. Coffinet, surveyor for the Commune, ordered braziers to be set round the trenches for the burning of juniper wood or, failing that, of thyme or sage to counteract the mephitic pall over the garden and spilling across the whole district. This order was ignored.

The inmates of the former convent, who were paying high odds for something like a comfortable and secure existence, sent a petition of complaint to the authorities, a petition studiously couched in unimpeachable patriotic style: 'Citizens, a large number of old people, drawn by the fresh air, as well as vine-growers, gardeners and citizens of all degrees, justly alarmed by finding in their neighbourhood ditches destined for the burial of conspirators felled by the sword of the law, represent to you the dangers to which they have become exposed. The number of cadavers interred in one of the trenches gives off a fetid miasma which must soon become pestilential if prompt and effective precautions are not taken, such as spreading a sufficient quantity of lime and covering the hole with a large layer of earth. Citizens, you will not allow men who, while they were alive, declared themselves enemies of the people and of the Republic to murder the people after they have died.'

Poyet visited the Picpus grave pits on a tour of inspection and his report identified two salient problems: in order to inhibit the putrid stink, he suggested covering the entire aperture of each ditch with joists and boards into which were cut trapdoors for access. Secondly, recent downpours of rain meant that the clayey soil of the area had become waterlogged and impermeable. It simply could not absorb any more blood under and round the scaffold in the place du Trône Renversé or in the Picpus site. A large hole some two metres deep had been excavated under the scaffold as a soak-away for the spouts of blood from the severed necks, but no decent provision had been made to cope with the inundation or the aftermath: the hole was merely covered over with planks after the executions. It did nothing to stifle the ever-fouler reek of the congealing blood. The acute problem of drainage was further aggravated by the gallons of water used to wash down the guillotine and the scaffold each evening.

Of the Picpus garden, Poyet concluded that the first ditch had been too liberally doused with water. Managing the detritus of these mass executions was a novel undertaking: they were learning as they went. All that was needed, Poyet advised, was a light sprinkling with earth of the latest infill of fresh corpses before the application of the recommended quantity of quicklime. He also concluded that the dimensions of the enormous third ditch should be reduced to the size of ditch number two.

A second report from the architects' office recommended the building of walls just under four metres high enclosing and confining the whole area, approximately 200 metres long by 26 across, of the grave pits.

Before this work could be put in hand, the Terror had ended. The men who helped end it were beginning to act more concertedly.

In mid-June, Vadier of the CGS, habitué of Barère's dinner parties in the house at Clichy, an ardent revolutionist and dechristianiser, a primary target of Robespierre's virulent hatred, had floated the rumour that the Incorruptible was caught up in a subversive group of religious dreamers, already infiltrated by CGS spies, centred on one Catherine Théot, a demented crone who preached a fantastical religion to her devotees: that she was the mother of the coming Messiah, that Robespierre, fulfilling a mission foretold by the prophet Ezekiel, was the Herald of the Last Days and the prophet of the New Dawn. These latter claims were detailed in a letter, possibly forged, found hidden under that favourite French locale for a cache, her mattress.

The raid by the CGS police on her house in the rue de la Contrescarpe in the crinkum-crankum tangle of streets in the Latin Quarter, discovered her in company with one Dom Gerle, a Carthusian monk, who had been a deputy in the old constituent Assembly, one of three priests whom the painter David, himself a member of the CGS, had depicted swearing the famous Tennis Court Oath, defying the threat to dissolve the first elected assembly. Compounding the embarrassment, Dom Gerle had a certificate of civism signed by Robespierre himself.

By implicating Robespierre in this circle of adventists, Vadier's aim was to discredit his apparent messianic view of his role in the Revolution *and* his toleration of old-regime Catholicism. The name Théot, close enough to *theos*, the Greek for 'god', reinforced the suspicion that in protecting the crazy visionary babbler, Robespierre was dallying with intimations of his own divinity.

The Théot case was brought by the CGS and the relevant papers delivered to Fouquier. On 26 June, Robespierre peremptorily summoned the public prosecutor to bring the dossier to the CPS. The Committee in session, 'I walked in,' said Fouquier, 'laid the papers on the table and Robespierre gathered them up. He had scarcely begun to read them when everybody slipped off. When we were alone, Robespierre said he would have to postpone a decision on the affair. I pointed out that he was required by decree to pursue it. He ordered me to drop it. I obeyed.'

Fouquier, the archetypal bureaucrat and no friend of Robespierre, stormed straight round to the office of the CGS and cried: 'He he *he* is opposed in the name of the CPS.' Of the 12 members of the CGS, only two, David and Le Bas, were partisans of Robespierre.

If the election of Fouché to the presidency of the Jacobins had been an affront to Robespierre, the subsequent election of Barère, his opponent in the CPS, and then Elie-Lacoste of the CGS, suggests that his ascendancy in the club was at hazard if not undermined. However, his sights were now firmly set on the indisputable ringleader of the opposition, even if the opposition was neither defined nor organised.

On 11 July, at the Jacobins, he delivered a eulogy of the martyred Jacobin hero of Lyon, Chalier, and proceeded to the main thrust of his homily: a scathing denunciation of the absent Fouché, who was not only 'a vile and despicable impostor whose intriguing was admission of his crimes, whose hands were contaminated with loot and stained with blood' but had 'persecuted the patriots of the Emancipated Town with a wiliness, a perfidy as cowardly as it was cruel'. An essential part of Robespierre's technique was to distance himself from the more erratic actions of the men sent out by the CPS to bring the Terror to the outlying corners of France and thereby insinuate that the renegades, as he now painted them, had acted expressly, wilfully, artfully against the wishes of the government in Paris. Since the representatives on mission could rarely produce any documentary proof of explicit orders amid the vagaries emanating from the green room in the Tuileries, this was a safe enough tactic. Robespierre then proposed that Fouché be 'invited to come to the Society to defend himself' and then backed, if he did not actually frame, the motion demanded by Couthon to exclude Fouché from the club.

Fouché wrote asking the club 'to suspend their judgement until the CPS and the CGS had delivered their report on his private and public conduct'. This was bold and astute: it effectively set the Jacobins against the Committees as well as the Convention by calling into question the legitimacy of any move they had or might make against him in what was and always had been a *private* arena, a mere political club, however much Robespierre and his myrmidons might wish to regard the acts and proposals of the Jacobins as in no way distinct from the public realm.

This confusion of power and authority lay at the heart of the Jacobin tyranny; its usurping of the representative body through the auspices of Robespierre, Saint-Just and Couthon, in particular, whose role as leading men in the CPS and the Jacobins seemed to legiti-mate their authority without due reference to the Convention. They might stand up in the Convention and deliver their reports, their proposals for decrees, their judgements on counter-revolution, their denunciations of crime, but it was in the green room and the Jacobins that the real work was done; or so it seemed to those excluded from both or either.

Fouché's letter was read out in the club on 14 July – the date was not loosely chosen – and Robespierre rose to speak: 'I begin by asserting that Fouché the man does not interest me at all. I was able to associate with him because I believed him to be a patriot; when I denounced him here, it was less because of the crimes he has committed in the past than because he has gone into hiding in order to commit others and because I regard him as the chief of the conspiracy which it is our task to unmask. I have read the letter you have just heard carefully and it is clearly written by a man who refuses to justify himself to his fellow citizens in person. This is how tyranny begins. A man who will not answer to a popular society is a man who opposes their very existence.'

Deploring Fouché's neglect of the society (as if he would stroll into the viper's nest now) and his appeal to the Convention for help against the Jacobins, he went on: 'Is he afraid that crime is written plainly in his doleful face, that 6,000 glances fixed on him will see his soul laid bare in his eyes and that, despite his natural gift in hiding his thoughts, one will read them there? Is he afraid that whatever words he chooses cannot conceal the hesitations and contradictions of guilt?'

Did the sharp remembrance of Fouché's jilting of his sister Charlotte still needle him, the frequent visits and attentions he had paid her, the behaviour which one could only interpret in one way, the fact that he had spoken of marriage? Such a bitter memory was surely as long as his capacity to overlook it was meagre. It made the hyperbole (6,000 hostile faces turned on Fouché), his final gibes, the more acerbic.

Fouché was, that night, excluded from the Jacobin club.

'Let us,' said Robespierre, 'separate ourselves from the cheats and the intriguers and they will be unable to divide us. Thus will the divine charm of virtue and of friendship unite us.'

It is a measure of his remoteness that he could speak thus as the ghastly butchery of the Great Terror went on, as tensions within the circles of government stretched tauter – within the CPS itself, between the CPS and the CGS – and murmurings in the outer corridors grew more distinct.

'What is important,' wrote Hesdin, 'is that the tigers are quarrelling.'

# NINETEEN

# *Thermidor*

Because half a dozen grasshoppers under a fern make the
field ring with their importunate chink . . . do not imagine
that those who make the noise are the only inhabitants of
the field.

Edmund Burke *Reflections on the Revolution in France*

FOUCHÉ LIVED IN constant fear of arrest, never sleeping more
than a night in the same place, moving along the chain of sympathetic deputies, each of them as terrified as he of seeing their name
on a list of the proscribed. The list would surely be published soon,
the final tally of the accused. And this was Fouché's sole weapon:
if he could convince a man that his name was on the list that
Robespierre was compiling, he could put it to him that it was now
or never – act or go to the guillotine. However much Robespierre
might vaporise about the Convention 'in general' being pure, which
put it above fear and above crime, he also said that the Convention
had 'nothing in common with the conspirators it currently shelters
in its midst'. He was not saying who they were; to rally support
Fouché played on the uncertainty, on the paranoid fear which characterised Robespierre's every utterance. Had it not been said of
Robespierre that he aspired to sole mastery not from ambition but
from fear?

Fouché, as too his immediate allies Fréron, Tallien and Barras,
was guilty of extremist actions committed in the name of the CPS,
but they were all out on a limb. No documents existed to implicate
any member of the Committee, no material evidence to prove that

the representatives of the people on mission – in Bordeaux, Toulon, Lyon – had acted under any authority but their own or that they had not exceeded their powers. Robespierre would undoubtedly strike at them as instigators of excessive terrorism, in line with his injunction never to overstep the letter of the law; at Fouché in particular: the Lyon Jacobins detested him and complained bitterly to their loyal friend in Paris about his high-handed behaviour, his cruelty, his arrogance.

Fouché's grouping was no faction but rather a disparate collection of men – the remnants of those factions already expunged, the deputies to right, left and centre who were revolted by the Great Terror but paralysed by a sense of impotence in the face of the all-powerful CPS, and, naturally, those of the CGS who reviled the new tyrant.

If Barère of the CPS could be relied on to go with a general drift against Robespierre, Couthon and Saint-Just, two other members were less secure. Indeed, Fouché learnt that Collot d'Herbois and Billaud-Varenne were contemplating a reconciliation with the hardliners. He approached them with a stark choice: 'If you allow Robespierre to take our heads, who will be there to save yours?'

In the midst of this frantic consolidation of opposition, Fouché's daughter, scarcely a year old, fell ill and died of a fever in the family home. Fouché dared not visit the dying child, for fear of arrest, but, on 6 Thermidor (20 July) he joined his wife and accompanied the coffin to the cemetery. If his nerve had ever threatened to fail him in the weeks since his public banishment, it steadied now in the awful, the absolute silence of his dead child's graveside. Two days later he struck.

On 7 Thermidor Robespierre took his dog Brount for a walk in the Marbeuf gardens. He stopped to talk to a young child, gave her a silver coin and walked on. That night he spent writing and rewriting a long speech to mark his return, the following day, to the Convention, for the first time in four weeks. The time had come to make the decisive strike at his enemies.

At 11 a.m. on 8 Thermidor, in the national Convention hall, the stenographers sat ready, in a box set aside for their use, to scribble their verbatim record of the proceedings.

Rising to stand before a packed session, Robespierre asked for and was granted leave to speak. He wore the dandyish silk coat and breeches, the powdered wig, of the fashion before the Revolution.

He wore spectacles as much to distract from the pinched and cringing expression of his face as because of his poor eyesight.

His manner of speechmaking never varied: his delivery was laboured, his sentences so lengthy that, whenever he paused, pushing the spectacles up on his forehead, the impression was that he had finished. But, having tracked with his eyes every corner of the room, he lowered the spectacles once more over his eyes and continued piling more phrases into an already prolix sentence.

This day he walked across the narrow aisle, sheaf of papers in hand, spectacles anchored like a tiara in his powdered wig, and ascended the rostrum. In the deathly silence he stood a long while without saying a word, quizzing the drawn faces along the benches in front and to the side with that expressionless, myopic stare which could flush the guilt out by its unspoken interrogation, its mere suggestion. (Barras records how a member of the Convention, attention wandering, suddenly caught Robespierre staring at him as he was putting his hand to his temple; hurriedly he lowered it. 'He'll suppose I am thinking something suspicious.') In this way, by the very tension of his silence, the menace of the words he was ready to uncoil, he imposed his will. Finally, he pulled the green-tinted spectacles down on to the bridge of his nose, adjusted them and, in the thin, reedy voice which carried only in the penetrating silence his sinister presence commanded, began the long oratory of his veiled threat.

Men called him a tyrant, he whined: he was no such thing, rather a slave of Liberty, his life one of martyrdom to the Nation. He promised, yes, revelation of a terrible truth and its corollary, Death. Virtuous men need have nothing to fear. But two things animated the governance of the nation: Terror and Virtue, the one ensuring the purity of the other. But there existed a vast and complex plot to destroy public liberty and there were traitors signatory to it even in the heart of the Convention; even certain members of the CPS. He knew who they were. The traitors must be punished, the Committees purged and reorganised. The People was virtuous even if acts of the individuals who comprised it might not be.

'By what misadventure has this grand accusation of dictatorship suddenly fallen on the head of one of the members of this assembly? Strange project of a man to engage the national Convention in committing suicide one by one with its own hands to clear a way to absolute power for him. Let others perceive the ridiculous side of these charges: it is for me to see only the atrocity of them. However, this word "dictatorship" exerts magic effects – it blights liberty, it debases government, it destroys the Republic, it degrades all the revolutionary institutions that are introduced as the work of one man on his own; it focuses on one point all hatreds, all the daggers of fanatism and of aristocracy.'

He stopped abruptly. He seemed to hesitate.

Billaud-Varenne stood and declared: 'This speech incriminates the Committees; it must be examined rigorously and in detail.'

Charlier, deputy for the Marne, in his turn said that this examination should be made the responsibility of the Committees.

Robespierre cried out: 'What? Would I have the nerve to come here and to confide in the bosom of the Convention those truths which I consider vital to the safety of the nation only for my speech to be examined by the members whom I accuse?'

The speech lasted two hours, the list of traitors hinted at but not disclosed. It was a masterly show of manipulation, for everyone present knew – suspects and Robespierrists alike – that Saint-Just would bring the list to the rostrum the next day and read out the names in that heartless voice. That is how they worked: the Incorruptible to preach the new testament of guilt; the Angel of Death to deliver the judgement.

At last Robespierre ended and, in the unmanning silence, gazed slowly round the room. Suddenly a burst of ecstatic applause broke along the Jacobin benches; it swelled through the hall. Robespierre was back in command, so he must have believed; he had cowed them, made them once again bow to his will.

However, Bourdon de l'Oise, informed by Joseph Fouché, leader of the conspiracy against Robespierre, that his name was on the list, rose to his feet – what had he to lose? – and shouted: 'I oppose the publication of this list. These are grave accusations which demand proof.'

Robespierre was stunned, taken aback, and, while he hesitated, Pierre Joseph Cambon of the Finance Committee, whom Robespierre *had* named, hustled him aside on the rostrum and bellowed: 'Before I am dishonoured, I will speak to France. It is time to tell the whole truth. One man, one man alone has paralysed the will of the national Convention. And that man is the man who has just spoken. It is *Robespierre*. Therefore: judge him.'

There was uproar, a clamour on every side for the names on the list. Robespierre stood his ground, refusing stubbornly, like a petulant child, to be drawn.

Panis confronted him, claiming that Robespierre had drawn up a list and that 'my name is on it'.

The hall resounded with the deputies chanting: 'The list, the list' but Robespierre would not bend.

A voice goaded him: 'And Fouché? What of Fouché?'

Robespierre was being offered a sop – Fouché's hostility was an open secret – but he rejected it. His power depended on absolute control of information. Name Fouché and he must name the others. Drily he said: 'My only responsibility is to the call of duty' and left the session. It was 5 p.m.

Later that evening he went to the Jacobin club to rally support among his faithful supporters in the vast vaulted gallery of the library in the former Dominican monastery on the site of the Marché Saint-Honoré: the walls lined with bookshelves, transverse bars to prevent the theft of books; on three sides, tiers of benches for members; the centre of the hall lined with seats for the public. This was his spiritual home, his power base, the womb of pure patriotism and revolutionary right thinking. If, in his absence, the mood of the Convention had changed, he was still master here.

When he asked to speak, Billaud-Varenne and Collot d'Herbois, neither of whom had attended the club for four months, butted in and demanded their turn to be heard. Their supporters cheered them on, shouting: 'Robespierre has no right to preference.' But Robespierre's partisans howled the claque down and he took the stand – just as in ancient Sparta, where the passing or casting out of laws was decided by volume of opponents shouting for or against.

Robespierre proceeded to read out, in its entirety, the speech he had delivered that afternoon in the Convention. In a peroration with which he had not graced the Convention, he ended: 'Brothers and friends, you have just listened to my last will and testament. My enemies, rather those of the Republic, are so numerous, so powerful, that I cannot delude myself I can escape their blows for very long . . . whatever happens, you will always remember me with honour in your virtuous hearts . . . If you lend me your support, the traitors will undergo the same punishment as their forerunners. If you abandon me, you will see with what calm I know how to drink the hemlock.'

David, the painter, burst out: 'I will drink it with you' and the rest shouted deliriously: 'All of us, all of us.'

Now Collot d'Herbois, struggling to the rostrum through the crowd, shouted into the din, recalling the services he had rendered to the Society of the Friends of the Constitution, the formal title of the Jacobin club. It was futile. Then Billaud-Varenne joined him, screaming: 'I no longer recognise the Jacobins.'

Amid a tumult of noise, Couthon, crippled and confined in a wheelchair, moved up to the stand.

'Citizens,' he said, 'I am convinced that the facts relayed by Robespierre are true. However, I believe we cannot shed too much light on them, for this is the most deep-seated conspiracy of any to this date.'

(Voices: 'Yes. Yes.')

'It is certain that there are pure men in the Committees but it is no less certain that there are criminals in the same Committees. And so, I too demand a debate, not about Robespierre's speech, but about the conspiracy. Let us see here on this rostrum before us the conspirators, we will cross-examine them, we will observe their blushes, we will listen to their wavering responses; they will pale in the presence of the people, they will be overwhelmed and they will perish.'

Couthon's motion was adopted in a storm of applause, everyone in the hall on his feet, hats flying in the air, and chanting: 'The conspirators to the guillotine', they made for Billaud-Varenne and Collot d'Herbois. Billaud managed to escape, but Collot was not so fly – they grabbed him, ripped the coat off his back and tore his shirt before he wriggled free.

Dumas, the Jacobins' president, called them to order and adjourned the meeting to the revolutionary Tribunal.

It was shortly before midnight.

Collot and Billaud went straight to the Tuileries, where the CPS and the CGS were in joint session; Robespierre returned home. The cabal made the rounds of the deputies, giving them heart or scaring them into solidarity.

At this joint meeting of the Committees, Barère, a trimmer, a man always inclined to test the prevailing mood before committing himself, prevaricated no longer. They were, he said, every one of them, subsiding into a sort of lethargy of indecision and inaction. He railed at them: 'Who are you, then, you insolent pygmies, that you want to divide what is left of our country among a cripple, a child and a scoundrel [Couthon, Saint-Just, Robespierre]?' That, at any rate, is what he claimed to have said. Under pressure, Saint-Just finally yielded and agreed to draft a report on the current political situation and the measures being taken by the government to deal with it, and to submit the text to the Committee before he presented it in the Convention the next day. This report, a regular function of his role in the CPS, he had agreed to draw up three days earlier but had still not done so.

The meeting broke up in the early hours. Carnot, Collot, Billaud and Barère stayed on to draft various measures: a decree relieving General Hanriot of command of the Paris national Guard and replacing him with six subordinate legion commanders who would assume the command in rotation. Another to divest Lescot-Fleuriot, the mayor of Paris, and the executive council of the Commune of jurisdiction over the political security of the Convent; this authority would pass to a new board in which each of the six legionary commanders would have a voice. Since these proposals would need the approval of the Convention, Barère prepared a speech to mollify and induce them to sign. He also prepared a proclamation in the name of the Convention summoning the French people to stand behind their representatives. 'Against the Paris mob' was the unspoken message.

Most importantly, this budget of emergency legislation would trammel the Commune and the national Guard, who had, in tandem, so effectively intimidated the Convention for so long. Fouché and the others would hold the deputies of the centre in line. With Collot in the chair, Robespierre could be denied the floor. He must not be allowed to speak. Saint-Just they had in line; so they thought. But after leaving the stormy meeting to write his report he had gone instead to Robespierre and been turned. He spent all night preparing a speech denouncing the traitors at the very heart of government.

At noon on 9 Thermidor, as the Committee members waited in the corridor outside the Convention to take their seats, a messenger brought a note from Saint-Just: 'You froze my will and closed up my heart; but I have determined to trample my cowardly promises underfoot. I intend to open my heart directly to the Convention.' It was plain enough: Collot and Billaud, Carnot and Barère were about to be condemned as conspirators. Tallien, reading the dismay in their faces, came over and exhorted them to stay firm. Collot, as president for the day, had already taken his seat in the hall. As the benches filled, the room felt, someone said, like 'a volcano with a boiling crater'.

Robespierre, Couthon and Saint-Just entered the room to a huge burst of applause from the Jacobins. Robespierre, in jonquil knee breeches and white stockings, the robin's-egg-blue coat draped over his shoulders, looked calm and self-assured.

Saint-Just, in a chamois-coloured coat, pearl-grey breeches, white waistcoat, with high stock that emphasised that way he had of holding his head like the host of the Eucharist, strode to the rostrum. The conspirators had agreed the signal: a Saint-Just trademark cliché, his routine allusion to the Tarpeian rock, a high bluff in Republican Rome from which traitors were hurled to their death.

He began: 'The course of events has indicated that this rostrum may be the Tarpeian rock for the man who . . .' Immediately Tallien hurried towards the rostrum and cried: 'I demand to be heard.' Saint-Just protested, he was speaking for the CPS. Collot rang his bell furiously, drowning him out. Tallien continued: Saint-Just had no right to speak for the two Committees, which by law must speak through a spokesman: 'I demand that the veil be torn away.' Other conspirators in the hall stood up: 'It must be, it must be.'

Tallien's fervour was sharpened by the fact that he was desperate to save his mistress, Thérésia Cabarrus, the former marquise de Fontenay, stewing in prison.

Neither Saint-Just nor Robespierre could get to the rostrum. Now Billaud denounced Robespierre for the cryptic threats he had made the day before. Further, he named the Robespierrists as the real conspirators. 'These people are planning to murder the Convention.' He glanced up at the gallery. 'I see one of those men who dared menace the Convention sitting in our midst now.'

Cries of 'Arrest him' and the police, primed, moved in to whisk the man away.

Saint-Just's friend Le Bas tried to approach the rostrum but was shoved aside as Tallien rejoined: 'I asked a moment ago that the veil be torn aside. It is now ripped asunder. The conspirators are soon to be unmasked and annihilated. Liberty will triumph.' He went on: 'I was at the Jacobins last night and I shuddered for my country. I saw the army of a new Cromwell being formed.' (For the revolutionaries, Cromwell was the archetypal dictator.) And, drawing from inside his coat a dagger, he flourished it histrionically and declared: 'I have armed myself with a dagger which I will drive into his breast if the Convention does not have the courage to decree his arrest.'

Cries of 'Down with the tyrant.'

Saint-Just did nothing, suddenly utterly deflated. For a year they had been in undisputed control; opposed for the first time, that control, that insidious domination, had crumbled. For the rest of the session, four long hours, he stood motionless, arms folded, next to the tribune, in a near-catatonic stupor.

When Robespierre tried once more to speak he was peremptorily shouted down, Collot ringing his bell. At once there were cries of 'Barère to the rostrum', the catchphrase signalling the moment when Barère would step up to deliver a *carmagnole*, a paean of victory, florid, overwrought, dripping with patriotic sentiment and revolutionary rodomontade in praise of the brave armies of the Republic. And so he came, Tallien stepped down and Barère, calm and urbane, read his request, his sweetly worded appeal to their reason: it was for the Convention, he said, to save the unity of the government by taking action on 'several individuals who are discharging important duties'.

Collot stepped down and handed over occupancy of the president's chair to Thuriot.

Now Tallien went to the rostrum again and moved the decree to arrest Hanriot, Robespierre's 'general' in the Commune, and Dumas, president of the revolutionary Tribunal.

Robespierre, his face quite drained of colour, beads of sweat pilling on his brow, attempted once more to get to the rostrum; once again his voice was drowned out by the bell.

At this point the deputy from the Aveyron, one Louchet, an obscure individual and yet a member of the Mountain, seeing his moment in history writ large, suddenly rose and cried out: 'I demand the arrest of Robespierre.' It unleashed a storm of voices: 'To the vote. To the vote, To the vote.'

It was a little after 1.30 p.m.

As Robespierre struggled once more to appeal to them, the Mountain howled back: 'Down with the tyrant' and 'Get away from here, the ghosts of Danton and Camille Desmoulins reject you.'

Fréron remarked: 'Ah, it's hard to beat a tyrant down.'

Thuriot rang the bell furiously at Robespierre as he made his appeal: 'For the last time, President of assassins, I demand the right to speak.' (Others report that he said: 'By what right have you made yourself president of these assassins?')

Tallien: 'The monster has insulted the Convention.'

Robespierre now appealed to the centre – 'Men of virtue, men of purity, I appeal to you. Give me the leave to speak which these assassins have refused me.' This they refused and like a hunted animal he scrambled up, panting, to the empty seats on the right. Remnants of this party who had escaped the guillotine shrank from him in horror. One cried: 'Monster. You are sitting where Condorcet and Vergniaud once sat.'

Vadier added his voice: 'According to Robespierre, he is the only one defending liberty . . . and he's forever saying: "They're harassing me, they won't let me speak" and, of course, no one else has anything of any use to say because they can't get a look in – Robespierre always gets his way. "So and so is conspiring against me," he whinges, "me, the Republic's truest ally." That's a new one.'

Everyone laughed. Robespierre coughed, trying to clear his throat, but no words came; a deputy jeered bitterly: 'Danton's blood chokes him.'

Renewed cries of: 'Bill of indictment. Bill of indictment.'

Thuriot put the question to the house. The vote was taken, the decree of arrest against Robespierre, Couthon, Saint-Just, Le Bas outlawing each one passed *nem. con.* And the entire Convention stood and shouts rang out of 'Long live the Republic', to which Robespierre retorted: 'The Republic is lost. The brigands triumph.' They were the last words he ever said in the Convention hall, which he had kept to heel for so long. It was a year to the day since he had entered the CPS.

The police searched out Hanriot, the commander of the national Guard in Paris, arrested him, stripped him of his command and took him for detention to the Hôtel de Brienne, the headquarters of the CGS. As planned, political responsibility for Paris was handed over to the mayor, the national agent and each in turn of the six new national Guard commanders. The deputies also voted a proclamation calling on the people of Paris to stand behind the Convention and not lose in one day the precious gains of six years.

When an usher approached the bench where he had sought refuge and handed him the order of arrest, Robespierre seemed not to notice. His naturally pessimistic and depressive temperament had darkened. His will, his psyche had collapsed. Eventually he and the others were rounded up and brought to the bar below the president's chair, where, at around five o'clock, they were placed under formal arrest. They, together with Robespierre's brother Augustin, were immediately escorted by a cordon of guards to the Hôtel de Brienne and, it being dinner time, they were served a meal of soup, coarse-salted capon, roast lamb and two bottles of burgundy.

Not to be outdone, the Convention declared a two-hour dinner recess for itself. At this great moment of crisis in her governance, France's legislators took themselves to the dining table.

An hour earlier 44 prisoners had been assembled in the court-yard of the Conciergerie, ready to be taken to the guillotine. Sanson, acutely aware of disturbances in the Faubourg Saint-Antoine, suggested to Fouquier that the executions might be deferred. There was every chance of a riot. 'Justice must take its course,' Fouquier replied, and the tumbrels transporting this last batch of cruelly unlucky souls trundled off. The list included one Vermandois, a canon of Chartres cathedral. There was no one of that name, no canons in the gaol. Fouquier's envoy, in a sweat, insisted: 'I must have a canon.' Eventually, after a lot of searching, the gaolers lit on an individual named Courlet-Vermantois, former soldier, son of a councillor of Dijon; he had absolutely no connection with the cathedral, but was assigned the indictment against Vermandois.

Two writers went to their death that day: the poet Roucher and the playwright André Chénier. Roucher wrote a steady flow of letters to his daughter from inside Saint-Lazare.

. . . alone here in my cell, seeing none and seen by none of my fellow inmates, my desk lit by the light from the window, a free space of two feet, my feet on my carpet folded in two, my legs wrapped in a muff of flecked calico, I might almost be taken for a Sybarite and yet I am no more than a poor republican, a friend of studies and a great enemy of the cold. Ovid said, I think, 'adversity often stimulates and inspires us'.

. . . Oh he is so very right. Freedom loves to sprawl and never has enough room; misfortune learns how to confine itself and somehow knows how to find some space for repose. If the lessons of the past were not routinely lost for us in the future, the great landowners in here would be a rich font of thought in the days of their liberty, thought which would add to their future joys. When one has seen how little there is of real need in life, one can, one must, recognise the truth of the saying 'Oh useless necessities'.

But Roucher spoke with eloquence not available to most of the wretches incarcerated in the prisons of revolutionary France and with a philosophical hauteur to which most could never attain. The misery, deprivation, fear, torpor, rage, anguish, despair which afflicted them all at one time or another and many of them, in soul-destroying conflict, constantly, could not be assuaged by fine words or noble sentiment, alas. Nor can even the modest effort of an otherwise obscure man or woman given brief notoriety by mention in the dreadful registers of the Terror's bureaucracy to rise above tears in the transition from the putrid straw of the prison cell to the tumbrel and the scaffold be allowed to efface the disgusting travesty of all decency and promise of liberty that this revolutionary justice presented. For most of them, let Avoye Paville Costard be a spokesman, a name given the souvenir they all merit, of the needless, the futile torment they endured. Twenty-six years old, she wrote from the Conciergerie to Fouquier in an access of grief following the execution of her young lover:

'Why did you condemn him? Because he loved his God, his Catholic religion . . . and his king . . . Life is impossible for me under a regime such as yours where one sees only massacre and pillage. Before my beloved's death, I suffered patiently the evils heaped upon me . . . Now, there is nothing left for me, I have lost my love. Strike me down, put an end to a life which has become hateful, a life which I cannot endure without horror.' She was executed the next day.

Chénier, 31 years old, went with Roucher in the same cart and lamented the death of an adored husband and father; Roucher lamented the death of this young man of virtue, of brilliant genius and full of hope. Chénier said: 'I have done nothing for posterity', then, tapping his forehead, he was heard to add: 'But I did have something in there.'

The rest of the batch were mostly humble and obscure members of the petite bourgeoisie, but also six former nobles and the 23-year-old Princesse de Monaco, who had been denounced by the prison fly, Ferrières-Sauveboeuf. Claiming to be pregnant, she won herself a precious day's reprieve, but expressly so that she might be able to cut her own hair with a piece of glass. She plaited it and entrusted it to the prison·porter on his honour to give it to her children. In a last letter to them she told them she had stolen another day of life, not from fear but because she wanted them to have the last fond memento of her she could give them, rather than let it fall into the hands of the executioner. 'I have passed another day in this agony of suspense [a few words elided] do not repine.' She asked that they place the plait under glass and cover it with black crêpe, to be brought out a few times a year as a souvenir of the mother who loved them, and regretted her death only because she could no longer help them. She commended to their care their elderly grandfather.

In the cart, she comforted the woman standing next to her, Cécile Quévrain, 22-year-old chambermaid of the comtesse de Narbonne, accused of emigrating with her mistress and sheltering and succouring other émigrés on their return to France: 'Courage, my dear friend, courage. It's only crime that gives way to weakness.'

By 7 p.m., according to the minutes of the military escort, all the prisoners had been guillotined.

From the Hôtel de Brienne, Robespierre and the others were dispersed to separate prisons. News spread fast: informers, messengers scurried across to the Paris Commune offices in the Hôtel de Ville, where the mayor, Lescot-Fleuriot, immediately issued orders to all prisons in the city, which were under his jurisdiction and responsibility, to refuse admission to these prisoners. He also sent a message to the Jacobins asking them to muster as many men – and women – prepared for a fight as quickly as they could to defend the Hôtel de Ville. He then ordered all belfries to ring the tocsin and drummers of the national Guard at their posts to beat the general alarm tattoo. Within an hour a formidable mob had gathered in the square outside the building. Their objective: to rescue Robespierre and save *their* revolution.

A coach had taken Robespierre across the river to the Luxembourg prison. The chief warder, obedient to the orders from the Hôtel de Ville, refused him entry. News that he was being taken there had spread fast. A mob had gathered in the rue Tournon in front of the prison. Surrounding the coach, they shouted: 'To the Commune. To the

Commune.' He was their leader, they would have him with them. Robespierre asked to be taken instead to the administration of the municipal police on the Quai des Orfèvres: it was nearer than the Hôtel de Ville, and very close to the Palais de Justice, the revolutionary Tribunal, the Conciergerie: nerve centre of the revolutionary justice he had shaped. He arrived, haggard, wan, bewildered at about 8.30 p.m. He was greeted warmly: 'Rest easy. Are you not among friends?'

Paris was in ferment. Hanriot once again nominally in charge. His artillerymen, always reckoning themselves of higher status by virtue of greater firepower, remained staunch behind him, more loyal to the rebels than the infantry battalions of the sections, who grumbled openly about being made to risk their lives in defence of a government led by their so-called champion, Robespierre, a regime which had given them little in the way of food, voice or liberty. The artillery had trundled its guns round to the CGS headquarters, led by Coffinhal, presiding judge of the revolutionary Tribunal. Altogether some 3,000 troops of Hanriot's national Guard took over the building and liberated Hanriot. From there they advanced across the river to the national Assembly building. But Hanriot had never been more than a slovenly incompetent, four of the six appointed legion commanders refused to obey any orders issuing from him. He did not press his advantage and order the force at his command to terrify the Convention into submission, as they had done so resolutely in the past. Lamely, he ordered the gunners to withdraw from the Tuileries gardens.

Inside the building, the reconvened Convention passed a decree outlawing Hanriot and Lescot-Fleuriot, with his entire municipal administration, and appointing Barras commander-in-chief of the national Guard in Hanriot's stead. The legal definition 'outlaw' signified that formal identification of the prisoner was the only evidence required for conviction. The brothers Robespierre, Couthon, Saint-Just, Le Bas and their accomplices were named as the leaders of 'the plot against the national representation' and charged with treason.

Lescot-Fleuriot, told where Robespierre had taken refuge, sent a message to him appealing him to come at once to the Hôtel de Ville and put himself at the head of his people. Robespierre did not reply.

The Commune remained devoid of leadership, of direction, of clear orders; the former valet Hanriot, glassy-eyed with drink,

Robespierre in a funk, cowering, listless in the police station, trapped in an inertia, a variant of that abstraction in which he was always rapt. 'I was,' he said, 'born to detect crime not to punish it.'

Lescot-Fleuriot sent a second message: 'You no longer belong to yourself. You belong to your country now.' A second time, Robespierre did not reply.

The third message came in the shape of a large armed force led by members of a newly formed Executive Committee, comprising staunch Robespierrists – Payan, Coffinhal and others: 'We need your advice. You must come here at once.' The other outlaws of the CPS were already there. Robespierre responded at last, if reluctantly. He set out for the Hôtel de Ville, arrived at around 11 p.m., entered the building unobserved, by a back stairway, and joined the other insurgents in an upstairs room.

In those hours of Robespierre's prevarication, Barras had organised a substantial force. More and more of the city sections, hitherto loyal almost by definition to the Commune, had declared for the Convention. This was solid indication of the hatred Robespierre had sown; he had silenced all dissent, plated them over with a crust of the dread he instilled: now that he was broken he had no hold on them.

The disaffection seeped like a chill into Hanriot's force and the assembled mob outside the Hôtel de Ville. Waiting for orders which did not come, torn by ambivalent loyalties, and with what had seemed a firm target no longer clear to the view, they had been drained of will and energy by the long inertia, and as the dismay at what they might face stole over them, they slipped away in growing numbers. A brief burst of thundershot rain broke out of the leaden heat of the stifling night skies. Whatever resolve still glued them together cracked. By 1 a.m. the square was deserted.

In the Hôtel de Ville there was frantic activity. The Executive Committee for what they were now calling the Revolutionary Commune of 9 Thermidor issued a decree ordering the arrest of a number of members of the Convention, but Robespierre remained in a torpor, incapable of either action or decision. Lescot-Fleuriot begged him to sign an appeal, drawn up by Payan and others, to the sections to come to the aid of the Commune: 'People, rise up, let us not destroy the fruits of 10 August and 31 May, let us hurl all traitors to their tombs.'

Couthon urged him to make a similar appeal to the army. Ever the lawyer, the nit-picking man of detail, the prude, he replied: 'In whose name am I to sign it?'

'In the name of the Convention,' Couthon replied. 'Isn't that still where we are?'

Robespierre leaned towards his brother and said: 'In my view, it should be in the name of the French people.'

He finally agreed at about 2 a.m. and, even as Barras' men entered the building, stormed up the stairs and burst into the room where he sat, he had signed the first two letters of his name, Ro : . . , and stopped, stricken with indecision, lacking the force of will and heart. It was entirely characteristic. Sheltering within the protective carapace of the law, he was firm. Naked of its armour, he succumbed to the morbid lassitude of doubt.

Hearing the commotion, Philippe Le Bas, Duplay's son-in-law, blew his brains out. Some accounts claim that, as he raised the pistol, Saint-Just implored Le Bas to kill him first, to which Le Bas replied: 'Fool, I have more important things to do.' Augustin Robespierre, in an access of despair, leapt from the window and landed, grievously hurt, at the feet of one of Barras' men. The municipal officer Gobeau stabbed himself in the chest, not fatally, with a stiletto. Couthon lay sprawled comatose, his skull fractured, halfway down the stairs, having fallen down or been pushed by a soldier.

Hanriot jumped – or was pushed by Coffinhal – from another window and fell into a midden, where he lay senseless till he was found several hours later.

Robespierre carried a pistol and when the door burst open he had it raised to his mouth (the preferred angle of a suicide attempt) but, distracted by the noise, his arm jerked, he yanked at the trigger, and instead of entering his brain the bullet went through his cheek and shattered and lodged in his lower jaw. A gendarme, Merda, who may or may not have snatched at Robespierre's pistol or indeed loosed off his own pistol, claimed the glory of wounding the monster. For this presence of mind and for aiming with a brilliant accuracy so as not to have robbed the guillotine of such a victim, he was promoted and died a general and baron.

Couthon was taken to the Hôtel de Dieu hospital. The others, a corpse and four maimed and wounded, remained briefly under guard in the room; only Saint-Just was uninjured. Pall-bearers arrived with stretchers and transported Robespierre to the doors of the

Convention, which, at 3.30 a.m., remained in permanent emergency session. Charlier, then presiding, addressed the hall: 'The coward Robespierre is outside. Do you want him to come in?' The response was immediate, violent: 'No. No. No', to which Thuriot added that 'the corpse of a tyrant could not but bring with it the plague' and demanded that 'the sword of the law should strike the prisoner and his accomplices without delay'.

Robespierre was carried to the antechamber of the CPS and laid on a table, his head resting on a small deal box containing samples of army rations. In his hand he clutched, still, his pistol case, on which was inscribed: 'In the name of the great monarch, Lecourt, purveyor to the King and his troops, rue Saint-Honoré, next to Pulley Street [rue des Poulies], Paris.' His shirt, breeches and blue coat were torn and dishevelled, his stockings round his ankles, his face a piteous mask of blood and gore. Sightseers trooped in to gaze and jeer at him, the stricken creature who had terrorised them.

'Your majesty appears to be in distress.'

One paused a long while before whispering: 'Yes, Robespierre, there *is* a God.'

A deputy of the Convention who saw him said later: 'This man who had been the cause of so much anguish to others, suffered as much pain and torment as any mortal could stand before he died.'

At 6 a.m. two army surgeons arrived to dress and bandage Robespierre's wounds. He sat up on the table and supported himself on his hands. They washed his face before one surgeon searched inside the jaw. He pulled out two teeth which had been uprooted. Stanching the blood-soaked interior of the broken lower jaw with linen pledgets, he then extracted the bullet with a larding needle (a hollow tube, pointed at one end, rather larger than a knitting needle, used by butchers for drawing a string of fat through meat). Again he washed the face of fresh flows of blood and laid a strip of linen bandage on the wound, held in place with a ribbon tied under the jaw to support it. He dressed the upper face. Throughout this grisly procedure Robespierre made a few convulsive movements and rolled his eyes to the ceiling, but otherwise remained quite impassive through what must have been intense pain.

When the surgeon had finished, Robespierre, reverting childlike to the courtesy of the old regime, whispered: 'Thank you, Monsieur.'

This impassivity was imputed by one journalist to his being rigid with terror.

At 11 a.m., under armed escort, the outlaws, Robespierre and 21 others, were taken to the Conciergerie and at 2 p.m. in the afternoon, in a short judicial procedure before the revolutionary tribunal, more truncated even than its usual practice, two municipal officers formally established the identity of each man, Robespierre first. Asked: 'Are you indeed Maximilien Robespierre, aged 35 [he was 36], born in Arras, deputy in the national Convention?' he made a sign with his head, two court employees corroborated the identity and the president of the court pronounced him an outlaw and sentenced him to death.

The Convention, on the initiative of Elie-Lacoste, of the CGS, had ordered the guillotine to be transferred back to its original site on the place de la Révolution and in the prison of Port-Libre one of a small company of prisoners wrote: 'the storm which had been rumbling for several days broke at last; we could support the loss of our liberty at Port-Libre: we knew each other, we had friends and acquaintances. Suddenly, on 7 Thermidor at 2 a.m., lists of transfer were handed round and we had to climb into the funereal carts, 45 of us, not knowing where we were going. Among the transfers I saw Coittant, Laroche, Quoinat, Vigée. Several of the people on the list bought themselves off it.'

They were moved to the Carmes prison, a long, slow journey through the dark streets, with a strong escort of mounted gendarmerie. At the prison they were herded into a fetid stable and left for several hours before being marched in fours to corridors or cells infected with the stink of latrines, where, by morning, the humidity was so high they were poached with sweat and plucking exhaustedly at their clothes. At 10.30 a.m., bitten by insects of all sorts, dying of hunger, they were given a bit of bread.

Other detainees slumped here and there in undress – shirt, trousers, filthy, bare legs, handkerchief round head, hair long and uncombed, the men many days unshaven; women in short dresses or country smocks.

But Coittant and the others had been reprieved: due to go to the guillotine the following day, they were replaced by a more distinguished batch.

At 6 p.m. three tumbrels drew up in the courtyard of the Conciergerie. In the first, the gravely hurt – the two Robespierres,

Couthon and Hanriot, still daubed with manure, one eye dangling from its socket, the four of them 'looking like bandits ambushed in the forest by the gendarmerie', wrote an eyewitness. In what contrast Saint-Just, his fawn breeches and white waistcoat immaculate, his head erect, face a morgue of indifference.

The others: mayor Lescot-Fleuriot, national agent Payan, president of the revolutionary tribunal Dumas, Vivier, who had presided over the Jacobins' meeting on the evening of 9 Thermidor, Hanriot's adjutant the general and former marquis Lavalette, the municipal officer Gobeau, scarcely alive, 11 members of the general council of the Commune, including the cobbler Simon, guardian of the Dauphin in the Temple.

The journey took an hour and a half. The streets were crammed, the crowds in a fever of jubilation and disbelief that it was over. A woman rushed out and grabbed the edge of the tumbrel in which sat Robespierre and spat at him: 'Villain. Your death makes me drunk with joy. Go down to hell with the curses of all wives and mothers.'

The rue Saint-Honoré was all but impassable, the tumbrels slowed to a near stop, the jeering and howled insults deafening. Outside the Duplays' house, they stopped. A child ran up to the door and sloshed a basinful of ox's blood over it. A group of women danced a jig. Others sang, tossed hats in the air, exulting, delirious with joy, then joined the throng behind the carts, a great troupe of celebration.

When at last they reached the scaffold, through a deep press of spectators, the crippled Couthon, near insensible, it was who went first. They had to carry him up and bundle him on to the plank. It took ten minutes to get his twisted body into position but on his side.

Saint-Just, as haughty as any caricatural aristocrat, remained impervious, as aloof from any swirl of emotion, as in all his dealings: he had dispensed the judgements of death in the name of an ideal, he had spoken of terror with clinical indifference to the effect it produced in human hearts. He went to his own death unaffected, it seemed, by the workings of that terror on his own mind and body, his face impassive, his eyes staring into the abstractions of his metaphysic, a distant possibility that none but the fanatic can conceive of, the sacred host of his head held high until it was no longer his to command and he went into that long sleep whose mortal version he had ever denied could be enjoyed by the true revolutionary. 'There is no rest for the revolutionary,' he had said, 'except in the grave.' The line was found in a leather-bound notebook in his desk at the CPS, together with: 'Love is the recollection of happiness.'

Robespierre was the last but one to die. His face drained of colour, he bowed his head as he mounted the scaffold, stepping in the blood of those who had gone before him, his once elegant figure as soiled and stained as Marat's: the ruined blue coat slung across his shoulders, the rest of his clothes torn and filthy, his jaw swathed in a foul bandage. Sanson removed the coat and then ripped off the bandage. A gush of blood poured out, the lower jaw detached itself from the upper bone and Robespierre let forth a terrible cry of agony. When, seconds later, the executioner held up his head, 'it presented the most horrendous image one could imagine, a monstrous, an inhuman face'.

His Calvary had lasted for 17 hours of agony. Reporting in the *Journal Universel* on 11 Thermidor (29 July), when 61 others of the Commune and municipal administration associated with them followed them to the scaffold, Audouin wrote: 'Robespierre's death lasted a long time.'

The corpses were removed to the Errancis cemetery, in a plot of land adjoining the Monceau Park. Earlier that day the joint Committees, the CPS and the CCS, issued an order 'relating to the dead bodies of the conspirators' and requesting that a 'large quantity of quicklime be spread over the remains of the tyrants to dissolve them so as to make it impossible ever to identify them'.

Let the several fictive death masks of Robespierre, worked up from contemporary drawings and paintings, symbolise the tangle of lies and distortions, of hyperbole and misconstruction, the great wash of greater and lesser mendacity which swamped the Revolution which paraded truth and true as if they were new ideals never open to the claim of humankind. The face, pock-marked with smallpox scars, the skull, all but in two pieces, shortly to be eaten away by quicklime, was naught but a mask, a mask of Terror.

# Postscript

They called up the street and the street has dispatched them.
*Max Weber* on the leaders of the abortive Bolshevik coup in
Berlin, 1919

T HE TERROR was the product of culpable complicity; of its proponents, Robespierre was the most reviled because, for all his apostrophising of the sovereign people in abstract, he had no love or
affection for, no understanding of, flesh and blood *people*.

Lecointre de Versailles took Billaud-Varenne aside. 'Robespierre
left the CPS on 12 May because, according to you, having had his
way for six months he was faced with opposition and left without
saying a word. So, I ask you, Billaud, with your supposed gentle
nature, humane, averse to bloodshed – or so the good Carnot attests,
from pliancy rather than veracity – what decree did you draw up or
propose in the interim? What humane order did you give? Not one.
And yet the tyrant was no longer in your midst. I consulted the
register of those accounted for by the guillotine between 12 May
and 26 July, 54 days when it was in action; I find 1,285 executed
and 278 acquitted. Then I look up the 54 days which preceded
Robespierre's absence from the CPS and I find only 557 guillotined
and 182 acquitted.'

By failing to resist evil with force they were responsible for the
spread of evil.

If the realpolitik of their excuse is to be believed – that in allowing
the barbarous Prairial law to take its murderous course they provoked
the revulsion that led to the fall of Robespierre – the conclusion must

be that the disgrace of the Terror had plunged them all into moral bankruptcy.

Perhaps 35–40,000 persons all told, including those who succumbed in prisons, lost their lives in the Terror. Of the 16,594 people who, condemned by courts, went to the guillotine, only 878 were of noble birth, a mere 6.25 per cent of the total; Paris and the Paris region, the South-east and the West accounted for 14,498 and the 551 executed in the three departments of the North – Nord, Pas-de-Calais and Somme – were almost all victims of the ferocious Le Bon.

In six departments there was no death sentence passed during the Terror: Aube, Basses-Alpes, Corsica, Hautes-Alpes, Haute-Saône, Seine-et-Marne; in four others, excluding Paris, over 1,000.

By far the majority of the victims was drawn from those so-called beneficiaries of the Revolution, the small people and the hated bourgeoisie and professions, that class from whose milieu came the men who directed the Terror.

The regions on which the infernal machine worked its worst devastation were those where love of King and God was strongest and most deep-rooted. Neither attachment blinded the peasants of the Vendée or the muscadins of Lyon to the inequalities of the old regime: the injustice of privilege was widely hated and roundly complained of. But whereas the poor in Paris had a violent, dogmatic hatred of conspicuous wealth, of corrupt churchmen, of an incompetent court, the one cause they shared with the poor in the rest of France, in both town and country, was the oppression of hunger and the abject failure of the monarchical government to remove it. When the republican government, in its turn, failed quite as signally, the rest of France, by and large, blamed the Republic while Paris insisted on blaming the old culprits – the egoistical villains behind the famine pact – and persisted in its belief that the Revolution had but one object: to root out and exterminate the serpents by whose cunning and self-interest the evils of the old regime were being perpetuated. For the poor of Paris had no natural allies until the revolutionary intellectuals, radicals, writers and journalists, *lawyers* took up their cause.

Elsewhere the atavistic ties between landowners and landworkers, prone as such affiliation was to long resentments and the imbalance of grinding hardship on one side and a life of ease on the other, were nonetheless strong. The bonds of the land are similar to those of family; cap-in-hand deference and the (often notional) obligations of *noblesse oblige* (noble birth) may seem to have little to do with affection or honest dealing, but they underscored perceptions of humanity and the natural order which do not lean much towards equality. Any attempt to sweep away the innate hierarchical structure of human society will succumb to the griefs of insanity and at the same time destroy at source the true impulse of charity by which inequality is best mollified.

Reprehensible this may be in theory, and the Jacobins based their entire programme of social demolition on it; however, hierarchy has a curious affinity with one of the most potent elements in social cohesion: communality. The Terror, through the surveillance committees of communes across the country, waged spiteful war on community and on mutual trust by disseminating the deadly toxin of suspicion, fear, envy.

The common foe had been a heartless authority which imposed crippling levies on a much-belaboured people. But that authority, making its visitations in the shape of the intendants and local magistrates, was a nameless entity: it came upon them like plague, crop failure, the bitter cold of winter. Should they blame God, who had made them poor and vulnerable? The King, who did nothing to ameliorate their misery? Recriminations aside, neither God nor the King could be a target of blame. Whom, then, to castigate? Naturally the rich, the merchants, factory owners, slave-traders, tax farmers, grand office-holders, and, yes, the wealthy aristocrats (a distinct minority), who did nothing and lived in luxury on the ill-gotten proceeds of their doing nothing, ill-gotten through the sweat of other men's toil.

The sansculotte was a man who earned his living 'by the sweat of his brow' and the most obvious target of sansculotte fury was the man who exploited that. Peasants have always grumbled about farmers and always will, but their conservatism runs deep. Rancour at the new rich, especially the new rich scrambling for place, privilege and social recognition, was quite another thing: it offended the old order. The bourgeois had not even the excuse of being a vital, an essential part of the hierarchy, the chain of being which went from lowliest subject up to the King and on to the Creator. What did they do precisely? Whom did they serve but themselves; whom exploit but the poor, the weak, the hungry? And all at the cost of social cohesion. For threaded through the chain of being was a pulse of human feeling, irrational, maybe, but nonetheless potent, which made sense, even if obliquely, of what society was and, more important, could be. Not, however, in some fanciful paradise, promise of which taps dangerously into that other human failing which vitiated the apparatus of the Terror: gullibility.

Danton, in Jean Anouilh's caustic take on the Revolution, *Pauvre Bitos Le dîner des têtes*, exposes the sterility of Robespierre's vision, sterile because it was shaped by a hollow intelligence, worse, in a hollow heart, by a man who could *do* nothing. An arid, graceless, mechanic of politics, with thin lips which had never smiled, well-manicured nails which had never touched anything, large eyes which never *saw* anything.

> As for me, without the Revolution, I could have been a cartwright or a blacksmith and made an honest living with hammer and red-hot iron; Camille could have played the clavichord or painted; Saint-Just had the skill to break in horses or to have been a gunsmith; the poor fellow Louis XVI himself wouldn't have made a bad locksmith . . . You? You didn't know how to do anything with your hands. All you knew was how to talk. An ugly little lawyer. You recall what I said about you during the trial? That bugger there isn't even capable of cooking an egg.

It was the man who had no life of his own, who devoted his waking hours to a sublime nonsense: that by destroying so much real life it was possible to remake an imagined life and that in striving to forge a republic of love, harmony, liberty and happiness, he and those who seconded him brought into being such a monstrous, repulsive travesty of it.

# The Revolutionary Calendar

| | |
|---|---|
| Vendémiaire | 22 September–21 October |
| Brumaire | 22 October–20 November |
| Frimaire | 21 November–20 December |
| Nivôse | 21 December–19 January |
| Pluviôse | 20 January–18 February |
| Ventôse | 19 February–20 March |
| Germinal | 21 March–19 April |
| Floréal | 20 April–19 May |
| Prairial | 20 May–18 June |
| Messidor | 19 June–18 July |
| Thermidor | 19 July–17 August |
| Fructidor* | 18 August–16 September |

*five supplementary days, the *sansculottides*, tacked on to the end of Fructidor, made up the full year. The calendar was used from September 1792, at the start of Year I, until Year IX, 1800–1801.

# Bibliography

I CHEERFULLY ACKNOWLEDGE the huge debt I owe to the myriad authors who have toiled painstakingly and undaunted through the mass of archive material in a number of libraries. Without their meticulous scrutiny, their dogged quest for hitherto unconsidered trifles, the task of writing this book would have been impossible. Moreover, my own sorties into various archives were invaluably guided by the researches of all those named below and I have drawn shamelessly on passages – many of them already familiar to me as to any student of the period – quoted in specialist studies.

Daniel Arasse *La Guillotine et l'imaginaire de la Terreur* (Paris, 1987)

Jean-Marie Artarit *Dominique Dillon, Curé, Vendéen et révolutionnaire* (Centre vendéen de recherches historiques, 1995); *Robespierre* (La Table Ronde, 2003)

Antoine de Baecque *La Gloire et l'Effroi* (Grasset, Paris, 1997)

Florence de Baudus *Le Lien du Sang* (Editions du Rocher, 2000)

Olivier Blanc *La Dernière Lettre: Prisons et Condamnés de la Révolution* (Editions Robert Laffont, Paris, 1984); *Les Espions de la Révolution et de l'Empire, Les hommes de Londres, histoire secrète de la Terreur*

Thomas Carlyle *The French Revolution* (1837)

John Laurence Carr *Robespierre* (Constable, 1972)

Louis-Marie Clenet *Les Colonnes Infernales* (Perrin, 1993)

Jean-Baptiste Cléry *Journal of Occurrences at the Temple* (Folio edition, 1974)

Richard Cobb *The People's Armies* (Yale University Press, 1987); *The Police and the People, French Popular Protest 1789–1820* (Oxford, 1970)

Leonard Cowie *Documents and Debates: The French Revolution* (Macmillan, 1987)

Albert Croquez and Georges Loublie *Fouquier-Tinville, l'accusateur public* (Paris, 1945)

C.A. Dauban, ed. *Les Prisons de Paris sous la Révolution* (Paris, 1870)

Christopher Dawson *The Gods of Revolution* (Sidgwick and Jackson, 1972)

Camille Desmoulins *Le Vieux Cordelier* (Paris, 1936)

William Doyle *The Oxford History of the French Revolution* (Clarendon Press, 1989)

Abbé Edgeworth de Firmont *The King's Last Hours* (Folio edition, 1974)

W.D. Edmonds *Jacobinism and the Revolt of Lyon 1789–1793*

Alan Forrest *Society and Politics in Revolutionary Bordeaux* (Oxford, 1975)

Anatole France *Les Dieux ont Soif* (Editions Gallimard, 1989)

François Furet and Mona Ozouf *Dictionnaire Critique de la Révolution Française* (Flammarion, 1992)

Alain Gerard *Les Vendéens* (Centre vendéen de recherches historiques, 2001); *'Par principe d'humanité . . .' la Terreur et la Vendée* (Fayard; 1999)

Leo Gershoy *Bertrand Barère: a reluctant Terrorist* (Princeton, 1962)

James Logan Godfrey *Revolutionary Justice* (Paris Tribunal, 1793–95)

Lisa-Jane Graham *If the King only Knew* (University Press of Virginia, 2000)

Donald Greer *The Incidence of the Terror during the French Revolution* (Harvard University Press, 1935)

John Hardman, ed. *French Revolution Documents* Volume II (Blackwell, 1973)

Colin Haydon and William Doyle, eds *Robespierre* (Cambridge University Press, 1999)

Jacques Hébert *Le Père Duchesne*

Raoul Hesdin *Journal of a Spy in Paris 1794*

Christopher Hibbert *The French Revolution* (Allen Lane, London, 1980)

Hubert C. Johnson *The Midi in Revolution* (Princeton, 1986)

Michael L. Kennedy *The Jacobin Clubs in the French Revolution 1793–95* (Princeton, 1982)

G. Lenotre *Episodes of the French Revolution of Britanny; The Guillotine and its Servants; La vie à Paris pendant la Révolution; Le baron de Batz* (Paris, early 20th century)

Stanley Loomis *Paris in the Terror* (Jonathan Cape, 1965)

Colin Lucas *The Structure of the Terror: Javogues and the Loire* (Oxford, 1973)

Jean-Paul Marat *Oeuvres*

Marcel Marion *Dictionnaire des institutions de la France 17th–18th centuries* (Paris, 1923)

R.R. Palmer *Twelve who Ruled* (Princeton, 1941)

Georges Pernoud and Sabine Flaissier *Documents of the French Revolution* (Secker and Warburg, 1960)

Marcel-Vincent Postic *Carrier et la Terreur à Nantes* (L'Harmattan, 2001)

J.M. Roberts, ed. *French Revolution Documents Volume II* (Oxford, 1966)

Maximilien Robespierre *Oeuvres* (Paris, 1968)

George Rudé *The Crowd in the French Revolution* (Oxford, 1959); *The French Revolution* (Weidenfeld and Nicholson, 1988)

Louis-Antoine Léon de Saint-Just *Oeuvres*

Simon Schama *Citizens* (Penguin, 1989)

William Scott *Terror and Repression in Revolutionary Marseille* (London, 1973)

Joseph Shearing *The Angel of the Assassination* (Heinemann 1935)

Albert Soboul *Les Sans-culottes* (Princeton, 1980)

J.M. Thompson *Leaders of the French Revolution* (Basil Blackwell, 1965)

Jean Tulard *Joseph Fouché* (Librarie Arthème Fayard, 1998)

Peter Vansittart *Voices of the Revolution* (Collins, 1989)

J.M. Wallace and J.McManners, eds *France: Government and Society* (Methuen, 1970)

D.G. Wright *Revolution and Terror in France 1789–1795* (Longman, 1974)

Arthur Young *Travels in France* (Cambridge, 1929)

Municipal Archives, Nantes

National Archives and Bibliothèque historique de la ville, Paris

Memoirs: Beugny, Riouffe, Laboureau, Mme de la Rochejacquelin, Charles Nodier, Bertrand Barère de Vieuzac, Joseph Fiévée [journalist]

# Index